THE EXUMA GUIDE
A CRUISING GUIDE TO THE EXUMA CAYS

Approaches, routes, anchorages, dive sights, flora, fauna, history, and lore
of
The Exuma Cays
by
Stephen J. Pavlidis

(Exumian Coat of Arms*)

SEAWORTHY PUBLICATIONS
PORT WASHINGTON, WISCONSIN

Published in the USA by: **Seaworthy Publications, 17125C W. Bluemound Rd., Suite 200, Brookfield, WI. 53005**
First Printing, January 1995
Second Printing, May 1995
Second Edition, June 1997

CAUTION: Although the author has, as in the previous edition, taken extreme care to provide the most accurate and reliable charts possible for use in this second edition. Nevertheless, the charts in this guide are designed to be used in conjunction with DMA, NOAA, and other government charts and publications. The Author and Publisher take no responsibility for their misuse.

The Author wishes to thank the following for their help in this effort. First and foremost, my friend and partner, Ray Darville, Warden of the Exuma Cays Land And Sea Park, without whose help this book would not have been possible, just saying thanks seems too little for all you have done; also, Kelly Becker, what can I say, once again you have proven as much a part of this guide as anyone, I often feel that you and Ray should be co-authors, thanks. I would like to offer my heartfelt thanks to Steve Dodge of Abaco, my cartographic mentor, who taught me how to create highly refined, accurate charts. And to Steve's son Jeff, whose software makes it all possible. A deep debt of gratitude is also due the following; Peter and Alison Albury of Highborne Cay for their help and encouragement; Terry Bain and his mother Corene, for their help with the history of Little Farmer's Cay and the waters in that area; Lee Bakewell of the S/V *Winterlude* for his help with the programming; Dwight Brice, also known as BM, for his help around Forbes Hill; George and Sue Brown, co-skippers of S/V *Pod Logic*, for their help with the soundings and checking my GPS waypoints; Bugger Bob and his wife Nancy for their help in the central Exumas; Carolina Skiff, Inc., for the 16' Carolina Skiff whose 4" draft allowed us to go many places that the ordinary dinghy would have to be portaged while still being able to handle the roughest seas in the cuts; Dan Doyle, skipper of the R/V *Sea Dragon,* for his unceasing help with the charts and diving sites; Richard Ellis for his help with the waters around Musha Cay; Pat Farquharson for his help with the Pipe Creek area; Peggy Hall for all her contributions on Exuma Park; Bob Head of the Caribbean Marine Research Center and his staff for their help with the CMRC and surrounding waters; Chris Lloyd of BASRSA in Nassau for his help; Anita Martinec and Bob Rader for their help on Exuma Park and Crab Cay; Sandy and Michael Minns for their assistance with this guide and with cruisers in general; Nicolas and Dragan Popov of Island Expeditions for their invaluable assistance and photographs; John Sutter, S/V *Madeline*, for his help with the soundings; Tom and Kathy on *Flying Jinny VII* for the use of their Turtle Charts; Carolyn Wardle for her help with the section on Ham Radio; Wojo, skipper of the S/V *Cat Ppalu* for his help with the diving sites; Tommy Young for his help in the Cave Cay-Rudder Cut Cay area; and thanks to the many cruisers who offered their input, suggestions, and experiences. Last but certainly not least, I would like to express my deepest appreciation to the genuinely warm and friendly people of the Exumas for all their help in the production of this guide, I hope that this guide can in some way benefit you also.

The Publisher expresses sincere thanks to the following contributing artists: Cover art, *"Tida Wave* At Rest" by Jack Blackman, depicts the famous Staniel Cay sloop *Tida Wave,* winner of several Family Islands Regattas, laying in her cradle on Staniel Cay just off Staniel Cay Creek. Sketches of The Exumas that appear on section pages are courtesy of Don Reynolds, owner of Tree House Studio, Sanford, FL; done while cruising The Exumas in his self-built Roberts 36' cutter, *Ppalu.* Back cover photo courtesy of Nicolas Popov/Island Expeditions.

Library of Congress Cataloging-in-Publication Data

Pavlidis, Stephen J.
    The Exuma guide : a cruising guide to the Exuma Cays : approaches,
routes, anchorages, dive sites, flora, fauna, history, and lore of
the Exuma Cays / by Stephen J. Pavlidis. - - 2nd ed.
        p.   cm.
    Includes bibliographical references (p.   ) and index.
    ISBN 0-9639566-7-1
    1. Boats and boating--Bahamas--Exuma--Guidebooks. 2. Exuma
(Bahamas)--History. 3. Exuma (Bahamas)--Guidebooks.   4. Nautical
charts--Bahamas--Exuma.   I. Title.
GV776.24.E88P48   1997
797.1'097296--dc21   97-23745
                                                              CIP

Other books by Stephen J. Pavlidis:
A Cruising Guide To The Exuma Cays Land And Sea Park; with Ray Darville, ISBN 0-9638306

Preceding page: *THE EXUMIAN COAT OF ARMS*
    The *Dexter* (left) half of The Exumian Coat of Arms incorporates the bearings of Lord John Rolle. The *Sinister* (right) half displays an onion and a section of straw plait used to make baskets and hats. The light, sandy soil of The Exumas is well suited for the cultivation of onions and during the season thousands of bags are shipped to Nassau by mail boat. Plait can be found in almost every Exumian home and although most plait is sold in the coil to vendors in Nassau as raw material for their goods, much is turned into hats, bags, and mats by the local ladies.

THE EXUMA GUIDE

A CRUISING GUIDE
TO
THE EXUMA CAYS

SEAWORTHY PUBLICATIONS
PORT WASHINGTON, WISCONSIN

Dedication:

FOR MY PARENTS,

ELIZABETH AND BASIL,

FOR INTRODUCING ME TO

THE BEACH,

THE SEA,

AND BOATS.

STEPHEN

TABLE OF CONTENTS

THE EXUMA GUIDE
A CRUISING GUIDE TO
THE EXUMA CAYS

Sou-Sou East as fly the crow,
To Exuma we will go.

Sail her down, sail her down,
Sail her down to George Town.

Highbourne Cay the first we see,
Yellow Bank is by the lee.

Harvey Cay is in the moon,
Farmer's Cay is coming soon.

Now we come to Galliot,
Out into the ocean we must go.

Children's Bay is passing fast,
Stocking Island come at last.

Nassau gal is all behind,
George Town gal is on my mind.

A wiggle and a jiggle and a jamboree,
Great Exuma is the place for me.

Exuma song, author unknown

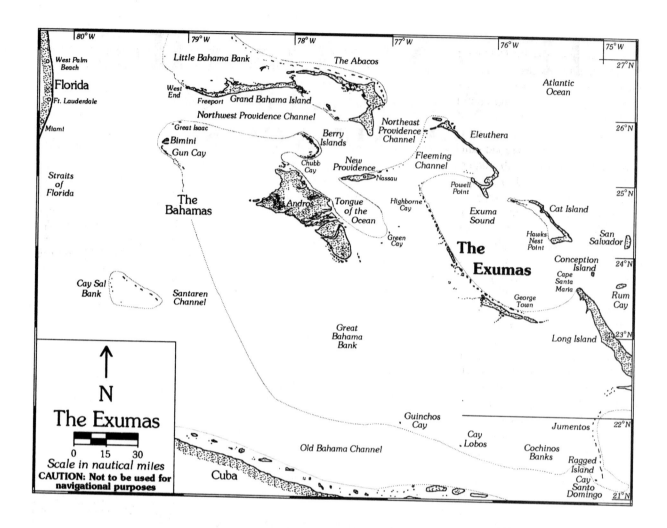

ROUTES TO THE EXUMAS

Southeast of Nassau in the central Bahamas, directly on the much traveled path to and from the Caribbean islands, lie the Exuma Cays. Stretching for 140 miles from Sail Rocks in the north to Sandy Cay in the south, the Exumas lie on the edge of the Great Bahama Bank at Exuma Sound and are the primary destination of some skippers while only a stopover for others. Most vessels arrive in the Exumas from either of two places, south Florida or the Caribbean.

From southern Florida there are several routes to take. Of those vessels departing U.S. ports and heading directly to the Exumas the majority make a stop in Nassau for provisioning or clearing in prior to beginning their Exuma cruise. Most skippers cross the Great Bahama Bank on the Gun Cay-Chubb Cay-Nassau route while others sail directly to Nassau in deep water via the Northwest Providence Channel. Those with plenty of time to spend may cross the Gulf Stream to West End, Grand Bahama, cruise the Abacos, and then go offshore to Eleuthera, Nassau, or through the Fleeming Channel to Beacon Cay. From Eleuthera the most popular jumping off spot to the Exumas is at Powell Point, only about 30 miles from the cays. A few skippers elect to take the less traveled routes, passing south of New Providence from Andros, or passing south of Andros from the Cay Sal Bank.

Except for those skippers who elect to cruise through the Jumentos, vessels arriving from the Caribbean usually pass north of Cape Santa Maria on Long Island to enter Exuma Sound.

INTRODUCTION

To begin with, I wish to thank all the supporters of *The Exuma Guide*. All the cruisers who have made this publication, in the words of many of you, the *"Bible"* of Exumas cruising. To those of you who have written to me, called me on VHF or SSB, dinghied over to *IV Play,* or stopped me at the Park or on some cay to offer your suggestions, thank you. Your contributions have made this second edition that much better. So many of you seem hesitant to point out my errors or omissions while others are happy to be my editor. Whichever you are, please, keep responding, your contributions make you a part of this publication.

The theme for this second edition may well be changes. The biggest changes in this second edition are the Charts. I am now able to abandon the Sketch Chart format and create some very accurate charts employing latitude and longitude lines. With the help of my cartographic mentor, Steve Dodge (*A Cruising Guide To Abaco*), I have constructed a similar hydrographic system and have resounded the Exumas and the results are to be found within. You can now accurately plot your position on the pages within this book, something many of you missed in the first edition. You will also notice that the land masses are shaded for better definition. That was one of the biggest complaints about the first edition. That and the fact that I opened up some previously "secret" anchorages that some people wanted to remain that way. To these people I apologize. They must realize that when boaters see masts in some out of the way spot, they will ultimately endeavor to gain entry. I feel obligated to enable them to do just that, safely and securely. You will just have to live with it.

There have been quite a few changes in the Exumas too since the first edition of this guide was published in January of 1995. In October of 1996, Hurricane Lili's destructive path crossed right over Great Exuma sinking about two dozen vessels in the George Town area, destroying a few homes and a lot of roofs. The hurricane has changed nothing in the routes shown in this book. I have re-sounded each of the routes in the guide over the winter of 1996-1997 and found no differences. One of the most noticeable effects of Lili is the destruction of some of the flora. Many of the trees, especially the palms, have lost a lot of their foliage. The large tree over looking the straw market in downtown George Town lost a number of its limbs resulting in a loss of shade for the ladies in the booths underneath the sawn stumps of its once majestic arms.

There has been a lot of controversy in the George Town area over the last couple of years concerning cruisers violating Bahamian Customs regulations. Remember, you are in a foreign country and are expected to obey their laws. Any violation by a cruiser reflects upon the entire cruising community. George Town has even begun to enforce anchor light regulations on a small scale. We cruisers have no one to blame but ourselves for this by failing to display anchor lights in a crowded and busy anchorage.

The biggest changes in the Exumas have come from the long arm of commercial and private development. Highborne Cay, Hall's Pond Cay, Bell Island, Little Bell Island (Cambridge Cay), Wild Tamarind (formerly Rat Cay), Cave Cay, Musha Cay, Rudder Cut Cay, and Little Lansing Cay have all been purchased by new owners and development has either already begun or is in the planning stages on all of those cays. Except for Little Bell Island, cruisers have lost the opportunity to go ashore on all these cays. The safe anchorage inside the pond at Rudder Cut Cay has become off-limits to boaters due to construction in 1997. I find myself using the sentence "Visits ashore must be by invitation only." more and more throughout this book.

When will it all end? Five years from now? Ten? When it does end, how much of the Exumas will resemble south Florida? Who knows? I could sit here and predict all sorts of dire tales of woe emanating from these islands in the future. I could. But I won't. For one reason and one reason only. The islands of the Exumas seem to always claim what is theirs. History has shown us this. The Lucayans, the Buccaneers, the Loyalists. The Exuma Cays have survived our shenanigans for hundreds of years and the only signs of our passing are some stone ruins. I have faith. I have a feeling that the Exuma Cays will weather even the wealthiest, cold-hearted developer. I have a feeling that the Exuma Cays will even weather us cruisers. It's very satisfying to know that the Exumas will always be here. When will you be here?

Stephen J. Pavlidis

S/V IV Play

A HISTORY OF THE EXUMAS

Isles where Columbus first unfurled
The Spanish flag in the Western World.
Isles where the pirates once held sway,
And scuttled ships off many a cay.
Isles of summer and endless June,
Velvet nights and a golden moon.
Waters of turquoise and lazuli,
Whitest of beaches and sapphire sea.
Isles of romance, story and song,
Of gallant deeds and bitter wrong.

Anonymous
Printed in *Postage Stamps And*
Postal History Of The Bahamas;
by Harold C. D. Gisburn

This chapter is intended to acquaint the visitor to the Exuma Cays with some of the history of The Bahamas, and in particular, the Exumas. From the earliest pre-Columbian inhabitants to the current generation of the descendants of freed slaves, the inhabitants of the Exumas, along with the surrounding waters and the physical layout of the cays themselves, all share and contribute to a fascinating history. The one constant throughout the history of the Exumas is the sea. She has deposited all the inhabitants of the Exumas at one time or another, and with her reefs, rocks, and shoals, she has doomed some to these cays, while others she has protected and nurtured. As the years progress and Exumians enter periods of feast or famine, you will notice an underlying theme of profit from the sea, from harvesting sponges to blockade running, rum running, and drug smuggling. Today the sea brings the Exumas another high tide of good fortune. Waves of cruisers, and their money, are being deposited ashore up and down the entire island chain. Visitors bask in the clear, warm waters, enjoying the ambiance of the island lifestyle while local guides take their charges to sample some of the best fishing and diving in the world. The sea will always be intricately woven into the fabric of the Exumas and this is as it should be.

The Bahamas are fairly simple geologically and visitors often mistakenly believe the cays to be volcanic in origin. They are basically Tertiary limestone, that is, limestone that was laid down as windblown deposits in the geological period know as the Tertiary, approximately 1,000,000-2,000,000 years ago. A gradual subsidence produced an immense plateau which the action of the sea divided into great canyons such as the Florida Straits, The Northeast and Northwest Providence Channels, The Tongue Of The Ocean, Exuma Sound, and The Crooked Island Passage. Most of the present aspect of The Bahamas has been produced in geologically recent time by coral formation during the four glacial and interglacial epochs. Nowhere in The Bahamas is any rock other than limestone found. If you happen to be out diving and find a piece of granite, it is most likely a ballast stone from an old sailing vessel that may have sunk nearby.

The cays themselves are very flat and low lying with few hills over 100' high, the highest hill in The Bahamas, on Cat Island, is little more than 200' high. The external limestone is worn razor sharp by the action of wind and wave and the cays themselves are honeycombed with caves and cave holes. The soil, fertile but extremely thin, is usually found lodged in shallow depressions and often in cave holes. Some of the cays are so pockmarked by cave holes that they are impossible to traverse let alone farm. Fresh water is found close to the surface, often gathering in cave holes after rain. Wells worked too hard or too deep often only produce brackish water, a mixture of fresh water and the underlying salt water. Salt water "holes" are often found inland and are sometimes connected to the sea by a subterranean passage. The cays themselves tend to be covered with various cacti, scrub brush, flowers, and trees. While this is indeed a harsh environment, the climate is one of the best in the world. The sea temperature is ideal for coral formation while the air temperature remains between 50° and 90°. One nineteenth century visitor to The Bahamas coined a phrase when, because of their climate, he called the cays "The Isles of Perpetual June."

The Exumas have had many names. The first map of the new world, produced by Juan de la Casa in 1500, showed the Exumas with the name *Yumey*. The Turin map of 1523, showed the Exumas Cays as little more than rocky blobs named *Suma*. These names were further corrupted to *Xuma* by 1741 and *I Cumey* in 1804.

THE FIRST INHABITANTS

Although many Exumians can trace their roots back to the Loyalists or their slaves, no one can claim a family history of over three hundred years. The first *Homo Sapiens* to make their appearance in The Bahamas were the Siboneys, a peaceful race of fisher-folk who migrated down the Florida and Yucatan peninsulas island hopping to Cuba, Hispaniola, and Jamaica well before the time of Christ. Their name came from their successors' words for *cave dweller*. Little is certain as to the lifestyle of the Siboneys. Other than some finds in a cave in Andros, the Siboneys left few clues as to their culture and range, leading researchers to conclude that they either were very few in number, or only visited The Bahamas temporarily. Without archeological evidence we will never know for sure if the Siboneys may have inhabited the Exumas, but it is highly likely that they passed through in their wanderings. Their scant remains found in the Greater Antilles indicate that those Siboney who were not enslaved became nomadic fugitives from later Amerindian migrants.

The first inhabitants of whom there is evidence are the Lucayans. The Lucayans were in fact Arawaks, a term that meant *meat eaters* in their language. They originated in South America where their descendants are still to be found in the northern parts of Venezuela and the Guianas. They colonized the Caribbean in dugout canoes, a specimen of which in Jamaica was 96' long with an 8' beam and carried as many as 150 rowers. The relatively peaceful Arawaks, although they were brave warriors, were forced to keep on the move by the pressure of the far fiercer Caribs. The Caribs were a cannibalistic group whose chief aim seemed to be murdering the Arawak men and enslaving their women. They would castrate young Arawaks and fatten them up with rich diets and prevent them from engaging in any form of labor to insure tender flesh. The Carib religion promised a paradise for the courageous warrior where the Arawaks he killed would serve him as slaves while assuring the coward that he would be doomed to a hell wherein he would eternally serve an Arawak master. A handful of Caribs survive to this day in Dominica though even less is known of their early culture than that of the Arawaks.

In their search for peace, the Arawaks pushed their canoes northward into the Caribbean, reaching Hispaniola around 200 A.D. and then settling in Cuba and Jamaica over the next two hundred years. They reached the Exumas sometime around 500-600 A.D. in the last wave of their migration. Here they became know as *luddu-cairi* or *luko-kayo* meaning *island people*.

The Caribs were never far behind the Arawaks. By the time Columbus discovered the Lucayans on San Salvador, the Caribs had conquered the Lesser Antilles and were raiding Puerto Rico and Hispaniola. Columbus noted scars on the bodies of some of the Lucayans and through sign language was told that people on neighboring islands wanted to capture them and that they defended themselves.

Lucayans built circular, conical houses of wood and thatch and survived on conch, fish, hutia, and plants. They were basket makers and were adept at manufacturing polished stone implements. Lucayan pottery is called palmettoware and was tempered with bits of conch shell to improve the quality. With the exception of some small gold decorations, the Lucayans had no knowledge of the use of metal. They slept in hammocks, a habit Spanish seamen soon picked up. There seems to have been some commerce between the Lucayans and their Arawak cousins in Cuba and Hispaniola.

The Lucayans were a handsome people, almost oriental in appearance, with broad faces and foreheads flattened in infancy by tying them to boards. This practice was designed to add distinction to their appearance as well as hardening the bone as protection against blows. Mayans and Egyptians shared this unique custom at one time as did an Indian tribe in Montana called the Flatheads. Lucayans wore their coarse hair in bangs in the front and long in the back. For the most part they wore no clothing although they painted their faces, and sometimes their entire bodies, with red, black, and white pigments. They decorated themselves with tattoos, necklaces, bracelets, bones, and feathers. Their chiefs, or *caciques*, were allowed to practice polygamy and served as chief, judge, and priest in their culture. The Lucayans had a class structure and the caciques enjoyed all the benefits afforded to their position. The cacique's canoe was the only one that was painted. When traveling by land they were borne in litters, their children carried on the shoulders of the servants. After death, the cacique was buried along with supplies for the journey to *Coyaba* along with one or two of their favorite wives.

Lucayans were lovers of peace and simple pleasures with a gentle and generous nature, sharing anything they had with Columbus and his men. Next to singing and dancing, the Lucayans loved *batos*, an organized ball game similar to volleyball and soccer. Though they had no written language, their spoken language was described as "soft and not less liquid than Latin." Some 20 Lucayan words and their derivatives survive to this day. Avocado, barbecue, canoe, Carib, cannibal, cassava, cay, guava, hammock, hurricane, iguana, maize, manatee, perogue, potato, and tobacco are all Lucayan in origin.

It was the Arawaks of Cuba who taught Columbus and his people their custom of smoking the *cohiba* plant in their strange Y-shaped pipes called *tobacco*. The tubes of the Y were inserted in their nostrils and the smoke inhaled until the smoker fell into a stupor. The Spaniards quickly picked up this habit although they did not inhale to the point of intoxication. Although Columbus never reported seeing the Lucayans smoke, he described a leaf that he found a Lucayan carrying in his canoe as being highly valued by the Lucayans.

The Spaniards originally thought the Lucayans had no religion leading Columbus to believe they would readily become Christians. They actually had a highly developed religion with two supreme beings, a male and a female, and a belief in an afterlife. They also believed in numerous spirit beings called *zemis* who lived in sacred trees, carved images, and in relics of the dead. The zemis had to be appeased with great festivals in their honor. To induce visions of the future, the Lucayans ground into a powder a potent narcotic called *yopo* which they then snorted up the nostrils. The drug is still in use by Amerindians in Venezuela to this day. A Lucayan chief, while under the influence of yopo, foresaw the destruction of his civilization by ". . . strange blonde men in winged canoes."

The landing of Columbus (who had red hair) in San Salvador in 1492 sounded the death knell for the Lucayan civilization. Columbus brought back some Lucayans in chains, and it was not long before King Ferdinand of Spain authorized raiding parties to the "useless islands." The Spaniards made some 500 journeys to The Bahamas to enslave the Lucayans for their mines and plantations in Cuba and Hispaniola. In 1517 there were an estimated 20,000-40,000 Lucayans in The Bahamas and their price fluctuated at around 4 gold pesos each. The asking price skyrocketed to 150 pesos each for these excellent divers when rich pearl beds were discovered off Venezuela and Trinidad. The Spaniards played upon an Arawak superstition and enticed many Lucayans to board ships with promises of returning them to South America, their ancient homeland and the place where their souls would go when they died, *Coyaba*. Many Lucayans did not go willingly, choosing instead to fight the heavily armed Spaniards. Others, even mothers with small children, committed suicide by drinking the juice of the cassava plant to avoid a life of wretchedness at the hands of the cruel Spaniards. The rest died of starvation and ill-treatment while in bondage and a very few lived to old age. By the early 1520's, this peaceful, innocent civilization, who had only lived to satisfy nature without all the trappings of laws and governments, were obliterated from the face of the Earth and sadly reduced to a footnote in history.

PRIVATEERS, BUCCANEERS, AND PIRATES

After the time of the Lucayans, the Exumas had few visitors until the 1600's. Details of this era are sketchy at best and there are huge gaps in the substantiated history of the cays. Vincente Pinzon, Captain of the *Nina* on Columbus' first expedition, lost two ships off the Exumas in 1499. After a fleet of Spanish ships sank off Abaco in 1595, Spain lost interest in The Bahamas with its reefs, shallow waters, rocks and shoals, and concentrated primarily on its interests in Cuba and Hispaniola. The English however, were right on the heels of the Spanish. Soon the British were busy setting up a colony in Nassau and William Sayle's Eleuthera Adventurers were struggling to gain a foothold in Eleuthera. During this period the only inhabitants in the Exumas were involved in the salt industry. The only visitors were passing ships in search of salt, and privateers.

As Spanish shipping activity increased throughout The Bahamas the era of privateering began. Spanish ships, laden with the riches of the New World, would pass through Bahamian waters on their way back to Spain making wrecking prosperous in the outer islands. It is said that if a crewman were lucky enough to survive the wreck, it was uncertain as to whether he would survive the wreckers. If the Spanish knew of the location of their wrecks they would send crews to salvage the valuables. Bahamian wreckers would drive off the intruders and loot what they had salvaged. The Spaniards retaliated by seizing Bahamian vessels, committing robberies, and taking Bahamian settlers to Havana as prisoners. Proprietary Bahamian Governor John Clarke commissioned privateers to plunder and destroy the marauding Spanish. England soon joined other nations in opposing the forces of France which gave Bahamian privateers freedom to operate against French flag vessels also. As captains became wise to the ways of the wreckers and privateers, wrecks became fewer and fewer, the privateers had to find other uses for their talents. This was not difficult, the era of the buccaneers was in full swing.

The original buccaneers (*boucaniers*), the forerunners of the pirates, were based in northern Hispaniola. They were a wild group of men from France, Holland, and England, indentured servants, seafarers, and adventurers. They wore colorful, picturesque garb and hunted the semi-wild cattle and pigs on the island, descendants of escapees from Spanish farms. They roasted the meat over fires called *boucans* and would sell this smoked meat product, along with hides and tallow, to passing ships. Hispaniola soon became the location of a huge illicit meat and hides trade. The boucaniers quickly learned to live less off hunting and to rely more on their commerce with Spanish ships, first in canoes, then "acquiring" ships, and finally in small flotillas.

From 1629 to 1641, English buccaneers were organized as a company using the island of Providence off the Nicaraguan coast as a base. The 1630's were a very prosperous era for the Providence based buccaneers. Their prosperity ended abruptly in 1641 when the Spanish invaded the island and massacred every settler they could find. The few who escaped shifted their base of operations to Tortuga, an island off the northern coast of Hispaniola, only 55 miles from Inagua in the southern Bahamas. Recruits from every European trading nation began to pour in. By the middle 1600's the buccaneers formed armed bands who were accustomed to hardship, had strong codes of honor that they chose to live by, and were extremely well led. For over 75 years these buccaneers were the scourge of the Spanish fleet.

Most prominent of the buccaneers were Edward Mansfield and the legendary Sir Henry Morgan. In 1664, Mansfield conceived of a permanent settlement upon a small Bahamian Island, New Providence, and Henry Morgan agreed. The proprietary government in Charles Town (renamed Nassau in 1695) was favorable to the buccaneers and Charles Town became quite the haven for these *brethren of the coast*. Mansfield's early and untimely death created confusion in the leadership of the buccaneers and Morgan set them off on a course of plunder and profit. The years between 1671 and 1686 were a time of buccaneer ascendancy. The buccaneers had the backing of major European finance against the Spanish empire. After the capture of Jamaica in 1655, Port Royal, just outside Kingston, became the headquarters for English buccaneers and remained so for 20 years. Under Sir Thomas Modyford and Sir Henry Morgan their achievements reached a climax. The Treaty of Madrid with Spain in 1670, the death of Henry Morgan in 1688, and finally the destruction by earthquake of Port Royal in 1692 dispersed these Jamaican based buccaneers.

There is no fine line as to when the buccaneers became pirates. Webster's Dictionary offers little difference between the two. History suggests that the code of honor of the early buccaneers was forgotten and the bands degenerated into piracy. The buccaneers had articles call *chasseparties* which allocated duties, rewards, and compensations. In all things, their brotherhood was expected to observe a rigid code of honor called *la coutume de la côte*, which roughly translated means *the custom of the coast*. Despite their code and the chasseparties, the English and the French buccaneers were always quarreling. The number of English buccaneers at Tortuga having to rely on French protection increased year by year. The Jamaican and Carolina legislatures passed severe acts against them and the buccaneers became less and less particular about their prey. By 1685 their own people were even calling them pirates. Whatever unity there was between the British and French buccaneers dissolved when their two countries went to war after William of Orange ascended the English Throne in 1689. This struggle was to last 126 years with only one long break. Loyal English were no longer welcome in Hispaniola and when the Anglo-French fighting reached the Caribbean in 1691, the last of the English pirates left the safety of Tortuga and settled in The Bahamas.

The English pirates began to take on bigger game. Bermudan and colonial American ships trading between the Turks, Inagua, and the Colonies became fair game. The Exuma Cays were perfect places where the pirates could hide and spring out to take any vessels they fancied. One Captain said, "As surely as spiders abound where there are nooks and crannies, so have pirates sprung up whenever there is a nest of islands offering creeks and shallows, headlands, rocks and reefs-facilities, in short, for lurking, for surprise, for attack, for escape." They felt safe in the Exumas because of their knowledge of the waters and because of the ineffectual, if not sympathetic, government in Nassau.

Nassau in the 1690's had become, in the words of then Proprietary Governor Nicholas Webb, ". . . a common retreat for pirates and illegal traders" and a ". . . receptacle for all rogues." Harsh words for a man who was not far removed from the ranks of the pirates, of course there is the possibility he was bragging. Nassau had as leaders during the latter 1600's, a succession of men who were little better than pirates themselves, "pirate-brokers" as they were described. The government was as corrupt as it could get. Hog Island, now Paradise Island in Nassau, was granted to a former Governor, the unscrupulous Nicholas Trott for £50. When asked by pirates for permission to land at Nassau and take on water, Trott asked for and received 20 pieces of eight for each pirate who landed in Nassau, 40 pieces for their Captain, and £1,000 in plunder. When he received reports that the French had taken Exuma with three ships and 320 men, he gave the pirates permission to stay. Later on, the whole of the Exumas was granted to one Henry Palmer, the whale and rock-fishing rights to two others.

In 1701, a merchant, Captain Elias Haskett came to Nassau to fill the vacant governorship. He found "disaffection and insecurity" was the rule in Nassau. When he attempted to imprison the pirate Read Elding he stirred up a rebellion. His skull was broken by a pistol butt and he was expelled to New York aboard a small ketch.

Haskett was no saint himself, having arrived in Nassau to avoid creditors in England. His rule as governor was described as tyrannical.

The Spanish and French, realizing the worth of Nassau and The Bahamas against their fleets, attacked Nassau in October of 1703. They plundered the town, spiked the guns, killed many of the men, and left with eighty prisoners including then Acting-Governor Ellis Lightwood. The Spanish returned in 1706 to finish the job. The population of The Bahamas in 1706 was between 400-500 families, mainly scattered over New Providence, Eleuthera, Cat Island, and Exuma. Pirates had free run of the area for the next ten years. By 1713 there were an estimated 1,000 active pirates operating in Bahamian waters. One of their favorite areas was the south anchorage at Warderick Wells from which they could take any vessel attempting The Wide Opening on the way to Nassau.

Some of the most notorious pirates to be found in the pages of history were lurking in Bahamian waters during these years. Mary Read and Anne Bonney, the "lady" pirates who sailed with Calico Jack Rackham, Stede Bonnet the Gentleman Pirate, Benjamin Hornigold, Charles Vane, Captain Kidd, and of course, Edward Teach, better known as Blackbeard. If any one particular pirate could embody the spirit of the era and of piracy itself, none would be better suited for it than Blackbeard. From 1713 until 1716 he teamed up with Hornigold and was based in Nassau along with Captains Jennings, Burgess, and White. Blackbeard's independent pirate career lasted only two years, from 1716, when he acquired his first ship, the *Queen Anne's Revenge*, until his death in 1718.

A stranger piratical trio could not be found than Calico Jack Rackham, Anne Bonney, and Mary Read. Anne Bonney and her penniless sailor husband moved to Nassau seeking employment. There she met Calico Jack who soon swept her off her feet. She eloped with him, heading off to sea in men's clothes. Calico Jack put her ashore with friends in Jamaica when she became pregnant until such time as she gave birth and could rejoin him. She later accompanied Calico Jack on all his exploits. Mary Read, raised as a boy by her grandmother, joined an army unit as a cadet and fought bravely. She fell in love and eventually married another soldier who at first did not realize she was a woman. After her husband died, she again dressed as a man and went on board a vessel bound for the West Indies. She joined up with a group of privateers under Woodes Rogers on the island of Providence. Mary Read claimed she detested the life of the pirate, however, when some of the crew mutinied and returned to their former lifestyle, with them went Mary Read. She wound up on board Calico Jack's ship and no one had guessed she was a woman. And then along came Anne Bonney. Bonney thought Read was a rather handsome fellow and became enamored of her, forcing her to reveal her secret. Calico Jack, noticing the partiality Bonney was showing to Read, threatened to shoot Read. Once again her secret had to be revealed. Read later fell in love with another crewmember and revealed herself to him. When her lover fell into a disagreement with another crewmember and the two were to duel ashore in three hours, Read found out, engaged the crewmember in an argument, and promptly killed him. When Calico Jack finally surrendered and was removed from his ship in Nassau, Anne Bonney, Mary Read, and one other crewman were the last fighters on deck, the rest of the crew fleeing below. Mary Read tried in vain to rouse the crew, finally killing one and wounding another before the lady buccaneers were captured. In court they asked to speak to the judge whereupon they promptly announced, "My Lord, we plead our bellies." Both women were pregnant and English law at the time forbade hanging a mother-to-be no matter how serious her crime. Mary Read later became ill and died, thus cheating the hangman. Anne Bonney, through the intercession of some notable Jamaican planters, escaped the noose and was never executed. Calico Jack, while awaiting execution, was allowed a brief visit with Anne Bonney. Instead of consoling Rackham, she only told him that she was sorry to see him there, and that if he had fought like a man he would not have to die like a dog. No one knows exactly what happened to Anne Bonney, she soon disappeared from the pages of history but she apparently died a free woman. South of Warderick Wells are a series of rocks named after Edward Teach, Anne Bonney and Mary Read.

Many grisly tales have been told and handed down over the years about the exploits of the Bahamian pirates. For the most part they seemed to have lacked the thieves honor of the earlier buccaneers. The notorious Captain Charles Vane hung a member of the crew of a captured vessel at the yardarm only to cut him down prematurely and hack him to death with a cutlass. On another occasion he tied a crewmember to the bowsprit with matches burning down to his eyes and a loaded pistol in his mouth to force him to disclose the location of the ship's money. A pirate named Spriggs went even further. He ordered his captives hoisted to the maintop and released. Those who survived the crippling fall were free to go.

In London, constant argument and complaint was beginning to stir officials to action. The Crown received letters of complaint from citizens, captains, and Governors of every maritime colony. Finally the Crown took action. In 1717 a Royal Proclamation was read in Nassau to some 300 gathered pirates offering pardon for those who surrendered immediately. Only five pirates, one of which was the notorious Captain William Jennings, took advantage of the offer and went to Bermuda. The Crown realized that The Bahamas needed a strong governor who was backed by force and began a search for the right man. Stepping forth was Woodes Rogers.

Like Blackbeard, Woodes Rogers was a Bristol seaman and an ex-privateer. He had already earned a portion of fame for his around the world privateering voyage of 1708-1711 during which he captured some twenty odd ships. It was on this voyage that his vessel rescued Alexander Selkirk from the island of Juan Fernández. Rogers' account of this gave Daniel Defoe the inspiration for *Robinson Crusoe*. In 1718 Rogers was proclaimed "Captain-General and Governor-in-Chief," the first Royal Governor of The Bahamas. Woodes Rogers, as a privateer, had previous dealings with the likes of Vane, Rackham, and Hornigold in places as diverse as Madagascar and Providence, he knew them and their ways well. Armed with the Amnesty Declaration he set sail for Nassau in the company of four British warships arriving off Eleuthera on July 20, 1718. Residents of Harbour Island came out to greet him and warn Rogers that there were over 1,000 pirates in Nassau and that Vane had no intention of surrendering. Six nights later Rogers and his fleet lay off Nassau. At dawn Vane hoisted the skull and crossbones, burned a French vessel he had captured, fired a gun in contempt at Rogers, and with his second-in-command, Calico Jack Rackham, set full sail out the shallow eastern entrance of the harbor. Rogers, with his deeper draft boats, could not follow Vane across the banks. Within three days, Vane and Rackham had captured two vessels bound for Nassau. With their prizes intact they landed on a small island to divide their booty. Some reports say this was in the Abacos while others say it was in the south anchorage at Warderick Wells. It is more likely to have been somewhere in the Exumas. In Exuma Sound, Vane would be free of interference by Rogers' ships, they could not cross the banks and the voyage around Eleuthera would cause a considerable delay, giving them little chance of finding Vane with his head start. If Vane had headed north to the Abacos, he likely would have drawn the attention of Woodes Rogers swifter vessels once off the banks. He could not outrun or outgun Rogers' warships. Vane was never seen in The Bahamas again and was eventually executed in Jamaica in 1720.

After Vane's departure, Rogers landed and walked ashore between two lines of about 300 pirates who fired their guns into the air while cheering for "good King George." Rogers immediately set about proclaiming martial law and securing the town and all vessels within the harbour. He rebuilt and strengthened the fort and garrison, reformed the government, and put everyone to work. One pirate, John Augur, had accepted the offer of amnesty but soon reverted to piracy. The ex-pirate Hornigold was sent to bring him to justice. Augur and thirteen others were captured in the Exumas after a bloody fight, three died of their wounds on the way back to Nassau. Calico Jack Rackham eventually surrendered to Rogers in Nassau in May of 1719 but there were still some 2,000 pirates at large. The Spanish attempted to attack Nassau again in February of 1720 only to be repelled by two warships and furious musket fire. In failing health, Woodes Rogers left Nassau in March of 1721 for England. After spending his personal fortune on rebuilding Nassau, he received no help from The Crown and spent some time in prison for debt. The savior of Nassau in a debtor's prison, this was his reward.

But Woodes Rogers was to make a comeback. He returned to Nassau on August 25, 1729 for his second term as Governor with the benefit of a salary of £400. He died in Nassau on July 15, 1732. He had succeeded in ridding Nassau of pirates and the lawless capitol had a new future. He gave The Bahamas their first motto: *Expulsis Piratus-Restuta Commercia* or *Pirates Expelled-Commerce Restored.*

Privateering continued through the remainder of the 18th and 19th centuries. Many Spanish and French vessels were taken and the claims were settled in a fair, civilized, and legal manor in Nassau's Admiralty Court. Although a few rogue bands of pirates would occasionally visit these waters, they were primarily a threat only to the residents of The Bahamas. The long era of piracy and bloodshed was drawing to a close in the Caribbean and The Bahamas. Except for Eleuthera, there were no permanent settlements in the Bahamian out-islands around this time, the only inhabitants were fisherman, turtlers, wood cutters, and salt exporters. The Exumas returned to a quieter time, when the roar of cannons and the clash of swords no longer competed against the crashing surf or the call of the gulls. But there were invaders just over the horizon and the sounds of the pirate's sea chanteys would soon be replaced by the work songs of the slaves. The Exumas were about to be discovered by the Loyalists.

THE LOYALISTS

Across the Gulf Stream in North America rebellion was brewing. The Stamp Act of 1765 was the beginning of the end for British rule in the Colonies. The American Revolution was getting underway and it was as much a revolt as it was a civil war. An estimated 20% of the population of the Colonies was fiercely loyal to the Crown and hostile to the American cause while many more were neutral or passive.

Known as Tories, the Loyalists favored reconciliation with the Crown. Many stood to lose jobs, commerce, or prestige if the upstart rebels were victorious. Many Loyalists suffered greatly at the hands of the Patriots. Some were socially ostracized and their businesses boycotted, others who refused to sign loyalty oaths to the rebellion were accused of treason and often had all their land and possessions confiscated. Still more were tarred and feathered in the name of Patriotism. Many Loyalists were sent to the notorious Simsburg Copper Mines in Connecticut. They worked in holes 150' below the surface and so many died there that the mine was known as the "Catacomb of Loyalty." The Patriots became even more hostile and vengeful after the defeat of Cornwallis at Yorktown in 1781. Many Loyalists, including some future Exuma residents, sought refuge in eastern Florida as Florida was not involved in the American Revolution.

The Treaty of Versailles on January 20, 1783 restored The Bahamas to England and gave Florida to Spain. The Loyalists in Florida felt cheated that Florida was being traded for The Bahamas and were irate at having to move again. No longer safe in colonial America, they looked to the nearby Bahamas with hope. Investigators were sent to the islands for the express purpose of surveying the land and making a report on the suitability of the land areas for plantations. They found that salt was big industry. Seasonal workers from Nassau produced enough salt from the ponds of Exuma as early as 1728 to supply all of America. The cays were covered with large hardwoods such as madeira, lignum vitae, and braziletto spawning some small logging activity. The few settlers they found were engaged primarily in farming. A report by a Lt. Mowbray in 1785 describes the ". . . Harbour of Great Exuma as the safest and best Harbour in the Bahamas Islands." He suggested that the harbor, now Elizabeth Harbour at George Town, become a port of entry to prevent smuggling and assist the salt trade but the harbor's lack of depth prevented it from becoming a more important harbor such as Nassau. The British Brig. Gen. McArthur reported that 650 Loyalists in Abaco from east Florida were prepared to go to Exuma, ". . . attracted by the goodness of the harbour and the fertility of the soil." The investigators report on the lush vegetation, the good harbour, and the beautiful, rich waters encouraged the Loyalists to believe that a new life, comfortably similar to the old one that they were quite accustomed to under Crown rule, was very possible in the Exumas.

This was a time when some wild schemes were implemented including one which suggested organizing a new military force to attempt to retake the southern colonies. As time passed and their hopes began to fade, the Loyalists throughout the colonies realized that they had to act now to make the best of a bad situation. They began preparing to move. The Crown would provide free transportation for the east Florida Loyalists from the port of St. Mary's. Many Loyalists secured their own means of evacuation with many heading to Nassau before settling on the outer islands. It is estimated that 80,000-100,000 Loyalists and their slaves left the new United States with the great majority settling in the Canadian Maritime Provinces, especially Nova Scotia. A few returned to England while others sailed to Jamaica, Dominica, and The Bahamas. With few exceptions, most Loyalists who settled in the Exumas from 1783 and onwards came from the southern colonies, particularly South Carolina, Georgia, and Florida. The population of The Bahamas tripled in a few short years after the arrival of the Loyalists. The population of the Exumas in 1783 was 32, 17 whites and 15 slaves. Three years later in 1786 the population was 704, 66 whites and 638 slaves. The population of The Bahamas was more than tripling in a very short time. Most of the Loyalists who settled in Exuma were farmers while those that settled further north in the Abacos were primarily businessmen and boat builders.

The most well-known of the Exuma Loyalists must be Denys and Lord John Rolle. Denys Rolle was a Loyalist who lost his land in Florida and in 1783 was given equal compensation in The Bahamas by the Crown. He packed all his belongings including his slaves and livestock aboard the good ship *Peace And Plenty* and sent them to Exuma. His overseers had instructions to establish a cotton plantation on a large tract of land on Great Exuma to which he had title. Denys Rolle, who never visited Exuma, died in 1797 and was succeeded by his son Lord John Rolle, a member of Parliament and the second Baron of Stevenstone. Lord John Rolle controlled some 2300 acres (in absentia-he too reportedly never visited Exuma) and was the largest slaveholder with 376 slaves.

Rolle and the other Loyalists tried to recreate the life they had lived in the southern colonies by establishing huge cotton plantations, complete with elegant mansions, separate stone kitchens, and slave quarters. Although the early cotton crops were successful, by the beginning of the 1800's it was becoming increasingly evident that cotton as a staple cash crop would not succeed. The failure could be contributed to three things. Primarily it was the attack of the chenille, a ravenous caterpillar that still survives to this day in the cays. The thin soil of the cays was rapidly depleted and there was a scarcity of fertilizer, there being very little stock for manure production. Worst of all, the government in London did virtually nothing to assist the farmers in their plight. Lord Rolle tried to move his holdings to Trinidad in 1828 but the Crown refused him permission.

The end of the slave trade in 1807 and the abolition of slavery in 1834 deprived the owners of their indispensable work force and drew to a close the era of King Cotton. The mansions quickly decayed in the tropical climate leaving very little to demonstrate the original lifestyle of the Loyalists although The Hermitage Estate in Williams Town is very much the way it stood two hundred years ago. The Hermitage Estate processed cotton for the Kelsall family who arrived in Exuma in 1790 aboard the schooner *Eliza*.

With the abolition of slavery, hundreds of freed slaves found themselves in a survival situation. No longer would they have to pick cotton for overseers and masters whom they never saw, instead they would have to learn to fend for themselves. They learned to survive as fishermen, earning their living off the rich bounty of the sea. As subsistence farmers they had to adapt to the unyielding soil and a lack of resources. They kept alive their traditions of Junkanoo, bush medicine, and Obeah, or magic. Their foods, music, and dance are all now a part of the Bahamian culture.

The majority of the freed slaves adopted the surnames of their owners (this is why Rolle is the most common surname in the Exumas today). You won't have to look far to find names like Clarke, Dames, Ferguson Forbes, Hall, Kelsall, McCay, Moore, Moss, Mowbray, Nixon, Panton, Ramsey, or Winfree. You will also find certain settlements named after these Loyalists. There's Forbes Hill, Jolie Hall, Moss Town, Ramsey, there's even a Panton Cove in the Berrys.

The settlements of Rolle Town, Rolleville, Mt. Thompson, and Steventon were named after Lord Rolle's plantations. There is some confusion as to what became of Lord Rolle's holdings after his slaves were freed. Some reports indicate that Lord Rolle deeded his holdings to his slaves who in gratitude adopted his surname. Other reports suggest that the freed slaves took to homesteading his lands, hoping that distance and the confusion of the times would allow them to settle the lands permanently. Whatever actually occurred, the former Rolle estate remains to this day as common property, generation land, deeded in perpetuity to all Rolles and controlled by locally elected officials. You will also find generation land in other families with roots in these times.

Many took to plying the old Bahamian trade of wrecking, salvaging the cargoes of ships that came to grief in the shallow waters of The Bahamas. Some of these Exuma wreckers sailed far and wide in search of cargo venturing to the waters off Florida and Hispaniola.

The salt industry came into its own in the 1800's. Salt was in great demand for the preservation of meat and fish and Williams Town on Little Exuma was the center of this production employing 200 people at one time. There stands today a huge stone column built over 200 years ago to mark the area as a salt producer for passing ships who would take their cargoes to Nova Scotia and North America.

All in all, the years following the abolition of slavery were a peaceful time when the inhabitants lived off the bounty of the sea and land, much as the earlier Lucayans had done. Poverty was the byword but prosperity was just around the corner. Once again, across the Gulf Stream, a war was brewing. The restlessness that was to become the American Civil War was already being felt in Nassau, and Exumians stood to make a profit on it.

THE AMERICAN CIVIL WAR YEARS AND BLOCKADE RUNNING

Towards the end of the 1850's The Bahamas was eagerly anticipating the age of steam. A steamship company opened a Nassau office in 1842 just to deal with the burgeoning Bahamian sponge industry. Many far-sighted Bahamians knew that very little stood in the way of Nassau becoming the winter resort of North America. An act to encourage steamship navigation between New York and Nassau was passed in 1851 but the arrival of the first steamship, the *SS Jewess*, burnt to the waterline, ended that affair. In 1859 an agreement was reached with the Cunard line and Nassau was added as a regular stop on their New York to Havana run. The Royal Victoria Hotel was built to accommodate the expected influx of North American visitors but it surely would have gone bankrupt had it relied on those expected visitors in the following years. The ill-fated Royal Victoria Hotel was to become the headquarters of the Bahamian blockade runners in the American Civil War.

On April 12, 1861, Confederate troops opened fire upon Fort Sumter in Charleston Harbor and four years of America's bloodiest war began. The southern states lacked the manufacturing capabilities of their northern counterparts and had to rely on imports to carry on the war effort. Realizing this, President Lincoln ordered a blockade of all southern ports very early in the war. At first, the Federal Navy was unprepared to enforce the blockade and blockade running entailed little risk, but as the north mobilized, the blockade tightened. Ship builders, ship owners, seamen, and adventurers were all drawn by the huge profits involved with blockade running. Anyone with a vessel and a little luck stood to make a lot of money by supplying the South with much needed supplies from abroad while taking southern cotton to market in Nassau.

After the capture of New Orleans in April of 1862, blockade running became increasingly hazardous. Over 150 ships were employed in the blockade of Charleston and Wilmington alone. As the strength of the blockade increased, so did profits, some blockade runners could make $300,000 for a round trip. Their vessels were long, lean, shallow-draft side-wheelers capable of high speed. They were usually painted a slate gray to decrease their visibility and they burned anthracite coal so that the smoke from their funnels would not betray their position. Some blockade runners were built with a goal of only three trips whereby they would have paid for themselves with plenty of profit to spare.

Many Exumians jumped at the opportunity to share in this windfall and headed to Nassau. Even Exumians without ships could expect high wages for blockade running. The Captain would receive £1,000 and 10 bales of cotton, the pilot received £1,000 with 5 bales of cotton, the purser and first officer each received £300 and 2 bales, and even the ordinary seaman was paid £20 a month with a bonus of £10 for each completed trip. There were rich rewards for the blockaders as well as those who dared their lines. When the U.S.S. *Magnolia* caught the blockade runner *Memphis* in July of 1862, each Lieutenant received $38,318 and ordinary seamen drew $1,700 apiece. If this may not seem like a lot to you, remember that at this time labor unions in America were seeking a wage of $1.00 a day.

Nassau has probably never experienced a more frenzied period than during this short time. Shops were packed, streets were crowded, and money was spent as fast as it was made. Even the lowliest seaman could afford champagne and rich food. Not since the days of the buccaneers and pirates had Nassau known such prosperity. The Royal Victoria Hotel was the scene of nightly parties attended by diplomats, Confederate and British Officers, blockade runners, newspaper correspondents, advertisers, and all sorts of rogues that controlled the ingress and egress of goods and services from Nassau, characters as rich and as colorful as almost any of the pirate era. The sudden wealth in Nassau allowed Bay Street to be widened, new buildings to spring up, and land prices to increase by 300-400%. The public debt of £47,786 was paid off almost overnight and the Bahamas Police Force was created by an act of 1864. But good fortune rarely lasts long and this sudden prosperity had to come to an end, it could not go on forever.

The blockaders, now numbering over 300 ships, besides having control over almost all the Atlantic coast ports, would often enter Bahamian waters in search of the blockade runners. They would lie in wait in the waters around Great Stirrup Cay in the Berrys waiting for blockade runners heading to or leaving Nassau. At one time or another they were accused of using Exuma and Inagua to water their ships. Not all blockade runners found and stayed upon the road to wealth. Many were caught and imprisoned while still more died in wrecks or from Federal gunfire. By 1863, half the blockade runners that left Nassau never made it to their destinations, two were sunk within a mile of the shore of Eleuthera. Sherman's march to the sea in 1865 successfully cut off the southern ports from the interior ending the Bahamian gold rush. Nassau and The Bahamas had reaped the last of that golden harvest.

THE BIRTH OF TOURISM

With the loss of revenue at the end of the American Civil War Nassau quickly slid into a horrendous depression. The new street lamps on Bay Street remained unlit and the Royal Victoria Hotel was put up for sale but no offers were tendered. Although poverty was endemic throughout The Bahamas, the outer islands such as the Exumas suffered least as they profited least and while some men had made fortunes during the Civil War years, most could only look forward to a return to the ways of fishing and farming.

After the war the salt industry quickly collapsed because of a high tariff imposed by America, however the sponge industry was still going strong. In 1841, a shipwrecked Frenchman, Gustave Renouard, began exporting Bahamian sponges to Paris and Nassau soon became the sponge emporium of the New World. It is estimated that at one time 265 schooners, 322 sloops, and over 2800 open boats plied Bahamian waters in search of sponges with nearly 6,000 Bahamians making their living from the harvest in places like the Bight of Abaco, Long Island, The Great Bahama Bank, The Jumentos, and the Exumas. Spongers worked the northern Exumas from Nassau to Sandy Cay just north of Sail Rocks, down to Farmer's Cay and westward to Green Cay on the Tongue of the Ocean. In 1870, Key West was established as a sponging center and it was Bahamian *conchs*, white Bahamians, who formed the bulk of that city's population. In 1892 there were 8,000 Bahamians in Key West's population of 25,000. This was typical as the Bahamian population in the Out Islands steadily declined from 1871-1921. The sponging prosperity continued until 1939 when an epidemic fungus killed off 90% of the Bahamian sponges within two years plunging the Bahamian economy into a brief depression. Although Bahamian sponges are once again commercially available, the modern sponging industry is only a reminder of the richness of that vanished era.

Many former blockade runners returned to that old Bahamian standby of wrecking; wrecks have always been considered a regular and predictable means of income in the islands. The hurricane of October, 1866, provided a banner year for the wreckers but this prosperity would also be fleeting. The Imperial Lighthouse Service, in spite of some violent opposition, erected beacons and the first truly accurate charts of The Bahamas were drawn up. Lighthouses sprang up throughout The Bahamas and year by year the number of wrecks became fewer and their value less. More and more wreckers found themselves involved in heated competition with one another. A minister in Hopetown, Abaco, was facing his congregation one Sunday morning (they had their backs to the sea) when he noticed a ship coming to grief upon the rocks. He told his flock to bow their heads and close their eyes for a minute of silence. The deacon ducked out and the churchgoers soon realized what was transpiring and a race to the wreck ensued. The church members later turned the altar around so that they might have the view of the reefs.

Many Bahamians found a market for their crafts. Examples of Bahamian straw-work and shell-work were exhibited at several International Expositions from 1851-1886. Bahamians were stressing Bahamian products and were gaining attention. Conch shell exports, primarily to cameo brooch makers in France and Italy, steadily rose during the 1850's only to settle back down by 1860. Around 1875, many Bahamians began growing tobacco with the first cigars being exported in 1878. Unfortunately many cigar aficionados found the Bahamian tobacco to be inferior to that of Cuba or Jamaica and the industry died. Abaco turned to shipbuilding and boat builders crafted some fine vessels but the industry never really flourished. There was a huge pineapple industry on Eleuthera and Cat Island with its best year in 1890 when 700,000 dozen were exported. The Bahamas was the first commercial producer of pineapples on a large scale and the word *pineapple* became synonymous with *The Bahamas* by the mid to late 1800's. The industry began declining from 1902 onwards but The Bahamas still grow some of the sweetest pineapples you will find anywhere. The Exumas were not blessed with the soil that could produce those exquisite pineapples that Eleuthera and Cat Island became famous for, so Exuma farmers went from crop to crop searching for something that could grow in the cays and enable them to turn a profit. In the 1880's they discovered sisal.

Sisal, a cousin of the Mexican *agave* plant, is sometimes called a century plant and grows with very little care. The leaves sprout long, wide, and flat from a central core and have sharp needle-like points on each tip. You can spot a sisal plant by its tall, thin, central stalk, sometimes rising 15' or more straight up with small leaves and branches at its conical shaped upper end. The fibers are put through a soaking and beating process and the pulp dried, twisted into twine, and then made into rope. America was a major consumer of sisal, buying not only from The Bahamas, but from Mexico and the Philippines also. By 1890 the sisal boom was on in the Exumas. By the mid 1890's the market for sisal began to slide but was revived temporarily by the Spanish American War in 1898 and peaked during the years 1902-1903. The Bahamian sisal industry had a few more good years during World War I but by the 1930's the industry was finished. Manufacturers had many problems with Bahamian sisal. Unlike the sisal produced in Mexico and the Philippines, Bahamian sisal had a higher salt content which would often play havoc on American machinery. One prison in the U.S. had a million dollars worth of machinery quickly rendered useless from rust by running Bahamian sisal through its rollers. Today, sisal plants can still be seen sprouting their towering central cores toward the sky up and down the Exuma chain.

The first two decades of the twentieth century saw The Bahamas mired in poverty but with a future that held much promise. Bahamians came to realize that their greatest assets were all around them, the pure white beaches, the beautiful blue-green waters, and a winter climate that was described as early as 1651 as being ". . . good and wholesome." In 1851, the Bahamian Government planted the seeds of an ambitious program of promoting tourism that would not truly come into its own for almost another century but would bring The Bahamas true, and hopefully lasting prosperity.

The only obstacle to be becoming a tourist haven for wealthy Americans lay in getting the tourists to The Bahamas. The Bahamian government signed navigation acts in 1851, 1857, and 1879 aimed at promoting interest in Nassau from steamship companies. Contracts were signed with the companies in 1851, 1859, and 1879 and tourists began flowing into Nassau, actually it was more of a trickling. The early efforts at promoting tourism seemed jinxed by fatal misfortune. Besides the loss of the *Jewess*, five other ships either sunk or burned before 1895 with considerable loss of life. The best tourist year before the 1900's was in 1870 when Nassau had over 500 winter visitors. In 1890, regular steamship service began between Nassau and Florida with a cable being laid between Nassau and Jupiter, Florida in 1892.

In 1898, the fourth and most important Hotel and Steamship Act was signed with H. M. Flagler of Florida fame. Flagler built the Colonial Hotel in Nassau which would one day become the British Colonial Hotel. In 1914, the government created a Development Board specifically charged to increase tourism in the islands of The Bahamas. Exuma would not reap any benefits from the early tourism campaign, discovery of these cays by tourists was still a long way away. Flagler's enterprises failed but tourism itself continued to grow slightly each year with Nassau and The Bahamas becoming established as a bona fide tourist haven with tourists arriving in increasing numbers up until the outbreak of World War I.

World War I did much to bring The Bahamas closer to the outside world. Many Bahamians traveled away from home for the first time with many out-islanders passing through Nassau and widening their outlooks. The Bahamas sent their first contingent of combat soldiers to France in 1915. These "Gallant Thirty" were soon followed by more between 1915-1917, all in all, 650 Bahamians went to war and 50 never returned. At home, sponge and sisal prices remained high throughout the war but the latter years brought shortages of many items and inflated prices on almost all staples.

The end of the war was greeted with great cheer, Church and ships bells ringing and Bahamians dancing in the streets. The returning soldiers found sisal and sponge prices rapidly dropping and the economy taking its usual roller-coaster plunge. But once again, as it always seems to happen in these islands, the sea would bring a new wealth to the inhabitants. Once again, Bahamian mariners would supply the American continent with what it needed most and was willing to pay highly for; liquor.

PROHIBITION AND RUM RUNNING

In December 1919, the United States passed the Volstead Act as the 18th amendment to the U.S. Constitution. This act, which became law in January of 1920, made it illegal to import, sell, or manufacture intoxicating liquors except for export or medicinal purposes. This was a blessing, a gift for The Bahamas. The proximity of The Bahamas to the eastern U.S. coast made the cays perfect places from which to illegally import alcohol into the U.S., a high risk, high profit business called bootlegging. Seeking to test the waters, exports of spirits to the U.S. in 1920 and 1921 were small. But when it soon became clear that the Bahamian government did not intend to support the U.S. Excise Service, more than 20 giant liquor concerns sprang up virtually overnight in Nassau. Anyone with a fast boat could reap the harvest and skippers and crews once again flocked from the outer islands to Nassau seeking a portion of the wealth. Fast powerboats soon began making runs from Bimini and West End, Grand Bahama, to Florida, while schooners would sail to "Rum Row" just off the New York-New Jersey coasts. For the first time planes were used to smuggle liquor to bases in the Florida Everglades. Exumian mariners found a market for their talents and were well compensated for their risk.

Bootlegging became a prime industry in The Bahamas from 1920-1933 in the same tradition as privateering, wrecking, and blockade running and Nassau again reigned supreme as the base of operations during the Prohibition years. The headquarters in Nassau was at the Lucerne Hotel, home to the annual "Bootleggers Ball," and the popular, and appropriately named, *Bucket of Blood*. Nassau's streets were busy again and money flowed freely in all circles. The outer islands lagged in the prosperity but some of the wealth did manage to trickle back home to the seaman's families. From past experience, Bahamians knew the well would one day run dry and began to invest more of their money in The Bahamas with $4-5 million dollars being invested in Bahamian real estate and buildings in the 1920's with many notable family fortunes being made during this era.

As if following a script, the end of the prosperity quickly came and the Bahamian economy took another swift downward plunge. The repeal of Prohibition ended the positive cash flow that The Bahamas so enjoyed for thirteen years. Tom Lavelle, the bartender at the old Lucerne Hotel, summed up the final days when he said, "Boys, those days are gone, we've got to go to work now."

THE TOURISM BOOM

The years between the repeal of Prohibition and World War II found The Bahamas once again deep in a severe depression. Although locally grown foods were cheap, work was scarce. In Exuma, as in all the Out Islands, inhabitants returned to the ways of farming and fishing. The end of the sponge industry to a fungus in 1939 dealt the already hard pressed islanders another deadly blow, there were several actual cases of starvation reported.

When World War II began, The Bahamas raised a contingent of soldiers that were put into service with the Northern Caribbean Regiment, and of the 1100 Bahamians in service, only 14 did not return. The War brought some minor economic benefits. Tourism enjoyed a small boom in the winter of 1940-1941 and The Bahamas suddenly blossomed into a haven for rich British refugees eager to escape rationing, shortages, and the horrors of war. Real estate prices climbed higher and Nassau society received a new lease on life when the Duke of Windsor, ex-King Edward, arrived as Governor. The Duke initiated policies to assist Out Island farmers and opened an Infant Welfare Clinic in Nassau. In 1940 the British Government leased a site at George Town, Exuma to the U.S. Navy for 99 years and the Navy opened a seaplane base using local labor at American wages, a tremendous lift for the depressed Exumians.

V.J. Day, August 14, 1945, brought celebrations reminiscent of the scenes at the end of World War I, but unlike previous events, did not bring about the traditional slump to the economy. The next three decades after the war brought an unparalleled burst of expansion and success. A soaring tourism industry and increasing investments breathed new life into the Bahamian economy. Government revenue multiplied which in turn raised the standard of living throughout the cays and brought about a steady progress towards full political self-determination. The Bahamas were on the road to independence and little would stand in their way.

The increase in tourism after World War II can in no small way be contributed to an improvement in air service. An increasing number of daily flights into Nassau brought the cays that much closer to visitors who were tired of overcrowded Florida and were wary of the political turmoil in Cuba. Of no less importance was Nassau's old world charm, cheap goods, and the beautiful waters and comfortable climate. By the mid-1960's, there were 43 airports and over 40 hotels spread throughout the Bahamian Out Islands. Nassau was receiving 7,500 visitors a day and the Out Islands up to 4,000. The primary motivation of the new tourism movement was the promotional advertising undertaken by the Development Board which was to become the Ministry of Tourism in January of 1964.

The Bahamas was becoming known as a year-round destination instead of seasonal. Money was pouring into the country and it was being invested as fast as it arrived. Throughout the Out Islands, wealthy Bahamians and foreigners alike were purchasing property and building houses as prime residences and vacation retreats and many sub-divided developments sprang up in the Out Islands. One notable location on Great Exuma promised ". . . a place away from it all." Twenty thousand adjacent lots were sold on the strength of that slogan although actual construction only occurred on less than 5% of the lots. The Exumas were beginning to get a trickle of tourists and even a few scant yachts began arriving in the cays. Most of the incoming wealth that flowed into The Bahamas was concentrated in the Nassau-Grand Bahama Island areas while in the Exumas, wages were still low, work was scarce, and the cost of living grew by 100% in the 1950's. Those not farming and fishing became involved with earning their living off the tourists. Bahamian Independence was a welcome event but seemed overshadowed somewhat by the new prospects for instant wealth that blew in from South America.

DRUG SMUGGLING

The Bahamas, as you have seen, has gone through many periods of feast or famine. Throughout the times of the wreckers, privateers, pirates, blockade runners, and bootleggers, when the money flowed, it flowed like a river, but the 1970's and 1980's would bring a flow of money of tidal wave proportions. Once again America demanded and The Bahamas supplied, this time it was marijuana and cocaine. The Bahamas became an important staging area for fast boats and planes delivering South American and Jamaican goods to the U.S. shore. Places like Abaco and Andros were vital links in the system but neither gained the notoriety of the Exumas when it came to the smuggling business. The center of all the action in Exuma was at Norman's Cay.

In January of 1979 a newly registered Bahamian company called International Dutch Resources Ltd. bought half of the 650 acre island. The $900,000 purchase price included the old Norman's Cay Yacht Club with its dock, airstrip, grocery and liquor store, and 10 rental units. A Colombian of German ancestry, Carlos Lehder, was the controlling shareholder of International Dutch Resources Ltd. Lehder first appeared on Norman's Cay in 1977 and shortly thereafter purchased a villa. He systematically began purchasing other properties, threatening and intimidating when he could not get his way. After he purchased the marina and airstrip he sank over $5 million into renovations, lengthening the airstrip and enlarging the dock. He had already been smuggling Medellin Cartel cocaine from Norman's since 1978 to airstrips in Florida and south Georgia. Boaters and visitors to the cay were discouraged, often chased away by gun toting guards. The airstrip soon became a hub of activity and aroused suspicions.

The DEA organized a task force called Operation Caribe and targeted Carlos Lehder. Agents disguised as boaters feigned mechanical breakdown's in the anchorage while other agents set up surveillance from Shroud Cay and from a Coast Guard cutter offshore. A September 14, 1979 raid by Bahamian police officers netted 33 Germans, Americans, and Colombians. Lehder was apprehended attempting to flee in a small boat. He told officials he thought the raiding party was coming to kidnap him. Lehder's people were allegedly warned of the raid by a Bahamian official and arrangements were made to have the cay spotless. Lehder and his inner circle were actually on Wax Cay at the time of the raid. A Bahamian police official released Lehder uncharged after he turned over a suitcase which is said to have contained $250,000. His men were released and back on the cay within 48 hours. An irate DEA official stated that Lehder not only owned Norman's Cay, he owned ". . . the whole damned country." Some very famous names were allegedly associated with his operation including Fidel Castro, Manuel Noriega, and Robert L. Vesco, the fugitive American financier who was living just south of Norman's Cay on Cistern Cay at this time. NBC News broadcast a report on September 5, 1983, implicating the Bahamian Government including the Prime Minister, but no charges were ever filed, either in the U.S. or The Bahamas, on any high ranking government member.

The DEA began to choke off Lehder's cash flow by arresting his pilots and confiscating his shipments. Finally on January 8, 1981, a 39 count indictment was handed down in the United States naming Lehder and 13 others. Lehder was not overly concerned as he continued to enjoy the freedom that Norman's Cay and the Bahamian government offered him. By 1983 Lehder had seriously curtailed his Norman's Cay activities and had not been on the cay for over 6 months. His men had ransacked all the villas on the cay. A new plane destined to smuggle cocaine for Lehder crashed into the shallow waters east of the marina dock where it remains to this day. Lehder began living in Columbia as a fugitive and was finally captured by Colombian authorities on February 5, 1987, just outside Medellin and extradited to the United States. On May 19, 1988, Carlos Lehder was convicted and sentenced to life without parole plus 135 years. Norman's Cay today reflects little of Lehder's lawless days except for some bullet holes in the buildings on the southern end of the island and the plane that rests in silent tribute in the anchorage.

Besides what transpired at Norman's Cay, a few other people up and down the cays were involved in one form or another with drug smuggling. The horror story of a sailboat with four dead bodies aboard in the 1970's was kept very hush-hush and few can, or will, remember exactly what happened. It is suspected that money earned during this time was invested in the Exumas, increasing the standard of living and paving the way for today's visitors to enjoy the cays even more. Very little is mentioned about this period, local inhabitants are very tight lipped on the subject. Maybe it is too recent, maybe people are afraid to implicate themselves or someone else, most folks simply want to forget. This is probably best. Exumians did what Exumians have always done, they profited from the sea, and the air.

THE EXUMAS TODAY

Visitors today will find the Exumas highly tourism oriented. George Town has an international airport and there are a half-dozen marinas strung throughout the islands with more planned. There are some excellent restaurants and bars to enjoy and George Town has quite a few hotels. Tourist dollars are a vital part of the Exumian economy and most Exumians make their living from the tourist trade in some way, whether it be as a guide, a cook, or a craft maker. Exuma visitors are steadily growing year by year with no end in sight for the boom. More and more investors are looking at the Exumas with an eye towards commercial development and real estate prices reflect this interest. Even the smaller cays in the Exumas are being bought up almost as quickly as they come on the market.

The sea is once again bringing a share of wealth to the Exumas from the numerous cruising boats that visit the area every year. It is likely that a charter company will open up for business in the not too distant future. As the Exumas become more and more like south Florida, do condos or an all inclusive resort lurk over the horizon? One must wonder what the future will bring. History would suggest this prosperity to be short lived but for some reason that seems unlikely. Time will dictate the next chapter in the history of the Exumas so in the meantime, drink deep of the islands and enjoy, whatever lies in the future of the Exumas, one thing is fairly certain, the Exumas will endure and prosper.

FLORA AND FAUNA

The Exuma Cays are home to some interesting species of flora and fauna that are uniquely Bahamian and found few other places in The Bahamas. While a study of the flora and fauna of the Exumas could comprise volumes in itself, we will only touch upon the subject to acquaint the cruiser with what they will likely encounter in the Exumas.

FAUNA

We will begin our study of the fauna of the Exumas with a look at the mammals you will find throughout the cays. Mammals are any creatures of the class *Mammalia*. These are warm blooded and their young are nurtured with milk secreted from the female mammary gland, hence the name. With the exception of bats because of their ability to fly, mammals are relatively poor colonizers of islands. Cuba and Hispaniola seem to be the source of terrestrial vertebrates in The Bahamas.

The mammals you are most likely to come across in the Exumas will be rats, bats, and hutia. Next to rodents, bats are the most abundant species on earth. There are 12 species of bats in The Bahamas but the most predominate are the three genera of leaf-nosed bats. These creatures are characterized by a leaf shaped appendage on their snout that is actually their "radar dish." They are nocturnal and feed primarily on fruits and small insects. While the term "bat" usually conjures up images of blood sucking vampires, the only creatures that need to worry about bats on these cays are the mosquitoes.

There are two species of rats in the Exumas, the brown Norway rat and the black rat. While both are nocturnal, the black rat adapts better to forest and field with very little water supply. The brown Norway rat requires a steady water supply and so it is often found near man and his dwellings.

Another rodent you may come across is the "hutia," pronounced "who-tia." The early Lucayans kept them as pets and for food. The early Loyalists described them as ". . . a coney with a rat's tail." With their chunky bodies, stubby necks, short ears and tails, they resemble guinea pigs although they are cousins to the porcupine, chinchilla, and capybara. When they walk through the bush they waddle but when they are on the beach they tend to hop like rabbits. They are nocturnal and feed primarily on the leaves, bark, and branch tips of four or five species of plants from which they also obtain their water. Once widespread throughout The Bahamas they were nearly exterminated by hunting and the predation of dogs and cats. The only place to find these creatures now is within the boundaries of The Exuma Cays Land And Sea Park. Eleven hutia were placed on Little Wax Cay in 1973 and thirteen on Warderick Wells Cay in 1981. Both groups have multiplied profusely and are rapidly devouring all vegetation within their habitat. There seems to be a conflict in the Park as there is an endangered species, the hutia, rapidly devouring endangered species of plants. Exuma Park and The Bahamas National Trust are working on resolving the problem without endangering either the hutia or the plants.

Amphibians are represented in the Exumas by a few species of frogs such as the Cuban tree frog, the eastern narrow-mouthed toad, and a species of greenhouse frog. The Cuban tree frog is frequently seen on walls and windows and is attracted to house lights in search of insects. Although it is usually whitish or gray, it can change its color very quickly. If handled it will produce an irritating mucus so wash your hands immediately after handling one.

Reptiles are abundant in the Exumas. You will see curly-tailed lizards, noticeable by their tail which curls up and over their back, on almost every cay. Anoles, such as the Bahamian green anole or the Bahamian brown anole, are also common. The green anole is very similar to the small lizard sold in pet stores in the U.S. and is sometimes mistakenly called a chameleon although it does have the ability to change its shading. You will often see it clinging to branches extending its dewlap, the bright orange sack under its throat, as a threat display.

There are four species of snakes in The Bahamas. None are poisonous and all are to be found in the Exumas. The most common snake is the brown racer who prefers to hunt lizards and insects. The Bahamas fowl snake is a relative of the boa constrictor and is usually about 2'-3' in length although some have been reported growing to 6'. There is a rarely seen pygmy boa which is often called a golden boa because of its coloration. This snake prefers lizards for its diet and only grows to 12"-14." The worm or blind snake is rarely seen except after a heavy rain and grows to about 5". It is easily mistaken for an earthworm which is quite uncommon in The Bahamas. Rest assured that these snakes are more scared of you than you are of them. Far too many have been killed by hysterical people who know nothing of snakes except to irrationally fear them.

There are no fresh water turtles native to the Exumas but there are three types of sea turtles to be found. The green turtle is probably the best known because of its abundance and the fact it is the principal source of turtle soup. It may grow to 4' and weigh between 250 and 500 pounds. The carapace, its shell, has an olive brown color on the upper side with the scutes, (the scales), shiny and yellow with green and black spots. The green turtle feeds primarily on marine plants, turtle grass, and eel grass. The hawksbill turtle is easily identified by its attractive shell made up of multi-colored translucent plates. The carapace is dark brown with yellow and reddish streaks on the scutes. The hawksbill turtle is smaller than the green turtle, only growing to about 3' and about 100 pounds. It is omnivorous and prefers a diet of animal origin including jellyfish, sponges, sea urchins, crustaceans, and sea grasses. The loggerhead turtle is the largest of the three, easily attaining a length of over 4' and weighing in at over 500 pounds. It is characterized by a heart-shaped carapace, reddish-brown in color and its long, broad head with two pairs of prefrontal scutes and a strong, horny, beak. The loggerhead is primarily carnivorous and feeds on mollusks, crustaceans, fish, jellyfish, and occasionally sea grasses. Small loggerhead turtles were tagged, weighed, and then released into the creeks of Shroud Cay in The Exuma Cays Land And Sea Park in 1983.

Photo courtesy of Nicolas Popov/Island Expeditions

Rock iguana.

The reptile that most cruisers want to see is the rock iguana of the northern Exumas that is found nowhere else in The Bahamas. They are relatives of the iguanas that were used as dinosaurs in the old horror movies. In pre-Columbian times the rock iguana was far more numerous than today and inhabited almost every major Bahamian island and cay. The former abundance of iguanas is evidenced by the number of "Guana Cays" still on the charts. The few iguanas left now are protected by Bahamian law although some Bahamians still hunt them for food. There are two colonies of them at S.W. Allan's Cay and Leaf Cay in the northern Exumas. The Bahamas National Trust, in an effort to preserve the species and broaden their territory introduced two iguanas from Allan's to Warderick Wells. Ping, an 11 year old male, and Ling, a 7 year old female were placed there on March 23, 1990. Rock iguanas are generally of a dark, dirty color with shades of red around the head and upper portions of the limbs. The legs are dark and the skin has a criss-cross pattern to it and their eyes are deep red. They have a serrated ridge of skin along the spine that is used to bleed off excess heat. Their most remarkable feature is their third eye. Known as the *pineal eye*, it is located under a triangle of clear skin just behind the meridian of the other two eyes. The pineal eye is found in many lizards, including several iguanids, and is a very well developed organ with a lens and retina while in others it is a degenerative gland with few light receiving abilities. Despite intensive research, the function of the pineal eye is little understood though some scientists suspect it is involved with the detection of day length, necessary for the reproductive cycle of the lizard.

Bird watchers will have a field day in the Exumas. The list of birds sighted in the Exumas is long indeed and includes woodstar hummingbirds, owls, red-legged thrushes, mockingbirds, and the reclusive Audubon's shearwater. The bananaquit, also know as the Bahama honeycreeper is very common throughout the cays. These small, sooty-black birds with yellow breasts and pale throats can be seen throughout the year. Leaving a small dish of sugar on your boat will certainly entice some of them to pay you a visit for dinner. As you travel along, you are likely to hear the song of the mockingbird. These may be either the North American mockingbird or the Bahamian mockingbird, which prefers more secluded areas. The white-crowned pigeon is a dark gray bird that is about the same size as a domestic pigeon and was an important game bird throughout The Bahamas for many years. It is not unusual to be anchored off an outlying, uninhabited cay and hear their soft cooing well into the night. The white tailed tropic bird is one of the most beautiful, graceful birds you will see in the Exumas. Sometimes called a *bosun bird*, the tropic bird shows up in numbers in March, usually from Shroud Cay to Hall's Pond Cay, but they have been seen as far south as the Brigantines and Great Exuma. The tropic bird is about the size of a large pigeon and is white with dark patches over the eyes and on the wings. Its most striking feature is its long, sinuous tail feathers and their aerial acrobatics, mating maneuvers, are a delight to witness. The osprey, sometimes called a fishhawk, may be seen in the more isolated areas perched on a rock or beach, calmly watching and waiting for a meal. Found from Maine to the southern Bahamas, the North American and West Indian osprey can both be found in the Exumas. Osprey build massive nests in trees, stumps, and often on rocks. These nests may be inhabited by succeeding generations of osprey for upwards of 60 years and are so conspicuous that they are used as navigational landmarks by the local fishermen. Some of the more isolated cays in the Exumas are rookeries so please do not disturb any nesting birds that you may come across.

As far as insects go, the sandflies and mosquitoes are everywhere and it seems that only the wind can stop their vicious attacks. Screens and bug sprays are a must on windless nights. Some locals say that they only bite in season while others say that the season is all year long. The sandfly is probably the most loathed of all the creatures in The Bahamas. These infamous *no-seeums* seem to be little more than teeth with wings. They can inflict tiny welts which are more irritating and last longer than the bites of mosquitoes many times their size. There are two types of sandflies in the Bahamas, they are the night-feeding *Ferocious Sandfly* (aptly named), and the day-feeding *Becquaert's Sandfly*. As there are day and night-feeders, it seems that the torment will last 24 hours a day. The Ferocious Sandfly reaches its peak feeding hours during twilight and around midnight. It is the female searching for a blood meal that bites. They occur year-round but are most active during the rainy seasons from June to August and from October to December. Wind seems to provide the only effective relief from them. Ferocious Sandfly feeding seems to cease when the wind increases to 6 knots however the Becquaert Sandfly is much more determined and may continue to feed until the wind picks up to 15 knots. Some people use a 50-50 mix of water and "Avon Skin-So-Soft" spread on unprotected skin as a repellent.

As you walk along you may encounter the large web of the crab spider. Make sure that if you walk into one of these webs that you do not pick up the spider as a hitchhiker. Their bite is mildly toxic and can be very painful. There are black widow spiders and small scorpions in the Exumas so take precautions when around loose rocks, heaps of trash, and in the leaf litter of palm trees. Termites are also common and often will build large nests that are plainly visible. The termite nests are even marked on the trail maps of Warderick Wells which are available at the Park Headquarters.

One of the oddest insects you may run across is the giant bat moth. Called *brujas* by the nearby Cubans, they are considered corporate spirits. They grow up to 8" across and will indeed startle you at night as they hysterically flap their wings to get out of your path. It is easy to see how people mistake them for bats.

EPIFAUNA

Plants and animals living on or in the ocean bottom are called the *benthos*. Nearly 16% of all living animal species are benthic. Animals that live on the ocean bottom or on rocks, shells, seaweeds, pilings, etc. are called *epifauna* and make up about 80% of all benthic animals. Animals that live buried in the sea bottom such as clams and worms are know as the *infauna*. There are 30,000 species of infauna compared with 125,000 species of epifauna. The larvae of benthic animals are an extremely important part of plankton, one of the building blocks of the marine food chain. It is estimated that 75% of all benthic animals have a planktonic larval stage. Most benthic animals live in less than 600' of water due to the availability of food at those depths. The epifauna includes corals, crustaceans, echinoderms, fish, mollusks, and sponges.

Coral is a product of benthic animals and the prudent mariner has a deeply ingrained respect for coral reefs. These massive, extremely complex environments, with an insatiable appetite for ships and sailors, are far better understood today than they were a few centuries ago when European adventurers first braved these waters.

There are two types of coral reefs in The Bahamas. The isolated coral patch reefs which often occur in channels, or at deep drop-offs adjacent to soft coral areas, can be very small and found some distance inward on the banks. The fringing reefs are the large reef systems that you will find along the windward side of the cays and rocks. The term *coral reef* may be a bit of a misnomer. Although the dominant organism in Bahamian reefs is coral, reefs are built not only by corals, but by algae, worms, sponges and mollusks, all combining to create a reef out of calcium carbonate.   Reef-building, or *hermatypic* corals, require clear water of generally less than 150' and water temperatures that seldom, and not for very long, drop below 70° Fahrenheit. This generally limits coral reefs to the shallow waters between the Tropics of Cancer and Capricorn, and to the eastern shores of the continents, since the western shores, because of the Earth's rotation and prevailing winds, are subject to upwellings of cold water from the ocean depths. Even though most of The Bahamas are north of the limits of suitable conditions for hermatypic corals, the Gulf Stream warms the surrounding waters to within the tolerance of reef-building corals.

Coral is the hard, stony skeleton of calcium carbonate secreted by certain marine polyps. These polyps are only a veneer of life on a coral reef. Like the heartwood of a tree, the interior of a coral colony is inactive, mere rock, the skeletons of ancestral polyps, layered generation upon generation. Like reading the rings of trees, scientists are able to read the history of the sea in cores taken from the interior of corals. Coral rock is accreted differentially according to day length, season, water temperature and salinity. We know from fossil corals that day length has been increasing over time. Corals during the Devonian Era, 400 million years ago, experienced 400 days per year. Modern science has recently been able to chemically alter coral, changing the calcium carbonate to calcium phosphate, the same material as bone. This allows coral to be implanted in the human body as a replacement for weakened or damaged bone.

The polyps that form coral are known as *cnidarians* and are any of a phylum of invertebrate animals, mostly marine, including jellyfish, *hydrozoans,* and *anthozoans. Cnidarians* have two basic forms, the *polyp* and the *medusa*. The polyp is tubular, radially symmetrical, and has a simple internal cavity that aids in digestion. The medusa consists of an epidermis, gastrodermis, and tentacles, which are actually an extension of the body that is designed to reach out and grab food. Fire coral is an excellent example of a medusa. One cnidarian to be found in great numbers (and avoided) in the Exumas is the *thimble jellyfish*. The thimble jellyfish is dark brown and about the size and shape of a thimble, hence the name. The larger ones, as big as the end of your finger, are known for their painful sting. Found in great numbers throughout the Exumas in spring and early summer, it is not unusual to see a great brown spot in the water, sometimes 100' or more across, that appears to be a reef, but in reality is a massing of these creatures. Use caution and do not swim among these jellyfish.

Coral has few natural predators. The number and variety of animals that eat coral polyps are just now becoming understood by researchers. Certain stars, shrimp, crabs and butterfly fish specialize in eating the mucus coating of the coral colonies. The Foureye Butterfly Fish actually bites off the polyps themselves. The 8" green bristle worm, a voracious predator, can chew away the living parts of entire segments of staghorn coral. Parrot fish take bites out of coral and turn them into fine sand in the process of feeding on algae. Man is the principal destroyer of coral. Since the times of the earliest settlers in these islands, the bark of the Jamaican Dogwood, *Ichthyomethia piscipula*, has been used to poison reef fish. No one is really sure of the damage this practice did to the reefs. Dynamiting reefs to stun fish was a widespread practice in The Bahamas until recently. Except for a massive ship grounding, few events could be more catastrophic to a reef. The use of bleach to drive crawfish from their holes in the reef is currently destroying vast stretches of reefs in The Bahamas. Dive on some of the reefs around Manjack and Powell in the Abacos and you will see what bleach can do to a living reef. Remember when diving around coral that it is a living organism. It grows very slowly, averaging about an inch a year. Never stand on it, break it, touch it, or kick sand on it, this can smother it. It is illegal to remove live coral in The Bahamas and the penalties are quite stiff.

Corals can be *branching, encrusting,* or *hemispheric.* Branching corals grow quite erect such as racks of elkhorn or staghorn coral or sea fans. Fire corals are encrusting, meaning they encrust a base upon which to grow, yet they are not true corals, they are actually related to jellyfish. Forming massive, branching, plate-like colonies, they are often found encrusting soft coral species. Their plates may be box-like and yellow, white, or brown in color. Blade fire coral is similar to branching fire coral and forms thin, irregular, upright blades or plates. If in doubt about a coral, don't touch it. Encrusting corals such as pencil coral or cactus coral can be found in shallow water but are more abundant in deeper water. Hemispheric corals, such as brain coral, form huge rounded heads that often grow to

6' in diameter and more. Star corals are an abundant hard coral that form huge mountainous domes or boulders as colonies. They also form multi-lobed heads and knobs and can also be encrusting. This coral is a major reef builder and may vary in color from green to yellow.

Crustaceans are any of a subphylum of arthropods and include shrimp, crabs, barnacles, and lobsters that usually live in water and have gills, mandibles, two pairs of antenna, and two compound eyes. They may have three or more pairs of walking legs and pairs of specialized appendages called maxillae. Crustaceans have a hard, chitonous covering, or shell, called a carapace which they periodically shed when moulting.

Barnacles, after a free-swimming larval stage, become the scourge of ship bottoms increasing fuel consumption while decreasing maneuverability. They are shrimp-like animals that cement themselves to rocks, pilings, docks, or ship's bottoms, as well as other animals such as whales. It is a little known fact that Mocha Dick, the white whale that was the real life inspiration for Melville's *Moby Dick* appeared white because of the many barnacles that covered him. The adhesive strength of the cement that the barnacle secretes from a gland in its antennae has been tested at the National Institute for Dental Research in the U.S. at up to 22 pounds per square inch of contact area with a tensile strength of over 5,000 pounds. The acorn barnacle forms cone-shaped plates around itself while the goose barnacle secretes a two-part shell and attaches itself by a fleshy stalk. To feed, barnacles open their shell plates and extend their six leathery feet into the water, trapping plankton. Louis Agassiz, the American naturalist who classified over 2000 species of fish in the Amazon, once described a barnacle as ". . . a shrimp-like animal standing on its head in a limestone house kicking food into its mouth."

The giant hermit crab has a rusty red color with a granular, stony appearance and stalked blue eyes. Often found living in a queen conch shell, the giant hermit crab has red and white banded antennas and two massive claws, the right one slightly larger than the left. It is commonly found along rocky shorelines and sandy shoal areas. The small, three colored hermit crab has blue legs with white bands and orange joints. Its tiny claws are equal in size and are red or maroon with white tips. The blue crab, the common edible crab of the Atlantic coast, has a greenish-tan carapace with legs and claws of bright blue with red spines. Younger blue crabs may have pale blue legs. The four pairs of legs are well adapted for swimming and the last pair has flat round paddle-like appendages. Its claws are of equal size. It prefers sandy to muddy bottoms in shallow water. The mangrove crab is a quick little creature that has a mottled dark green color on its smooth carapace. The legs are often reddish with equal size claws with hairs on their outer surface. The carapace is nearly square. It inhabits sandy shorelines in and around mangroves and under rocks. The yellow box crab has a yellow carapace covered with nodules and ridges. Seven teeth or spines form a crest on its flattened claws. This crab has a "can opener" arrangement of fingers on its right claw that is used to pry open shells when feeding. It prefers sandy bottoms in shallow water where it sometimes burrows into the sand. Spider crabs, which from claw to claw may measure over 2', can be found prowling the grottos and reefs.

At home on the most arid islands, land crabs are yet tied to the sea. They spend their juvenile life stages as plankton and their long marches to the sea during summer months enable the females to release their offspring, up to several hundred thousand eggs, into the water. Being fundamentally creatures of the sea, they respire by means of gills that must be kept moist. For this reason, land crabs must dig their burrows deep enough to reach the water table and is why they are included in the section on *Epifauna* instead of the section on *Fauna*. Their are four species of land crab including one species of hermit crab in The Bahamas. Two of the species are commonly eaten, the giant white crab and the black crab. The giant white crab may exceed 2' from claw to claw while the black crab is said to be the more succulent of the two. The land hermit crab is only distantly related to its marine cousins. It inserts its abdomen into the vacated shell of a marine or land snail and carries the shell around wherever it goes. It has a large, muscular, blue claw that serves as a weapon, feeding utensil, and a trapdoor to its home.

The crustacean that most cruisers search so incessantly for is the spiny lobster, a clawless relative of the Maine lobster. It has a spiny carapace and legs and is colored brownish blue to dark red with yellow spots on its tail. It has no claws for defense but has spines over the eyes to protect it from some predators. Along with the spiny lobster there are the smooth tailed lobster, spotted lobster, and the unique slipper lobster with its blunt, squared-off head. The lobster is one of the most important marine creatures in the Caribbean as it provides a living for many of the islanders you will come across in your cruising. Unfortunately, the spiny lobster is getting increasingly difficult to find in sufficient numbers and size. They are in danger of being over-fished. Considerate cruisers to these areas only take what they need and do not try to fill up their freezers.

The spiny lobster mate and lay eggs when the ocean is warm, usually from March through July. When lobsters mate the male and female lie face to face and the male leaves a sticky fluid on the female's belly. This hardens into a black patch called a *tar spot* which contains thousands of sperm. If you see a female with a tar spot you know she will soon lay eggs. The female lays many bright orange eggs and carries them beneath her tail, scraping the tar spot as she lays them to release the sperm. A female carrying eggs is called a *berried* lobster because the eggs look like thousands of tiny berries. The female carries the eggs until they hatch, protecting them from predators and fanning them with water to prevent the growth of fungi and bacteria. After 1-4 weeks the eggs are a dark brown and ready to hatch. A larger, older female may lay up to three times more eggs than a smaller, younger lobster. Bear that in mind when you venture forth on a lobster hunt.

The newly hatched lobsters look nothing like their parents. They have flat, clear bodies with long, thin legs. They do not crawl on the bottom but drift in the sea. Lobsters must float in the sea for their first 6-12 months of life. They drift in company with baby conchs, crabs, clams, and fish. After their plankton stage, they go through a metamorphosis where they change into the shape of a small lobster. These young lobsters can swim and so they head for shore. The juvenile lobsters settle in shallow areas like mangroves, grass beds, or shallow reefs. They may also hide in the weeds growing under boats, on weed encrusted mooring lines, and dock pilings. Their clear bodies are now marked with pale yellow and brown. If you see what you think is a baby lobster, that is, it looks like a very small lobster, it is probably at least a year old. As the lobsters age, they move out to the coral reefs to breed and spawn. In places known for only small lobsters, it is probably because the lobsters have grown and moved to other areas. Most lobsters begin to mate at 3-5 years. At this age they are about 8"-10" long from head to tail. Lobsters can live more than 40 years and can reach 3' or more from head to tail, the difficult part is in avoiding predators for that long.

A lobster, as it grows, must shed its shell from time to time in a process called moulting. As it breaks out of its old shell, backing out where the tail joins the body, it wears only its soft skin-like shell. This soft skin swells to a larger size and the lobster has room to grow inside it until it is time to moult again. From the larval stage to a bottom dwelling juvenile, a lobster may moult 11 times.

Lobsters eat mainly snails and clams but they may also eat worms, crabs, shrimp, urchins, sponges, and small fish. On the other hand, snappers, grouper, octopus, sharks, and rays all dine on lobster with humans consuming the most lobster of all.

One of the most intriguing things about the lobster is the lobster march. A lobster, or crawfish, march is an amazing spectacle. Believed to be triggered by waning Autumn light, these marches tend to be single minded affairs. Typically a migrating group consists of 2-75 or more lobsters moving single file, head to tail, sometimes for weeks at a time and covering hundreds of miles. Occasionally they bivouac on a patch reef where they provide a bonanza for the lucky fisherman. Unsure of the reason for the marches, some biologists believe their annual exodus to be a behavioral artifact from ages past when the crawfish had to migrate from the cold northern waters to the warmer southern waters in the fall. When confined to a pool at Bimini's Lerner Marine Laboratory, a group of migrating crawfish marched around the periphery of their enclosure continuously, day and night, for two weeks.

Echinoderm means prickly or spiny skin. All echinoderms possess an internal skeleton and a radial body. Their most distinctive characteristic is their water vascular system composed of canals with tiny tube *podia*, tube feet. Typical echinoderms are starfish, sea urchins, the sea biscuit, the sea cucumber, and the sand dollar. If you find an echinoderm that feels soggy, it is most likely sick. When the water vascular system is functioning properly the echinoderm is full of water and is kept stiff and rigid. The one echinoderm to watch out for is the black, long-spined sea urchin. It has a brittle shell with numerous movable spines projecting from it. If stepped on or handled, these barbed spines break off under the skin and become firmly embedded. Hours of pain and swelling are to follow. Remove as many of the fragments as possible and apply antiseptic or ammonia (urine will suffice) if stung. The urchin may be several inches wide with spines of up to 16". This creature is primarily nocturnal, preferring to hide in holes in coral or rocks in the daytime with only its spines sticking out. One might think that the spiny sea urchin has no natural predators but it is consumed by at least 15 species of fish including trigger fish and snails. The most spectacular echinoderm may well be the intricately fretted basket star. By day, basket stars are tightly wadded into fist-like balls that are attached to sponges or gorgonians. By night it expands to as much as a yard across, grasping for its planktonic prey with its widespread, branching arms. The sea cucumber, though not usually eaten in this part of the world, is known in the Orient as *trepang* and is considered a delicacy. Shaped like the vegetable it is named after, the sea cucumber is green, soft and leathery, and grows between 2"-18" long. It can usually be found in the soft sand or mud below the low water mark. This strange creature eats mud that it sucks off of the tentacles that ring its mouth, breathes through its anus, manufactures iron, and synthesizes opal which it stores inside its body. Oddest of all, it defends itself by expelling all of its internal organs through its anus and then growing back a new set over a period of time after the coast is clear. The green sea urchin, *Stronglyocentrosus droebachiensis*, the owner of the world's longest scientific name, has gonads that are prized as a delicacy.

With a multitude of fish dictionaries, fish encyclopedias, and field guides to fishes of certain areas, the amount of information on fish is staggering. The average boater probably has one or two reference books on fish aboard and many cruisers hardly go a few days without catching or eating fish. Anything written here would likely be a boring repetition of material found elsewhere, and a simple listing (very long) of the fish found in the waters of the Exumas would accomplish very little. The average visitor to the Exumas is most likely familiar with the more common fish but may not understand the behavior and lifestyle of fish and how that is linked to their appearance.

While some fish rely on speed to catch their prey, others rely on stealth. Prickly spines make certain fish unattractive to predators, while others depend on their ability to outrun or evade the hunters. This diversity of reef fish did not just happen, it is a product of the need to survive, to feed. A fish that cannot feed, cannot survive. If you understand how fish compete for food and how that competition has created the diverse species, you can make an educated guess at any reef fish that swims by. In the midst of the competition for food, an advantage can be gained by specializing. Species may become more efficient at obtaining a particular food supply by selecting their feeding time or place. Some fish are nocturnal feeders while others prefer certain depths, bottom types, or corals. Specialization is possible because seasonal changes on the reefs are minimal. Life on the reef is much the same day to day, month to month, century to century. For example, a butterfly fish feeds almost exclusively on certain species of coral polyps. It plucks these from the reef with its tubular snout and it has a slender body that allows it to prowl the narrow reef crevices. Imagine what would happen if the corals it feeds on began shedding their polyps every fall like leaves on a tree. This fish, with its specialized snout, would find itself poorly suited for obtaining any other kind of food until the polyps returned. If it were unable to adapt, the species would likely become extinct. The specialization on and over the reefs takes a variety of forms but their appearance is the logical result of natural selection. The fish you are likely to find can be broken down into five very general groups, the camouflage experts, the high speed predators, the reef dwellers, the large reef predators, and the schooling fish.

Some fish rely on camouflage to survive and although some of these fish may be in plain sight, it might take you a second look before you realize what they are. These masters of disguise may be found on the reef, the bottom, or occasionally free swimming. Having reduced swim bladders, they usually don't swim far or often, preferring to stay motionless awaiting passing prey, and then surprising them at close range. Although exposed to predators, their camouflage makes them difficult to detect. They usually will have spines and sharp, pointed, bony plates on the head. Some species possess poison glands that can deliver an extremely painful dose through their spines.

The angler fish uses its disguise most efficiently. Not only does its appearance conceal it, it aids in attracting dinner. The fleshy tabs drooping from its retractable dorsal fin above the angler fish's head lures smaller fish in close where, with one swift gulp, it disposes of one course and then awaits the next. Flatfishes, such as the flounder, are usually found lying just under the sand on the bottom awaiting their prey to swim by. They have pigment cells on their upper side (flatfishes lie either right side or left side up, they cannot change). Their nervous system controls these cells enabling them to blend in with their surroundings. Scorpion fish, and their cousins the stone fish, are found right in among the corals on the reef. Easily overlooked, they are decorated with fleshy tabs, warts, and lumps of a mottled brown or tan color. They have poison glands associated with their spines. Do not attempt to handle these fish.

Stealth tactics are also used by fish that live above the bottom and the reef. Such fish usually have elongated, almost cigar like forms. Pipe fish, trumpet fish, and flute fish prey on small invertebrates by appearing as small sticks or reeds floating above the bottom. Needle fish and barracuda are often seen floating, immobile, as if just some sort of debris. Their stabilizing fins are located well to the rear of their elongated bodies where they act like the stabilizing feathers on an arrow. The barracuda has a fearsome reputation but if proper precautions are taken you may learn to swim with them. They tend to be highly curious of divers, following you wherever you may swim around the reef. Barracuda move water over their gills by the action of opening and closing their mouths which makes the uninitiated diver wary as it can be a fearsome display. When diving, do not wear shiny objects such as bracelets, earrings, or necklaces as they may be attracted by the shiny flash and think it is a food fish. Most barracuda attacks that are not provoked happen when spearfishing. Barracuda are highly territorial and may resent your taking what they deem is their dinner. They have been known to swim up with blinding speed and take the fish right off your spear. Most of the fish that you will catch when trolling on the banks will be barracudas. Many people eat barracuda and delight in its sweet taste. There is a gray area when it comes to whether or not it is safe to eat barracuda due to ciguatera poisoning. The locals have a simple method of determining the edibility of barracuda. They say that if you catch one well out on the banks, away from the reefs, they are edible. The ones you catch offshore or in the cuts are the ones you will have to worry about.

Feeding over and around the reefs, but not making use of its living space, you will see the high speed predators. These fish are always moving, usually at a considerable speed and have developed smoothly tapered bodies for minimum water disturbance. Mackerel and tuna have ideal bodies for this type of foraging. Their scales are set so deep that they appear smooth and slick and their heads and eyes are contoured for smooth water flow. Even their fins fold away into pockets in the body wall. These fish tend to have nonfunctional air bladders so they can swim quickly from one depth to another. Their tails are usually narrow, stiff, and forked. Though not efficient at slow speeds or for quick acceleration, they are ideal for the upper speed ranges where it is important for a tail to move back and forth through the water rapidly. These fish are very muscular and when swimming at high speeds appear almost immobile. Their speed and coloration are excellent defenses. They are dark blue or green above, silver along the flanks, and white along the belly. From above they appear the color of the deep sea, from below they appear to blend into the daylight filtering down from the surface, and from the side the reflected light aids in masking them entirely. Besides the mackerel and tuna, which are not very common around reefs, another fast predator that you will likely see are the jacks, especially around the deeper portions of the reefs. Jacks are very curious fish and may swim along with you for a while.

There are two groups of reef dwellers that make their home in and among the various coral formations, holes, and crevices in the reef. In the first group are the small fishes seen flitting in and out of the reef or hovering motionless nearby. These fish, such as the butterfly fish, trigger fish, or the angel fish, are usually disc-shaped and slender. With their pectoral fins high on their sides and centered, they are highly maneuverable and have precise control of their position. This allows them to feed even amid the strong tidal surge that flows over the reef. For the most part, they cannot swim at high speed, but when threatened, they can turn on a dime and dart into the recesses of the reef for safety. When trigger fish are threatened, they retreat to a crevice or hole where they raise and lock their first dorsal spine with a *trigger* device located in their second dorsal spine. They then lower their pelvis and become wedged in. This group of reef dwelling fish often have brilliant stripes, bands, or bars, and are the most colorful inhabitants of the reef. These displays act to break up their outline and may even send courting or territorial signals to members of their own species. In the language of the reef, stripes seem to indicate cleaning behavior, giving their owners an immunity to predation. While some juvenile angel fish have been observed cleaning other fish, blue-striped neon and shark-nosed gobies devote their entire lives to removing parasites from their neighbors. Setting up cleaning stations on the reef, they make themselves as conspicuous as possible in order to draw in clients. Fish that are troubled by parasites can be seen swimming around these stations, patiently awaiting their turn.

Deep within the maze of meandering passageways in the reef, with no need for precise control of motion, you will find the other group of reef dwellers, the eels. Eels have elongated bodies with small fins set far apart. Since their feeding habits consist of briefly darting from their hiding places, a lack of precise control does not pose a problem. Eels are nocturnal explorers of the reef when they travel at all. Rarely does their entire body leave the protection of the reef during the day, even when attempting to seize a meal. Certain wrasses have been given license to clean their teeth without harm. Eels must continually pump water over their gills for respiration giving them the fearsome appearance of gnashing their teeth. There is a record of one eel living to 88 years of age.

The large reef predators, although not excessively streamlined or extremely fast, can be very quick over short distances. While not perfectly camouflaged, they can be difficult to spot, and, even though they are not bristling with spines, their size and speed makes them less subject to predation. This group consists of snappers, groupers, and squirrel fish. Snappers generally cruise the reef all day, alone or in groups, and capture their food with short bursts of speed while groupers on the other hand are more sedentary preferring to stay partially hidden in the reef awaiting passing prey. When stalking prey, they tend to stay on the bottom where their coloration aids in camouflaging them. Their large spots, blotches, and stripes break up the outline of the grouper making it difficult to pick out on the reef. They have fine scales that are covered with a mucus that helps to keep them from getting stuck in the reef. The squirrel fish is generally nocturnal and is one of the principal feeders after dark although they are often seen in the daytime hovering in the shadows. They have large eyes and reddish tones and although they are not as large as the grouper or snapper, they are more common. Squirrel fish are muscular and are protected from predation by an array of prominent spiny rays on their fins and sharp edges on their gills and head.

For the schooling fish, wandering en masse over the reefs has special advantages if a fish is not a large predator or highly specialized. Always exposed to predators while grazing on the reef, schooling fish rely on safety in numbers and when threatened may seek shelter or tighten up the school and move away rapidly. Predators can be confused or intimidated by large schools reducing the odds of a single fish being eaten. Schooling fish vary widely in appearance but tend to be the most easily seen and approached of any of the other groups. Damsel fish, parrot fish, and wrasses are examples of schooling fish. The sergeant major, a damsel fish, is one of the most prolific characters you will find on the reefs, seeming to be everywhere in large numbers. Parrot fish have large, heavy scales and a prominent beak that is used to literally take bites out of the reef. Wrasses are smaller with finer scales. They feed on algae, plankton, and small invertebrates. Neither parrot fish nor wrasses are strong swimmers. Surgeon fish are common on reefs and often form large schools. They get their name from their lance-like spine located on either side of the base of their tail. The coloration of this spine stands out against their normal color patterns warning predators of its presence.

Sharks should probably be included in the category of large reef predators but they are likely to be seen anywhere on the banks or in the Sound. Although many commercial divers running charter operations in the cays may feed them and swear that they are not as dangerous as their reputation, for the non-professional, the best thing to do is get out of the water when a shark is in the vicinity. Many local fishermen claim that if one is going to get bit it will probably be in October when some of the species are mating. Lemons, makos, tigers, black tips, gray reef sharks, and hammerheads may be found anywhere in the Exumas. Parts of Elizabeth Harbour in George Town seem plagued with occasional visits by these voracious feeders. Nurse sharks, which resemble large catfish, are generally quite docile towards man unless provoked. Large groups of nurse sharks mate in the tidal creek on the eastern shore of Ship Channel Cay from March to June.

Mollusks, with over 100,000 living and 35,000 fossil species, have no internal supporting skeleton, instead they secrete a shell that serves to protect their body. Species below the tide line need the shell as a refuge from attacks of predators while inter tidal species use the shell to prevent drying out during low tide. Mollusks usually have highly developed sense organs, eyes or antennas. Mollusks use a foot, a muscular organ, for movement. Mollusks include squid, octopus, snails, clams, oysters, chitons, limpets, nerites, periwinkles, ceriths, murex, augers, miters, helmets, pen shells, and cockles. In the Exumas the focus is on only one mollusk, the conch, in particular, the Queen Conch.

If you have ever picked up a seashell and listened for the ocean, chances are it was a conch shell. Who isn't familiar with the conch shell, its size and shape and the beautiful pink enamel-like finish of the inside? Its firm, white meat, marketed for thousands of years, can be found served up as cracked conch, scorched, as fritters, in a stew, creole, or raw with lime in a conch salad. Early islanders exported the conch shell as far as the territory of the Hopewell Indian tribes in Ohio. Exports of 300,000 shells to Europe were not uncommon in the nineteenth century. In the 1930's and 1940's a strong curio trade prevailed and countless young conch were caught and their shells shipped to shell distributors in Florida. Today the trade is aimed at the tourists who buy hundreds of thousands of full size shells and manufactured items every year.

The Queen Conch, as befits its calm existence and provident nature, has always served as a symbol of peace, joy, and life. Caribbean sailing vessels of old sometimes hoisted a conch to the yardarm as a symbol of peaceful intent. Joyful conch trumpets may be heard at sundown all over the Caribbean and Bahamas, their mournful wail once told of fish for sale. Key West, Florida has proclaimed itself *The Conch Republic* and its natives *conchs*.

Conch shell was an essential material to islanders before metal arrived from Europe. Log canoes were scraped out with conch shells while hammers, chisels, and adzes were fashioned from it by Arawak Indians. Conch shells have been used for decorative and symbolic items for centuries. Conch are found extensively in sea grass beds and sandy, muddy areas feeding on turtle grass in relatively shallow water while juvenile conch are found closer to the shoreline.

The male conch has a black arm over his right eye while the female has a groove that runs down the right side of her foot. The female conch lays her egg mass only on a clean sand or gravel bottom. The conch eggs are very small, smaller than grains of sand and hidden inside a string of sticky jelly that the female lays from her foot. The female conch lays this jelly string back and forth until it forms a firm egg mass. The egg mass is a crescent-shaped lump about 4"-6" long that, in a few days, will hatch into baby conch. Baby conch are so tiny that you would need a magnifying glass to see one properly. Ten could fit into one drop of water. The newborn conch, about the size of a period on this page, has two round lobes rimmed with many short hairs that beat back and forth to help the conch swim and move food into its mouth. The baby conch will drift in the sea for about three weeks feeding on microscopic plants. The conch then sinks to the sea bottom and undergoes a metamorphosis and its lobes disappear. It develops a long snout with a mouth at the end, and a foot with a claw. It will never swim again. The baby conch now buries itself into the sand and hides for approximately one year while it continues feeding on small plants and growing larger. A conch grows its own shell which it makes larger as its body grows. When a conch is a few months old its shell is white, but by the time it is 5 or 6 months old its shell is white with streaks of dark brown. By the time you are likely to notice a conch on the sea bottom they are usually over a year old and their shells are no longer streaked. Their shells are now pinkish to yellowish brown with pink or yellow inside the lip. As the conch grow, they are called *round* or *roller* because their shell is like a round spiral. As it grows the spiral gets bigger. When it is 3 years old the conch has reached full shell size, now it grows a broad lip on its shell. This new lip is a sign that the conch is about to reach maturity. Once the conch has a broad lip, it is as big as it will ever grow. Conch may live to about 20 or more years naturally, and the lip keeps growing thicker and thicker with age and becoming darker with orange or gray. The splines, or horns on the shell, once long and sharp, become blunt and stubby. In its old age, the conch's shell is eroded by boring worms and sponges and becomes covered with corals and weed. Old conch are called *samba conch* or *sanga conch*. Experienced conch fishermen will tell you that these old conch are often poisonous and should be left alone. It is speculated that conch acquire a cumulative toxin from the food they eat, just as barracuda and jacks do.

Photo Courtesy of Nicolas Popov/Island Expeditions

Conch Fishermen.

Although a conch produces large numbers of eggs, most of the newborns are eaten when still very small. Many kinds of fish, crabs, crawfish, stingray, shark, turtle, and octopus eat young conch. While older, broader lipped conch are safe from most of these animals, the loggerhead turtle, stingray, and octopus can also devour large conch. The loggerheads have been known to crush conch shells in their jaws. Moderately sized conchs have been found in the stomachs of sharks. As with the lobster, man is their greatest consumer. In the U.S. alone, about 2.5 million pounds of meat from around 10 million conch are consumed yearly. Many millions more are exported to the Orient, Europe, or eaten locally throughout the islands. It is not unusual to see great mounds of conch shells littering islands and beaches. There is a reason that the shells are ashore instead of in the water. It is said that if you throw a conch shell back into the water, conch will no longer inhabit that area and move on. It is more likely that the reason you won't find old conch shells in the water is that conch divers don't want to spend most of their time diving for empty shells.

If you have ever caught and cleaned conch, you have probably encountered the conch fish. The conch fish is not a parasite, it only seeks shelter in the protective shell of its host and as many as five conch fish have been recovered from a single conch. The conch fish, actually a cardinal fish, is nocturnal, leaving its host at night to browse among the blades of turtle grass for small shrimp and other crustaceans. Besides the Queen Conch, there are four other species of conch in and around the Caribbean. The Roostertail Conch, the Milk Conch, the Fighting Conch, and the Hawkwing Conch. Do not confuse a helmet with a conch. A helmet feeds on sea urchins, it does not feed on plants and has no hooked claw.

You will likely come across many species of sponge on your Exuma cruise. The Exumas were once an important sponging ground in the Bahamian sponge industry. The entire northern Exumas, from Nassau to Sandy

Cay north of Sail Rocks, down to Farmer's and westward to Green Cay on the Tongue of the Ocean, was thick with sponges and spongers. Nassau was the home to an unusual "silent" sponge auction where, in complete silence, buyers would examine the sponge lots and write down their bids. The era ended abruptly in 1939 when an epidemic fungus killed off 90% of the Bahamian sponges within two years, but sponging is once again alive in The Bahamas in the Bight of Abaco, southward to Long Island, Ragged Island, and the Jumentos.

Sponges are remarkable creatures. It was not until 1825 that biologists agreed that sponges were animals and not plants. Even today, zoologists are uncertain as to the exact position sponges occupy in the animal kingdom. Sponges are the least complex of all multi-cellular organisms as they lack organization of cells into tissues and organs. The individual cells of sponges exhibit a considerable degree of independence from each other, yet at the same time are able to unite and cooperate in a complex system. No one has really explained whether a sponge is an individual or a colony of individuals. An experiment performed on sponges involved the sieving of a small freshwater sponge, *Scyon*, into hundreds of pieces to form a chunky broth of sponge cells. Left overnight, the sponge cells began to join together and reassemble themselves into several smaller sponges. An amazing feat of regeneration that is well beyond the capabilities of more complex organisms.

Sponges are of the phylum *Porifera*, which means *hole boring*. It is through these holes that water is drawn and filtered removing micro-organic particles for food. Even a small sponge may filter up to 100 liters per hour of sea water. You can observe the flow of water through a sponge by squirting a little food coloring around the base of a healthy sponge. You will see a colored flume shoot out of the large central opening. It is common to find other invertebrates such as brittle stars, shrimp, and worms living in the canals of a sponge. Sponges may drill into the hard substrate and anchor themselves, live on top of either live or dead coral, or grow amorphously in lobes or branches. You can find over 50 species of sponges in the Exumas but avoid the red sponges. When touched they can cause itching, swelling, and a painful, irritating rash. Some other species will stain your hands if touched. The red boring sponges excavate tiny galleries for themselves in calcium carbonate rock and shell. Although seemingly insignificant, the sponges inflict tremendous damage on non-living reef material, particularly under shelves or coral and in the caverns that undermine patch reefs, cavities which they helped build.

The loggerhead sponge, a large commercial species that resembles a sediment covered old tire, sometimes harbors several species of pistol shrimp. Pistol shrimp, as they become adults, become trapped inside the internal passageways of their host sponge where they steal food from the collared cells. Pistol shrimp derive their name from the loud concussion made when they forcibly articulate their front claws. This concussion may ward off and even stun small animals nearby. This cacophony of snaps and clicks from the hundreds, sometimes thousands of shrimps locked inside a loggerhead sponge is a familiar sound to any experienced Bahamian sponge diver.

The sponge *Discodermia dissoluta*, abundant in Bahamian waters, generates a chemical called *discodermolide*. Researchers are hoping that this substance, a very effective immuno-suppressive agent, may help lessen organ rejection in patients after transplant surgery.

FLORA

"The trees are as green and leafy as those of Castille in the months of April and May."
- Christopher Columbus upon landing at San Salvador

There are over 1300 species of plants in The Bahamas most of which can be found in the Exumas. Some orchids, trees, cacti, and grasses are rare or endangered. It is not possible to cover every tree, flower, and bush in the Exumas in the scope of this guide, but quite possible to acquaint you with the most common flora to be found on the cays.

The most important plant to know and avoid is poisonwood. It is a member of the sumac family and is as nasty as any poison ivy or poison oak you have ever encountered. Poisonwood may be small and bushy, or tall and tree-like growing to 15'. The way to recognize it is by its leaves. The leaves are smooth and shiny green above and pale underneath with occasional brown patches or dots. The groups of five, oval-shaped, droopy leaves mark this as poisonwood. It has a light brown bark which flakes to show the orange underbark. The bark and leaves will cause severe itching and burning and can develop into quite a sore rash. Calamine lotion, kerosene, or the sap of the gumelemi tree all help in relieving the itching.

The Australian Pine, also known as the *casuarina*, is an invader in the Bahamas. Sometimes called *shee-oaks* because of the sound the wind makes in their branches, these trees were brought to south Florida in the 1800's and quickly spread to The Bahamas by the 1930's. Reaching heights of 70', they are often used as navigational landmarks as they can usually be seen from seaward before the islands themselves. Many people stroll beneath the casuarina totally oblivious to their destructive nature. Casuarinas denude Bahamian landscapes of all their native flora and replace it with a carpet of smothering needles which are in reality not needles at all but photosynthetic stems. These stems accumulate in mats making the soil very acidic and killing off competing plants. Very little can live beneath an Australian Pine.

Lignum Vitae, sometimes called the *tree of life,* is one of the hardest woods known and is the national tree of The Bahamas. It is impregnated with fragrant resins that make it naturally self-lubricating and ideal for use aboard ship as bearings, bushings, blocks, and rollers. Once known as the *sailor's cure,* the Indians of Hispaniola used a decoction of Lignum Vitae as a treatment for syphilis. Lignum Vitae was in great demand after the return of Columbus in 1493. It seems that the Spanish were afflicted with an epidemic of the disease and proved to be a very eager market for it.

Madeira was once very prevalent throughout the Exumas but is very rare now due to the lumber trade. Madeira, the Bahamian term for mahogany, was first used by the Arawak Indians in the Caribbean. Besides being prized for its esthetic qualities, it is quite useful in boat building. The old shipbuilder's loved its "...durableness, resisting gunshots, and burying the shot without splintering."

The silver top palm and the thatch palm, found growing on almost every cay, are cornerstones of Bahamian culture and economy. Over 250 years ago the governor of The Bahamas imported artisans from Bermuda to teach the locals plaiting. Since that time Bahamians have woven the leaves of these plants into baskets, hats, ropes, shoes, mats and thatch for the roofs over their heads.

EPIFLORA

Plants that live under the sea are called *epiflora.* Attached epiflora are found only in the inter tidal and subtidal zones, the only benthic zones reached by light. Epiflora consists primarily of the seaweeds, algae, mangroves, and the sea grasses.

Of the sea grasses, turtle grass is the most significant as well as the most prolific species in The Bahamas. Turtle grass forms very stable communities in dense beds on the sea floor and are so easily seen from the deck of a boat or by air that they are often used as navigational landmarks. Numerous crustaceans, mollusks, and fish feed on and inhabit the turtle grass communities. Conch are usually found in turtle grass beds. Turtle grass is very broad bladed and grows to about 6 or 8 inches. It is not a true grass but rather a member of a family of aquatic flowering plants. Along with turtle grass you may find manatee grass with its shoelace-like blades, shoal grass which has narrow, round leaves, and the common eel grass which has long grass-like leaves.

Aside from the marine grasses, which grow wholly submerged, the other flowering marine plants are the mangroves which grow partially submerged along tropical seashores around the world. Mangroves are basically terrestrial plants with special adaptations allowing them to utilize salt water by removing the salt and then secreting it in glands found on the leaves. For matters of convenience, the four species mentioned here, the red, black, white, and gray or buttonwood mangrove are all called mangroves, however, the red mangrove is the only true mangrove. The four "mangrove" species actually represent three different families of plants. Each type of mangrove has unique environmental requirements that do not suit the others and so they are seldom seen intermingling with the others. Mangroves are land builders, slowly recovering the ocean floor and converting it into dry land and usually appear in sequence. As each mangrove species colonizes an area it transforms it into a slightly more terrestrial environment making it less suitable for itself. This process is called ecological succession. The red mangrove grows closest to the water's edge where its red roots firmly anchor it in the unstable ground despite the uprooting pressure of wind and wave (which is why you should tie off to mangroves in the event of a hurricane). Its tangled roots, home to countless sea creatures, stifle water currents and augment sedimentation which, after years of accumulation, become sufficiently permanent to support the next in line of the mangrove procession, the mud dwelling black mangrove. Black mangroves are recognized by their snorkels, i.e., breathing roots or *pneumatophores,* which stick straight up out of the mud providing aeration for their underground roots. The black mangrove transforms the mud into hard ground where the white mangrove takes over and in turn yields to the gray mangrove or buttonwood. The buttonwood is a tree that grows to a height of 15 to 25 feet with numerous twisting branches that are highly prized as driftwood.

Algae are relatively simple plants that have changed little since the dawn of cellular life on this planet. Benthic life depends on the photosynthetic algae as its primary food source, the first step in the food chain. Brown algae known as sargassum weed, originates far out into the Atlantic Ocean in an area between the West Indies and Africa known as the Sargasso Sea and can be found littering windward beaches throughout The Bahamas. It makes up the weedlines that fishermen find so rewarding. Green algae coats docks and tidal rocks with a slippery slime while some types form a miniature forest that resemble shaving brushes. One species known as the *mermaids wine glass*, clutter wooden pilings and floating debris like so many tiny parasols on a beach. You are likely to find this algae growing under your boat on your unpainted grounding plates. There are three types of red algae in the Exumas which form brittle, pink crusts on docks, rocks, and the undersides of unpainted dinghies. The famous pink sands of some Bahamian beaches derive their color from the pulverized skeletons of this algae and not, as is generally believed, from crushed shells. In certain areas, calcareous algae of this type completely dominate the corals and are the primary reef builders creating what are called *algal ridges*. Although there are two known algal ridges in The Bahamas, neither one is in the Exumas, one lies off the southern shore of Plana Cay and the other is just off the eastern shore of Booby Cay.

Without a doubt, the rarest, and arguably the most important living creatures in the Exumas, are the blue-green, reef-forming algae known as *stromatolites*. Stromatolite reefs are the oldest evidence of life on Earth with some fossil stromatolites dating back 3.5 billion years (the Earth is estimated to be 4 billion years old). Stromatolites were the dominant reef-forming material for 3 billion years and helped to create the conditions by which life could develop upon the Earth.

The Earth 3.5 billion years ago was not at all like it is today. Try to visualize the environment at that time. There is no oxygen in the atmosphere or in the water. It will be 3 billion years before primitive animals such as jellyfish, corals, worms, and trilobites will appear on the scene. The only living creatures are the stromatolites. Being plant life, the stromatolites use carbon dioxide and liberate oxygen into the water and atmosphere. After billions of years the stromatolites produced enough oxygen to allow animal life to develop. Stromatolites reefs are created by tiny hair-like bacteria called blue-green algae, or *cyanobacteria*. Being plants, they require sunlight for photosynthesis and position themselves with respect to the sunlight. As they grow, they trap sediment and cement it together into tightly packed layers of limestone. These mounds are called *stromatolites*, a Greek term meaning *mattress rocks* because they grow and accumulate layers of sediment piled one on top of another. Creating mounds or columns as they grow, the deeper layers become cemented into limestone and form the rigid bases for the upper levels which remain living and extremely fragile. Fossilized stromatolites are found in the largest iron ore deposits on Earth. Much of the ore from which lead and zinc are mined in Tennessee and Missouri contains stromatolites. It is reported that the spacing and shape of stromatolites aids geologists in predicting where to dig to obtain the richest mineral deposits. For years, scientists thought stromatolites were extinct. Some believed they became prey to primitive animals that grazed on the algae, while another theory was that the algae was unable to bind the coarse-grained sediment produced by the remains of higher plants and animals. In the 1950's, living stromatolites were found in a very briny saltwater tidal flat in Shark Bay, Australia. In 1983 and 1984 stromatolites were found in the Exumas off Stocking Island, Lee Stocking Island, and in The Exuma Cays Land And Sea Park. These stromatolites are estimated to be about 2000 years old.

Please, whatever you do, do not touch or walk upon these stromatolite reefs, they are very fragile and you can destroy them without even knowing it. Besides, there is little to see without a microscope. Stromatolites were the first living creatures on this planet, please treat them with the care and respect you would an aged family member.

THE BASICS

ANCHORING

Just as important as getting your vessel moving and keeping her heading along your chosen course quickly and efficiently is the fine art of keeping your vessel from moving. Nowhere is this more important than when you are anchoring in the Exuma Cays. Many of the anchorages in this book are swept by swift tidal currents, sometimes up to 2.5 knots, and to avoid bumping into your neighbor in the middle of the night or putting your vessel on the rocks or beach, two anchors, such as in a Bahamian Moor, are required.

Anchor choice is basically a personal preference. Some cruisers prefer CQRs, while others swear by a Bruce or a Danforth. Of the "Big Three," you will find that a Danforth holds as well as a CQR or Bruce in sandy bottoms while the CQR or Bruce is preferred when anchoring in rocky bottoms. Whatever your choice of anchor, you must deploy your anchor correctly and with sufficient scope to hold you when the tide changes, if a front approaches, or if a squall should blow through at 2:00 a.m. (which seems to be the time they choose to blow through). Your anchor should have a length of chain (at least 15') shackled to your anchor to keep your rode from chafing against coral or rocks and to create a catenary curve that helps absorb shock loads while lowering the angle of pull on your anchor. Too high an angle may cause your anchor to pull up and out of the bottom. Some cruisers prefer all chain rodes with a nylon snubber to absorb the shock loads. This is an excellent arrangement but a windlass may be needed unless you prefer the workout involved with hauling in the chain and anchor every time you move.

In many of the lee side anchorages in the Exumas you may lie comfortably to one anchor. When setting your anchor do not just drop it and let your rode run out, piling itself on top of your anchor. Lower your anchor to the bottom and deploy the rode as you fall back with the current or wind until you have at least a 5:1 scope out, 7:1 is preferable but not always possible in places such as the holes on Stocking Island where setting two, and even three anchors, is the norm. When calculating the amount of scope required, be sure to allow for high tide as well as the height of your anchor roller or fairlead above the water. Without being precise, you can figure on a 2½'-3½' tidal rise in the Exumas although occasionally you may find a 4' rise such as during neap tides, a little more during a full moon and a little less with no moon. When you have secured your rode, back down with the engine at about ½ throttle to set the anchor. If you have not succeeded in securing your anchor, try again. To check the set it is best to dive on your anchors or at the very least, look at their set through a glass bottom bucket from your dinghy. You may find that you will have to set them by hand, especially in rocky areas.

If there are other boats in the anchorage when you arrive and they are riding to two anchors, or if you are in an area beset by tidal currents, it is best to set two anchors in a Bahamian Moor. Although one anchor may be fine if you have the swinging room, when the tide changes it may pull out and fail to reset. These anchorages are often very crowded and while you may swing wide on your one anchor and not find yourself endangered by the rocks or beach, you and your neighbor may go bump in the night because his two anchors have kept him in one spot. If unsure the best thing to do is follow the lead of those boats that are there before you. Conversely, if you arrive at an anchorage and everyone is on one anchor and you choose to set two, do so outside the swing radius of the other boats. If you are riding on one anchor and find that you are lying to the wind but that the swell is rolling you, you can position another anchor at an angle off the stern so as to align your bow into the swell making for a more comfortable night.

To set a Bahamian Moor you must first decide where you wish for your vessel to settle. You will lay out two anchors, one up-current and one down-current of that spot, the two anchors keeping you swinging in a small circle. Head into the current to where you will drop your first anchor and set it properly. Let out as much scope as you can, setting your anchor on the way by snubbing it, until you are at the spot where you are to drop your down-current anchor. If the wind has pushed you to one side or the other of the tidal stream, you will have to power up to the position where you will set your second anchor. Lower your second anchor and pull your vessel back up current on your first rode, paying out the rode for the second anchor and setting it as you maneuver back up current to your chosen spot. You may want to dive on your anchors to check their set. Keeping your rodes tight will keep you swinging in a tighter circle. Check your anchor rodes daily as they will twist together and make it extremely difficult to undo them in an emergency.

In some tight anchorages you will be unable to set your anchors 180° apart. An alternative is to set them 90° apart in a "Y" configuration perpendicular to the wind. In the holes on Stocking Island you may even choose to use three anchors to keep your swing radius as small as possible. A skipper with a large swing radius in very tight quarters is apt to find out what his neighbors think of his anchoring technique as soon as the wind shifts. Responsible anchoring cannot be overstressed.

Always set an anchor light. Some cruisers feel this is unimportant in some of the more isolated anchorages in the Exumas. What they probably do not understand is that many Exumians run these islands at all hours of the night, even on moonless nights, and an anchor light protects your vessel as well as theirs.

Anchorages on the eastern shores of the Exuma Cays are all daytime anchorages only due to the prevailing winds and should be used only in settled or westerly weather. Never anchor in coral, even with your dinghy anchor. An anchor can do a great deal of damage to a very fragile ecosystem that will take years to recover if it is to recover at all. Besides, sand holds so much better anyway.

In summer months and on into the early fall, or when there is no wind, you may wish to anchor a good distance from shore to keep away from the relentless biting insects. Cays with a lot of vegetation or mangroves will have a higher concentration of biting insects.

Proper anchoring etiquette should by practiced at all times. For instance, if the anchorage is wide and roomy and only one boat is at anchor, do not anchor right on top of them, give your neighbor a little breathing room and some solitude. You would probably appreciate the same consideration should the situation be reversed. All to often cruisers exhibit a herding instinct where they seek the comfort of other nearby cruisers, anchoring much too close at times.

Many boaters, after a long, hard day in rough seas or bad weather, anxiously await the peace and tranquillity of a calm anchorage. The last thing they want is noise and wake. If you have a dog aboard that loves to bark, be considerate of your neighbors who do not wish to hear him. They do have that right. Jet skis can be a lot of fun, but only if you are astride one. Many cruisers have little tolerance for the incessant buzzing back and forth of high speed jet skis. It is a good show of manners to slowly leave the anchorage where you can have your high speed fun and games and not disturb anyone. Water skiing is prohibited within 200 ft. of the shoreline in The Bahamas unless the skier is approaching or leaving the shore at a speed of 3 knots or less. If at all possible, avoid running your generators at sunset or after dark. At sunset, many cruisers are sitting in their cockpits enjoying cocktails and watching the sun go down and do not want a generator disturbing their soft conversations. Many powerboats use a lot of electricity by running all sorts of lights at night. Some will leave on huge floodlights for one reason or another with no idea of the amount of glare and light it produces in nearby cockpits to other boaters. This is not an incrimination of all powerboaters, only the careless few. The vast majority of powerboaters are very considerate and professional and do not approve of their noisy, blinding, cousins. Courtesy shown is usually courtesy returned.

CHARTERING

Currently there are no charter operations in the Exumas except for the rental of small outboards at Sampson Cay, Staniel Cay, and George Town. Some charter companies in south Florida will allow you to take their boats to the Exumas and some will even let you drop them off there. For information, contact your charter broker. The only charter company in The Bahamas that services the Exumas is Marine Services of Eleuthera in Hatchet Bay, Eleuthera. They have a fleet of Cabo Rico's and some newly acquired catamarans. You can contact Marine Services of Eleuthera in the United States at 242-335-0186.

Students wishing to do research in The Bahamas, and the Exumas in particular, should contact Nicolas and Dragan Popov of Island Expeditions at P.O. Box CB11934, Love Beach #4C, Nassau, N.P., The Bahamas, 242-327-8659. Island Expeditions has several sailing trips each year throughout the Exumas and a very good humpback whale study program.

CHARTS

For navigational purposes use NOS Chart 11013, and DMA charts 26253, 26257, 26286, 26301, 26303, and 26305. The BBA, the Better Boating Association, Box 407, Needham, Ma. 01292, makes an excellent 17" x 22" chart kit with reproductions of U.S. government charts and color photographs. *The Yachtsman's Guide To The*

Bahamas, edited by Meredith Fields, Tropic Isle Publishers, has some excellent sketch charts of the Exumas and should be aboard every vessel cruising The Bahamas.

CLOTHING

If you are heading to the Exumas you will enter a tropical climate where the theme for clothing is light. You will most likely live in shorts and T-shirts (if that much). Long pants and sturdy, comfortable shoes are preferred when hiking for protection from the bush and the rugged terrain. Long sleeved shirts (or old cotton pajamas) and wide brimmed hats are important in keeping the sun off you. Polarized sunglasses (helpful for piloting) and suntan lotion (suntan oil tends to leave a long lasting greasy smear all over everything) should be included in your gear. In winter months it is advisable to bring something warm to wear, especially in the evenings. Long pants and sweaters are usually adequate and a light jacket would be a good idea as some frontal passages will occasionally drop the temperature below 60° F.

It is important that men and women dress appropriately when entering settlements. Skimpy bathing suits for men as well as women are excellent for the beach or boat but in town they are not apropos. Men should wear shirts in town as some Exumians are quick to remind you to cover up. Remember, you are a visitor here and that entails a certain responsibility.

CURRENCY

The legally acceptable currency of The Bahamas is the Bahamian dollar whose value is on par with the American dollar. American money is readily acceptable throughout the islands at stores, marinas hotels, etc. Bahamian money comes in 1¢, 5¢, 10¢, 25¢, 50¢, $1, $3, (yes, a three-dollar bill), $5, $10, $20, $50, and $100 denominations.

CUSTOMS AND IMMIGRATION

Bahamian Ports of Entry

ABACO: Green Turtle Cay, Marsh Harbour, Spanish Cay, Walker's Cay
ANDROS: Congo Town, Fresh Creek, Mangrove Cay, Morgan's Bluff
BERRY ISLANDS: Chubb Cay (Chubb Cay Marina), Great Harbour Cay (Great Harbour Cay Marina)
BIMINI: Alice Town (North Bimini)
CAT CAY: Cat Cay
ELEUTHERA: Governor's Harbour, Hatchet Bay, Harbour Island, Powell Point, Rock Sound, Spanish Wells
EXUMA: George Town
GRAND BAHAMA: Freeport Harbour, Lucaya Marina, Port Lucaya, West End, Xanadu Marina
INAGUA: Matthew Town
LONG ISLAND: Stella Maris
NEW PROVIDENCE: Nassau (any marina)
MAYAGUANA: Abraham's Bay
RAGGED ISLAND: Duncan Town
SAN SALVADOR: Cockburn Town

All vessels entering Bahamian waters must clear in with Customs and Immigration officials at the nearest port of entry listed above. Failure to report within 24 hours may subject you to a penalty and make you liable for confiscation and forfeiture of your vessel. When approaching your selected port of entry be sure to fly your yellow "Q" flag. Tie up to a dock or marina and await the officials if directed. In places like Bimini (where the dockmasters will usually have the necessary forms for you) or Green Turtle Cay, only the captain of the vessel may go ashore to arrange clearance and no other shore contact is permitted until pratique is granted. Some of the marinas that you use may levy a charge for using their dock, Cat Cay in particular. If they do not charge you, good manners suggest that you at least make a fuel purchase. There is only one port of entry in the Exumas and that is in George Town at the Government Dock in Elizabeth Harbour. This is a popular clearing in spot for boats northbound from the Caribbean although most southbound vessels usually clear in long before they reach the Exumas.

During normal working hours, 9:00 a.m. to 5:30 p.m., Monday through Friday, no charge other than necessary transportation costs is charged for the clearance of pleasure vessels. If arriving outside these hours or on holidays you may expect to pay overtime charges of 1½-2 times the normal pay of the officer. These charges are per boat so don't expect to split them up amongst the members of your flotilla. U.S. citizens need proof of citizenship, a passport (not required) or Voter Registration Card. Canadian and British visitors also do not need passports. Visas are not required for visitors from the U.S., Canada, and persons from any British Commonwealth country. If you are flying in and returning by way of a boat in transit you need some proof that you are able to leave the country. It is suggested that you purchase a round trip ticket and leave the return reservation open. When you return aboard your boat you may then cash in your unused ticket or use it for a future flight. Check with the airline when buying your ticket as to their policy in this matter.

If yours is a pleasure vessel with no dutiable cargo, the captain will fill out a Maritime Declaration of Health, Inwards Report for pleasure vessels, and a crew list. Do not mistakenly call your crew "passengers" or it may be interpreted that you are running a charter. An International Marine Declaration of Health in duplicate will be accepted in lieu of a Bill of Health from vessels arriving in The Bahamas. Smallpox vaccination certificates and cholera inoculation certificates are required only if the vessel is arriving directly from an infected area. Each crew member will fill out and sign an Immigration Card. You will be asked to keep the small tab off the card and return it by mail after you leave The Bahamas. You can ask for and receive a stay of up to six months however some Immigration Officials will only give three or four months for reasons that are clear only to them. This is an inconsistency that one sees every now and then as you talk to different cruisers and find out about their clearing-in adventure. An Immigration official in Nassau explained that it is up to the individual officer to determine how long a stay to permit. If you have guests flying in they also must have a return trip ticket and proof of citizenship.

The captain will be issued a Cruising Permit (Transire) for the vessel that is valid for up to 12 months. This permit must be presented to any Customs official or other proper officer (if requested) while in The Bahamas. If you wish to keep your vessel in Bahamian waters for longer than one year without paying import duties, special arrangements must be made with Customs. The owner may extend the one year stay for up to three years by paying a fee of $500 per year after the first year. Import duties are now 7.5% for vessels of 30 to 100 feet while vessels less than 30' are charged 22.5%. Spare parts for installation aboard your vessel are duty free. If the parts are imported as cargo they are subject to a 6% duty.

If you plan to do any fishing during your stay you must purchase a fishing permit which is good for up to six reels. Acquiring a fishing permit for more than six reels is costly and only for the serious fisherman. For the non-commercial fisherman the Permit costs $20 for three months; a huge price increase from the old cost of $20 per year. Please familiarize yourself with the rules and regulations on the reverse side of the permit. There are strict penalties for violations, especially within the boundaries of The Exuma Cays Land And Sea Park.

If you have pets on board they must have an import permit. An application for the permit may be requested by writing to the Director of the Department of Agriculture, P.O. Box N-3704, Nassau, Bahamas (242-325-7413, fax # 242-325-3960). Return the completed application with a $10.00 fee in the form of a Postal Money Order or International Money Order payable to the Public Treasury. This will hasten the process of obtaining your permit although you should allow three to four weeks processing time. Rabies certificates are required of all animals over three months old and must be more than 10 days but less than 9 months old and should be presented when you clear Customs and Immigration.

Non-residents of The Bahamas entering aboard a foreign vessel are not required to obtain permits nor pay duties on firearms during their visit to the islands. This exemption is for three months following the arrival of the vessel at a designated port of entry. After three months a certificate must be obtained from the Commissioner of Police. All firearms must be kept safe from theft under lock and key and be declared on your cruising permit with an accurate count of all ammunition. Firearms may not be used in Bahamian waters nor taken ashore. Hunters should contact the Department of Agriculture and Fisheries in Nassau for information on hunting in the Exumas. Completely forbidden are tear gas pens, military arms such as artillery, flame-throwers, machine guns, and automatic weapons. Exempt are toy guns, dummy firearms, flare guns, and spear guns designed for underwater use.

Certain items may be brought in duty free including personal effects such as wearing apparel, ship's stores, 1 quart of alcoholic beverage, 1 quart of wine, 1 pound in weight of tobacco or 200 cigarettes or 50 cigars.

As soon as the captain has cleared Customs, you may take down your yellow "Q" flag and replace it with the Bahamian courtesy flag.

American flag vessels are not required to obtain clearance when departing U.S. ports. If you are clearing back into the United States you must, upon entry, call the U.S. Customs Service to clear in. On May 9, 1994, the old routing of clearing in if arriving between Sebastian Inlet and Naples, Florida, at one of 27 U.S. Customs Reporting Stations located throughout south Florida was changed. The new law requires you to go a nearby telephone immediately upon arrival and dock nearby. You can dial 1-800-432-1216, 1-800-458-4239, or 1-800-451-0393 to get a Customs Agent on the line to arrange clearance. When you have Customs on the phone you will need to give them your vessel's name and registration number, the owner's name, the Captain's name and date of birth, all passenger names and dates of birth, a list of all foreign ports visited and the duration of your stay there, a list of guns aboard, the total value of all purchases, your Customs User Fee decal number if one has been issued, and whether you have anything to declare (total of all purchases, fresh fruit, vegetables, or meat). If you do not have a decal you may be directed to the nearest U.S. Customs station to purchase one within 48 hours. Decals may be purchased prior to departing on your voyage by ordering an application (Customs Form #339) and submitting the completed application with a $25.00 fee (Money Order or check drawn on U.S. bank) to U.S. Customs Service, National Finance Center, P.O. Box 198151, Atlanta, Georgia 30384.

Each resident of the United States, including minors, may take home duty-free purchases up to $600 U.S. if they have been outside the U.S. for more than 48 hours and have not taken this exemption in 30 days. This includes up to 2 liters of liquor per person over 21 provided that one liter is manufactured in The Bahamas or a member of the Caribbean Basin Initiative (CBI). A family may pool their exemptions. Articles of up to $1000 in excess of the duty-free $600 allowance are assessed at a flat rate of 10%. For example, a family of four may bring back up to $2400 worth of duty-free goods. If they were to bring back $6400 worth of goods, they would have to pay a duty of $400 on the $4000 above the duty-free allowance. This flat rate may only be used once every 30 days. If the returning U.S. resident is not entitled to the duty-free allowance because of the 30 day or 48 hour restrictions, they may still bring back $25 worth of personal or household items. This exemption may not be pooled. Antiques are admitted to the U.S. duty-free if they are over 100 years old. The Bahamian store selling the antique should provide you with a form indicating the value and certifying the age of the object. Importation of fruits, plants, meats, poultry, and dairy products is generally prohibited. More than $10,000 in U.S. or foreign coin, currency, traveler's checks, money orders, and negotiable instruments or investment securities in bearer form must be reported to Customs. Importation of Bahamian tortoise or turtle shell goods is prohibited. Many medicines purchased over the counter in The Bahamas such as 222, a codeine-aspirin-caffeine compound, are not allowed entry. Although you can buy Cuban cigars in Nassau, enjoy them on your cruise and do not attempt to bring them back into the U.S. The U.S. Customs Service frowns on Americans spending money on Cuban products. Hopefully that will change in a few years.

Any number of gifts may be sent to the U.S. from The Bahamas and the recipient will pay no duty provided that the gift is worth U.S. $50 or less. If the value is over U.S. $50, duty and tax is charged on the full value. The following regulations must be complied with. Only $50 worth of gifts may be received by the U.S. addressee in one day. The value of the gifts must be clearly written on the package as well as the words "Unsolicited Gift." No alcoholic beverages or tobacco may be sent. Perfume with value of more than $5 may not be sent. Persons in the U.S. are not allowed to send money to The Bahamas for gifts to be shipped to them duty-free, the gifts must be unsolicited. Persons may not mail a gift addressed to themselves. For more information, contact the U.S. Customs Service before you leave or call them in Nassau at 242-327-7126.

Canadian residents may take advantage of three categories of duty-free exemption. If you have been out of Canada for 24 hours, you may make a verbal declaration to claim a CDN$20 duty-free allowance any number of times per year. This exemption does not include alcohol or tobacco. If you have been out of the country for 48 hours, any number of times per year, a written declaration must be made and you may claim a CDN$100 allowance. This allowance can include up to 200 cigarettes, 50 cigars, or 2 lbs. of tobacco, and 1.1 liters of alcohol per person. If you have been out of Canada for over 7 days, you may make a written declaration and claim a CDN$300 exemption including the above mentioned amounts of tobacco and alcohol. After a trip abroad for 48 hours or more you are entitled to a special 20% tax rate on goods valued up to CDN$300 over and above the CDN$100 and CDN$300 personal exemption. For importation of tobacco the claimant must be 16 years of age. For alcohol, the claimant must have attained the legal age prescribed by the laws of the provincial or territorial authority at the point of entry.

Unsolicited gifts may be sent to Canada duty-free as long as they are valued under CDN$400 and do not contain alcoholic beverages, tobacco products, or advertising matter. If the value is above CDN$400 the recipient must pay regular duty and tax on the excess amount.

Photo courtesy of Nicolas Popov/Island Expeditions

Defence Force Vessels.

THE DEFENCE FORCE

The Royal Bahamas Defence Force came into existence officially on March 31, 1980. Their duties include defending The Bahamas, stopping drug smuggling, illegal immigration, poaching, and to provide assistance to mariners whenever and wherever they can. They have a fleet of 26 coastal and inshore patrol craft along with 2 aircraft. The Defence Force has over 850 personnel including 65 officers and 74 women.

I have been associated with a number of Defence Force personnel through my efforts at Exuma Park and I have developed a healthy respect for these men and women. Every officer and seaman that I have met has been highly intelligent, articulate, dedicated, and very professional in regards to their duties. These are not the thugs and hoodlums that so many cruisers have come to fear over the last few years. As late as 1991, horror stories were coming out of Nassau concerning improprieties during routine boardings. The Defence Force has taken corrective steps and reports of trouble caused by boarding parties are almost non-existent now. There is no reason to dread the gray boats as they approach. The Defence force has a very difficult job to do and it often becomes necessary for them to board private pleasure vessels in routine searches. The boarding party will do everything they can to be polite and professional, however, due to the violent nature of the criminals they seek, standard procedure is to be armed. Unfortunately, in the process of protecting themselves, they inadvertently intimidate cruisers. Please do not be alarmed if a crewman bearing an automatic weapon stays in your cockpit while the officer conducts a search below decks in your presence. If you are boarded you will be asked to sign a statement saying that the search was carried out politely and in the presence of the owner or skipper. It is not unusual for the Defence Force to enter an anchorage and board all the vessels in the anchorage. Normally they will not board a vessel that is unoccupied, preferring to keep an eye out for your return.

Cruisers often ask why single me out, why search my boat? What are they looking for? Besides the obvious problem with drugs, The Bahamas has problems with people smuggling illegal weapons and ammunition into the country with bullets selling for $5 and more a piece on the street in Nassau. You must keep accurate records on all your weapons and ammunition and make sure you record them on your cruising permit when you check in.

The Defence Force also must defend the richness of the marine fisheries in The Bahamas. It is not unknown for a boat to cross over from the states without a permit and fill up its freezers with Bahamian caught fish, conch, and lobster. In 1997, a boat from south Florida was boarded upon its return to Florida and the owners and crew arrested and charged under the Lacy Act. The Defence Force, if they board your vessel, will probably want to see your fishing permit and ask you whether you have any fish aboard. For most cruisers this does not pose a problem. If, however, you have 100 dolphin aboard, you will find yourself in a world of well deserved trouble.

DINGHY SAFETY

Most cruisers spend a considerable amount of time in their dinghies exploring the waters and islands in the vicinity of their anchorage. Their workhorse of a dinghy faithfully serves multiple duty to ferry crews to and from shore, bring piles of provisions back to the mother vessel, and take her owners to remote areas to dive and fish. Although these same cruisers may take great precautions in their mother vessel to insure the safety and survival of their crew and vessel with EPIRBS, life rafts, and abandon ship kits, few skippers concern themselves as seriously with their dinghies. Most dinghies carry some sort of small tool kit, spare spark plugs, and a patch/repair kit which is fine if you are only going between your boat and town or the beach. When you start venturing farther away from your mother vessel to seek out that special reef or to investigate some neighboring cays it is time to get serious.

It is not unknown for a dinghy engine to fail beyond repair or run out of gas miles from the mothership. Once the skipper gets past the "it won't happen to me" mindset he or she may begin to prepare for the worst by carrying some simple survival gear in their dink. Don't laugh. These are practical suggestions born of real experiences. I have seen people forced to spend a night or two in a dinghy and these few items would have made their adventure less of an ordeal if not entirely unnecessary. I know of two men who drifted from Eleuthera to Exuma Park over a forty-eight hour period in thirty knot winds and six to eight foot seas. Personally I have run out of gas and used flares to attract some local attention even though one of my boat mates was ready to dive in and swim for the nearest island to fetch assistance. Now I never leave in my dinghy without my little survival bag aboard.

Topping the list of what to bring is extra gas for obvious reasons. Next, a handheld VHF radio for equally obvious reasons. If there are any other boats around this will be your best chance for getting some assistance. If possible tell your neighbors where you're going and to keep an ear tuned to Ch. 16. A couple of handheld and parachute flares is also a good investment to attract the attention of passing boaters or those ashore. I've seen Bahamians carry a large coffee can containing a rag soaked in oil lying in the bottom. If they get in trouble lighting the rag will produce an abundant amount of smoke which can be seen from quite a distance and bring help.

A good anchor and plenty of line is also high on the list. Now I don't mean one of those small three pound anchors with thirty feet of line that is only used on the beach to keep your dinghy from drifting to Cuba while you're munching on grilled dolphin and downing *Kaliks*. It may pay to sacrifice the onboard room and carry a substantial anchor with a couple of feet of chain and at least 100' of line, more is better. You may find yourself having to anchor in three to five foot seas in forty feet of water. Just as you would go oversize on your mother vessel do the same with your dinghy. If you are being blown away from land a good anchor and plenty of line gives you a good chance of staying put where someone may find you.

A dinghy should be equipped with survival water, a bottle or some small foil packages manufactured by a company such as DATREX. It would be a good idea to throw in a few MRE's. These are the modern, tastier version of K-Rations which our armed forces survived on for years. Each MRE also contains vital survival components such as matches and toilet paper. Another handy item that does not take up much room is a foil survival blanket. They really work and take up as much space as a couple of packs of cigarettes. Use your imagination in building a dinghy safety bag. Picture yourself drifting away from your anchorage at 2 knots with no help in sight. What would you need or want aboard if that were to happen?

These suggestions are not for everybody. Some cruisers do not venture far enough away from their mothership to warrant carrying a survival bag. Some are probably still convinced it won't happen to them. Some simply don't have the room. If I had to take only one item it would be a handheld VHF.

One final word. If you find yourself dinghying around The Exumas and you find you must go far out of your way to skirt a large sandbank lying to leeward of a cay, bear in mind that even though the sandbanks stretch out quite a ways to the west, there is usually a channel of slightly deeper water nearer the shoreline of the cays. Usually deep enough for a dinghy.

DIVING

From shallow water reef dives to deep water wall drop-offs, the diving in the Exumas is as good as it gets anywhere and much better than most places. You don't need SCUBA equipment to enjoy the undersea delights that are available, many reefs lie in less than 30' and are easily accessible to those with snorkels, dinghies, and curiosity. For those with SCUBA gear, the deeper waters open up and reveal some truly breathtaking scenery such as Ocean Cay Wall or The Walled City. The Banks drop off sharply to the deep basin of Exuma Sound for almost the entire 140 miles of the Exumas and the wall drop-off usually begins in around 60'-80' of water.

Although the waters in the Exuma Cays are crystal clear and the obstructions plainly visible in the ambient light, divers must take proper precautions when diving in areas of current. Experienced divers are well aware of this but it must be stated for novices and snorkelers. Tidal fluctuations can produce strong currents which must be taken into account when diving. Waves breaking over the and around inshore reefs can create strong surges which can push or pull you into some very sharp coral. For safety's sake, only experienced divers should penetrate the wrecks and caves in the Exumas. Ed Haxby at Exuma Fantasea in George Town is an experienced cave diver and should be approached if you have any questions or need any assistance concerning diving in the area.

For those seeking a charter operation there are some very professional dive boats operating in the Exumas. At the top of the list is the 65' R/V *Sea Dragon* and Captain Dan Doyle. Dan is based in Nassau and is the guru of dive boat operators in this area, he's been doing this for over 22 years. His charters are filled by word-of-mouth referrals and repeat customers who often book tours years in advance. You can contact Dan in the U.S. at 305-522-0161. Captain Doyle specializes in Exuma diving although he often takes charters to the other Out Islands for diving. The 95' R/V *Sea Fever*, owned and operated by Captain Dan Guarino, specializes in Bahamian diving. Captain Guarino has a very thorough knowledge of the Exumas, Berrys, Cat Cay, the Joulters, and the Cay Sal Bank. He can be reached in the U.S. at 800-44-FEVER. For a professional diving guide service to the Exumas and Eleuthera try Custom Aquatics I Nassau at 242-362-1492. Captain Francis Young has 20 years of experience in Bahamian waters. Captain Young offers diving as well as instruction. The 65' sailing catamaran *Cat Ppalu* and her very capable crew is based in Nassau and visits the Exumas on a regular basis. Call Blackbeard Cruises in the U.S. at 800-561-0111 for more information.

EYEBALL NAVIGATION

When you arrive on the Banks you will leave behind the normal deep-water navigational methods you so adeptly used to get yourself here. You will still use these skills when you traverse Exuma Sound but when on the Banks you must, and will, learn the art of eyeball navigation. To have an enjoyable and safe cruise you will need to be able to read the waters and acquiring this skill is not that difficult. The relationship between water color and depth is what eyeball navigation is based on.

I have often seen people who, in their home waters, would think nothing of cruising in 8' depths where they cannot see the bottom. However, when they arrive in The Bahamas, some are quite intimidated by 12' depths where every feature on the bottom is visible in the crystal clear water. This is normal and you'll soon get over it. The clarity of the water is your greatest ally when navigating on the Banks. Reefs, heads, rocks, and wrecks stand out distinctly in good visibility and are very easy to steer around. Channels between sandbanks appear as clearly as would an interstate highway back home. Once you learn to read the waters you will find that the entire area has really opened up to you and that you can take your vessel practically anywhere in safety with this knowledge. It is impossible teach you how to navigate by eye in this book, or any book for that matter. Eyeball navigation is a skill that only you can teach yourself when in these waters, in your boat, while underway. I will however, strive to give you the basics upon which to build experience. Remember, the water color will tell you what the depth is, you must however be able to read it. For the novice, the greatest obstacle may be to learn to trust what your eyes tell you once you have learned to read the waters.

> *"Water that's blue is deep and true;*
> *As it shades to green, the water gets lean;*
> *White or yellow will ground a fellow;*
> *If the water is brown, you'll run hard aground;*
> *If the water is black, you'd better tack."*

This simple little ditty pretty much sums up the relationship between color and depth. Blue water, such as in Exuma Sound or in some of the deeper areas inside the cuts, is usually 40' or more in depth and poses little threat to navigation except for the occasional rock or head which juts up to just below the surface near shore. Green water, which will range from about 3'-40' is the most difficult to read. It will take you a while to get used to the color differences between an 8' depth and a 12' depth. With practice, and an eye on the depth sounder, you will soon begin to recognize the subtle differences in depths and steer accordingly. Before long you will pride yourself on being able to look at stretch of water and call out its depth almost as well as anyone who lives in these waters. The lighter the green, the shallower the water. Water that shifts from green to yellow or white is showing you the sand on the bottom and warns you that there is little water in that area. Brown signifies a rocky bar or reef with little water over it. Stay clear and use caution when approaching a brown bar even in your dinghy, they love to eat inflatables. Black can mean either a grassy patch with questionable depth, or a reef or coral head. Reefs and heads are easy to steer around if you have enough room in the channel. Grassy patches can be confusing. Until you get close you may not be able to discern the depth of water over the grass. Coral heads rising up out of grassy patches (very profuse in the Elizabeth Harbour area) are often surrounded by a ring of white sand which will help you pick them out. If in doubt, go around.

Along with reading the color of the water, the surface appearance of the water can also indicate what lies ahead. For instance, if heading north through Pudding Cut in the Brigantines, there is a shallow sandbar that you must dogleg around. It juts out from the western sandbank into the deep water channel that you are following. In the wrong light you will never see it and go aground on a soft sandbank with only about 1' of water over it. The only indication it is there is by noticing the flow of water over it. Even in bad light you can see the water turbulence as it flows onto or off the bar depending on the tidal flow. For another example, there is a channel with a 7' depth at low water on the northwestern shore of Darby Island. In the middle of the channel is a mound of sand and grass with only 3' over it at low water. The only way to tell that it is there in bad light is by the water turbulence over it. Ripples, eddies, wavelets, current flow, all tell you a story about what causes them. Look at each one and try to picture what is causing the turbulence. It could be that the current must flow around a head. It may be that the water is falling off a shallow area into deeper water or just the opposite, the turbulence is an upwelling where the current is pushing water up onto a bank. The waters will usually tell you what lies underneath them, it is up to you to decipher the message.

As a general rule of thumb, if you stay in the blue or darker green water, and avoid brown bars and heads, you will most likely stay out of trouble. Soon enough your adventurous spirit will take over and you will begin entering the lighter green water, often using the Braille method of sounding the bottom with your keel as you explore more and more of these cays. That's part of the fun of cruising the Exumas. Most of the bottom is soft sand and you can usually pull yourself off either with the help of your dinghy, by using a kedge, or by waiting on the tide.

Misjudging water depths is not the only way that cruisers can have a bad experience in these waters. With the exception of bad weather, there are three ways that most cruisers get in trouble in the Exumas, and to some extent everywhere. All are reasonably within your power to correct.

The first is negligence. Not paying attention to where you are and where you are going is the quickest way to plant your keel on Mother Earth. Taking shortcuts is also not recommended. This guide encourages boaters to get off the beaten track and explore, that is part of what cruising is all about, but trying to cut the corners on the sandbanks too close is not advised. The thinking seems to be "If I cut it a little close here I might be able to save some time and I won't have to go that extra quarter mile around the tip." What usually happens is that the skipper wastes much more time waiting on the tide to rise or someone to pull him off than he would have saved by giving the area a wide berth. Don't be in a hurry. If you see an area where the depth is in doubt, say over the top of a coral head, don't fall in to the bad habit of saying, "Well, it looks okay, I went over the last one with no problems, I'll give it a try." There are more than a few who have come to regret that line of thinking.

The second problem cruisers have is with visibility, or the lack of it. If you cannot see the dangers lurking beneath the surface, you cannot avoid them. Plan your passages according to the available light. Quite often you will leave your anchorage and head east into Exuma Sound in the morning sun and then arrive at your destination only to enter the cut heading westward with the afternoon sun in your eyes. If you are heading eastward into the rising sun, try to do so a little later in the morning when the sun is not such an obstacle. If planning to enter the cuts from Exuma Sound try to do so before too late in the afternoon when the sun will again be in your eyes. A good pair of polarized sunglasses is necessary. After adjusting to the differences in color involved with wearing sunglasses, you will soon come to appreciate the polarized lenses as they remove most of the sun's glare and reflection on the water.

The local mariners who must run these waters on a daily basis prefer sunny days with just a little wind. Cloudy days and calm days mask obstructions. Often passing clouds will cast a shadow that looks just like an area of deep water. The sun will occasionally burst through highlighting small areas and making them appear bright green and too shallow for navigation. If in doubt take it slow and easy with one eye on your depth sounder. Experienced mariners often *sun tack*. Sailors are well acquainted with tacking. A sailboat cannot sail into the wind, they can only sail to one side or the other of it. If the wind is coming from 12 o'clock, a sailboat can only, at best, steer towards 11 o'clock or 1 o'clock. Tacking the sun is similar. When the sun is low and in front of you at 12 o'clock it creates an immense reflection on the water and you cannot see the dangers directly in front of your boat. However, your visibility improves slightly as you steer towards 11 o'clock or 1 o'clock. The further you steer away from the sun the better your visibility gets. Taking the time to sun tack may make a trip a little longer but there is no need to hurry in the Exumas.

Cruising the banks to the west of the Exumas at night is not recommended. Although the experienced skipper can discern some difference in water depth with the available light on calm, full moon nights, running these waters at night is a dangerous proposition at best, even for those that know the area well. If you are in Exuma Sound, stay a couple of miles out to give the cays a wide berth as they are low and hard to see on moonless nights.

The third way cruisers get in trouble is improper timing, which obviously relates to the first two means of getting in trouble. If the tide is ebbing and you wish to enter a cut from Exuma Sound with a strong onshore wind, you may find you are in a place you would rather not be. Try to plan your passages to take the fullest advantage of the tide if possible. There can be quite a difference in the seastate in a cut at ebb and flood tide.

The tidal currents in some of the passes in the Exumas run from 2-4 knots in places. When you try to steer across one of these areas you may find yourself quickly and forcibly pushed to one side of your courseline or the other. Vigilance at the helm is the best way to counteract this problem. When anchoring, do not attempt to anchor a vessel with a 6' draft in 8' of water at high tide or you will wake up with the distinct feeling that something is not quite right with your vessel. To be on the safe side, allow for a 3½' tidal fall, minimum, at all times. Spring and full moon tides are slightly more.

Many skippers get in trouble when they have to follow a schedule, when they have to be somewhere at a certain time to pick up or drop off guests. If you are planning something along these lines, allow plenty of time and arrive early, it is safer than having to face bad conditions in order to make your destination in time. Many skippers have to get to George Town to pick up or drop off guests at a certain time. In their haste to get there on time they often go out into Exuma Sound in far less than perfect conditions. This is not always necessary. You can take a cab from Barretarre (See Norman at Fisherman's Inn) to the airport to drop off or pick up your guests. This way you can avoid going out into Exuma Sound in bad weather. The cab ride is about the same price as in George Town.

If you take the proper precautions and keep your eyes open, you will have a safe and most enjoyable cruise. By the end of your Exuma cruise you will undoubtedly be quite adept at eyeball navigation, a real "eye pilot."

FISHING

Fishing in The Bahamas is hard to beat. Trolling in the Gulf Stream, the Atlantic Ocean, Exuma Sound, or Crooked Island Passage you are likely to hook a dolphin, wahoo, or tuna, all excellent eating. Trolling on the banks you will usually catch a barracuda although it is possible to bring up a snapper, jack, or grouper. Bonefish can be found in the tidal flats scattered throughout the islands. Chris Lloyd of BASRA in Nassau offers this little ditty to those who are unsure what color lure to use for trolling offshore. Chris says:

Red and black-
Wahoo attack.
Yellow and green-
Dolphin fishing machine.

Chris works Monday through Friday and BASRA HQ in Nassau Harbour and is quite an authority on fishing Bahamian waters. If you have any questions stop in and ask Chris. He loves visitors and is a wealth of fishing and diving information. Chris reminds us that the cooler months are ripe for wahoo while dolphin are more abundant from March through May.

The back of your fishing permit will have a brief but incomplete description of the fishing regulations in The Bahamas. Only six lines are permitted in the water at one time unless you have paid for a commercial permit (very expensive). SCUBA is illegal for the taking of marine life and an air compressor such as a Third Lung or similar type of apparatus, must have a permit issued by the Minister of Agriculture. Spearguns are illegal for fishing in The Bahamas and are illegal to have aboard. You may only use a Hawaiian Sling or pole spear for spearfishing. It is illegal to use bleach, firearms, or explosives for fishing. Spear fishing is illegal within one mile of New Providence and within 200 yards of any of the Exuma Cays. The capture of bonefish by net is illegal as is their purchase or sale. Conch, with a daily limit of 10 per person, may not be taken if they do not have a well formed, flared lip. Possession of a hawksbill turtle is prohibited. The minimum size for a green turtle is 24" and for a loggerhead, 30". The bag limit for kingfish, dolphin, and wahoo is a maximum combination of 6 fish per person aboard.

Crawfish, the spiny lobster that is such a treat as well as being a large part of the economy for local fishermen, has a closed season from April 1-August 1. The minimum limits are a carapace length of 3 3/8" and a 6" tail length. It is illegal to posses a berried (egg laying) female or to remove the eggs from a female. You may not take any corals while in the Bahamas.

Within the boundaries of The Exuma Cays Land And Sea Park you may not take any marine or animal life. The Park is 22 miles long and 8 miles wide stretching from Wax Cay Cut in the north to Conch Cut in the south. The no-fishing zone includes the four miles of water on either side of the cays.

In the Exumas there are far fewer jobs than there are people looking for jobs. The people here must eke out a living the best way they can. Remember that when you are fishing. Please catch just enough to eat and maybe put some away for tomorrow. So often cruisers come through this area with huge freezers just waiting to be filled to the brim to help their owners offset vacation costs. If you over-fish an area you may be taking food out of the mouths of children. To protect the livelihood of the people of the Exumas, some of the richer fishing spots in the Exumas will not be mentioned in this guide.

Conch can usually be found on the bottom in beds of sea grass or soft corals where they prefer to feed. They are usually in areas with a swift current such as in the cuts between cays. The conch that you don't plan to eat right away can be left in a dive bag hanging in the water or may be put on a stringer. Punch or drill a small hole in the lip of the conch shell and string four or five together and set them on the bottom, they won't go far. After you clean the conch, save the tough orange colored skin and put it in your freezer for later, it is an excellent fish bait and a small piece of it should be placed on all lures to give them an attractive aroma for the fish you are seeking.

The reefs in the Exumas can provide you with a plentiful supply of fish such as grouper, snapper, hogfish, turbots (trigger fish), and grunts. How many you can get is dependent on your skill with the spear. Grouper are especially wary and prefer holes to hide in.

When trolling in Exuma Sound, the drop-offs are excellent for game and food fish. You may find yourself hooking a dolphin, wahoo, shark, kingfish, or tuna. The absolute best deep water fishing in the Exumas is along the wall drop-off in 80' of water and more from Sail Rocks to Norman's Cay. The ODAS buoys, when they are not being used by the research vessels during underwater testing, are excellent places to fish. Fish love to congregate under these buoys and around the cables that keep them in position. Too many fishing boats have a tendency to spook them and they may stop biting if more than one or two boats are present. Bonefish can be found on the shallow flats. Compass Cay, Pipe Creek, Norman's Pond Cay, and the flats between Harvey Cay and Staniel Cay are all good for bonefish. In the southern Exumas, the area around Barretarre and the western side of Great Exuma, and the shallows in the vicinity of The Ferry are popular spots with many local guides for hire.

Crawfish, the clawless spiny lobster, is the principal delicacy that most cruisers search so hard for and which are getting increasingly difficult to find. They prefer to hide during the day under ledges, and rocks, and in holes where the only visible sign of them will be a pair of antennae resembling some sort of sea fan jutting out from their hiding spot. If you are fortunate enough to spear a few, and they are large enough, do not overlook the succulent meat in the base of the antennae and in the legs. So many cruisers ignore these pieces and just take the tail. Watch a Bahamian as they prepare a lobster, very little goes to waste.

FLIGHTS

There are two main airstrips for commercial flights entering and leaving the Exumas. The first is at Staniel Cay, serviced by Island Express direct from Fort Lauderdale, Florida. For information about rates with Island Express call (in the U.S.) 305-359-0380. George Town has a large international airport serviced by Island Express and Bahamasair. For information on Bahamasair flights call 242-322-4737 or in the U.S. call 800-222-4262. Remember that when you fly out of The Bahamas you will be charged a $15 departure tax.

Charter flights can be arranged throughout the Exumas, you can even be picked up at your boat by seaplane. In Nassau call Capt. Paul Harding at 242-393-2522 or 242-393-1179. He can carry up to four passengers with limited baggage on his seaplane and up to six with baggage on his Navajo. At Sampson Cay you will find Rosie Mitchell, who with her seaplane, can also be called on for charter. To reach Rosie call Sampson Cay on VHF ch. 16. When in

Staniel Cay, contact the Staniel Cay Yacht Club on VHF ch. 16 and they can help arrange a charter for you out of Staniel Cay.

GARBAGE

Garbage disposal is a major problem that we all must contend with while cruising. Nobody likes having bags of garbage stashed away in lockers or on deck while we search for a disposal site. Some marinas in the Exumas will take your garbage for a small fee. There is a dump on Norman's Cay but so many cruisers do not take the time to walk the ¼ mile to the end of the road and the dump. They wind up tossing their bags of garbage anywhere along the path and the next person that comes along gets the mistaken impression that this is the proper thing to do. Besides being unsanitary, this reflects badly on all cruisers. Nothing is worse than entering this paradise only to discover some ignorant cruiser has dumped his bags of garbage in the bushes. Please do not add to this problem. Many people separate the cans and bottles (wash them first to remove any smells while being stored), food scraps, and paper and plastic garbage for easier disposal. Food scraps may be thrown overboard on an outgoing tide while the paper and plastic can be burned and the ashes buried. The cans and bottles may be sunk in the deep waters of Exuma Sound, at least 5 miles offshore. Cut off both ends of the cans and break the bottles overboard as you sink them. If you cannot implement a garbage disposal policy aboard your vessel, stay home, don't come to these beautiful islands. Do not abuse what you use.

GPS

Even with today's crop of sophisticated Loran receivers, accuracy of this system south of Nassau should be viewed as suspect at best. In the search for reliable positioning, more and more skippers are turning to that electronic marvel called GPS as their main source of navigational data. It is a truly remarkable system offering very accurate positioning around the clock anywhere in the world. Nowadays anyone with a couple of hundred dollars can become an instant navigator. Although GPS is excellent for offshore use, it must be used with care on the Bahamas Banks.

In this Guide are certain GPS waypoints both on the Exuma Sound and Banks sides of the Cays. Banks waypoints often mark the western or southwestern tips of the sandbanks that work out in a southwesterly direction from the cays. If you attempt to steer from waypoint to waypoint you may absentmindedly go aground on a sandbank that has recently formed or possibly you will run up on the same sandbank you are trying to avoid. If you are using your GPS to arrive in the Exumas from Nassau, do not forget to keep your eyes peeled when crossing the Yellow Banks. GPS will not find and dodge the coral heads for you. You must use your eyes at all times on the banks. Trust your eyes and not the GPS when on the banks.

The waypoints on the Exuma Sound side of the cays are intended to put you approximately ¼-½ nautical mile off your intended destination so you can pilot your way in from there. If you intend to run waypoint to waypoint in Exuma Sound you must avoid the off lying Three Sisters Rocks near Barretarre (not to be confused with the Three Sisters Rocks off Mt. Thompson or off Hog Cay) and, in the vicinity of Williams Town, you must avoid the off lying Black Cays.

GPS datum used is WGS 84.

HAM RADIO

All amateur radio operators will need a Bahamian Reciprocal licensee (C6A) to operate legally in the waters of The Bahamas. To obtain an application write to Mr. T. M. Deveaux, Batelco, P.O. Box N-3048, Nassau, N.P., Bahamas, or if you have questions call 242-323-4911, ext. 7553. Return the application with a photocopy of your license and a money order for $6 (payable to Batelco, money order or certified check, no personal checks) and allow two months for processing of a new application. Do not arrive in Nassau thinking that you can apply for and get a new C6A. Although you may apply at the office, it will still take almost two months to process the application. Renewals, good for one year, are also $6 and can be walked through the Batelco Office on John F. Kennedy Drive in Nassau or handled by mail usually within approximately 2-3 weeks. It is best to handle this prior to your cruise. If you change your call sign with an upgrade you only need to send Mr. Deveaux a letter explaining the situation, it would probably be a good idea to enclose a photocopy of your new license.

The Bahamas does not have a third-party agreement with the United States, this means that you cannot make a phone patch from The Bahamas to the U.S.. If you head offshore three miles you will be in international waters and can make a phone patch from there without using your C6A, you will be MM2 (Maritime Mobile) once you are three miles out. Currently, Bahamian regulations state that international waters begin three miles out from the nearest Bahamian land mass. The Bahamas is currently considering a plan to classify all waters within the Bahamian archipelago as being Bahamian waters. This would mean that if you were three miles out on the Banks you would not be in international waters, you would still be in Bahamian waters. Hams will want to stay abreast of this situation and check with Batelco as to the status of the ruling. An excellent source of information on the topic would be Carolyn Wardle, C6AGG, who runs the Bahamas Weather Net every morning. If you have any questions give her a shout after the net, she will be happy to share any information she has on the subject.

A Bahamian reciprocal license offers expanded frequency allocations compared to domestic U.S. regulations. Some amateurs may not be allowed to use these frequencies unless they have a C6A or the proper class of U.S. license. For example, if you possess a General Class license in the U.S., you will be unable to participate in the Bahamas Weather Net (7.096 MHz) unless you have a C6A and are within Bahamian territorial waters. You could listen but not transmit. Remember to always use your C6A call suffix when you transmit in Bahamian waters.

Domestic U.S. FCC regulations have recently been slackened concerning business communications on a personal basis but in The Bahamas this is still a gray area. Batelco has made no rulings concerning this situation so use caution when broaching the subject if you are using a Bahamian reciprocal call sign.

There is a 2 meter repeater in Nassau that operates on 146.940 MHz (down 600). Until recently there was a second 2-meter repeater in Nassau on 146.640 MHz (down 600), it is currently off-line and its future is uncertain. Local hams are in the process of building a new repeater on Overyonder Cay in the Pipe Creek area. Plans call for its completion by summer of 1997. It will operate on 146.880 out and 146.280 in. For more information you can check with Carolyn, C6AGG, on the Bahamas Weather Net on 3696 (LSB) every morning at 0720 local time.

The following is a listing of frequency allocations permitted by a Bahamian reciprocal license. Please note that a maximum output power of 250 watts (Peak Envelope Power) is allowed for A3A and A3J emissions only.

BAND	CW-MHz A1	VOICE -MHz A3, A3H	VOICE -MHz A3A	VOICE -MHz A3J
160M	1.800-2.000	1.800-2.000	1.800-2.000	1.800-2.000
80 M	3.500-4.000	3.600-4.000	3.600-4.000	3.600-4.000
40M	7.000-7.3000	7.040-7.300	7.040-7.300	7.040-7.300
30M	10.100-10.150			
20M	14.000-14.350	14.050-14.350	14.050-14.350	14.050-14.350
17M	18.068-18.168	18.110-18.168	18.110-18.168	18.110-18.168
15M	21.000-21.450	21.050-21.450	21.050-21.450	21.050-21.450
12M	24.890-24.920 24.930-24.990	24.930-24.990		24.930-24.990
10M	28.000-29.700	28.050-29.700		28.050-29.700
6M	50.000-54.000	50.000-54.000	50.000-54.000	50.000-54.000
2M	144.000-148.000	144.000-148.000	144.000-148.000	144.000-148.000
70CM	430.000-440.000	430.000-440.000	430.000-440.000	

Emission Types:
A1-CW-telegraphy by on-off keying of a carrier without the use of a modulated tone.
A3-Telephony, double sideband.
A3A-Telephony, single sideband, reduced carrier.
A3H-Telephony, single sideband, full carrier.
A3J-Telephony, single sideband, suppressed carrier.

The following is a listing of ham nets you may wish to participate in during your Exuma cruise.

NET NAME	FREQUENCY KHz	TIME
Waterway Net	7268	0745-0845 ET
Computer Net	7268	0900 ET-Fridays
CW Net-slow	7128	0630 ET-Mon., Wed., and Fri.
CW Net-fast	7128	0630 ET-Tues., Thurs., Sat., and Sun.
Bahamas Weather Net	7096-winter, 3696-summer	0720 ET
Bah. Amat. Radio Soc.	7140	0830-Sundays

Intercontinental Net	14300-14316 (changes often)	1100 UTC
Maritime Mobile Net	14300-14316 (changes often)	After Intercon. until around 0200 UTC
Caribbean Net	7230 (changes often)	1100-1200 UTC
Hurricane Watch Net	14325, 14275, 14175	When needed

HOLIDAYS

The following public holidays are observed in The Bahamas:

New Year's Day-January 1
Good Friday
Easter Sunday
Easter Monday
Whit Monday-six weeks after Easter
Labour Day-first Friday in June
Independence Day-July 10
Emancipation Day-first Monday in August
Discovery Day-October 12
Christmas Day-December 25
Boxing Day-December 26

Holidays that fall on Sunday are always observed on Monday. Holidays which fall on Saturday are also usually observed on Monday. Exumians, like most Bahamians, are very religious people, so expect stores and services to be closed on Sundays as well as on Holidays. Some businesses may be open all day on Saturday but may close for a half day on Wednesdays. A must see is the Junkanoo Parade that begins about 4:00 a.m. on Boxing Day and New Years Day in Nassau and Freeport.

HURRICANE HOLES

If you are going to be cruising in The Bahamas from June through November, hurricane season, you should always keep a lookout for a safe hurricane hole. You'll want to know where they are, what you can expect when you get there, and how far you are away from your first choice. Personally, this skipper prefers a narrow, deep, mangrove lined creek but if one isn't available I'll search for something equally suitable. In the northern and central Bahamas you're never too far away from some sort of refuge. Some holes are better than others but like the old adage advises: *Any port in a storm*. With that in mind let me offer a few of the places I consider hurricane holes. Bear in mind that if you ask ten different skippers what they look for in a hurricane hole you're likely to get ten different answers. Some of these holes may not meet your requirements. I offer them only for your consideration when seeking safety for your vessel. The final decision is yours and yours alone. For the best information concerning hurricane holes always check with the locals. They'll know the best spots.

To begin with, there is no such thing as a truly safe hurricane hole. I believe that given a strong enough hurricane, any harbour can be devastated. Keep this in mind as the places that I am going to recommend offer the best protection and, under most circumstances, give you a better than average chance of surviving a hurricane, but are by no means "safe" in the true meaning of the word. Although you may feel quite safe in your chosen hole please remember that no hurricane hole comes with a guarantee. Many factors will contribute to your survival. The physical location and protection the hole offers is your primary line of defense. But hand in hand with that is the way you secure your vessel, the tidal surge, other vessels around you, and the path and strength of the hurricane. Allow yourself plenty of time to get to your chosen location and to get settled. Only a fool would attempt to race a hurricane. One more thing, in The Bahamas, owners of cays who chain off or otherwise restrict entry to a harbour, are required by law to make their harbour open and available to mariners seeking shelter in an approaching hurricane, not just in bad weather or a front, but only in a hurricane.

Abaco

Abaco offers quite a few decent hurricane holes. The best protection lies in places like Treasure Cay where you can anchor in the narrow creeks surrounding the marina complex. There is a man-made canal complex called Leisure Lee lying just south of Treasure Cay on Great Abaco. Here you will find excellent protection from seas in 8' but you will have to tie off to the trees along the shore as the entire complex is dredged and the holding is not good.

Green Turtle Cay offers White Sound and Black Sound. I much prefer White Sound though there is a bit more fetch for seas to build up. Black Sound, though smaller, has a grassy bottom and a few concrete mooring blocks scattered about. At Man Of War you can choose either anchorage. Just to the south on Elbow Cay, Hope Town Harbour boasts very good protection. If you arrive early enough and your draft is shallow enough you may be able to work you way up the creek for better protection. There is an old hurricane chain stretched across the harbour that you may be able to secure your vessel to. Ask any local where to find the chain. Just a few miles away lies Marsh Harbour with that wonderful sand/mud bottom that anchors so love. The holding here is great but the harbour is open to the west for a fetch of over a mile. For small shallow draft (3') monohull vessels there is a small creek on the eastern side of the harbour just to the east of the Conch Inn Marina. Get there early. Farther south you might consider Little Harbour though it is open to the north with a 3' bar across the mouth. Between Marsh Harbour and Little Harbour lies Snake Cay which has excellent protection in its mangrove lined creeks. In the more northern Abacos you can try Hurricane Hole on the southeast end of Allan's Pensacola Cay. Here excellent protection can be found in 6'-8' of water but the bar at the entrance will only allow about 4' at high water. Small shallow draft vessels can work themselves well up into the creeks at Double Breasted Cay if unable to get to better protection to the south.

Andros

The numerous creeks that divide Andros into hundreds of tiny isles are only suitable for small, shallow draft vessels. An excellent spot for vessels drawing less than 4' is in the small pocket at Stafford Creek that lies north of the bridge. Enter only at high tide. If you draw over 6' and are in Andros when a hurricane threatens you would be better off to get to New Providence or someplace in the Exumas.

The Berry Islands

There are only three places to consider in the Berry Islands and two of them were hit hard by powerful Hurricane Andrew. Chub Cay Marina is a possibility if you didn't mind a slip or perhaps tying off between pilings. The marina was devastated by Andrew and quite a few boats destroyed. Something to remember when it's decision making time. Another possibility would be to work your way into Little Harbour. There is a winding channel into the inner anchorage where you can tuck into a narrow channel just north of the Darville's dock in 8'-11' of water with mangroves to the east and a shallow bar and a small cay to the west. Little Harbour is open to the north but there is a large shallow bank with 1'-3' over it just north of the mangroves. Ask the Darville's where they found their refrigerator after Andrew. By far the best place to be in a hurricane is in Bullock's Harbour at Great Harbour Cay Marina. Check with the dockmaster prior to arrival to make sure there is room at the marina as the holding in the harbor is poor.

Bimini

The best protection in the Biminis is up the creeks of South Bimini by way of Nixon's Harbour. Seven feet can get in over the bar at high tide where you'll find plenty of secure water inside. On the west side of South Bimini lies the entrance to the Port Royal canals. Five feet can make it over the bar with spots of 7'-10' inside. Be sure to tie up in vacant areas between houses. On the north side of South Bimini is another entrance to some small canals with a 4' bar at the entrance from the harbour at North Bimini. Take into consideration that these canals have plenty of wrecks lining the shores along with old rotten pilings jutting up here and there. The surrounding land is very low and the canals may become untenable in a high storm surge. From Bimini Harbour you can follow the deep water channel, 5' at MLW, northward to Bimini Bay Resort where you can find protection in a deep mangrove lined creek. There is only room for two or three boats here at best. As with any hurricane hole, get there early.

Cat Island

Unless you have a small, shallow draft vessel and can get up Orange Creek or Bennett's Creek along the western shore of Cat Island, your only choice may be Hawksnest Creek on the southwestern tip of Cat Island. Six feet can enter here at MLW and work its way up the creek. Bennett's Harbour offers good protection but it is small and open to the north.

Crooked/Acklins

The only protection here will be found in the maze of creeks between French Wells and Turtle Sound for boats with drafts of 3' or less, or by going through The Going Through towards the Bight of Acklins. Here you will find a maze of shallow creeks leading to numerous small mangrove lined holes, perfect little hidey-holes for the shallow draft cruiser (up to 4' or less draft) seeking shelter.

Eleuthera

There are a few holes in Eleuthera but they all suffered considerable damage from Andrew. Royal Island offers excellent protection and good holding with a number of large concrete moorings. During Andrew the fleet washed up on one shore only to be washed up on the other shore after the eye passed. Hatchet Bay is often considered a prime hurricane hole but it too has a history of damage as the hulls along the shore will testify. At Spanish Wells you will find Muddy Hole lying off the creek between Russell Island and St. George's Cay. Muddy Hole is the local hurricane hole and 4'-5' can enter here at MLW if you get there early. Every boat (and there are a lot of them) at Spanish Wells will be heading there also. Some skippers like Cape Eleuthera Marina at Powell Point but I wouldn't use it as shelter unless I had no other choice. The dogleg marina channel is open to the west and large seas easily work their way into the basin rocking and rolling everybody. The huge concrete breakwater at the bend in the dogleg has suffered considerable damage and offers testimony to the power of the seas that enter the marina. Just south of Powell Point lies No Name Harbour, Un-Named Harbour on some charts. Eight feet can enter here at MLW and 6' can work farther up the small coves that branch off and offer fair protection. You might consider tying your lines to the trees and setting your anchors ashore here, the holding is not that great being as this is a dredged harbour.

Exumas

The Exumas Cays are home to some of the best hurricane holes in The Bahamas. From the north you should consider the inner pond at Norman's Cay. The pond offers excellent protection and good holding although there is a mile long north-south fetch that could make things rough at best. Shroud Cay has some excellent creeks with a reputation as good hurricane holes. Dr. Evans Cottman rode out a fierce hurricane here as documented in his book *Out Island Doctor*. Compass Cay has a snug little cove for protection with moorings, a marina, and creeks for shallow draft vessels. Farther south at Sampson Cay you may be able to tie up in the marina on the eastern side of the complex in the shallow and well-protected basin. I have known people to anchor between the Majors just north of Staniel Cay for hurricane shelter though I personally would try to find someplace a little more protected. At the north end of Great Guana Cay lies a small, shallow creek that gives fair to good protection for one or two small vessels drawing less that 5'. Cave Cay is an excellent hurricane hole with room for four boats in 6' at MLW. Many experienced captains like the pond at Rudder Cut Cay as a refuge but I see the eastern shore as being very low. I believe a strong hurricane with a large storm surge and high tide might make this anchorage a death trap. If had time to choose I would go north for five miles to Cave Cay and hope it wasn't too crowded. The George Town area is home to what may be the finest holes in The Bahamas. Holes #0, #2, and #3 at Stocking Island are excellent hurricane holes in every sense offering protection from wind and wave. The only problem here is that these holes will be crowded and Hole #3 is usually full of stored boats with absentee owners. The inner cove at Red Shanks offers good protection if you can get in close to the mangroves. Another possibility is inside the western arm of Crab Cay.

Grand Bahama

If you're in the area of Grand Bahama Island you might consider tying up at Jack Tar Marina at West End. Although Jack Tar offers excellent protection a direct hit by a major hurricane would likely do some considerable damage to this complex. From the north of Grand Bahama you can consider entering Hawksbill Creek though it only has 2' over the bar at its entrance with 5'-6' inside at MLW. The Grand Lucayan Waterway offers very good protection. You can tie up anywhere deep within its concrete lined canals but you cannot pass under the Casuarina Bridge unless your height is less than 27' at high water. The canal has a fairly uniform depth of 5' throughout although the northern entrance has shoaled to around 4'-4.5' at MLW. Another option would be to tie up at Lucayan Marina or in the small coves surrounding the complex that offer some very good protection.

New Providence

Here, in the capitol of The Bahamas, Nassau Harbour has good holding along with a long east-west fetch. There are two hurricane chains crossing the harbour whose approximate locations are shown on the chart for Nassau. If you fortunate enough to know someone in Coral Harbour you may be able to use their dock to escape the seas. On the southwestern shore of Rose Island is the entrance to a very good hurricane hole shown as Salt Pond on charts. It is a circular harbour with a small island in the center. The water is easily a 50'-60' wide and 7'-9' deep. Anchor and tie off between the shore and the island. Get there early as everyone in Nassau and the northern Exumas will have the same idea.

Long Island

If I had to find a place to hide from a hurricane while visiting Long Island my first choice would be in the canals that wind behind the marina at Stella Maris. Some skippers have suggested Joe's Sound but I find the land to the west too low and a tidal surge like the one in Hurricane Lili (9'-14') would make this anchorage untenable. Another consideration is in the mangrove tidal creeks in the Dollar Harbour area but the best protection is hard to get into unless you have a draft of less than 4'.

The Jumentos and Ragged Island

There are only two possibilities here and both are in the vicinity of Ragged Island. A boat with a draft of less than 5' can work its way up the mangrove lined channel to anchor off the dock at Duncan Town. Just south of Ragged Island is a small hole called Boat Harbour that the Ragged Islanders use as a hurricane hole. There is 9' inside but there is a winding channel with a 3' bar at the entrance. Ask any Ragged Islander to help you find your way in if necessary; they'll be more than happy to help.

Southern Bahamas

If you are cruising the southern Bahamas from Crooked-Acklins to Mayaguana or Inagua you will not find a truly safe hole. Although I have heard about a large sailboat riding out Hurricane Klaus lying between Samana and Propeller Cay I would not attempt to test my luck. I would either head north to better protection at George Town or continue on to The Turks and Caicos for protection at Sellar's Pond or up the canals at Discovery Bay lying northeast of Five Cays, at Leeward Going Through, or up North Creek at Grand Turk. If I had enough time I would try to make Luperon, D.R., which is as good a hole as any in the Caribbean.

JUNKANOO

The culture of The Bahamas, its heart and soul, the eyes through which it sees and is seen, is Junkanoo, with its spirit, music, dancing, singing, costumes and color. Standing along Bay Street in Nassau in the early hours of Boxing Day or New Years Day, one cannot help getting caught up in the frenzy that is Junkanoo. Junkanoo must be experienced on the street, where the clamor of the bells, whistles, and goombay drums approaching in the distance creates an electric feeling in the crowd who sway and jostle with the building excitement. Its source of all this energy is the participants, organized groups and "scrap gangs," throbbing forward to the rhythm of the music. Groups vie in a heated competition for awards for best music, costumes, and dance.

Junkanoo was introduced to the American colonies by slaves from Africa's western coast. From there it quickly spread to Jamaica and The Bahamas. Its exact origins are unknown and the numerous derivations of the name *John Canoe* further complicate the matter. The West African name *Jananin Canno* was derived from a combination of the Quojas tribe's *Canno*, a supreme being, and *Janani*, who were the dead who became spirits and were seen as patrons or defenders of the tribe. The Jamaican *John Canoe* was known in eastern North Carolina as *John Kuner, John Kooner, John Canoe, Who-Who's, and Joncooner*. A West African trait often attributed to the origin of Junkanoo was an Ashanti figure know as *Jankomo*. *Jankomo* was famed for his dance where he took two steps forward and one step back, a from of Junkanoo dancing prevalent in today's festival. Some researchers theorized that the name is a corruption of the French *gens innconnus* which, roughly translated, means u*nknown people* or *masked people*.

Junkanoo developed as a celebration during the pre-emancipation days when slaves were allowed a special Christmas holiday. Not wanting to waste any of their holiday, they took to beginning their celebration well before dawn. It is said that the wild costumes, masks, and makeup were used by the slaves as a way to disguise themselves while exacting revenge upon masters and settling grudges with fellow slaves. During the late 1800's, Junkanoo began taking on added dimensions and significance for Bahamian people. It became a vehicle for political expression and a catalyst for social change. The Street Nuisance Act of 1899 was aimed directly at Junkanoo attempting to reduce the amount of noise and length of celebration of the event in the hopes that Junkanoo would extinguish itself. Junkanoo continued, albeit a little quieter. During the economic depression of the early 1900's, Junkanoo was characterized by rival masked and costumed gangs from the various districts of New Providence. Money was scarce and the costumes changed from cloth to paper mache and became more frightening and grotesque.

World War I saw the suspension of Junkanoo when the white inhabitants of Nassau felt the celebrations were unsuitable considering the wartime conditions and Junkanoo was banned from Bay Street until well after the war. It moved to the "over the hill" section of Nassau where it grew and prospered. The prosperous bootlegging period of the 1920's in The Bahamas was reflected in more flamboyant costumes and headdresses. Junkanoo moved back to Bay Street in 1923 when its potential for increasing tourism revenue became apparent. It was at this time that Junkanoo became a competition with prizes being awarded.

Junkanoo was again banned from Bay Street in 1942 when riots broke out due to labor unrest and all public gatherings were banned. Junkanoo still thrived on various parts of New Providence however and was back on Bay Street by 1947. Junkanoo today is basically the same with some minor changes. It is no longer considered a social taboo to participate in Junkanoo and more and more women are parading in this once male dominated event. Junkanoo is a national event on the edge of becoming an international festival.

The heart of Junkanoo is the music which has changed little over the last 50 years. A typical Junkanoo band consists of lead drums, second or bass drums (goombay), cowbells, clappers, bugles, trumpets, horns, conch shells, and whistles. A few obscure instruments, such as the fife, are no longer used. The drum is the core of the music. Drums are made every year from goat or sheep skin and represent a sacrifice, the spilling of blood to make a drum. Drummers often place a flame inside the drum to help produce various drum tones; this is called "bringing it up!"

The combined effect of the music, the bells and drums and horns, all fueled by the emotion of the participants, is overwhelming.

The costumes create a tremendous visual effect and are painstakingly manufactured by hand. The costumes are brightly colored and usually represent some theme. There are no weight restrictions on costumes and one single piece may weigh over 200 pounds. Competition among the various groups is fierce and members are very secretive about their upcoming productions.

If you plan to be in Nassau or Freeport around Christmas or New Year's, do not miss Junkanoo.

MAILBOATS

You do not have to own a yacht to see the Exumas, much less the entire Bahamas, by sea. You will find you can go almost anywhere within The Bahamas by mailboat. One need only approach the dockmaster on Potter's Cay (pronounced Porter's Cay in the Bahamian dialect) for schedules and costs. Shipping times are announced three times daily on ZNS radio in Nassau. The mailboats are subsidized by the Bahamian government for carrying the mail but they also take on freight and passengers. It is an inexpensive and rewarding way to see the Out Islands. If you book passage you will gain a different view of the Bahamian people as travel by mailboat is a cultural experience as well as being a mode of transportation. People on the outer islands would find life hard indeed if not for the mailboats, they are the lifeline of the Bahamian Out Islands and the arrival of the mailboat is somewhat of a celebration. Costs range from $30.00 for a trip to Little Farmer's Cay to slightly higher for George Town or Inagua. Some mailboats include food in the fare. The M/V's *Lady Francis, Etienne and Cephas,* and *Captain Moxey* all serve parts of the Exumas as of this writing with the *Grandmaster* serving George Town.

MEDICAL EMERGENCIES

There are two hospitals in Nassau, Princess Margaret Hospital on Shirley Street and Doctor's Hospital on the corner of Shirley Street and Collins Ave. On Lyford Cay on the island of New Providence is the Lyford Cay Hospital and Bahamas Heart Institute. In the Exumas, there is St. Luke's Clinic at Staniel Cay and government clinics at Black Point, and Little Farmer's Cay. The clinics at Steventon and George Town on Great Exuma have a Doctor in attendance. If more medical assistance is needed the patient will be flown into Nassau, usually to Princess Margaret Hospital. National Air Ambulance out of Ft. Lauderdale, Florida (305-359-9900 or 800-327-3710), can transport patients from The Bahamas to the United States. If you join DAN, the Divers Alert Network, for a small yearly fee, you are covered under their *Assist America Plan.* This program offers emergency evacuation for any accident or injury, diving related or not, to the nearest facility that can provide you with adequate care. After you have been stabilized to the satisfaction of the attending physician and the *Assist America* doctor, *Assist America* will arrange your transportation back to the United States, under medical supervision if necessary.

The Warden of Exuma Park., Ray Darville, can be contacted in an emergency on VHF ch. 16 24 hours a day. The Park Headquarters has the most extensive medial emergency kit between Nassau and Staniel Cay.

The Bahamas Air-Sea Rescue Association, BASRA, has stations in Nassau, Black Point, and George Town in the Exumas, and at Salt Pond in Long Island. All BASRA stations monitor VHF ch.16. BASRA Nassau, monitors VHF ch.16 and 2182 Khz and 4125 KHz on marine single sideband from 9:00am-5:00pm Monday through Saturday. BASRA, Nassau, can be reached by phone at 242-322-3877.

PHONING HOME

If you are expecting speedy phone connections you will find that the telephone service in The Bahamas to be quite frustrating. Although there is a Marine Operator in Nassau monitoring VHF ch. 27, there are no marine operators in the Out Islands and public phones are few and far between. If you are in an emergency situation you may find a helpful Bahamian with a cellular phone in their home but these are very expensive and usually out of the reach of the average person. If you have a cellular phone contact your nearest Batelco office to arrange for service while in The Bahamas.

Amateur radio operators may not patch through phone calls by ham radio from The Bahamas. If you have SSB capability, contact WOM or WOO in the States to place calls by sideband, an expensive proposition and not at all private. Most cays with settlements will have a Batelco office where you may place a phone call. If you call the States, try to get an *AT&T USA Direct* line (1-800-872-2881), the quality and rates are much better.

If you are calling The Bahamas the area code for all islands is now 242.

PROVISIONING

If you are on a tight budget, it would be best for you to stock up on provisions in the United States prior to your Exuma cruise. Take enough for the length of your cruise and then some. With few exceptions, prices in The Bahamas are considerably higher than American prices. Beer and cigarette prices will seem outrageous with cigarette prices some 2-3 times higher than in the States. The local Bahamian beer, *Kalik* (named after the sound that cow bells make when clanged together), is very good and more reasonably priced than foreign beers. Rum, as one would think, can be very inexpensive while American whiskies and certain Scotches are very high. Staples such as rice, beans, flour, and sugar are just slightly higher than U.S. prices. Vegetables can be quite reasonable in season. The vegetable market on Potter's Cay in Nassau is a good spot to pick up a large box of mixed vegetables for around $10.00 in season. Meats, soft drinks, and milk all are considerably higher than in America. As you shop the various markets throughout The Bahamas you will find some delightful items that are not sold in the U.S., foreign butter and meats for example. The shopping experience will give you the opportunity to purchase and enjoy some new treats. Of course, the prices on fresh fish, conch, and lobster are all open to bargaining with the local fishermen.

Good drinking water is available in the Exumas from some of the cisterns and wells on various cays. Well water will have a higher salt content than cistern water which is rainwater. Always check with the owners before you remove any water. The cistern at the clubhouse on Norman's Cay is very good as is the cistern water on Rudder Cut Cay. Most stores sell bottled water and you can buy reverse osmosis (watermaker) water at Highborne Cay Marina and in George Town next to Harbour View Laundry.

If you plan to dine out while in the islands, you will find the prices to be comparable to or higher than at home. It is common for dining establishments in The Bahamas to include a 15% gratuity in the check. There are excellent restaurants at Sampson Cay, Staniel Cay, Little Farmer's Cay, Barretarre, Rolleville, George Town and at the airport on Great Exuma. Janet on Highborne Cay will cater to your vessel, call *Cool Runner* on VHF ch.16.

TIDES AND CURRENTS

Tides in the Exumas flow in and out the cuts and passes from the banks to Exuma Sound and range from 20 minutes later than Nassau at Highbourne Cay, to 30 minutes later in Exuma Park. As a rule of thumb you can estimate the tidal rise and fall to be about 2½'-3½' at most times. Tides in the northern and central Exumas range from 0-.3' less than in Nassau while tides in George Town are the same time as Nassau although they are .5'-.6' less than the same tide in Nassau. Tides on the western side of Great Exuma Island lag George Town tides by approximately 1½-2½ hours. Tides in Nassau have a mean rise of 2.6'. Neap tides, those after the first and last quarter of the moon, rise approximately ½' less, while tides after new and full moons rise approximately ½' more. During Spring tides, when the moon is nearest the Earth, the range is increased by another ½'. Cruising through the Exumas during Spring full moon tides will give you some of the lowest lows and highest highs. It is quite easy to run aground at this time on some of the Banks routes. Boats with drafts of 5' have reportedly run aground in what is normally a 6' depth at low water during this time. To receive tidal information while in the Exumas see the section *Weather*.

When attempting to predict the state of tide at any time other than at slack tide, you can use the *Rule of Twelfths* for a generally reliable accuracy. To do this take the amount of tidal fluctuation and divide it into twelfths. For example, if high tide in Nassau is expected to be 3.0' and the low water datum is 0.0', the tidal fluctuation is 3', and each twelfth is 0.25' or 3". To predict the state of tide at different times you can use the *Rule of Twelfths* in the following table. The table is merely to demonstrate a point and uses an imaginary charted high tide of 3'. Always consult your chart tables or listen for tide information broadcasts and calculate accordingly.

TIME OF LOW WATER	TIDE DATUM-0 FEET
1 hour after low, add 1/12	¼ foot above datum-3"
2 hours after low, add 3/12	¾ feet above datum-9"
3 hours after low, add 6/12	1½ feet above datum-18"
4 hours after low, add 9/12	2¼ feet above datum-27"
5 hours after low, add 11/12	2¾ feet above datum-33"
6 hours after low, add 12/12	High Water-3'*

Caution: *assumes a 3' tidal fluctuation as an example.*

Chart tables give the times and heights of high and low water but not the time of the turning of the tide or slack water. Usually there is little difference between the times of high and low water and the beginning of ebb or flood currents, but in narrow channels, landlocked harbors, or on tidal creeks and rivers, the time of slack water may vary by several hours. In the Exumas, you will find that it is not unusual for the currents to continue their direction of flow long after charted predictions say they should change. Strong winds can play havoc on the navigator attempting to predict slack water. The current may often appear in places as a swift flowing river and care must be taken whenever crossing a stretch of strong current to avoid being swept out to sea or onto a bank or rocks. Some of the currents may flow from 2.5 to over 4 knots in places and in anchorages with a tidal flow two anchors is a must. The cuts to Exuma Sound may be impassable in adverse wind conditions or in heavy swells that may exist with or without any wind. The Wide Opening is particularly susceptible to these conditions. Even in moderate conditions, onshore winds against an outgoing tide can create very rough conditions. Some of the passes, cuts, and anchorages shown may be a real test of your ability. If in doubt, stay out. As with cruising anywhere, if you exercise caution you will have a safe and enjoyable cruise in the Exumas.

VHF

The regulations pertaining to the proper use of VHF in The Bahamas are basically identical to those in the United States. Batelco, The Bahamas Telecommunications Co. oversees all licensing for VHF, SSB, and Ham radio. Channel 16 is the designated channel for hailing and distress. Please shift all traffic to a working channel when you have made contact with your party.

People throughout The Exumas use the VHF as a telephone. Almost every household has a VHF while few can afford the luxury of a cellular phone. You will often hear businesses announcing their latest deals, or the local restaurant describing the delights of their upcoming seafood night and inviting you for a meal in exchange for a small amount of cash. Technically this is illegal and improper by American as well as Bahamian laws. Bear in mind that this is a way of life in the Bahamian Out-Islands and that you are a visitor here and only temporary. There are a few cruisers who bring with them into this paradise the very things that many of us are here to escape. Some of these peoples insist on playing radio vigilante, sitting by the VHF anxiously awaiting an opportunity to spring into action and place the restrictions of the dreaded "proper radio etiquette" that have been placed on them, upon someone else. If you are one of the *Radio Gestapo*, please relax. You are doing nothing but making an unpleasant situation intolerable and increasing your blood pressure in the process. This is just the way it is on ch.16 in The Exumas and you had best learn to live with it. There is absolutely nothing that you, the Bahamian Government, or Batelco can do to change things. Besides, you will find few other cruisers that will agree with you. If you don't wish to hear the ads or traffic, simply turn your radio off.

When you are using your VHF assume that at least a half-dozen of your neighbors will follow your conversation to another channel. Even if you have a "secret" channel it will not take too long to find you. It is a fact of life that everybody listens in to everybody else.

WEATHER

The weather throughout The Bahamas is tropical with a rainy season from June through October, coinciding with hurricane season. In the winter, temperatures in the Out Islands rarely fall below 60°F and generally are above 75°F in the daytime. During the summer months the lows are around 75°-78°F while the highs seldom rise above 90°F. Sea water temperatures normally vary between 74°F in February and 84°F in August.

Humidity is fairly high all year long, especially during the summer months, but there is usually a breeze to lessen the effect. In the summer, winds tend to be light, 10 knots or less from the southeast with more calms, especially at night. In the winter, the prevailing winds are east-southeast and stronger. It is not unusual to get a week of strong winds, 20 knots or better, during the winter months as fronts move through. These fronts tend to move through with regularity during the winter months and become more infrequent as spring approaches. The wind will usually be in the southeast or south before a front and will often be very light to calm. As the front approaches with its telltale bank of dark clouds on the western and northwestern horizon, the winds will steadily pick up and move into the southwest, west, and northwest as the front approaches. Strongest winds are usually from the west and northwest. After the front passes the winds will move into the north and northeast for a day or two before finally settling back into an east/southeast pattern until the next front. Winds just after the front tend to be strong and the temperature a little cooler. A front passing off the southeast Florida coast will usually be in Nassau in about 12-24 hours and from there it may arrive in the Exumas within 12-36 hours and points south a little later.

In the summer the weather pattern is typically scattered showers with the occasional line squall. Although the main concern during June through November is hurricanes, The Bahamas are more often visited by a tropical wave with its strong winds and drenching rains. Tropical waves, sometimes called easterly waves, are low pressure systems that can strengthen and turn into a tropical depression or hurricane. Cruisers visiting The Bahamas during hurricane season are advised to monitor weather broadcasts closely and take timely, appropriate action (also see previous section on *Hurricane Holes*).

Staying in touch with weather broadcasts presents little problem in The Bahamas, even if you don't have SSB or ham radio capabilities. From Nassau you can receive the local Bahamian radio station ZNS I at 1540 KHz which also broadcasts simultaneously on FM at 107.1 MHz. ZNS II on 1240 KHz and ZNS III at 810 KHz can usually be picked up in the northern Exumas. WINZ, 940 KHz from Miami, is on the air 24 hours with weather for southern Florida approximately every 10 minutes. Unfortunately this station is difficult to pick up at night. WGBS also from Miami at 710 KHz has weather four times an hour 24 hours a day. In the northern Exumas you can occasionally hear *Ranger* from Nassau giving the weather and tides at 0715 every morning. *Ranger* will place a call on VHF ch. 16 and then move to ch. 72 for weather information. Skippers can contact the Nassau Marine Operator on VHF ch. 27 and ask for the latest weather report from the Nassau Meteorological Office.

If you have ham radio capabilities you can pick up the Bahamas Weather Net every morning at 0720 on 3.696 Mhz, lower sideband. Carolyn Wardle, C6AGG, whose husband Nick is *Ranger* in Nassau, begins with the local weather forecast and tides from the Nassau Met. Office. Next, hams from all over the Bahamas check in with their local conditions which Carolyn later forwards to the Nassau Met. Office to assist in their forecasting. If you are interested in the approach of a front you can listen in and hear what conditions hams in the path of the front have experienced. All licensed amateur radio operators with current Bahamian reciprocals are invited to participate. The local conditions in the weather reports follow a specific order so listen in and give your conditions in the order indicated. If requested, Carolyn will send you some information on the types of clouds and their descriptions along with a log sheet. Be sure to thank Carolyn for her tireless efforts that benefit all mariners, not only those with ham licenses. Thanks Carolyn.

At 0745 on 7.268 MHz you can pick up the Waterway Net. Organized and maintained by the Waterway Radio and Cruising Club, this dedicated band of amateur radio operators begin the net with a synopsis of the weather for South Florida and then proceed to weather for The Bahamas (with tides), the southwest north Atlantic, the Caribbean Sea, and the Gulf Of Mexico. For a listing of marine weather frequencies, see *Appendix F: Weather Broadcast Frequencies.*

If you have marine SSB capabilities you can pick up BASRA's weather broadcasts every morning at 0700 on 4003 KHz, upper sideband. Later in the day you can pick up the guru of weather forecasters, Herb Hilgenberg, *Southbound II*, from Canada. After a short interruptions of Herb's service, he is once again operating, this time from his home in Canada. You can tune in to Herb on 12.359 MHz, upper sideband, at 2000 Zulu. On 6.501 MHz you can pick up the voice weather broadcasts from NMN four times a day at 0500, 1100, 1700, and 2300 EST.

Starting in the southern Bahamas and continuing on throughout the entire Caribbean, an SSB equipped vessel can pick up David Jones, call sign ZHB, who operates from his boat, *Misstine*. David is on the air each day at 0815-0830 AST (1215-1230 UTC) on 4.003 MHz and then moves up to 8.104 MHz from 0830-0915. He begins with a 24-48 hour wind and sea summary followed by a synoptic analysis and tropical conditions during hurricane season. After this he repeats the weather for those needing fills and finally he takes check-ins reporting local conditions. During hurricane season David relays the latest tropical storm advisories at 1815 AST on 6.224 MHz.

USING THE CHARTS

The first difference the reader will notice between this second edition and the original is the Charts. In the first edition the Sketch Charts were exactly that, Sketch Charts. Depths were plotted by cross bearings, a tedious process at best and not accurate enough for today's skipper armed with state-of-the-art navigational instruments. With the help of my friend Steve Dodge (*A Cruising Guide To Abaco*) I developed a sister hydrographic system using similar equipment and software written by Steve's son, Jeff. The system consists of a computer based GPS and Sonar combination that gives a GPS waypoint and depth every two seconds including the time of each observation. The software used records and stores this information in an onboard computer. Due to the speed of my data acquisition vessel (DAV), each identical lat/lon may have as many as ten or twenty separate soundings. Then, with the help of NOAA tide tables, the computer gives me accurate depths to one decimal place for each separate lat/lon pair on the data acquisition run. Another program purges all but the lowest depths for each lat/lon position (to two decimal places). At this point the actual plotting is begun including one fathom and ten fathom lines. This system allows me to construct some very accurate charts with lat/lon lines and a compass rose for plotting courses. Of course, my plotting is guided by the notes actually taken in the field in which I still rely on crossed bearings for setting up control points. On all cays I land the boat on a specific point of land and simply record GPS waypoints for a period of twenty minutes. The average of these waypoints is later used to check lat/lon placement.

The charts themselves are constructed from outline tracings of topographic maps from the Land And Surveys Dept. in Nassau. Lat/lon lines are place in accordance with these maps. These topos are drawn from aerial photos and are geographically located using ground plates at known positions on each of the islands. They are scanned into my computer and everything else is added using various graphics programs.

These charts are as accurate as I can make them and I believe them to be superior to any others on the market. They are indeed more detailed than all others showing many areas that are not covered, or are incorrectly represented by other publications. As I said in the first edition, I have taken thousands of soundings up and down the entire island chain, from Sail Rocks in the north to Sandy Cay in the south, and in and out all the cuts and passes in between them from 1993 until 1995. In 1996 I once again covered these areas with my new hydrographic system. I have again trod each and every shoreline and poked the bow of my data acquisition vessel into every nook and cranny in the process of re-sounding the Exuma Cays. However, it is not possible to plot every individual rock or coral head so pilotage by eye is still essential. On many of the routes in this guide you must be able to pick out the blue, deeper water as it snakes between sandbanks, rocky bars, and coral heads. Learn to trust your eyes. Remember that on the banks, sandbars and channels can shift over time so that once what was a channel may now be a sandbar. Never approach a cut or sandbar with the sun in your eyes, it should be above and behind you. Sunglasses with a polarized lens can be a big help in combating the glare of the sun on the water. With good visibility the sandbars and heads stand out and are clearly defined. As you gain experience you may even learn to read the subtle differences in the water surface as it flows over underwater obstructions.

I have included both deep draft vessel routes as well as some shallow draft vessel routes. Deep draft vessel routes will accommodate a draft of 6' minimum and often more with the assistance of the tide. Shallow draft vessel routes are for dinghies and small outboard powered boats with drafts of less than 3'. Shallow draft monohulls and multihulls very often use these same routes. If traveling in small, shoal draft vessels, dinghies, or small outboards, remember that even though there are sandbanks stretching out towards the banks, there is usually a channel of slightly deeper water near the shoreline along the western side of the cays.

All courses here are magnetic. In this guide I have included GPS latitude and longitude positions for the entrances to the cuts and to give locations for the positions of shoal areas. These GPS positions are only to be used in a general sense. The best aids to navigation when near these shoals and cuts are sharp eyesight and good light.

Not being a perfect world, I expect errors to occur. I would deeply appreciate any input and corrections that you may notice as you travel these waters. Please send your suggestions to Stephen J. Pavlidis, C/O Seaworthy Publications, 17125C W. Bluemound Road, Suite 200, Brookfield, WI, 53005-5914. If you see me anchored nearby, don't hesitate to stop to say hello and offer your input. Your suggestion may help improve the next edition of this guide.

The prudent navigator will not rely solely on any single aid to navigation, particularly on floating aids.

LIST OF CHARTS

CAUTION:

The approach and index charts are not to be used for navigational purposes.
Their design is strictly for orientation.
All charts are to be used in conjunction with the text.
All soundings are in feet at Mean Low Water.
All courses are magnetic.
Projection is transverse Mercator.
Datum used is WGS84.
Differences in latitude and longitude may exist between these charts and other charts of the area;
therefore the transfer of positions from one chart to another should be done by
bearings and distances from common features.

The author and publisher take no responsibility for the misuse of these charts. No warranties are either expressed or implied as to the usability of the information contained herein.

Note: Some official governmental charts (NOS Chart 11013, and DMA charts 26253, 26257, 26286, 26301, 26303, and 26305) do not show some of the reefs and heads charted in this guide. Always keep a good lookout when piloting in these waters.

Legend

— – —	large vessel route-6' draft		light
— · – ·	shallow vessel route		anchorage
+	rock or coral head		GPS waypoint
++++	reef		tower
═══	road		wreck--above hw
m	mooring		wreck-submerged
dm	dinghy mooring		building

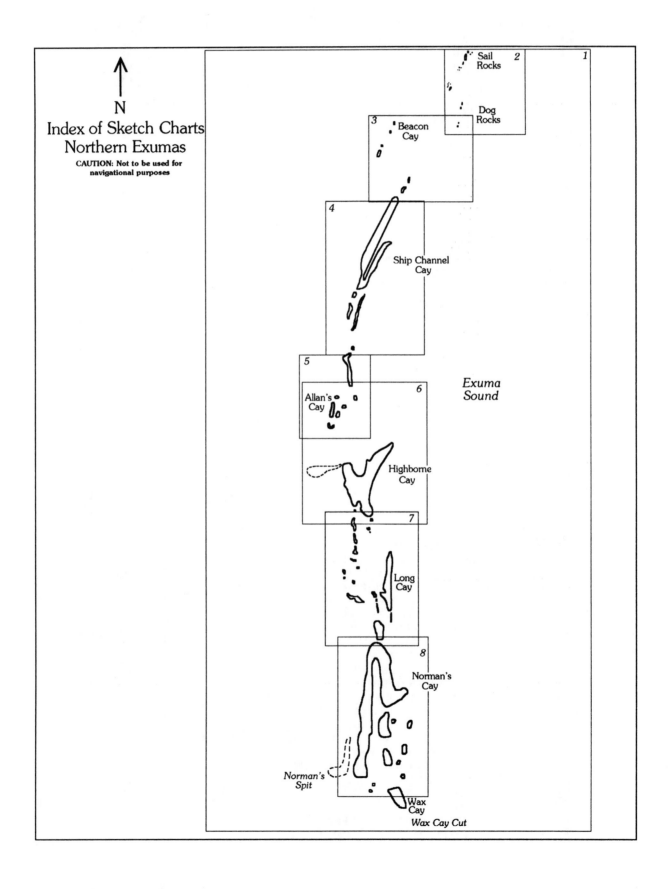

N

Index of Sketch Charts
Northern Exumas
CAUTION: Not to be used for
navigational purposes

Sail
Rocks   2   1

Dog
Rocks

3   Beacon
         Cay

4

Ship Channel
Cay

5

Exuma
Sound

6

Allan's
Cay

Highborne
Cay

7

Long
Cay

8

Norman's
Cay

Norman's
Spit

Wax
Cay

Wax Cay Cut

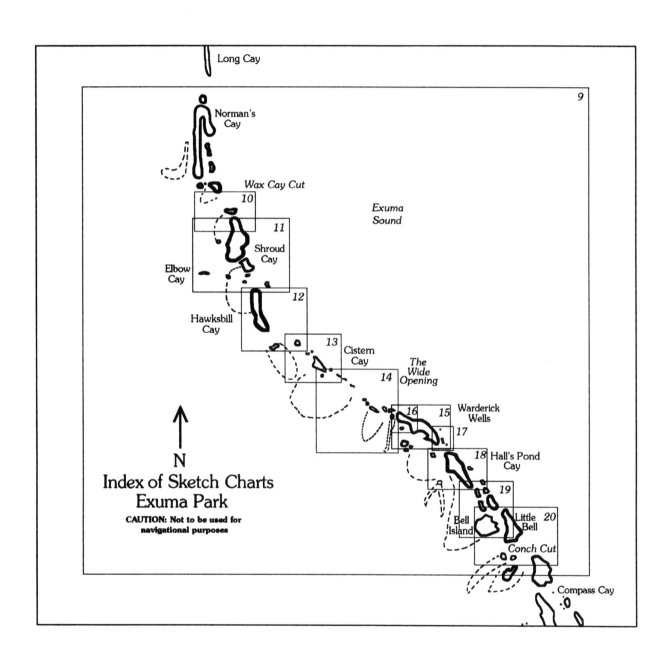

Long Cay

9

Norman's
Cay

Wax Cay Cut

10

11

*Exuma
Sound*

Shroud
Cay

Elbow
Cay

12

Hawksbill
Cay

13

Cistern
Cay

*The
Wide
Opening*

14

16   15

Warderick
Wells

17

18   Hall's Pond
Cay

N

Index of Sketch Charts
Exuma Park

**CAUTION: Not to be used for
navigational purposes**

19

Bell
Island

Little
Bell

20

Conch Cut

Compass Cay

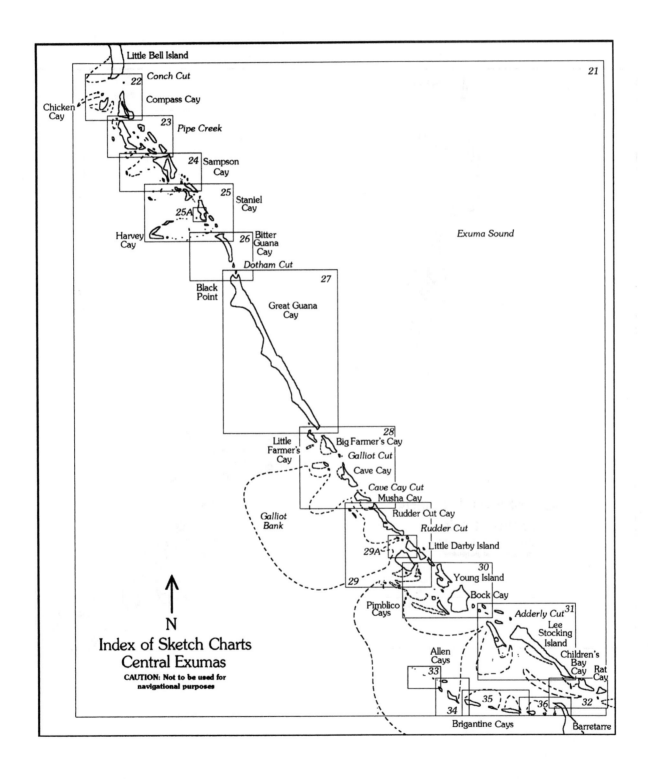

Little Bell Island

21

Conch Cut
22

Compass Cay

Chicken
Cay

23 Pipe Creek

24 Sampson
       Cay

25
      Staniel
      Cay

25A

Harvey
Cay

26 Bitter
      Guana
      Cay

Dotham Cut

Exuma Sound

Black
Point

27

Great Guana
Cay

Little
Farmer's
Cay

28
Big Farmer's Cay

Galliot Cut

Cave Cay

Cave Cay Cut
Musha Cay

Galliot
Bank

Rudder Cut Cay

Rudder Cut

Little Darby Island

29A

30
Young Island

29
Bock Cay

Pimblico
Cays

Adderly Cut *31*
Lee
Stocking
Island

Allen
Cays

Children's
Bay
Cay

Rat
Cay

33

35

34

36

32

N

Index of Sketch Charts
Central Exumas

**CAUTION: Not to be used for
navigational purposes**

Brigantine Cays

Barretarre

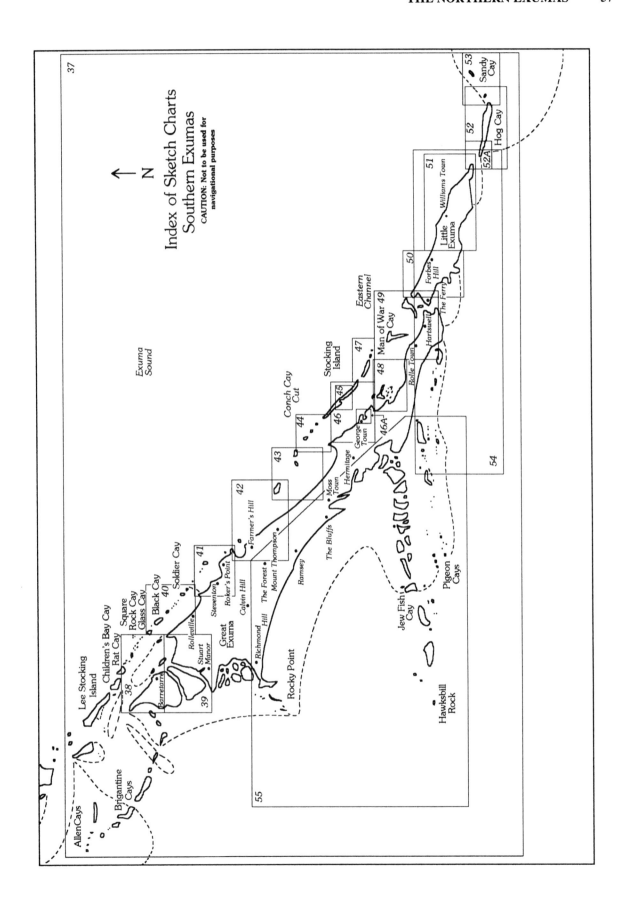

Index of Sketch Charts
Southern Exumas
CAUTION: Not to be used for
navigational purposes

THE
NORTHERN
EXUMAS

THE NORTHERN EXUMAS
Sail Rocks to Exuma Park

Let us begin our exploration of the Exumas at the northern end and work our way south. As you proceed on your cruise, you will undoubtedly become quite familiar with the names of the various cays and notice many with the same name. This is not unusual, for instance, any cay with a large, white patch of sand may be called White Bay Cay. Bird Cay may well be a small rock or cay where migratory birds nest. Hawksnest Rock usually refers to a rock or cay where osprey have constructed their nest and is normally occupied by succeeding generations of this bird. A small cay next to a larger one would likely be called Little which may often be corrupted to Lil or Lilly while the larger cay would understandably be called Big. Many cays were named after their owners. Mullins Cay, named after Elizabeth Mullins in 1789, has also been called Tommy Young Cay, Henderson Ferguson's Cay, F'eddy Bowe Cay, and Paul Clarke's Cay. Hog Cay (most likely a place where the owners or squatters kept hogs in a walled pasture), at the eastern end of Little Exuma was once known as Captain Mingo Rolle-God Rest the Dead Cay.

The cays are essentially limestone. They tend to be undercut along the shoreline with small caves and blow holes. Inland you will find caves and cave holes honeycombing some of the cays and just waiting to be explored by the amateur spelunker. At one time almost all these cays were covered with much larger trees such as madeira but they soon fell to the fledgling lumber industry. Now, with the exception of Great Exuma and a few other cays, you will find the cays to be covered with scrub brush, cactus, and smaller, stunted trees.

APPROACHES TO THE NORTHERN EXUMAS

There are two basic routes to take when cruising the Exumas, either inside on the Banks or outside in Exuma Sound. Vessels leaving Nassau will obviously take the Banks route until they reach the northern Exumas. Vessels arriving from Eleuthera, Cat Island, and Cape Santa Maria on the northern tip of Long Island will be approaching from Exuma Sound. Cruisers arriving from the western shore of Long Island or from the Jumentos must cross the banks which lie between Long Island, the southern Exumas, and the Jumentos. Heading south, all vessels will have to go out into Exuma Sound at some point unless you elect to take the mailboat route along the western shore of Exuma. By utilizing this route and passing through Hog Cay Cut, it is possible for vessels with drafts of less than 6' to parallel the western shore of Little Exuma to the Eastern Channel into Elizabeth Harbour and George Town and rarely get in water over 25' deep.

Voyaging in Exuma Sound offers few obstructions though it can get quite rough compared to the Banks. Strong winds on the Banks will create a short, steep chop with waves that are very close together. Exuma Sound, being very deep, is more similar to ocean sailing although Eleuthera and Cat Island afford a lee from the large ocean swells that originate far out in the Atlantic. Many a novice sailor has turned the corner at the north end of Long Island at Cape Santa Maria to be surprised at the size of the normal seas in the open ocean. Many have turned back, giving George Town a dubious reputation as "Chicken Harbour."

When approaching the northern Exumas from Nassau (Chart #EX-1), a vessel with a draft of 6' or less may begin its voyage at a point approximately 500 yards south of Porgee Rocks. The GPS waypoint for this position is 25° 03.50' N, 77° 14.55' W. Courses on *Chart #EX-1, Approaches to the Northern Exumas* begin from this position. Deeper draft vessels should steer for a point 2 miles south-southeast of Porgee Rocks. Taking up your course from this position will enable you to clear the heads and patch reefs that lie to the east of New Providence.

There is an area just south and southeast of Porgee Rocks that is locally known as the Five Fathom Bank. Here the water is 30' deep and is heavily affected by tidal currents. If you are heading to or leaving Nassau by the banks route you will pass over this area which will usually be the roughest part of your journey. If you are leaving Nassau and the conditions seem a little too rough for you, you might want to consider continuing on your course at least five miles to clear this bank as conditions often moderate once you pass the Five Fathom Bank.

The routes from Porgee Rocks to the northern Exumas cross the dreaded Yellow Banks which are indeed formidable but should pose no problem if the proper precautions are taken. The Yellow Banks is an area where the depths suddenly go from 20' to 12'-14' at low water and the bottom is besprinkled with dark coral heads and small patch reefs. A few of these heads have only 3'-4' of water over them but they are easily seen and you will have plenty of room to maneuver around them. The Yellow Banks begin about 13-14 miles southeast of Porgee Rocks so plan to arrive on the banks no earlier than 11:00 a.m. for good visibility. Earlier than this and the sun will be low and right in your eyes and you may not see the heads until you are almost on top of them.

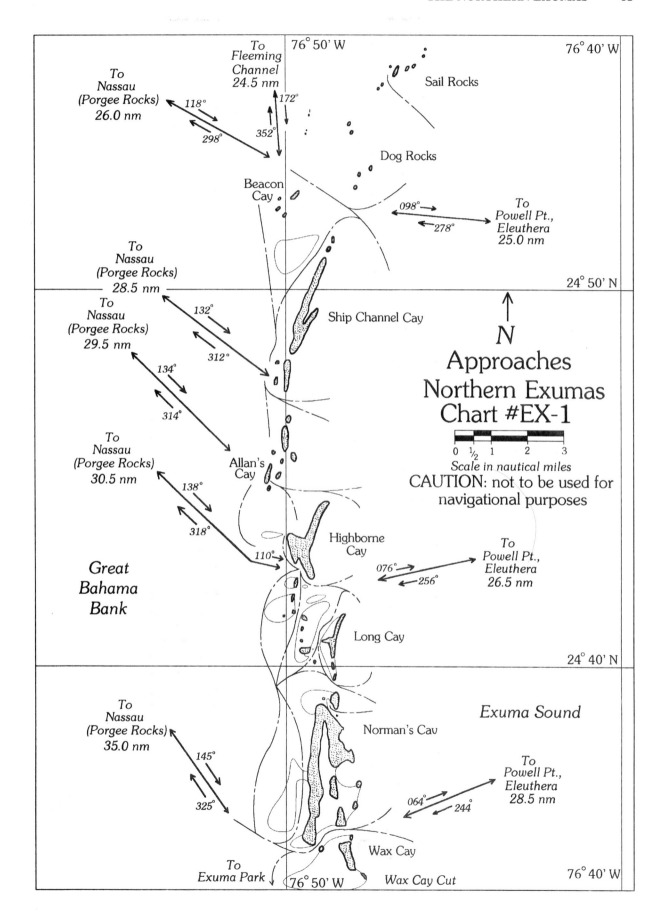

*To
Fleeming
Channel
24.5 nm*

76° 50' W

76° 40' W

Sail Rocks

*To
Nassau
(Porgee Rocks)
26.0 nm*

118°

172°

298°

352°

Dog Rocks

Beacon
Cay

098°

*To
Powell Pt.,
Eleuthera
25.0 nm*

278°

*To
Nassau
(Porgee Rocks)
28.5 nm*

24° 50' N

*To
Nassau
(Porgee Rocks)
29.5 nm*

132°

Ship Channel Cay

N

312°

134°

Approaches
Northern Exumas
Chart #EX-1

314°

0 ½ 1 2 3
Scale in nautical miles
CAUTION: not to be used for
navigational purposes

*To
Nassau
(Porgee Rocks)
30.5 nm*

138°

Allan's
Cay

318°

Highborne
Cay

*To
Powell Pt.,
Eleuthera
26.5 nm*

076°

110°

256°

*Great
Bahama
Bank*

Long Cay

24° 40' N

Exuma Sound

*To
Nassau
(Porgee Rocks)
35.0 nm*

Norman's Cay

145°

*To
Powell Pt.,
Eleuthera
28.5 nm*

325°

064°

244°

Wax Cay

*To
Exuma Park*

76° 50' W

Wax Cay Cut

76° 40' W

Remember that isolated coral heads may be found almost anywhere on the Banks side of the Exuma Cays, not just on the Yellow Banks. As ever, a good lookout is important. Although you may pass over most of these heads with plenty of room to spare, this type of cavalier attitude may cause you to find, as others have done in the past, that there is a head out there with your name on it. One mariner bragged about crossing the Yellow Banks numerous times, at all hours of the day and night (not recommended) until that one night that a head reached out and grabbed his keel. Luckily his pride suffered far worse than his vessel. Heads are quite a bit more numerous on the routes to Sail Rocks, Beacon Cay, Ship Channel Cay, and Allan's Cay. They are particularly thicker and shallower the closer you get to Sail Rocks, Beacon Cay, and Ship's Channel Cay. The heads are clearly visible in good light and easy to steer around in 10'-15' of water.

It is possible to steer a course of 180° from the position 2 miles to the south-southeast of Porgee Rocks for 11 miles and cross the area where the Yellow and White Banks meet. From this position you may then take up a course of 113° for approximately 21 nm to Allan's Cay. The heads here are more infrequent and generally have more water over them.

From Porgee Rocks, steering a course of 118° for 26.0 nm will bring you to a point just northwest of Beacon Cay and Ship Channel where you may enter the northern end of Exuma Sound. If you enter Exuma Sound from Ship Channel keep at least 1 mile off the eastern shore of Ship Channel to avoid these reef strewn waters. Entering Fleeming Channel (between Eleuthera and New Providence) from the Abacos, you may steer 172° for 24.5 nm to bring you to the position just northwest of Beacon Cay.

From Porgee Rocks to Allan's Cay it is 29.5 nm at 134°. Porgee Rocks to Highborne Cay is slightly more complicated as you must bypass Highborne Rocks which lie just south of the Allan's Cay group and west of Highborne Cay. Take up a course of 138° for 30.5 miles to a GPS waypoint at 24° 42.28' N, 76° 51.30' W to clear these rocks. From this position, take up a course of 110° until you can pick up the entrance range to the marina. To arrive at a position just west of Norman's Spit, steer 145° from Porgee Rocks for 35.0 nm to a GPS waypoint at 24° 35.64' N, 76° 51.96' W, this will place you approximately ¼ nm west of the stake that marks the southwestern tip of Norman's Spit.

From Eleuthera it is a deep water passage all the way from Powell Point, a popular jumping off spot. Steer 278° for 25.0 nm from Powell Point to arrive at Ship Channel and the entrance to the banks at Beacon Cay. Taking up a course of 256° for 26.5 nm from Powell Point will bring you to the southeastern entrance to Highborne Cay at Highborne Cay Cut. Those wishing to make landfall at Norman's Cay should steer 244° from Powell Point for 28.5 nm.

If arriving from the southern Exumas on the Sound side, keep at least ½ mile offshore once you clear the shoals and reefs to the east of Shroud Cay and Hawksbill Cay (stay 1 mile off in this vicinity) in Exuma Park. If heading north on the Banks side, once you clear Elbow Cay (Chart #EX-11) you need only stay two miles or more off the cays to avoid the conspicuous sandbanks that lie to the west of Norman's Cay and the stretch of rocks and shoals known as Highborne Rocks just to the west of Highborne Cay.

Those who wish a banks passage south to avoid Exuma Sound may follow the traditional mailboat route. Haitian vessels have also used this sailing route for the last 200 years. For more information on the mailboat route see the section *The Mailboat Route*.

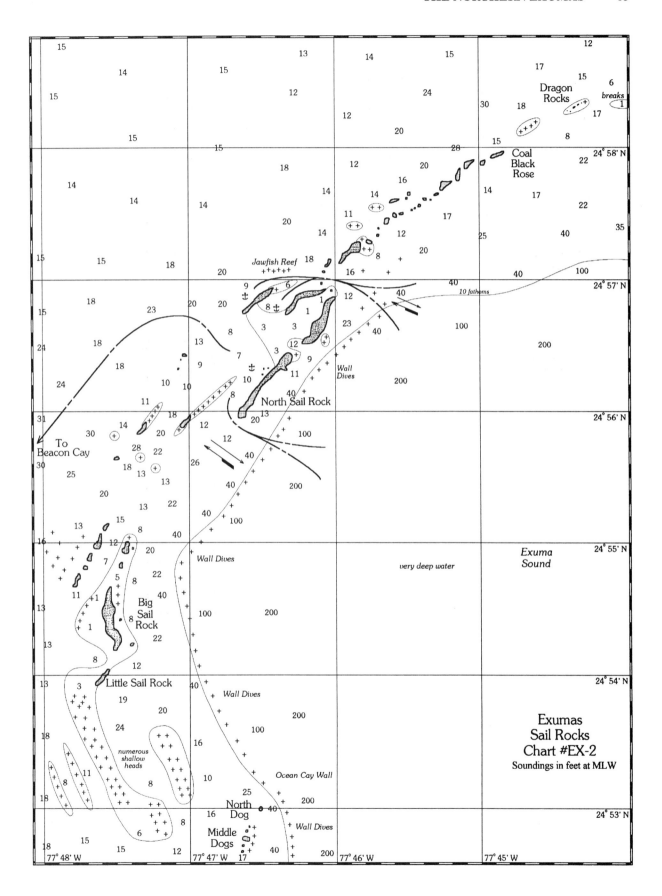

Exumas
Sail Rocks
Chart #EX-2
Soundings in feet at MLW

SAIL ROCKS

The Sail Rocks (Chart #EX-2), 62 in number, lie at the northernmost tip of the Exumas and range from 6' to ¾ mile in length. Starting with the Dragon Rocks and Coal Black Rose in the north there are 49 rocks bunched together stretching southward for 5½ miles. After a gap of one mile the remaining 13 rocks are strewn over another mile finishing up at Little Sail Rock. It is possible to sail from Nassau directly to Sail Rocks but this is not recommended due to the number of shallow coral heads on this route. We suggest you approach from Beacon Cay or Exuma Sound. Although it is possible to pass north of the Sail Rocks toward Eleuthera, if you attempt to pass from the northernmost of the Sail Rocks (Dragon Rocks) eastward, you will soon find yourself in a maze of shallows and bars. The area from Beacon Cay northward is not recommended for the novice mariner who is new to these waters and the art of eyeball navigation. For those first time visitors, it might be prudent to visit this area on the trip back when you are an accomplished "eye-pilot" so that the many reefs and heads in this area will pose less of a threat to you. Some of the reefs rise up out of 15'-20' of water quite abruptly and sometimes are not seen until you are on top of them.

The Sail Rocks are home for flocks of migratory sea birds and good fishing and diving abounds. The best fishing lies along the wall drop-off in 80'-100' of water which lies very close to the cays from the area of North Sail Rock southward. There are many large and colorful reef systems in the Sail Rocks area that will fascinate the diver in search of interesting diving far off the beaten track. The wall drop-off is an excellent dive almost anywhere along its length with the best areas lying just off North Sail Rock.

The closest anchorage for use in anything but settled weather is 8 miles to the south of Little Sail Rock (the southernmost Sail Rock) at Ship Channel Cay. There are good day anchorages in the lee of North Sail Rock where you can anchor in 8'-10' in settled weather. Entering from Exuma Sound pass the southern tip of North Sail Rock and head northeast into the anchorage. From here you can work you way through the maze of small patch reefs to anchor in the lee of the small unnamed cay that lies to the north of North Sail Rock. North of this cay is Jawfish Reef, a beautiful shallow water reef dive. You can reach this same anchorage by working your way northeastward from Beacon Cay along the western side of the Sail Rocks. Watch out for heads and small patch reefs on this route.

DOG ROCKS

The Dog Rocks (Chart #'s EX-2 & 3) are nine small cays divided into three sections, North Dog, Middle Dog, and South Dog. North Dog is often called Man Of War Rock by locals while South Dog is known as Ocean Rock or Jimmy Knowles. The Dog Rocks lie well to the east and northeast of Beacon Cay and are as barren as their neighbors the Sail Rocks. A surveyor in the 1920's wrote that they ". . . serve little purpose except to give the sea something to break over."

There are no anchorages in the immediate vicinity of the Dog Rocks although you can anchor in their lee in settled weather. It is possible to anchor just south of the Dog Rocks in the lee of Bluff Cay, Ship Beacon Cay, or Ship Channel Cay, and take your dinghy to investigate what the Dog Rocks have to offer. The redeeming features of these barren, isolated rocks is their close proximity to the drop off into Exuma Sound which offers excellent fishing and fantastic wall dives. The wall drop off comes so close to the Dog Rocks you can throw a rock from the North Dog Rock and it will land on the drop off. Ocean Cay Wall, a spectacular wall dive with many caves and crevices lies just east and north of North Dog Rock in 35'-90' of water. If you are heading north along the wall from Beacon Cay, put your lines out as soon as you are over the wall and troll in 80'-100' for dolphin, wahoo, shark, and other large fish.

BEACON CAY

Beacon Cay (Chart #EX-3), sometimes called North Rock, is the site of Beacon Cay Light (FL W+R ev 3 sec, 58ft, 8m), an important navigational aid in directing mariners from Nassau to Exuma Sound and the outer islands. Beacon Cay Light, now government maintained and automatic, once had two keepers who lived on the cay with their families. The ruins of their dwellings still stand and are a stark reminder of the harshness their life must have been on this isolated cay.

From Porgee Rocks take up a heading of 118° for 26 nautical miles to enter Ship Channel just north of Beacon Cay. A GPS waypoint at 24° 53.18' N, 76° 49.50' W will place you approximately 500 yards to the northwest of Beacon Cay.

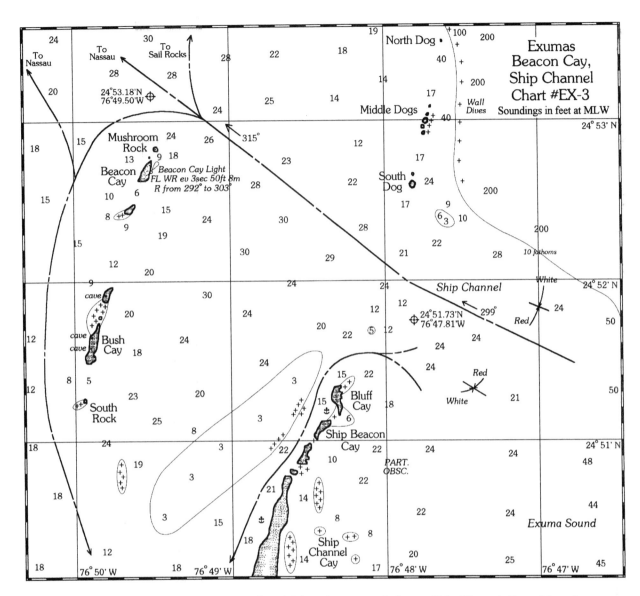

There are no protected anchorages in the vicinity, the nearest being at Ship Channel Cay, although you can anchor in the lee of Beacon Cay in settled weather. If you are heading into Exuma Sound, pass north of Beacon Cay and south of the Dog Rocks until you are in the deep waters of the Sound. Watch our for the 3' shallow area north of the channel and the 5' spot just south of the channel. Once in the vicinity of Beacon Cay, you can head south along the western shore of Beacon Cay and the small cays that lie to its south towards Ship Channel Cay.

From Exuma Sound, a GPS waypoint at 24° 51.73' N, 76° 47.81' W will place you approximately 2 miles southeast of Beacon Cay, just south of the Dog Rocks and north of Bluff Cay. The approach from Exuma Sound is on an approximate heading of 299° in the red sector of Beacon Cay Light. Approaching in the white sector from Exuma Sound may place you in jeopardy if you attempt to enter the channel from these directions, stay in the red which shows from 292°-303°. When in the vicinity of the GPS waypoint, or roughly midway between South Dog Rock and Bluff Cay, alter your course to 315° to pass north of Beacon Cay where you can then take up a heading of 298° for Porgee Rocks. It is possible to pass along the western shore of Bluff Cay and Ship Beacon Cay to anchor in their lee or to work your way along the western shore of Ship Channel Cay. Stay in the deep water between these cays and the very obvious sandbank that lies to their west.

Just north of Beacon Cay lies a small, barren, pockmarked and honeycombed cay named Mushroom Rock. South-southwest of Beacon Cay lies Bush Cay. Its name is a misnomer for the only flora is some cactus, grass, and a few shrubs barely 2' high. On the western side of Bush Cay, about 800' south of the northern end is a cave with several rooms and further south along the cliffs are several more caves and holes. Bush Cay is a nesting place for

Photo courtesy of Nicolas Popov/Island Expeditions

Ruins at Ship Channel Cay

several species of migratory seabirds. The small rock (500' x 200') just to the north of Bush Cay has a small cave on its west side.

Lying southeast of Beacon Cay and just south of Ship Channel is Bluff Cay, the northernmost of the Ship Channel Cay group, which generally refers to all the cays just to the north of the Allan's Cay group. The cay may be misnamed as there is no bluff on Bluff Cay but it is the home of a few species of seabirds. It is honeycombed with water filled holes, one of which is 25' wide and 3' deep with a sand beach. About 800' south of Bluff Cay lies Ship Beacon Cay. It is about 700' long and 100'-400' wide. Once the site of a stone beacon, there is little evidence of its ever being there except for a small pile of rocks about 8' in diameter which might have originally been a cairn.

SHIP CHANNEL CAY

Ship Channel Cay (Chart #'s EX-3 & 4), often overlooked, should be given serious consideration as your first stop on a southbound cruise. It has an excellent all-weather anchorage at its southern end between Little Ship Channel Cay and Long Rock with a narrow, shallow, entrance channel.

From Porgee Rocks, a course of 132° will bring you into the vicinity of the entrance to the anchorage (Chart #EX-4). Keep a good lookout for shallow heads on this route across the banks. A GPS waypoint at 24° 47.63' N, 76° 50.40' W will place you approximately ¼ mile west of the entrance channel. From this position pass close by the southern shore of the unnamed cay lying just south of Little Ship Channel Cay, between the unnamed cay and the reef that lies just to its south. The channel is extremely narrow with a 4' depth at low water so take it nice and easy through here. Head straight for the western shore of Long Rock and round up northward close to its shore to anchor in 7' at low water. The anchorage shallows out to the north. There are some excellent reefs for snorkelers between the anchorage and Ship Channel Cay in shallow water.

Photo courtesy of Nicolas Popov/Island Expeditions

Ship Channel Cay Anchorage.

If approaching from Exuma Sound a GPS waypoint at 24° 46.38' N, 76° 49.39' W places you approximately ¼ mile southeast of Long Rock Cut (Chart #EX-4). From this position steer approximately 290° to pass between the two small rocks shown on Chart #EX-4 in 18' of water. Once inside, head northward paralleling the western shore of the cays until you can enter the anchorage. Just to the west of the small rocks north of this cut lie two nice reefs, Lobster-No Lobster Reef and Close Mon Reef. Lobster-No Lobster Reef was named because you would sometimes find a lobster on it while other times you would not. You can find this reef by first lining up the southern end of the small unnamed cay that has Close Mon Reef off its western shore on an easterly heading, and then lining up the large square bush at the southern end of Long Rock with the northern tip of the same unnamed cay. Close Mon Reef is named because you have to get very "close mon" to the small cay it lies behind. Just to the west of Little Ship Channel Cay lie the remains of a large plane in about 15' of water. The plane was in the middle of a low level drug drop when it banked into a turn and caught its wing tip in the water and went down. To find the plane, head west in the area of Ship Channel Cay and Little Ship Channel Cay until you are in about 15'-20' of water. Look for a dark spot that resembles turtle grass. It may take a few minutes to locate the wreck but it makes for a good dive.

If you wish to pass through Long Rock Cut into Exuma sound, a GPS waypoint at 24° 46.78'N, 76° 50.30'W will place you approximately ¼ nm west of the cut between the two small rocks. Pass between the two rocks and head out into Exuma Sound on a heading of approximately 110°. Watch out for the small rocks just south of your course.

Ship Channel Cay itself is 3 miles long and almost 400' wide. One half mile southward of its northern tip is a hilly ridge approximately 35' high. At the south end of this ridge are numerous cave holes which contain salt water. The center section of this ridge is 30'-40' high with a sandy hill and a small beach just north of it. Before the boom of the lumber industry, 12' tall trees covered this cay and the light keepers on Beacon Cay used to come to Ship Channel Cay in search of wood for fuel. Cabbage palms are plentiful in the central section. South of this central section is an area of large white boulders, some up to 20' square and 6' high.

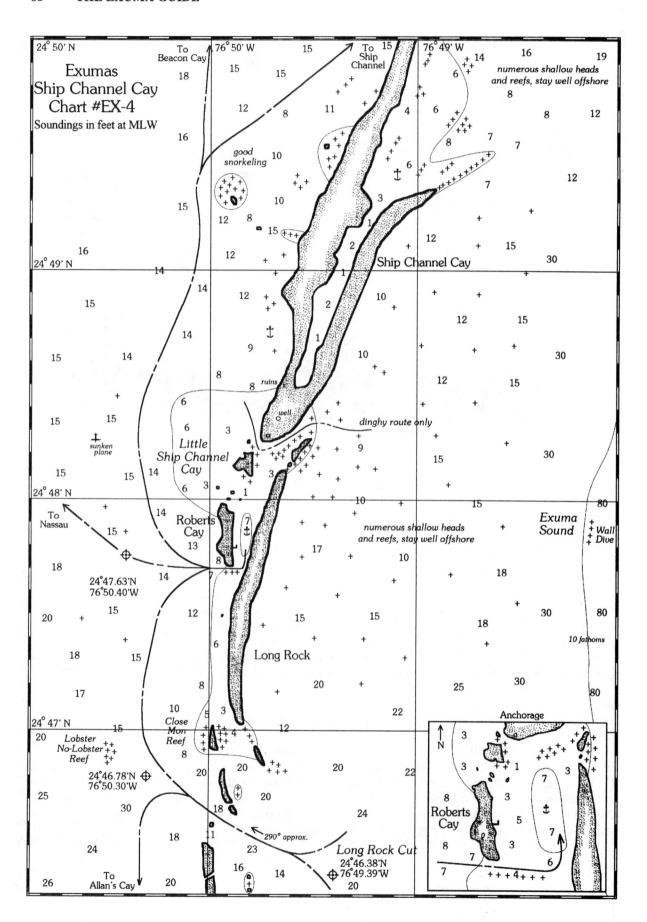

24° 50' N

To
Beacon Cay

76° 50' W

To
Ship
Channel

76° 49' W

Exumas
Ship Channel Cay
Chart #EX-4
Soundings in feet at MLW

numerous shallow heads
and reefs, stay well offshore

*good
snorkeling*

Ship Channel Cay

24° 49' N

ruins

well

dinghy route only

*Little
Ship Channel
Cay*

sunken
plane

24° 48' N

To
Nassau

*Roberts
Cay*

numerous shallow heads
and reefs, stay well offshore

*Exuma
Sound*

Wall
Dive

24°47.63'N
76°50.40'W

Long Rock

10 fathoms

24° 47' N

*Close
Mon
Reef*

Lobster
No-Lobster
Reef

24°46.78'N
76°50.30'W

290° approx.

Long Rock Cut
24°46.38'N
76°49.39'W

To
Allan's Cay

Anchorage

N

*Roberts
Cay*

The eastern shore of Ship Channel Cay is literally strewn with reefs, some quite large and shallow and this area must be given a wide berth (stay at least 1 mile off) by large boats although it is excellent for dinghy exploration. The wall drop-off along this shore has numerous wall diving opportunities, just pick a spot.   There is a large peninsula on the eastern side separated from the main section by a ½ mile long creek that is 600' wide in sections and 3' deep. This creek is a mating area for nurse sharks from March through June. If investigating the creek, easily accessible at high tide, please be careful that your dinghy engine doesn't hit a resting nurse shark. The anchorage inside the peninsula should be considered a daytime anchorage in settled weather only. To enter from Exuma Sound you will be kept quite busy at the helm dodging numerous reefs of staghorn and elkhorn coral. I do not recommend staying in this anchorage overnight. If the wind were to pick up and blow from the north or northeast you would be unable to eyeball your way out in the dark. There is little help in this area if you get in trouble.

Just south of the creek is a hill known as Claret Hill. South of this hill the land is high with white cliffs over 50' high that are visible for many miles. West of Claret Hill is a beach and small pond. Just north of the pond are the remains of an old road that leads to a well that is 20' deep and has been used by local mariners for generations. As everywhere throughout these cays, taste the water before you use it, it may have become brackish which is a common occurrence, especially after periods of no rain.

There are some nice ruins along the western shore and some Lucayan Indian artifacts were once found on this cay. At the southern end of the cay is the private terminus of Powerboat Adventures. There is a small cottage with tables and a beach that is used by the tourists that Powerboat Adventures bring to the cay on a daily basis. If you wish to visit the beach and trails, try to do so when Powerboat Adventures is not using the facilities. Ashore you may find wild chickens and a few pigs. The pigs, once wild, have now grown very used to visitors. They have even taken to drinking beer with the tourists. Be careful though, they do bite.

Little Ship Channel Cay is pockmarked with many small cave holes on its northeast tip. At one time turtlers used these salt water filled cave holes as holding pens for their catches. Good fishing and snorkeling abounds in this area. The unnamed cay just south of Little Ship Channel Cay is private and visits ashore must be by invitation only. In recent years cruisers have been coming ashore and helping themselves to water from the cistern without asking permission from the owner. If you need water, try the well on Ship Channel Cay, please respect the privacy of the owners of the cay.

Long Rock, often called Pimlico Cay, is 1¼ mile long and 100'-500' wide. It is a continuous ridge from north to south rising from 10'-35'. There are numerous coral heads and rocky bars on its eastern shore just inside the obvious brown bar with 10' of water over it. The cays south of Long Rock to the Allan's Cay group have no anchorages but are good for fishing and diving.

ALLAN'S CAY, LEAF CAY, S.W. ALLAN'S CAY

Allan's Cay (Chart # EX-5), one of the most popular anchorages in the northern Exumas, is quite often the first stop on a southbound Exuma Cruise. The principal attraction is the large population of rock iguanas (see *Flora and Fauna*) found on Leaf Cay and S.W. Allan's Cay. As you disembark from your dinghy on the beach you will soon notice the iguanas crawling out of the bush towards you. Although signs placed on the cay request that visitors do not feed the iguanas almost everybody ignores them. Consequently it almost seems as if the iguanas expect to be fed. Although rare, visitors have been bitten by the iguanas, they have poor eyesight and may think your ankle is a tasty tidbit. Rock iguanas are protected by law although some Bahamians still hunt them for food. Please do not take your dog ashore here to avoid confrontations with the iguanas.

Vessels approaching from Nassau can take up a course of 134° from Porgee Rocks for 29.5 miles to arrive at Allan's Cay. A GPS waypoint at 24° 44.74' N, 76° 50.91' W will place you approximately ¼ mile west of the entrance to the anchorage. Pilot your way in between Allan's Cay and S.W. Allan's Cay, avoid the small patch reef with 6' over it at low water which lies just to the west of the southern tip of Allan's Cay. You can anchor just north of S.W. Allan's Cay, in the deep water along the western shore of Leaf Cay (the best spot), or along the eastern shore of Allan's Cay. Watch out for the shallow sandbar between the two anchorages. Be advised that this anchorage can get quite rolly at times. Spongers and turtlers once used this anchorage and built kraals and turtle pens on these islands.

Vessels can pass through the Allan's Cay group to the east and into Exuma Sound (Chart # EX-6), or head south to the anchorage at the north end of Highborne Cay. On this route you will be kept quite busy at the helm avoiding patch reefs. As usual in the Exumas, good visibility is essential when traversing this area.

Snorkelers will delight in the abundance of reefs in the Allan's Cay-Highborne Cay area. Numerous patch reefs lie to the south and west of Leaf Cay, to the south of S.W. Allan's Cay, and throughout the waters between the

Allan's Cay group and Highborne Cay. Flat Rock Reef is a popular snorkel which lies along the western side of the easternmost large unnamed cay. Northwest of Allan's Cay lies Barracuda Shoal, an excellent snorkel. To find Barracuda Shoal line up the northern end of Allan's Cay and the conspicuous palm trees which surround the high house on the northern end of Highborne Cay. Proceed on that line heading roughly northwest of Allan's Cay until you are over the reef.

Photo courtesy of Nicolas Popov/Island Expeditions

A large population of rock iguanas live on Allan's Cay

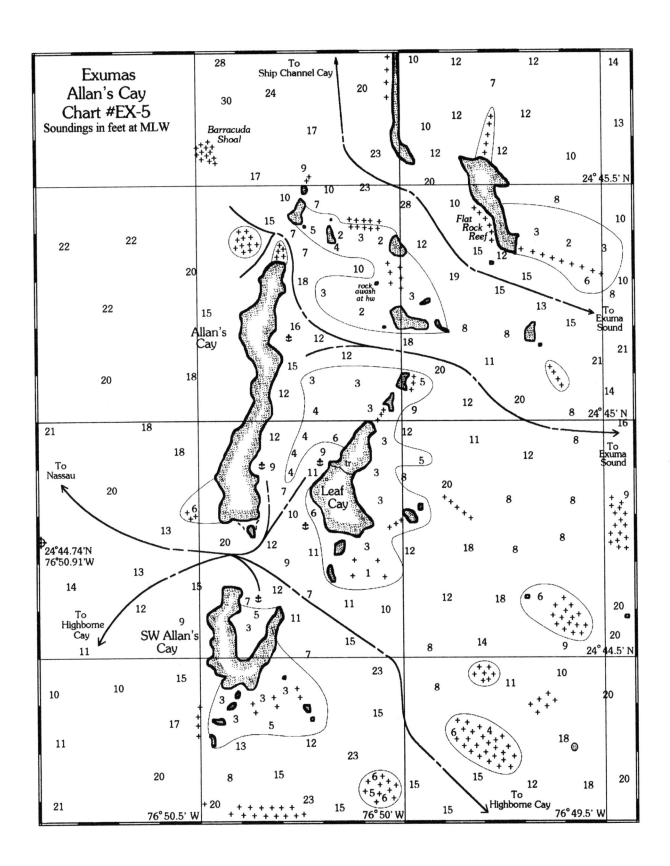

Exumas
Allan's Cay
Chart #EX-5
Soundings in feet at MLW

HIGHBORNE CAY

Highborne Cay (Chart # EX-6), 2½ miles long and encompassing almost 550 acres, is the northernmost inhabited island in the Exuma chain. Once called Little Norman's Cay and often shown on older charts as Hyburn or Highborn, this cay is shaped somewhat like the letter "H" and can be viewed as being in three sections. The eastern section is elevated and rocky, the middle section is a low lying sandy isthmus, and the western section consists mainly of black, rocky land about a mile long. Hills on the northern end of the cay rise to a height of 20'-102' while the southern end is lower and ends in a small hill about 35' high. The manager's house sits on a hill 102' above sea level about 1.7 miles from the marina. There are nine beaches surrounding the island. On the eastern shore you will find a mile long, curving beach, one of the most beautiful in The Bahamas. A map dating back to the 17th century shows a flowing channel of water across what is now the isthmus connecting the two larger, parallel portions of the cay. There is a spring near the southern end of the island, just ask Peter or Alison Albury, your genial hosts and managers of the cay, for directions. As you wander around the cay you will notice the beauty and cleanliness in which Peter and Alison take great pride. Please do nothing to mar this, do not remove any plants, and do not litter. The new owners of Highborne Cay ask that all visits ashore be confined to guests of the marina only.

Highborne Cay was purchased in the 1950's by a Philadelphia businessman who immediately began developing the island with a marina, houses, and paved roads. The cay was still owned by the same family until 1996. There are nine residences on the cay, five occupied by staff and four rental houses of two and three bedrooms each.

There are some ruins of the old Highborne Plantation dating back over 100 years towards the northern end of the island. The ruins of "South House" lie on a 40' hill and is 36' x 20' with walls 18" thick. It had 16 doors and windows and was surrounded by 10 terraces. It will take some searching to find these ruins as even the staff are unsure of their whereabouts. You may also see some ruins of pasture walls, stone walls built to keep in livestock. Various crops flourished during the plantation years, the principal being aloe, of which a large number are still in evidence. For a time aloe grew so profusely that the factory ran overtime to process the crop. Unfortunately, the high cost of processing and shipping to Florida failed to make the operation economically feasible. Watermelons once grew in such abundance here that the Nassau market could not absorb them.

After the abolition of the British slave trade in 1807, the Royal Navy would free any slaves seized on the high seas. One such cargo was seized in September of 1832 and 370 freed slaves were settled on Highborne Cay. A severe drought in 1833 killed many of the freed slaves and the survivors were taken to Nassau.

Highborne Cay Marina (242-355-1003) is the first marina you will find on your southbound Exuma cruise. It is an excellent, well kept marina with both gas and diesel. The fuel docks are open 8-12 and 2-5 every day with the exception of Wednesdays when Peter closes for the afternoon. Water is available and garbage may be disposed of for a small fee (free if you are a guest of the marina). There is a telephone and a small but well stocked grocery and liquor store on the cay. The store is open daily from 9-12 and 2-4 but is closed Wednesday afternoons and Sundays. Just ask Peter or Alison for a ride to the store. Highborne Cay Marina requests that visitors do not dispose of sewage in the harbor or barbecue aboard their vessels or on the dock. You are welcome to use Highborne Cay Marina's barbecue site ashore for this purpose. There is a catering service available ashore from Janet Miller. Call *Cool Runner* on VHF ch.16 and she will be happy to help you. Laundry can be taken care of by one of the cay's housekeepers, contact Alison for more information.

The new owners of Highborne Cay are expanding the marina to 40+ slips with the capacity to handle 200' vessels with drafts up to 10'. There will be 100 amp power available at the docks along with the current 30 amp and 50 amp service available. Plans tentatively include an upscale restaurant and bar. The area between the current moorings and the new construction has been dredged to 12'. The moorings may or may not stay, that is still up in the air for now. Construction is going on throughout 1997 so keep an eye out when entering the marina area. If you have any questions call Highborne Cay on VHF ch. 16.

To enter the marina area from Exuma Sound, a GPS waypoint at 24° 42.40' N, 76° 48.60' W places you ¼ mile east/southeast of Highborne Cay Cut. Head through the cut between Highborne Cay and the offlying rocks and round up towards the beach and marina keeping an eye out for the small reef that lies just off the small cay to the west of Highborne Cay. The reef is marked with an orange barrel, keep it to port when entering from Exuma Sound. Round the tip of the jetty and proceed to the marina docks.

If approaching across the banks from Nassau or Allan's Cay, the only obstruction is the rocky shoal known as Highborne Rocks which works out westward from Highborne for over 1½ miles. The shoal is easily seen when coming from Allan's and can be rounded by eye. When leaving Allan's Cay steer approximately southwest until you can clear the shoal area. Least water along this route is 8' at low tide.

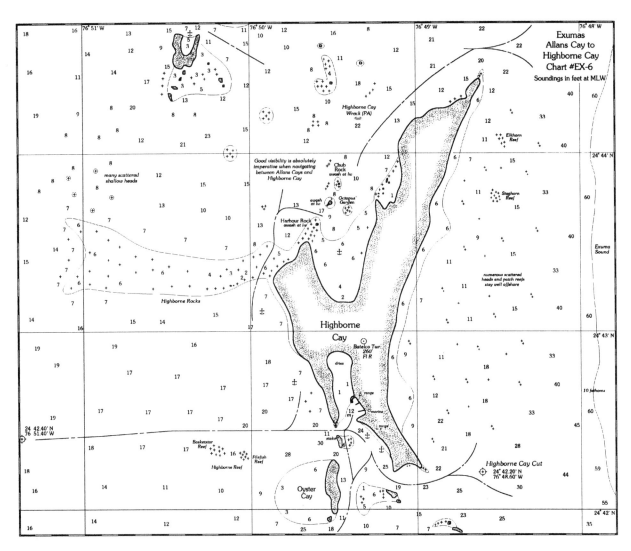

For those arriving from Nassau, a GPS waypoint at 24° 42.28' N, 76° 51.30' W will place you well to the southwest of Highborne Rocks. From this position take up an approximate heading of 96° magnetic until you approach the entrance into the marina and can pick up the range marks which lie due east. The area directly west of the entrance to the marina has plenty of deep water so strictly following these directions here is not absolutely necessary. Once past Highborne Rocks you can pilot by eye to the entrance to the marina or head eastward to anchor in the lee of Highborne Cay. The entrance to the marina area is just north of the small rock which has an orange pole on its northern end. Line up the orange range marks situated on Highborne Cay and head in on a bearing of 90°. Once inside, look to port and line up the orange range marks north of the marina and follow them in on an approximate heading of 15° until you can round the jetty into the marina area.

Vessels can anchor just south of the marina along the southeastern shore of Highborne Cay. Although this is an area with a lot of current and can get pretty rolly in strong southeasterlies, there are now four very secure moorings just off the marina. To inquire about a mooring call Peter or Alison on VHF ch. 16 (Highborne Cay). A good lee anchorage is along the western shore of Highborne Cay in 12'-15' of water off the long beach just south of Highborne Rocks. Vessels heading north from the marina can pass between Highborne Rocks and Highborne Cay to take advantage of the seldom used lee anchorage in the bight on the northern side of Highborne Cay. This anchorage is good in winds from east to south but is no place to be in a frontal passage. To clear the rocks proceed north along the shore and keep the eastern edge of the rocky bar and its accompanying highly visible sandbank close to port. Work your way between it and the shallow bar the works northward from Highborne Cay. A vessel with 6' draft can pass through here at high tide. Needless to say good visibility is essential on this passage. Once past Highborne

Rocks you must either detour around or pass between Harbour Rock and Chub Rock. There is a gorgeous reef called Octopus' Garden just inside the anchorage which will reward your efforts.

The Highborne Cay area has a lot to offer both snorkelers and SCUBA divers. The entire eastern shoreline is strewn with numerous shallow reefs and offers good snorkeling just off the beach. Highborne Cay Wall lies approximately 800 yards southeast of the northern tip of Highborne Cay. Start your dive when the northern tip of Highborne Cay bears 310° and the northern house on the hill bears 240°. Follow the sandy, coral covered slope to reach the wall at 60'. The wall ends straight down at 110' on a large lip followed by another slope.

Just off the eastern shore of Highborne Cay in 18'-20' of water lies Staghorn Reef. This is a large staghorn coral reef that is so concentrated one may have difficulty seeing the bottom. The staghorn coral is framed by enormous sculptured coral heads and magnificent brain coral formations with multitudes of colorful fish darting in and out. The reef lies approximately where the southern house on the hill bears 260° and the northern tip of Highborne Cay bears 360°. The reef lies about 500-600 yards offshore and the dark patch is easily recognizable. Just north of Staghorn Reef lies a huge stand of elkhorn coral appropriately named Elkhorn Reef.

Highborne Cay Reef is a group of coral heads and rocks in the shape of a wide channel about 300' wide lying in an east-west direction. It is actually two reefs that dive boat operators call Basketstar Reef and Filefish Reef. Between the heads and rocks are wide, sandy troughs and underwater dunes. Some of the heads reach a height of 6'. The area is rich in sea life but is subject to tides and current with the accompanying siltation. Slack tide is the best time to dive this reef. Highborne Cay Reef lies approximately 500 yards west of Highborne Cay Marina and the best spot is when the southern edge of Highborne Cay bears 110°.

Just off the northwest shore of Highborne Cay, in the lee of the island, lie the remains of a 16th century Bahamian shipwreck first discovered in 1965. Wrought iron ordinance, lead ammunition, small guns and breeches, rigging, chain, anchors, a wooden knife handle inlaid with gold, pottery, and numerous pieces of hardware and ballast stones were removed from the wreck and dated to the first half of the 16th century. The wreck lies in approximately 20' of water and is in an area of swift tidal currents sometimes reaching 3 knots. Although the identity of the vessel is unknown it was not a lightly built vessel as the salvage expedition soon learned. It was estimated to be over 19 meters long and 6 meters wide. The conclusion arrived at by the salvage team indicated that the ship probably anchored in the area to replenish its water supply from Highborne Cay but just what caused it to sink is unknown. Before leaving the site, members of the excavating expedition secured a Plexiglas sign to a pile of ballast stones with the following inscription: "Leave this site alone. There is no treasure here! These stones are the last remains of an historical shipwreck, part of the cultural heritage of the people of The Bahamas. It is protected by the Bahamian Govt. and removal of any objects is illegal. Take only pictures, leave only bubbles. Institute of Nautical Archaeology, R/V Coral Reef II, Sept. 1986." Please do not remove anything from this site.

HIGHBORNE CAY TO NORMAN'S CAY

The cays between Highborne and Norman's Cay (Chart # EX-7) offer excellent diving opportunities, easy access to the banks and the Sound, good fishing, a good lee anchorage, and one all-weather anchorage.

Long Cay, often called Spirit Cay or Sperrit Cay, is the largest cay in the group and lies on the edge of Exuma Sound. There is a lee anchorage just off its northwestern shore where boats of 5' draft can find suitable depth for anchoring. To enter the anchorage from Exuma Sound, round the northern tip of Long Cay and head close inshore until you find the spot you wish to drop the hook. The GPS waypoint for Highborne Cay Cut (24° 42.40' N, 76° 48.60' W) is a good position to use for your entrance.

South of Long Cay lies Long Cay Cut. A GPS waypoint at 24° 39.30' N, 76° 48.25' W will place you approximately ¼ mile east of the cut. Enter the cut by favoring the northern side of the channel, avoiding the rocky bar that works northward from the small rocks lying north of Saddleback Cay. Once inside, you can head southward past Norman's Cay by rounding the shallow bars to port and approaching Norman's Cay from the banks. If you wish to head north to the anchorage off Long Cay, pass between Lobster Cay and the small rock which lies just west of Long Cay.

To enter the Long Cay area from Highborne Cay you may head out into Exuma Sound and enter back onto the banks just north of Long Cay, between Long Cay and the shallow, rocky bar to its west. You may also follow the route that lies to the east of Oyster Cay heading southward towards Norman's Cay, staying close along the eastern shore of the cays south of Oyster Cay. Once past Lobster Cay (watch out for the 4' deep area at low water), turn to the northeast and pass between Lobster Cay and the small rock that lies to the west of Long Cay.

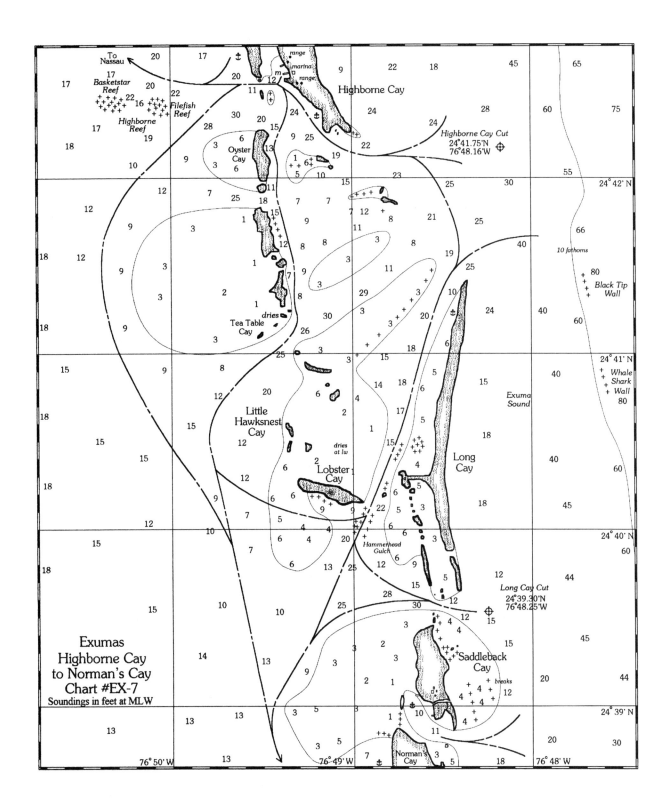

Exumas
Highborne Cay
to Norman's Cay
Chart #EX-7
Soundings in feet at MLW

Vessels leaving Highborne Cay for points south may pass to the west of Oyster Cay but must avoid the huge sandbank that lies to the west of Tea Table Cay.

There are numerous reefs between Long Cay and Tea Table Cay as well as a good snorkeling reef in 6'-10' of water in the bight about halfway down the western shore of Long Cay. South of the cut between Long Cay and Lobster Cay lies a beautiful reef known as Hammerhead Gulch in about 20' of water. Just to the northeast of Tea Table Cay is a beautiful drift snorkel when the tide is rising. The wall drop-offs that lie to the east of Long Cay offer stupendous dives for those with SCUBA gear. Directly east of the northern tip of Long Cay, in 60'-80' of water, lies Black Tip Wall. A little south of this dive site, also in about 80' of water, lies Whale Shark Wall. The entire drop-off, where the shallow banks plunge to the depths of Exuma Sound between Sail Rocks and Norman's Cay and usually starting in about 80' of water, are excellent places to troll a line for large fish. Do not fish south of Wax Cay Cut unless you are at least 4 miles offshore as you will be in the protected sanctuary of The Exuma Cays Land And Sea Park.

Saddleback Cay, originally called Little Norman's Cay, lies between Long Cay and Norman's Cay and has two conspicuous hills rising from 40'-60'. The small but secure anchorage, a good spot in a frontal passage, is entered from Exuma Sound between Saddleback Cay and the small rock just north of Norman's Cay (watch out for the shallow reefs just to the east of Saddleback Cay). The bottom is rocky and scoured due to the fierce current that flows through here. The best holding is in the sand on the eastern side of the anchorage. Saddleback Cay is private and visits ashore are by invitation only.

Vessels heading south for Norman's Cay from Highborne Cay should pass to the west of Lobster Cay and steer around the large shallow sandbank which works out from the north end of Norman's Cay. There are actually two sandbanks and a vessel with a 5' draft can pass between the two at low water (see Chart #'s EX-7 & 8). At this point you can pass between Norman's Spit and Norman's Cay in 5'-9' of water at low tide.

Photo by Stephen J. Pavlidis

Norman's Cay Anchorage.

NORMAN'S CAY

Norman's Cay (Chart # EX-8), one of the longest islands in the Exumas, is approximately 6 miles long and averages 1000' feet wide. Almost all of the cay is elevated with steep hills on the western shore that rise to 40'. There is a large unused and unlit antenna tower near the old clubhouse at the southern end of the island that is often mistaken for a Batelco Tower. A beach stretches for nearly the entire length of the western shore. Residents request that visitors confine themselves to the southern end of the island.

If there is one cay that a visitor has heard about long before visiting the Exumas, it is probably Norman's Cay. Norman's gained its notoriety during the late 1970's and early 1980's when it was used as a base for a very profitable cocaine smuggling operation (see *History-Drug Smuggling*) The only reminders are the bullet holes in some of the buildings on the south end of the cay and the airplane that rests in the anchorage. The residents today treasure the solitude and peace that once again reigns over Norman's Cay   The anchorages around Norman's Cay offer excellent protection from all directions. The most popular anchorage is at the south end of the island between the dock and the airplane. Entering from Exuma Sound, a GPS waypoint at 24° 35.76' N, 76° 47.48' W will place you approximately ¼ mile east of Norman's Cay Cut. Enter the cut on a heading of approximately 265° passing between the two large offlying cays to starboard and the two small rocks to port (see Chart # EX-8). Once past the plane, anchor with two anchors and allow for current. This anchorage will get a little rolly in strong easterly winds.

If entering this anchorage from the banks, a GPS waypoint at 24° 35.64' N, 76° 51.96' W will place you approximately ¼ mile west of the stake which marks the southwestern tip of Norman's Spit, the large sandbank which lies just to the southwest of Norman's Cay. When Wax Cay Cut bears 100°, steer for the cut until you can follow the deep water into the anchorage passing between Channel Cay and the shallow rocky bar to the south of Norman's Cay. There is a very visible sandbank that works northeastward from Channel Cay that must be left to starboard.

Photo by Stephen J. Pavlidis

Plane at Norman's Cay.

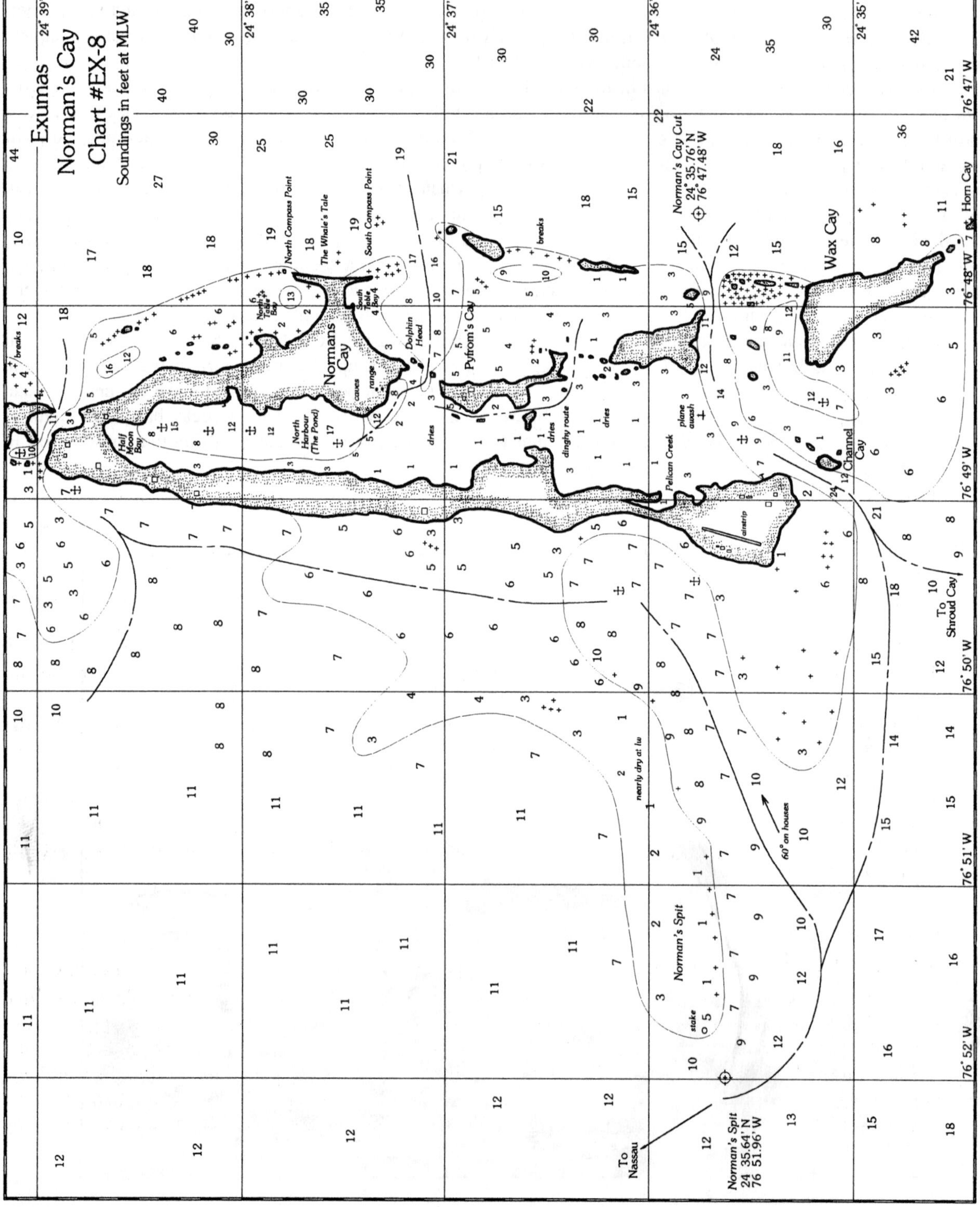

Exumas
Norman's Cay
Chart #EX-8
Soundings in feet at MLW

24° 39' N
24° 38' N
24° 37' N
24° 36' N
24° 35' N

76° 47' W
76° 48' W
76° 49' W
76° 50' W
76° 51' W
76° 52' W

Normans Cay

North Compass Point
The Whale's Tale
South Compass Point
North Turtle Bay
North Table
South Table
Half Moon Bay
North Harbour (The Pond)
range
canes
Dolphin Head
Pyfrom's Cay
dries
dinghy route
dries
Pelican Creek
plane
awash
airstrip
Channel Cay
Wax Cay
Horn Cay

Norman's Cay Cut
24° 35.76' N
76° 47.48' W

nearly dry at lw
60° on houses
Norman's Spit
stake
To Shroud Cay

To Nassau

Norman's Spit
24° 35.64' N
76° 51.96' W

breaks
breaks
breaks

The entire western shore of Norman's Cay offers a pleasant anchorage with good protection in prevailing winds. From Norman's Spit stake, pass south of the spit, it is easily seen in good light, until you can take up a 60° heading on the two houses on the southwestern shore of Norman's Cay. Once clear of Norman's Spit this 60° heading is not that critical, you will have deep water although you will have to steer around a few coral heads and small patch reefs which are easy to pick out in good light. Anchor anywhere you wish along the western shore of Norman's Cay. The area off the western shore of Norman's Cay has several small coral heads scattered about so keep a good lookout.

Approaching from the north, from the banks or Highborne Cay, you can steer for the northern tip of Norman's avoiding the large sandbank that works out from the northern end of the cay northward toward Lobster Cay. Parallel the shoreline of Norman's Cay as you head south staying at least 100 yards off. There is a shallow area by the large house about 1½ miles south of the northern tip that you must avoid. South of here you can easily pass between Norman's Spit and Norman's Cay and anchor wherever you wish.

The anchorage with the best protection, and one which should be considered if a hurricane threatens. is inside North Harbour, usually just called "the pond." The entrance is tricky but will handle a 6' draft at high tide. Most people do not attempt to enter the pond because they have heard it is extremely difficult and that many people run aground in the attempt. Most people run aground when they attempt to pass between the outlying cays and Pyfrom's Cay, an often recommended route. The waters here are very shallow and should not be attempted by any vessels except those with shoal draft, 3' or less. It is safer and easier to head outside into Exuma Sound and pass well to the east of these cays and enter the pond from Exuma Sound.

Once clear of the outlying cays and as you approach the small rocks leading to the entrance into the pond, you will see what appear to be two cannons, one on the southern rock and one on the northern rock pointing at each other. The cut between these two is the entrance to the channel which leads to the pond. There is a small deep water cut to the north of the northernmost cannon but do not use it, it shoals quickly just inside.

Once inside the cut look to starboard along the shore of Norman's Cay and you will see a small, privately maintained range, a large white pole with a shorter one in front. Line up the range and follow the dark water (4' at low water) until you can parallel the shoreline in 8' of water. Beware, there is some very shallow dark water that you must leave to port so don't let it confuse you, use your eyes and take it slow and easy through here. As you parallel the shore give the western tip a large berth to avoid the shallows that work out westward from it. Turn north into the pond and anchor wherever you wish. The pond is an excellent spot to ride out those fierce frontal passages in winter. It is said that hammerhead sharks frequent the pond.

Cave enthusiasts will enjoy the three caves at the entrance to the pond on the western tip as you enter the pond. Off the northwestern tip of Norman's Cay are several small caves, one with several rooms. About 50' south of this cave is another cave with a long, low passage leading north that may connect the two caves.

SCUBA divers will want to visit Dead Head Wall, a splendid wall dive in about 70' of water that is named after the Grateful Dead fan whose VW van lies on the reef (don't ask how it got there). To find it, line up the plane with the stand of trees which lie north of the small cabanas on the beach above the dock and proceed out to 70' of water.

There are some beautiful beaches on the Sound side north of Pyfrom's Cay. The interior of Norman's, although quite shallow, offers excellent dinghy exploration with mangrove creeks, ledges, bonefishing and conch. There is good diving just off the eastern shore on the many scattered heads and small rocks which line the shore especially north of the Whale's Tail.

WAX CAY

Wax Cay (Chart # EX-8) is easily distinguished by its high hills, the highest being 93'. Southwest of this hill is an old well that is now filled in while just to its west are some cave holes. This cay is best explored by dinghy from Norman's Cay. There are the remains of two houses on the cay that are very difficult to see from a dinghy. They were built by Carlos Lehder's people for Mr. Lehder to escape to with his closest companions when they needed a little break from the hectic pace of Norman's Cay. In the interior of the cay is a large mangrove swash that once was open to the sea but has since filled in. There are some excellent beaches along the cays western and northern shore and a beautiful small reef just off the southeastern shore. There is a large reef system between and to the west of the small rocks lying north of Wax Cay to Norman's Cay Cut.

THE
EXUMA CAYS
LAND AND SEA
PARK

THE EXUMA CAYS
LAND AND SEA PARK

The Exuma Cays Land And Sea Park is, without a doubt, the most pristine and possibly the most beautiful area in the Exumas. The Park, a designated replenishment area for all The Bahamas, is made up of 15 major cays and numerous smaller ones encompassing 176 square miles. The Park starts at Wax Cay Cut in the north and stretches southward some 22 miles to Conch Cut with an average width of 8 miles. There are no commercial developments within the Park and the only inhabited islands are privately owned.

With the continuing development of The Bahamas, Bahamians, as well as visitors, must come to grips with sensible conservation policies. It is getting increasingly difficult to find large conch in shallow water. Fishermen are having to search for them in deeper and deeper water. Lobsters also do not seem as plentiful as they did a generation ago. Dynamite and bleach have taken their toll on Bahamian reefs. A long look at some of the dead, bleached out reefs such as those around Manjack and Powell in the Abacos, gives one an appreciation of what is being accomplished in The Exuma Cays Land And Sea Park. This Park is for the young, your children, and your children's children. If marine life does not have a safe place to breed, simple arithmetic will reveal that a zero count is inevitable at today's catch rate. Repopulation of The Bahamas by conch, lobster, and fish is a major concern. Where will today's children and their children fish? Will they sit on the dock and reminisce about the old days when there were still a few fish around? Ask any old timer about the fishing around the Exumas, Abacos, or Long Island fifty years ago. They will expound upon the richness of sea life at that time, how the fish practically jumped into your boat, how multitudes of conch and lobster could be found in knee deep water. Compare that with what they think of the fishing today. Their eyes will sadden and they will likely shake their head and say "No mon, it ain't the same."

The greatest diversity of marine life in the Exumas occurs at the edge of the Banks where they drop off to the deep basins of Exuma Sound. This is the physical setting of The Exuma Cays Land And Sea Park. Since the taking of any plant, animal, or marine life, including corals and shells, is prohibited, researchers and visitors can view populations of land and marine life in their natural conditions, unspoiled by fishing and hunting. Curious grouper and lobster may approach to investigate you as you swim by instead of instinctively retreating into their holes. Here you will see reefs and coral formations that are uniquely Bahamian and have few rivals for sheer breathtaking splendor. Ashore you will find flora and fauna that are no longer found elsewhere in The Bahamas.

The Park has certain rules and regulations that all visitors must abide by. We strongly urge you to familiarize yourself with the regulations and the boundaries of the Park to make your visit more enjoyable and the Warden's job a little easier. One of the biggest dangers to the longevity of the Park is poaching. The depletion of fisheries outside the Park and the richness of the waters within the Park boundaries make this area prone to poaching. Whether it is a Bahamian trying to make a little money and put dinner on his table, or a visiting Yachtsman trolling within the boundaries, it is poaching and it is illegal. There are severe penalties for poaching and they are well deserved. Poachers are not only stealing from themselves, but from their children's future. The Park is 22 miles long and most vessels make that in half a day. Is that really too long to ask one to take in their fishing lines? There are thousands of square miles in Bahamian waters in which to fish. Please save these 176 for our future generations.

A HISTORY OF THE EXUMA CAYS LAND AND SEA PARK

The Bahamas National Trust shall be established for the purposes of promoting the permanent preservation for the benefit and enjoyment of The Bahamas of lands and tenements (including buildings) and submarine areas of beauty or natural or historic interest and as regards lands and submarine areas for the preservation (so far as practicable) of the natural aspect, features, and animal, plant and marine life.

Statute Law of The Bahamas
Chapter 355, Section 4
Paragraph 1

In 1953, a farsighted Superintendent of The Everglades National Park in Florida, Daniel B. Beard, began urging explorers, naturalists, and researchers of the importance of setting aside a section of the Exuma Cays as a buffer area, eventually to become a Land and Sea Park. Upon favorable response and cooperation he went ahead with his idea contacting various other conservationists and eventually the Governor and the Colonial Secretary of The Bahamas. His idea was received with enthusiasm and even received support from the Nassau newspapers.

In 1955, Colonel Ilia Tolstoy presented a proposal to the government that a stretch of the Exumas should be placed under protection. On February 13, 1956, Beard received a letter from the Governor of the Bahamas confirming that the Crown had set aside approximately 22 miles of the Exuma Cays from Shroud Cay to Little Bell Island inclusive. They were set aside for one year providing during that time, some organization would undertake to explore the possibility further and give concrete recommendations to the Bahamian Government. This organization would also be responsible for the financial support of the program.

Around this time Beard met Carleton Ray, then the Assistant Director of the New York Aquarium, who had spent a great deal of time in the Bahamas doing underwater photography and scientific research. Ray headed up a survey of the Exuma Cays to explore the feasibility of establishing a park. A one year extension was granted until June 30, 1958. Ray began his survey in late January, 1958.

Specific recommendations were made as a result of Carleton Ray's survey. Among those was the establishment of The Bahamas National Trust to oversee the proposed Parks in the Bahamas. Other recommendations included boundaries, regulations, the need for a Ranger (Warden) with a Ranger Station on Cistern Cay, and a Park Headquarters, originally called for at Norman's Cay instead of the current location at Warderick Wells.

Finally, on July 13, 1959, by a special act of Parliament, The Bahamas National Trust was incorporated and powers were conferred upon the Trust to allow it to set aside and care for places of historic interest and natural beauty. Thus was born the Exuma Cays Land And Sea Park.

BOUNDARIES

The Exuma Cays Land And Sea Park, beginning at Wax Cay Cut in the north, stretches southward some 22 miles to Conch Cut. It is approximately eight miles wide and encompasses 176 square miles. The boundaries, due to the lay of the cays, are anywhere between 3-5 miles off the land in either direction.

The boundaries of the Park are as follows: from the SW corner at 24° 14.417' N, 76° 36.033' W, along a line bearing 323° True for 22.14 nm to the NW corner at 24° 30.617' N, 76° 52.617' W. Then along a line bearing 058° True for 7.87 nm to the NE corner at 24° 35.500' N, 76° 45.833' W. Then along a line bearing 143° True for 22.92 nm to the SE corner at 24° 18.617' N, 76° 28.783' W. Then along a line bearing 244° True for 7.84 nm to the SW corner.

NATIONAL PARK REGULATIONS

BAHAMAS NATIONAL TRUST

1. The regulations for National Parks in The Bahamas are made under The Bahamas National Trust Act and operate in conjunction with all other laws of the Bahamas.
2. The hunting, trapping, netting, capture, or removal of any fish, turtle, crawfish, conch, whelk, or any marine and/or fisheries resource is prohibited.
3. The destruction, injury or removal of any living or dead plant life, beach sand, coral, sea fans or gorgonian from any National Park is prohibited.
4. The hunting, molestation, injury or destruction of any land animal or bird life and the taking or destruction of the eggs of any animal or bird life is prohibited in every National Park.
5. No person shall himself remain or permit any child or dog or any other domesticated animal in their care to remain in the vicinity of any active bird nest or other wildlife to a point which causes a disturbance to such nesting bird or other wildlife.
6. No person shall introduce or release any species or specimen of animal or plant into the land area of any National Park. Pet dogs are permitted only if they are accompanied and controlled by a responsible person at all times.
7. No person shall burn, place, dump, leave, bury or discharge any liquid or solid waste, sewerage, rubbish, garbage, oil, noxious or poisonous substance, nor leave any ash coals or embers whatsoever within any National Park, whether on land or at sea.
8. No person shall injure, deface, or remove any or part of any building, structure, sign, ruin or other artifact whether ancient or modern, nor any beach or seabed, sand, shell, fossil, rock, soil or other mineral whatsoever.
9. The posting of any sign, placard, advertisement or notice within any Park is prohibited as is the erection of any building, shed, or other structure.
10. No person shall display, use, fire or discharge any explosives, firearm, harpoon, or spear within any National Park save for the purpose of distress signaling. This does not apply to Peace Officers and/or Park Wardens.

11. No person shall, save in case of danger or emergency, cast or drop any anchor in any place where damage to a coral reef is likely to result nor place nor cause to be placed within any National Park any permanent moorings without prior written approval from The Bahamas National Trust and in strict conformity therewith.

12. No person shall operate or permit the operation of any vessel within any anchorage of the Exuma Cays Land and Sea Park at a speed above such vessel's idle speed (being the minimum speed at which such vessel's engine provides steerage).

13. No person shall operate, without lawful authority, any jet skis or similar personal water craft nor any air boat within any creek or anchorage in the Exuma Cays Land and Sea Park.

14. No vessel may remain for more than two weeks in any one anchorage on any visit to or voyage through the Exuma Cays Land and Sea Park.

15. No person on any private land within the boundary of any National Park shall construct any dock, structure, breakwater, sewerage outlet or overflow, etc. below the high water mark of the sea or draining or extending into the sea or dredge the sea bed adjacent thereto, without the written authority of The Bahamas National Trust and in strict compliance therewith.

16. It shall be an offense for any person to resist or obstruct, disturb or annoy any person lawfully and reasonably using any National Park or any Park Warden in the exercise of his duties.

17. These by-laws do not affect the existing rights of any person acting legally by virtue of any estate, right or interest in, over or affecting the privately owned lands within any National Park.

18. Permission may be granted in individual instances for the capture or removal of a designated number of land or sea animals or plants required for valid scientific research. In each instance the scientific institution concerned must obtain a permit from The Bahamas National Trust prior to capture or removal of the specimens.

19. Any person charged with an offense against any of these by-laws shall be liable on summary conviction to a penalty not exceeding $500 and to the confiscation of any boat, vessel or aircraft and of all the equipment, stores, provisions or other effects used for the purpose of committing the offense.

APPROACHES TO THE EXUMA CAYS LAND AND SEA PARK

Most vessels approaching from Nassau make stops at Allan's, Highbourne, and Norman's Cays before entering the northern boundaries of the Park (Chart # EX-9), however, it is possible to reach Warderick Wells in 10-12 hours with good weather if you can make 6 knots. If bound for Warderick Wells from Porgee Rocks, a course of 149° for 46.0 nm will bring you to a GPS waypoint • nm west of Elbow Cay at 24• 31.15'N, 76• 49.16'W (Chart # EX-9). Once clear of Elbow Cay you can take up a course of 137° to parallel the lie of the islands. Stand off three miles to avoid the shoals on the western side of the cays. If you choose to head south on the Sound side, stay at least ½ mile offshore. In the vicinity of Shroud Cay and Hawksbill Cay, stay at least 1 mile offshore to avoid the numerous rocks, heads, and small patch reefs to the east of these cays.

From Eleuthera it is a straight shot across Exuma Sound. The only hazard to navigation is the ODAS Buoy located at 24° 38.20' N, 76° 31.30' W in the northern end of Exuma Sound. This position is approximate as Exuma Sound is over 6000' deep in this area giving the ODAS Buoy a swing radius of over 1 mile. When the U.S. Navy conducts underwater tests in this area you will hear the research vessel *MONAB* make a call on VHF ch.16 prior to and during testing when they are moored to the buoy. When this underwater testing is in progress you must stay at least five miles away from the ODAS Buoy and the *MONAB*.

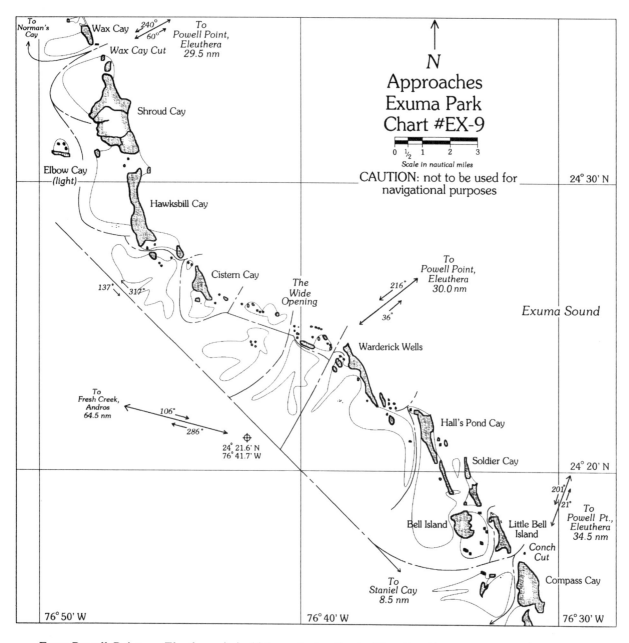

From Powell Point on Eleuthera, it is 29.5 nautical miles to Wax Cay Cut on a course of 240° magnetic. Steering a course of 216° for 30 nautical miles will bring you to the Wide Opening Channel while keeping a course of 201° for 34.2 nautical miles will bring you to Conch Cut.

When approaching Exuma Park from the south, you may follow the Banks route northward or you can head outside into Exuma Sound and deeper water. If approaching on the Banks from Staniel Cay or Sampson Cay, hold a course of 325° until you clear the shoals (which jut out onto the banks for two miles) west of The Rocky Dundas. The GPS latitude and longitude for the western tip of the shoal lying west of the Rocky Dundas is 24° 15.80' N, 76° 35.25' W. There is 7' at its westernmost end at mean low water and it is besprinkled with small heads and rocks. When Conch Cut bears due east you may continue on your course or steer 90° (favor the south side of the channel) and proceed to Conch Cut and the anchorages off Bell and Little Bell Island.

If approaching from the Sound side stay at least ½ mile offshore when off the cays in the southern Park. As you proceed north of The Wide Opening, stay at least 1 mile off to avoid the shallow water and reefs to the east of Shroud and Hawksbill. For sailors, a northbound voyage in Exuma Sound is usually a reach or broad reach with the prevailing winds. Beware of a rage at the cuts, even in moderate winds.

If you are heading towards the Park from Bennett's Harbour, Cat Island, a course of 256° magnetic will bring you to the entrance of Conch Cut, a distance of approximately 50 nautical miles across Exuma Sound. From Fresh Creek, Andros Town, Andros, take up a course of 106° magnetic for a point just a few miles southwest of Warderick Wells at 24° 21.60' N, 76° 41.70' W. Once you enter the banks from The Tongue Of The Ocean, you will have depths of 12' or better all the way to Warderick Wells. The distance along this route is approximately 64.5 nautical miles.

THE NORTHERN PARK

Wax Cay Cut to Warderick Wells

Approximately 40 miles southeast of Nassau, just south of Norman's Cay, lies the northern boundary to The Exuma Cays Land And Sea Park, at Wax Cay Cut. As you cruise the Park bear in mind that some of the cays in the Park are private property, The Exuma Cays Land And Sea Park asks you to please respect the rights and privacy of their owners.

LITTLE WAX CAY AND WAX CAY CUT

Little Wax Cay (Chart # EX-10), just south of Wax Cay Cut, is the northernmost large cay in the Park and is approximately ¼ mile long by ¼ mile wide. Originally called North Pigeon Cay, is has a bluff rising to 20' on its northwest shore and white cliffs on its eastern shore which rise to 50'. There is a large shallow sandbar on the west side and three breaking reefs to the east. It is best to give this eastern shore a wide berth unless exploring by dinghy. There are two small beaches on Little Wax Cay, one on the western shore and one in a bight on the eastern shore.

A century ago there were several sisal fields in the interior of Little Wax Cay. These were worked by squatters who lived on Hawksbill Cay, then called Shroud Cay. These squatters also did a good bit of buttonwood business, cutting the trees down and hauling them along a roadway to the western shore for shipment.

Little Wax Cay is now known as the home for a transplanted colony of hutia. Eleven hutia were introduced onto Little Wax Cay in 1973 and thirteen at Warderick Wells in 1981. In 1983, the hutia population on Little Wax Cay was estimated at over 750. When you look at Little Wax Cay you will see the brown, dead, and dying vegetation that is the result of hungry hutia. Exuma Park and The Bahamas National Trust are studying the problem and trying to develop an answer that will save the hutia and the cay. If you come ashore on Little Wax Cay please do not bring your dog so as to avoid any confrontations with the hutia.

Bush Hill, the first cay to the north of Little Wax Cay, is 1000' long, 200' wide, and rises to a height of 60'. Just north of Bush Hill lies Hawksnest Cay, 350' long and 150' wide. North of Hawksnest Cay lies Snuff Cay which is 200' long and 100' wide and rises to a height of 4'. Northward, across the cut, the southernmost cay off Wax Cay is called Horn Cay which rises to 18' on its west end. The northern boundary of Exuma Park runs between the south point of Wax Cay and the unnamed rock that lies between Wax Cay and Horn Cay.

Wax Cay Cut (Chart # EX-10) is the first deep water pass into Exuma Sound as you approach the Park from the north (and the only deep water pass until south of Hawksbill Cay). If approaching from Exuma Sound, a GPS position of 24° 34.76' N, 76° 47.01' W, will place you ½ mile to the NE of Wax Cay Cut. If you don't have a GPS and are approaching from the north or from Eleuthera, simply stay ½ mile or more offshore until the cut opens up to your SW. If approaching from the south, stay 1 mile off Hawksbill Cay and Shroud Cay. Wax Cay, just to your WNW has two conspicuous hills, one rising to 93'. Enter the cut between Horn Cay and Snuff Cay on a NE/SW line, favoring Snuff Cay to avoid the shallow, rocky bar that works out from the southern end of Horn Cay. Once inside you will find yourself in water anywhere from 25' to 45' deep. The channel bends slightly to the south and west, following the sand bank that lies to the west of Little Wax Cay. Once clear of Fire Coral Reef (breaks at low water), which lies well to the west of Bush Hill and Little Wax Cay, you can steer a course of 240°-260° which will take you well out onto the banks where you can round up past the sandy bar to starboard to enter Norman's Cay anchorage, or head south to Elbow Cay. There is a large, old-style ship's anchor embedded in Fire Coral Reef (which is aptly named). Divers should use caution on this reef, gloves are a must.

There are two marked anchorages in the deep water just at the cuts south and north of Little Wax Cay. These anchorages are not recommended as there are often fierce tidal currents of up to 3 or more knots in these areas. They are only shown here because some boaters like to anchor here in settled weather. It should go without saying that two anchors in these cuts are a must.

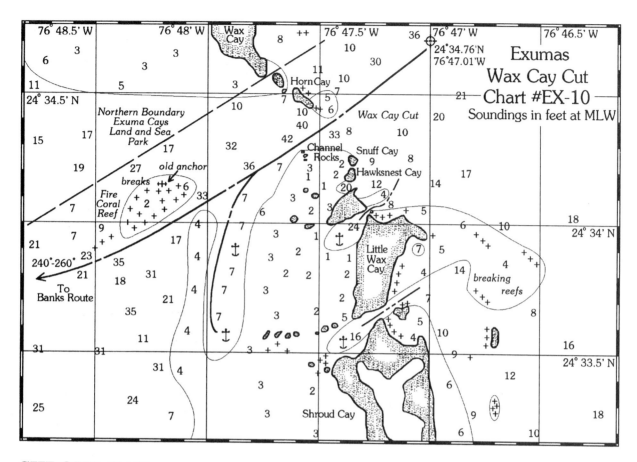

SHROUD CAY

Shroud Cay (Chart # EX-11) is actually a group of cays and rocks between which lies an extensive marl and mangrove salina. Shroud was the original name for the long narrow cay to the south which is now called Hawksbill Cay. Some of the older residents of the area maintain that the current charts are wrong and Hawksbill is Shroud and that is that. Shroud Cay's name came from its resemblance to the long narrow sheet, or shroud, used to wrap a body. In years past the various cays that make up the Shroud Cay Archipelago have been known as North Pigeon Cay, and Pigeon Cay. Some old charts show that Shroud Cay was once known as Hungry Hall, but according to some local fishermen, only the area between what is now Shroud Cay and Hawksbill Cay was called Hungry Hall by spongers during the heyday of the sponging era. The large eastern cay was originally called Big Pigeon Cay.

The entire eastern shore of Shroud Cay should only be explored by dinghy as it is shallow and laced with heads, rocks, and reefs. It is best to stay at least 1 mile offshore in this area if heading north or south in Exuma Sound. The best anchorages (Chart # EX-11) are on the west side, deep and well-protected from the prevailing winds and seas. Fresh Well Bay, also called Shroud Cay Anchorage, is just south of the three prominent rocks off the westernmost shoulder of Shroud Cay. From the Banks, head straight in for the beach (90°) and anchor in 8' within 75 yards of it. This is not a good anchorage when the winds go from south to west to north and you should think about heading north to Norman's Cay if a front is approaching. Just east of the rocks to the north of Fresh Well Bay, at the mouth of the creek, you will find a marked trail leading to a fresh water well. This natural well, one of the best in the Bahamas, has provided good water to visitors for more than a century and was a popular spot for sponging boats which worked the area in the early 1900's. The Bahamian Government placed a cement curb around the well in 1927.

The first Warden of Exuma Park, Beryl Nelson, cut steps into the stone path leading to the well from the banks side (by the small beach, you will see a sign) and built a handrail for it. The handrail (no longer there) was constructed from a salvaged spar off a Haitian vessel which wrecked near Wax Cay in 1980. From this anchorage, a vessel drawing 6' can work its way to the north around the offlying rocks and between the heads and sunken boat to anchor in 7' over a sand bottom.

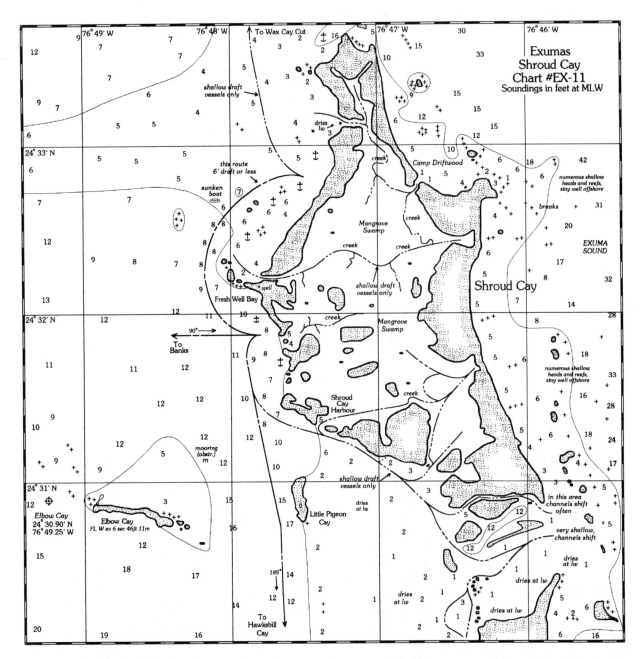

The entrance to Shroud Cay Harbour lies just to the south of Fresh Well Bay and about ½ mile northeast of Pigeon Cay. There is deep water inside once you clear the bar at the entrance (4½' at low water) but there is only room for one boat here. A small vessel with little draft can venture further in to tie off to the mangroves in case of severe weather. In his book *Out Island Doctor*, Dr. Evans W. Cottman recounts how he did this to ride out a hurricane. Dr. Cottman sailed his Bahamian ketch throughout these islands ministering to the isolated out-islanders. There is a radar reflector mounted on a pole marking the entrance to this harbor.

The chief delight of Shroud Cay is its variety of creeks which can only be explored by dinghy. The central tidal swamp forest of mangroves abounds in sea life. If you sneak up on the tangled root systems you may spot an assortment of grunts, groupers, schoolmasters, and even the occasional crawfish or shark. As you follow the winding, sandy-bottomed creeks, you may have to go from side to side to stay in the deep water, in some places 6', in others 6". It is best to explore them on a rising tide, about two hours before slack tide. The creeks, being so shallow and heated by the sun, will often be as warm as bath water. The currents can be swift and caution is a must for divers. Bear in mind that these creeks are breeding grounds and nurseries for many varieties of fish as well as conch and lobster. Try not to disturb these areas by churning up clouds of mud and keep the noise down if possible.

If you follow the northernmost creek as it winds its way into the interior of Shroud, you will come out on the Sound side by a wonderful small beach. There is a mailbox here where you can leave a message for the Warden or where the Warden may leave a newsletter for the passing cruiser. Beach your dinghy and walk around to the Sound side and you will see a path going up the hill, beyond which is a long curving beach. The path will lead you up to Camp Driftwood. Camp Driftwood is a very special place. A description of Camp Driftwood would not do it justice, you must see Camp Driftwood. In the 1960's, when there were not very many boats cruising the Exumas, a man named Ernest Scholtes began building Camp Driftwood. Ernest was a bit of a hermit, living on his sailboat just inside the creek on the Sound side. He cut steps into the 50' hill and carried sand in sail bags to build the trail. Along the way he would pick up a plank or a piece of driftwood and soon have a picnic table or bench. Coming across Camp Driftwood you might think that this was Robinson Crusoe's island. Scholtes and others have left behind treasures that were found on the beaches of the area. Shells, seabeans, floats, all manner of flotsam and jetsam decorate Camp Driftwood. At one time there was a jar with paper and pencils in it for people to leave notes behind. When Ernest Scholtes took ill one year, someone took the jar of notes and sent it to him as a get-well-quick wish. From the lookout at Camp Driftwood, or from the beach below, you can witness the aerial acrobatics of the tropicbirds when they nest in the area in March and April. It was off this beach that small loggerhead turtles were released in 1983. When you visit Camp Driftwood you must go beach combing first, this is so you can acquire the proper tolls for the passage and entrance to Camp Driftwood. Take your donations to the Guardians atop the hill and if accepted you will have free rein to roam Camp Driftwood.

When Carlos Lehder and his associates operated their thriving cocaine business from Norman's Cay, drug agents used the ridge at Camp Driftwood to spy on his operations. Agents set up a very sophisticated camera on the ridge and aimed it at the runway on Norman's. From this vantage point they were able to take photos of all the planes as they landed and took off, they were even able to capture the numbers off the smugglers fuselages. By the time they closed down Lehder's operation the agents had a fairly complete record of the comings and goings of his fleet of smugglers.

Just to the north of Shroud Cay Anchorage, by the trail to the well, is the entrance to another tidal creek. This creek will bring you to a dead end at a beautiful beach with a short walk over the hill to the beaches on the eastern shore of Shroud Cay. This creek once flowed into Exuma Sound at this point but over the years has filled in to its current condition. When you enter this creek from the west you will begin to see smaller creeks branching off the main stream. The first side creek to your right is not recommended. It is short, narrow, and has sharp rocky ledges along the western side that can rip an inflatable to shreds very quickly. About ¼ mile past this is another creek on the right that is worth exploring. Though it only goes back into the interior a few hundred yards, it is narrow and lined with mangroves on both sides. In places, the area may remind you of scenes from "The African Queen" with Humphrey Bogart and Katherine Hepburn. A little further along on the right a creek runs south to meet up with another creek that leads in from Shroud Cay Harbour in a vast tidal lake that dries at low water. About 300 yards from the end of the creek at the beach, a side creek on your left branches off to the north. This stream ties in with the northernmost creek just below Camp Driftwood.

From the entrance at Shroud Cay Harbour, a creek meanders to another beach with a short walk to the Sound side. This creek joins up with another creek that leads in from the south. These creeks are generally wider, deeper, and at their beginnings, rockier than their northern counterparts.

Hungry Hall, between Shroud Cay and Hawksbill Cay, is a pristine, windswept, wild and natural place. The channels in this shallow area are to be explored by dinghy on a rising tide as they silt in and change often.

LITTLE PIGEON CAY

Little Pigeon Cay (Chart #EX-11), originally called South Pigeon Cay and locally called Pigeon Cay, is private and visits ashore are by invitation only. There is deep water between Little Pigeon Cay and Elbow Cay which leads out to the Banks route, however, there is a shallow sandbank to the south and east of Little Pigeon Cay. Vessels heading south from Norman's Cay or the Shroud Cay anchorages can pass easily between Elbow Cay and Little Pigeon Cay with no obstructions except the large orange buoy that was placed there by a now defunct charter boat operation. The buoy lies northeast of Elbow Cay and west/northwest of the northern tip of Pigeon Cay, directly between the two cays. Once between Pigeon Cay and Elbow Cay steer 185° and avoid the huge sandbank that lies to the east and south of Little Pigeon Cay.

ELBOW CAY

Elbow Cay (Chart # EX-11), sometimes called "the elbows," lies just to the west-southwest of Shroud Cay. The cay has the distinction of having the only navigational light (FL W, 2 sec., 46 ft, 11m) to be found in the Park. Although Elbow Cay Light is one of the newest and most sophisticated lights installed in The Bahamas (originally placed in 1929), as with most navigational lights in the islands, do not rely on it to be working.

Elbow Cay is little more than a few scrub covered rocks and should be given a wide berth to the west due to a coral shoal that lies to its northwest. You can pass between Elbow Cay and Little Pigeon Cay but care must be taken to avoid the very obvious and shallow sand banks to the south and east of Little Pigeon Cay.

For those approaching from Nassau or skippers who wish to clear Elbow Cay to the west, a GPS waypoint at 24° 30.90' N, 76° 49.25' W will place you approximately ¼ nm west of Elbow Cay. Vessels passing too close to the northwestern shore of Elbow Cay may find themselves on top of some shallow reefs with less than 7' of water over them at low tide.

HAWKSBILL CAY

Hawksbill Cay (Chart # EX-12), originally called Shroud Cay, is one of the most beautiful cays in the Park, if not the entire Exumas. Uninhabited, it has several beaches on both the banks and Sound sides. Strolling along the beaches on the Sound side you will likely come across all types of flotsam and jetsam. Drums, containers, garbage, fishing floats and nets, all wash up on the windward sides of the cays but Hawksbill's eastern beaches seem particularly littered. The Park, when there are enough volunteers, will schedule a clean up day on the beaches to restore them to their natural beauty, albeit for a short while until the next blow.

On the southwest side of Hawksbill is a good anchorage with protection from the prevailing winds. It lies off the southwestern tip of the cay under a high bluff topped by a cairn. When approaching from the banks, take up a course of 90° on the bluffs just south of the offlying rocks. If approaching from the anchorages at Shroud, you can pass between Elbow Cay and Little Pigeon Cay, steering 185° to avoid the sandbank to the south and east of Little Pigeon Cay, until you pass abeam of these offlying rocks that lie just south of the long white beach. Give the rocks a wide berth as you take up a course of 90° into the anchorage. There are several shallow heads with only 2'-3' of water over them in this anchorage so keep a sharp lookout for them when you get within ¼ mile of the shore and steer around them. A vessel drawing no more than 6' can head north around the offlying rocks to anchor in some 7' pockets just off the long beach. Watch out for shallow heads in this area also. Ashore you will find a small creek that will take you and your dinghy well inland on a high tide. Remember to leave before the tide begins falling to avoid getting stuck in the creek.

Just north of the long white beach on the western side of Hawksbill Cay is a small beach with a marked trail that leads to the ruins of 10 houses and numerous outbuildings. There is a lot of small cactus growing in this area so you should wear shoes. The houses date from the Loyalist period, approximately 1783-1830. In 1785, The Crown gave a grant to the Russell family to settle on Hawksbill and the cay remained occupied by various families until about 1900. Near one of the houses lie the remains of a beehive oven surrounded by piles of conch shells. These ovens were used for cooking as well as to incinerate the conch shells for use in the making of mortar to line the walls of the houses. The same house is surrounded by a large grove of tamarind trees, the fruit of which is used for making beverages. Although there are some 10 houses, they are scattered about and you may have to do some walking and searching to find them all. Around the ruins themselves you will see some holes dug into the rocky ground for watering poultry and swine. Please do not remove any artifacts as they are protected by Park Regulations (See *National Park Regulations*). There is a large cave just to the north of the ruins on the western shore, you can see it from your dinghy.

The last known inhabitant of Hawksbill was a man known simply as "Rocker" who was married to a granddaughter of the original owner. Rocker and his wife, along with four other families, farmed the whole cay as well as every other cay within a day's sail on which cultivatable soil could be found. Sisal was commonly grown in the Bahamas at this time and may have been their major crop along with buttonwood and other hardwoods. Local legend is that Rocker bled to death from being bitten by a barracuda while wade fishing for bonefish.

On the southwest tip of Hawksbill lie the remains of an impressive stone pillar that was topped for years with an osprey nest. The pillar was toppled in 1979 by high winds associated with Hurricane David. There is a fresh water well near this cairn.

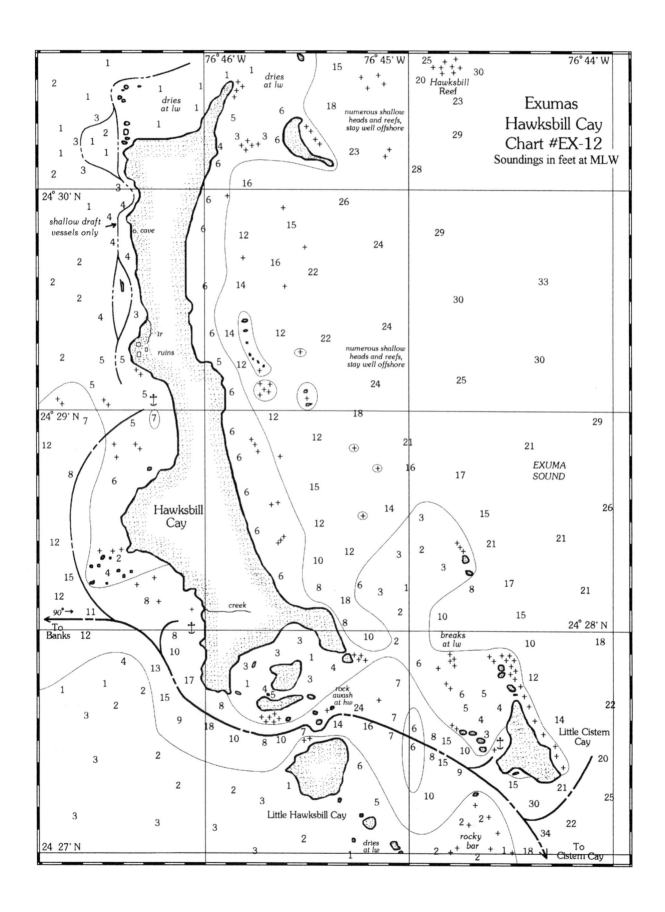

The south end of Hawksbill Cay is swept by strong tidal currents and is best explored by dinghy. There are some nice beaches in the bight along the southern shore. You will notice some moorings in the area. These are not placed by the Park, they are privately maintained and their holding is not to be trusted.

The eastern shore of Hawksbill Cay is comprised of two beautiful windward beaches. The area off these eastern beaches is not suitable for navigation except by small outboards and dinghies as it is strewn with shallow heads and submerged rocks. This area is excellent for snorkeling when the weather is calm.

LITTLE HAWKSBILL CAY

Little Hawksbill Cay (Chart # EX-12), originally known as Hawksbill Cay, is private and is rarely visited due to the tidal action around its northern and eastern shore. The only inhabitants are a pair of osprey. When approaching the Cistern Cay area from Hawksbill Cay, round the southern tip of Hawksbill Cay in deep water and head for the cut between Little Hawksbill and the two offlying rocks to its north. You will see a rocky bar and a small, partially submerged rock to port and just west of the pair of offlying rocks. Keep this bar and rock well to port but also keep an eye on the shallow rocky bar lying off the north shore of Little Hawksbill Cay. As you come around the rocky bar on your port, keep the northernmost offlying rock off Little Cistern lined up between the pair of offlying rocks directly in front of you and head straight for it, aiming between the pair of offlying rocks. Just before you reach the pair of rocks, take a dogleg to starboard around the southernmost rock, once again, keep an eye out for the shallow rocky bar to starboard off Little Hawksbill Cay. Although it is deep enough, it is not advisable to pass between the two rocks as there is a rock awash about 100 yards to the east of the rocks. Once past these rocks, take up a course for Little Cistern and watch out for the shallow sandbank you must pass over as you approach Little Cistern. These directions may make this passage sound a lot worse than it really is. With good light it is not much more difficult than maneuvering in a small, crowded anchorage.

LITTLE CISTERN CAY

Little Cistern Cay (Chart #'s EX-12 & 13) lies just to the north-northwest of Cistern Cay and to the southeast of Hawksbill Cay. Little Cistern Cay is 2000' long and 650' wide and encompasses about 30 acres. There is a nice little anchorage just off the beach on the western side of Little Cistern Cay. If you enter from Exuma Sound, pass along the south side of Little Cistern until clear of its southwestern tip and head northeast towards the beach. Upon entering you will see a large rocky bar, leave it to port and anchor between it and the beach. This anchorage is recommended in moderate weather only and is not the place to be in a frontal passage. Going ashore is not advised as the island is covered with poisonwood. Although unsuitable for humans, this is perfect for the white-crowned pigeon rookeries on Little Cistern. The young of the white-crowned pigeon feed exclusively on the fruit of the poisonwood tree.

CISTERN CAY

Cistern Cay (Chart # EX-13), originally named Big Cister for its fresh water hole, is privately owned. A former owner and resident was Robert Vesco, the renegade American financier who bilked $224 million from investors in the Investors Overseas Services Group. He purchased Cistern Cay in 1978 for $180,000. It is believed that he assisted Carlos Lehder, the infamous drug smuggler of Norman's Cay, in laundering money through Nassau banks. The cay, as well as Vesco's former residence, are now owned by different people. For information on renting the house (the former Vesco residence) and cabins that lie along the western point of Cistern along Molly's Beach, call 1-242-326-7875. As Cistern Cay is private, visits ashore are by invitation only.

To enter the Cistern Cay area from Exuma Sound (if approaching from the north stay 1 mile offshore until south of Hawksbill Cay), a GPS position of 24° 27.31' N, 76° 44.10' W will place you ½ mile to the ENE of the cut between Cistern Cay and Little Cistern Cay. From this point you may pass to the south of Little Cistern Cay in 20' of water, or pass between the outlying rocks north of Cistern Cay in 25' of water. If you approach through the offlying rocks, beware of the rocky shoal that works southward from the rocks on your starboard side. Proceeding southward, there is plenty of deep water between Cistern Cay and the shallow sandbank which lies approximately ½ mile off the western shore of Cistern Cay, parts of which are dry at low water. Approaching the south end of Cistern Cay, you must swing wide around the shallow banks south of Little Bitty Cistern Cay. Once around this bank you will enter The Wide Opening (Chart #'s EX-13 & 14) at which point you can proceed out into Exuma Sound via Coral Cut or head across The Wide Opening towards Warderick Wells.

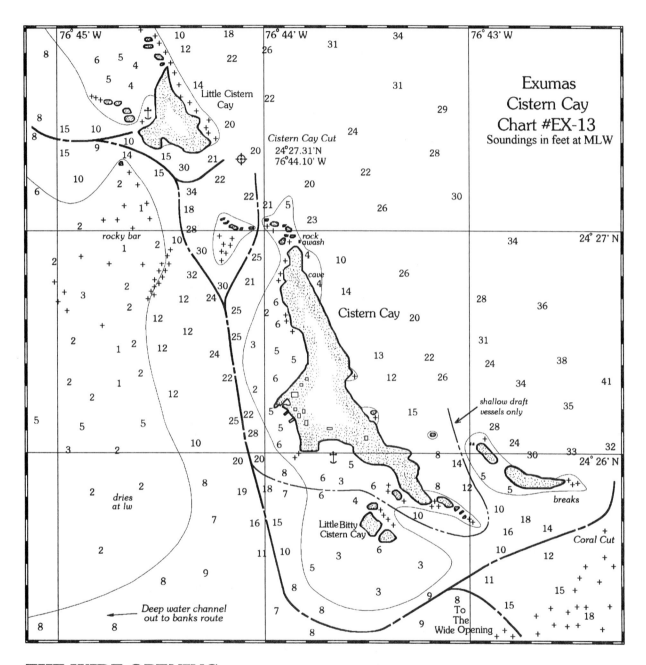

THE WIDE OPENING

The Wide Opening (Chart # EX-14) is the name for the area just to the southeast of Cistern Cay, where small rocky cays stretch for 5 miles to Warderick Wells. Although many people only use the term to describe the main channel (The Wide Opening Channel) from the Banks to the Sound, the entire area is now commonly referred to as The Wide Opening. The channel, being very wide and deep, was an easy entrance to the Banks for the old sailing ships, they could sail through it easily in any wind direction without having to tack. The Wide Opening Channel was the designated channel for the U.S. Navy between Exuma Sound and the banks during the Cuban Missile Crisis. The cays in The Wide Opening are exposed and windswept and offer no protection whatsoever. For refuge from the prevailing winds, head south to Warderick Wells or north to Hawksbill Cay.

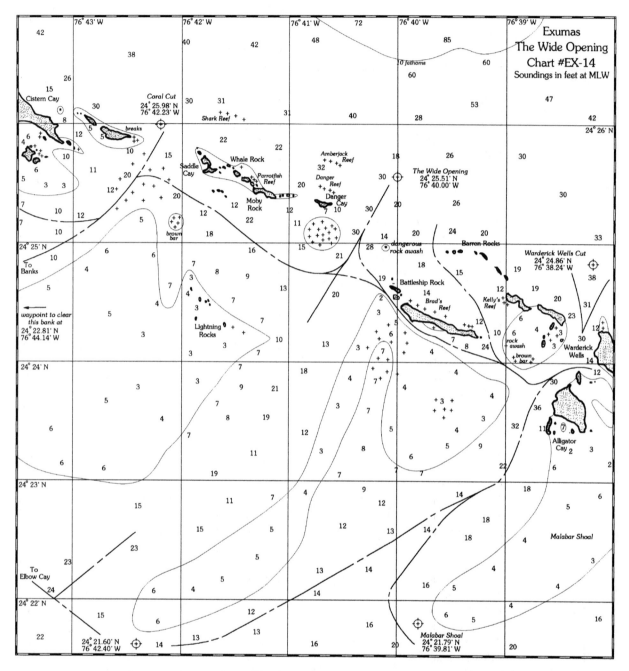

The current between the cays where the banks meet the Sound has created some of the most magnificent reefs in the Park. The reefs in the area of The Wide Opening are not for the novice diver. The Wide Opening abounds in strong currents, large fish (sharks), and diving is to be avoided in this area when the wind picks up. This warning is not intended to discourage diving on these reefs, rather it is merely a reminder for you to take the proper precautions as with diving anywhere.

There are two main channels from the banks to Exuma Sound through The Wide Opening, Coral Cut and The Wide Opening Channel. Although these are excellent channels, wide and deep, they can at times be very choppy due to their exposed location. A GPS position of 24° 25.98' N, 76° 42.23' W will place you ½ mile northeast of Coral Cut (an excellent drift dive by the way), and a GPS position of 24° 25.51' N, 76° 40.00' W will place you ½ mile northeast of The Wide Opening Channel. If you do not have a GPS, stay ½ mile offshore until you can line up in these channels on a NE/SW line. Coral Cut is just south of the large offlying cays south of Cistern Cay and The Wide Opening Channel is about midway between Cistern Cay and Warderick Wells. Both channels are very straightforward, wide, and deep. The Wide Opening Channel will take you all the way to the much traveled banks route that parallels the cays in a SE/NW direction.

From Cistern Cay, once you are in Coral Cut and wish to head across The Wide Opening towards Warderick Wells (calm weather and good visibility is essential here), steer a course for the southern side of Long Cay, the large cay just to the northwest of Warderick Wells. Keep an eye out for the rocky brown bar just southeast of Coral Cut and just northwest of Lightning Rocks (keep it on your starboard) and the rocky shoal south of Danger Cay (keep it to port). From Coral Cut the first major cay you come to will be Saddle Cay. It is 800' long, 250' wide, and 40' high. Just on the Sound side of Saddle Cay is a rock that is awash. It is called Whale Rock because it resembles a whale frolicking in the water. Southeast of Saddle lies Danger Cay, 900' long, 200' wide, and 20' high at its eastern hill. Just off Danger Cay in Exuma Sound, along a line just north of the western tip to northeast of the eastern tip, lies Danger Reef. Starting at around 30' deep, Danger Reef gradually slopes to 55'. Initially, the reef is flat and interspersed with sand gullies with many small corals based on coral rock. As the reef gradually gains depth, the coral formations form 15' gullies laced with a variety of tunnels.

After you cross The Wide Opening Channel, change course and head straight for Battleship Rock, the high (though not as high as Long Cay), bluff-sided, long rock just to the northwest of Long Cay. This is also sometimes called Steamer Cay, or depending on whom you ask, Hawkfish Rock (probably originally called Fishhawk Rock). It is 700' long, rises to 40', and is 100' wide at its western end. On this cay you will see an osprey nest that has been occupied by succeeding generations of osprey for the last 60 years. Turn to starboard close to the southwest side of Battleship Rock as soon as you can clear the tip of the sand bank that lies just south of Long Cay. Stay within 100 yards of the southern shore of Long Cay keeping an eye out for the shallow sandbank to starboard and a rocky bar to port just off the Long Cay shore. Once past the end of Long Cay steer for Alligator Cay.

Pass to the south of the southernmost rock in the shallow bank that lies to port on the north edge of Warderick Wells Cut. Here you can turn to port to head to the North Anchorage at Warderick Wells or turn to starboard to head out to the banks. Vessels drawing 6' or less, when entering from Exuma Sound, can pass to the north of Long Cay and around its southeastern tip to join up with the route to Warderick Wells. Watch out for the rock that is awash at high water just off the southern tip of Long Cay. Pass between this rock and the brown bar that lies to the east and southeast of Long Cay.

Long Cay, once known as West Shroud, is ½ mile long and comprises 20 acres. It rises from 10' at its northern end to 42' at its highest point. Long Cay is an Audubon Shearwater rookery, if you see any of these rare birds please do not disturb them. They prefer to nest on remote cays and only inhabit them at night. Three hundred feet from the northwest end, along the northeast shore, is an underground cave about 40' by 15' with a mouth to the sea that is about 15' wide. Blowholes from this cave lie 50'-60' inland. Long Cay is riddled with small caves and holes, many containing small bird bones and tunnels, some of which hold fresh water during the rainy season.

Lying parallel to the north shore of Long Cay is one of the most beautiful reefs in The Bahamas. Brad's Reef, a typical fringing reef, is rarely visited by cruisers because of its exposed location. It lies in just 8' of water a few yards off Long Cay and stretches for about 400 yards to 20' depths at the reef edge. From the northeast, sand gives way to an almost total cover of varied corals, dominated by large boulders of star coral and some brain coral, almost all in excellent condition with very little damage. There is a large stand of staghorn coral just east of the cay with a small beach that lies north of Long Cay.

If heading northwest across The Wide Opening from Warderick Wells, clear the southernmost rock and its bank and take up a course for Long Cay with the western point of Alligator Cay astern, then simply follow the above directions in reverse. After crossing The Wide Opening Channel, head for the gap between Little Bitty Cistern Cay and Cistern Cay leaving Battleship Rock on your stern. Keep a sharp eye out for the reefs and heads.

WARDERICK WELLS

Warderick Wells (Chart # EX-15), once called Waterish Wells and sometimes spelled Waderick Wells, like many other islands in The Bahamas with "wells" in the name, was once used by sailors as a source of fresh water. This fresh water, now brackish, flows to the Park Headquarters to fill some of the water needs of the Warden, Park volunteers, and any researchers who may be staying at the Headquarters. A half mile from the south of the northern end is a hill (Boo Boo Hill-70') with a slightly lower ridge that runs southward for approximately 250 yards. Boo Boo Hill, and the plaques and memorabilia placed there, is an excellent landmark when offshore. South of this ridge is a break of about 800' and then another ridge that rises to 20' and stretches to the southern end of the island. Along the western shore of Warderick Wells is a small boat channel that leads to the South Anchorage. This is recommended only for shoal draft vessels and dinghies.

Photo courtesy of Kelley Becker

The Author's boat moored in the North Anchorage at Warderick Wells.

THE NORTH ANCHORAGE

The north anchorage at Warderick Wells (Chart #EX-15) is one of the most popular anchorages in the Exuma chain. This is the hub of the Park, the home of the Park Headquarters. When approaching the north anchorage, the Park emphatically requests that you call them on VHF ch. 16 prior to your arrival. The Warden or the volunteer radio staff will then assign you a mooring (if you haven't already received a mooring assignment and if there are moorings available) and give you any assistance you may need in your approach. The Park will take reservations for a mooring one day in advance. Mooring assignments are given out every morning during the busy part of the season, usually January through May, at 9:00 am. Please do not call requesting a mooring before 8:00 am. Some inconsiderate cruisers think that the Park Warden and his wife have nothing to do all day and night except answer the radio as early as 6:00 am and as late as 11:00 pm. If you call well outside of office hours do not be alarmed if greeted by a less than cheerful voice that has been distracted from whatever it was doing to come and answer your non-emergency call. If for some reason you see that you will not be able to make your planned arrival at Warderick Wells, please notify the Park as soon as possible so they may give the mooring to another vessel.

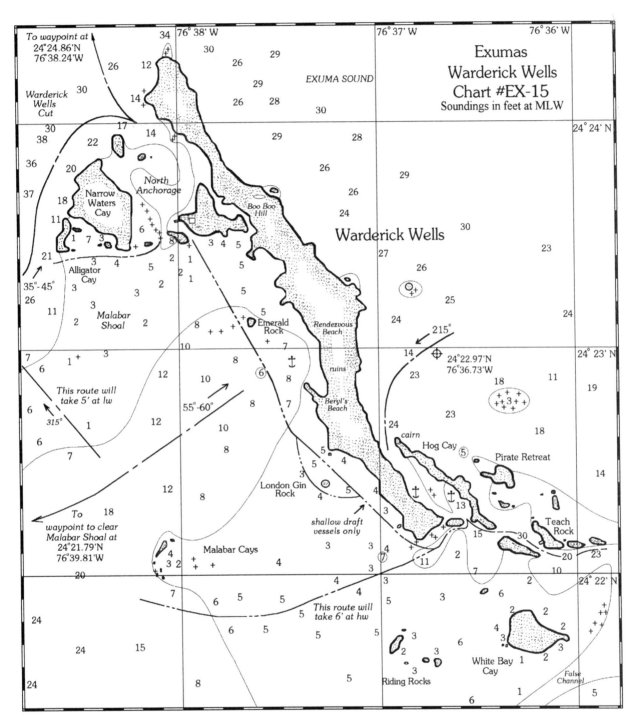

Due to damage to the turtle grass beds and siltation on the reefs in the area, anchoring is not allowed in the north anchorage at Warderick Wells. The bottom is poor holding in places and there is a very strong tidal flow through the narrow channel. The Park installed new moorings throughout the Park in the winter of 1993. There are 22 moorings in the north anchorage, 4 in the south anchorage, 2 at Hall's Pond Cay, and 2 dinghy moorings at the Rocky Dundas. Vessels use these moorings entirely at their own risk.

There are two types of moorings in use in the Park, the Halas mooring and the Manta mooring. The Halas mooring is used mainly in rock or coral. A hole is drilled in the coral or rock and then a stainless steel eyebolt, approximately 2' long, is placed in it and the hole is filled with concrete. The Manta type of mooring, used primarily in soft, sandy areas, consists of an 8' long shaft with an eyebolt on the top and a hinged, spade-shaped plate at the bottom. The mooring is pneumatically driven into the sand to a depth of 10'. An upward thrust is applied kicking the plate down into a locking position. The mooring is then tested with a predetermined upward pull. Although no anchors are allowed in the north anchorage, in extreme storm conditions setting out an extra anchor is allowed. Check with the Warden if you have any questions. During the "Storm of the Century," March 13, 1993, Warderick Wells experienced 70+ knot winds and every vessel (21) in the anchorage rode out the storm in comfort and safety. The only problems were due to skippers failing to eliminate chafe or using too much scope on their bridles.

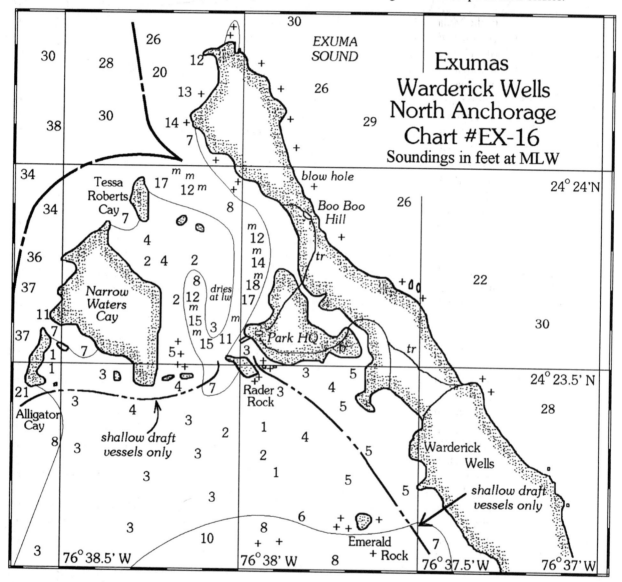

There is a charge for the use of the moorings, subject to change in 1998. As of this writing the fee is $15 for two nights, or, if you prefer, you may join the Exuma Park Support Fleet for $30 which entitles you to receive newsletters, a decal, and the use of the moorings without charge for the year. This arrangement works out well with the many cruisers who are only bound as far as George Town for the season and wish a mooring on the return trip. Although it is rare, there may be times when the 22 moorings in the north anchorage are filled and the Park must turn you away. The Warden or staff will suggest alternate anchorages. You may anchor in the south anchorage or just west of Warderick Wells near Emerald Rock or Malabar Cays.

Approaching from Exuma Sound (Chart # EX-15), a GPS position of 24° 24.86' N, 76° 38.24' W, lies ½ mile north of the entrance to Warderick Wells Cut on the Sound side. The entrance channel is wide, deep, and straightforward. Keep clear of the close lying heads at the northeastern end of Warderick Wells. As always, use caution when entering these cuts in adverse weather. Even in moderate weather onshore winds and an outgoing tide can build up quite a chop.

When approaching from the Banks you will find that the entrance lies between two shallow, sandy shoals that are easily seen in good light. Approaching on the banks side from the north you must clear the sandy shoal that reaches westward from the south end of the Wide Opening off Long Cay (Chart # EX-14). A GPS position of 24° 21.60' N, 76° 42.40' W, marks the southwestern end of the shoal. If you don't have a GPS, don't panic. The end of the shoal lies approximately halfway between Lightning Rocks and Malabar Cays, about 2½ miles to the west of Warderick Wells. Favor the Malabar Cays side and you will be in the entrance channel and can take up a course for Alligator Cay. When you clear the shoal, steer towards Alligator Cay on a heading of 70° (or simply eyeball your way in keeping the shoal well to port) until you get within ¼ mile, staying well clear of the shoal lying on your port side and Malabar Shoal which should lie well off your starboard side. As you approach Alligator Cay stay in the deep water (over 30') favoring the rocks and cays on your starboard side until the anchorage opens up to starboard. The deeper water lies closer to Alligator Cay, do not be afraid to stay within 150' of Narrow Water Cay and Alligator Cay. If you are approaching from the north and have turned too soon, you are now heading out The Wide Opening Channel. Don't worry, stay calm. If the weather is good you can go out into Exuma Sound and head in that way or you may take the route across the Wide Opening (see *The Northern Park-The Wide Opening*). At worst, you can turn around and head back out onto the banks and go around the shoal you prematurely turned to avoid. If you are leaving the north anchorage and heading north on the banks side, this shoal deceptively curves northwest giving you the impression that you have passed the end of the shoal. Many a mariner has been tricked by this only to run aground or have to alter course to clear the shoal that is suddenly once again in front of them.

Approaching from the south (Chart # EX-15), as you pass a mile to the west of Malabar Cays you will begin to see Malabar Shoal. Malabar Shoal lies basically southwest to northeast. Its southwestern tip lies approximately two miles southwest of Alligator Cay. A GPS position puts its southwestern tip at 24° 21.79' N, 76° 39.81' W with about 3'-4' at MLW. This shoal also has scattered rocks and heads along it. Once clear of its southwestern end, steer 35°-45° on the small hill that lies halfway between the northern end of Warderick Wells and the first beach to the south. This will lead you to Alligator Cay (which is hard to make out against the backdrop of Warderick Wells) in 12' of water that gets progressively deeper. Round Alligator Cay and favor the Alligator Cay and Narrow Water Cay shore until the entrance to the anchorage opens up. Vessels drawing 6' or less can take up a course of 315° from the westernmost edge of Malabar Cays to cross Malabar Shoal between two very visible shallow sandbars and save a mile. If in doubt, the passage around the end of the shoal does not add much more than a mile or so to the distance.

At the entrance to the north anchorage you will begin to see the white mooring buoys. The three outer buoys are for large vessels up to 150'. Smaller vessels will enter here and should keep close to the imaginary line between the buoys, staying at least one-third the distance off of the eastern shore until you pick up the dark grassy streak along the bottom. Beware of the brown bar and shoal jutting out of the eastern shore below the first beach. From here it is fairly straightforward, simply follow the channel around to your mooring. If you are to moor in the western arm of the anchorage, come past the Headquarters building generally heading south-southwest. You will see a turning buoy, keep this to starboard and as soon as you pass it, round up to starboard and steer for your mooring. Caution: at the southwest corner of the anchorage, past the Headquarters building and just opposite the turning buoy, you will see two small orange buoys. These are not moorings! They mark a beautiful soft coral reef with 3' at low water in some areas. It is bounded to the north by a sea grass bed and to the south by a small hard coral reef. This is an area with swift tidal currents, strongest between Rader Rock and Narrow Water Cay, so you may wish to examine it at slack tide, or drift snorkel over it. You may tie your dinghy up to the buoys but do not drop an anchor here. You may notice that there is some evidence of damage caused by careless anchoring on the northern end of the reef, please do not add to this.

After you have been assigned a mooring, prepare a line to run through the pennant and back to your own vessel. Many boaters make this a much more difficult and dangerous task than it needs to be. When you pick up the mooring pennant, attach it to the nearest cleat on your vessel and let it drift back and settle to its natural position lined up with the current or wind. Ready your own mooring line, motor forward, release the pennant from your cleat, and firmly attach your line to the eye of the pennant. Do not simply reeve your line through the eye, the constant motion of your line through the pennant in bad weather creates a sawing effect that will soon chafe through the pennant and may well set you adrift. There is a lot of current in the north anchorage so do not be alarmed when the tide changes and it seems like your vessel does not seem to know which way to lie, it will soon settle down with the flow. The Park accepts no responsibility for the use of their moorings.

In the center of the north anchorage, to starboard as you enter, between Warderick Wells and Tessa Roberts Cay, is a very conspicuous, large tidal flat that is exposed at low tide. The drop-off along the entrance channel is clearly visible. Some six-hole sand dollars and pen shells may be found in the algal turf below the tide line along with other mollusks and echinoderms. Remember, only look, do not remove any shells you may see.

About ¼ of the way down the entrance channel, at mooring #9, you will see on the bottom the burnt hull of a fiberglass sailboat. A gentleman once left his generator on while he went to dinner on another boat and the result is sitting on the bottom of the channel. Don't worry, even a 9' draft at low tide won't hit it (if you draw more than 9', simply steer around it, you have plenty of room). A 5' nurse shark makes its home in the hull now but is harmless. There are some other residents of the North Anchorage that you should know about. One is "Bubba," a 4' barracuda that loves to hang out under boats and feed on leftovers thrown overboard. Due to the abundance of boaters using

Photo courtesy of Nicolas Popov/Island Expeditions

Park Headquarters, Exuma Park.

the anchorage in winter, Bubba gets a little chubby come springtime and then thins down over the summer and the fall slow season. Bubba enjoys following divers and swimmers and is very curious. If he appears threatening, gnashing his teeth and writhing his body, don't be alarmed. This is only a display designed to ward off an apparent threat. You will find that he does that only when you are staring him down or moving towards him. A pair of lemon sharks, 4' Boo Boo and his 5½' big brother, The Harbormaster, have taken up residence in the harbor so keep an eye out for them when you go swimming. They seem harmless, Warden Ray Darville's three sons spent the entire summer swimming and diving with them. When in the water, if you move towards them, they move away. This is not a recommendation that you should swim with sharks, rather it points out that certain ones are familiar with humans and wary of them. These sharks are magnificent to look at and photograph, but if in doubt about any shark, by all means stay out of the water.

Between Rader Rock and Warderick Wells is a small reef that is typical of a "cut" environment that is seen between small cays. The tidal exchange of water is funneled through a small number of channel openings with sandy shoals to the east and west. The reef is approximately 60 yards long and consists of a soft coral shallow water reef, a shallow sill area, and a steep drop off with isolated coral heads. If snorkeling over this reef, due to the swift tidal action here, awaiting slack tide or drifting with the current may be prudent for the weaker swimmer.

Along the southeast side of Alligator Cay in shallow water you will see some small buoys. Please do not disturb them, they are collectors for an ongoing research project.

To visit the Park Headquarters, you may land your dinghy at either the beach to the northeast of the Headquarters or at the small beach just to the south. You may tie up at the dock but you must leave room for the Park patrol boat.

From any location in the anchorage you will see Boo Boo Hill. It is the high hill with the cairn and markers on it. Boaters have been leaving the names of their boats up there for years, carved or painted on anything from driftwood, to fishing floats, to old outboard motors. The view from Boo Boo Hill alone is worth the small climb. It is told that the boatload of missionaries that wrecked off Warderick Wells are buried on Boo Boo Hill and the cairn on Boo Boo Hill was erected long ago in their honor. Just below and to the south of Boo Boo Hill is Boo Boo Beach on the Sound side. Just to the northwest of Boo Boo Hill and along the same ridge you will see a small weather station. This is part of an ongoing study to monitor weather conditions in this section of the Exumas.

The eastern side of Warderick Wells, especially around the northern end, is great for dinghy exploring in calm weather. The rocky cliffs are pockmarked with holes and small caves waiting for the adventurous snorkeler.

Warderick Wells is criss-crossed with trails cut by various Wardens and volunteers over the years. We have a few marked on the charts but for a complete listing you can pick up a free trail map at the Headquarters. When walking, please stay on the trails to avoid damaging the fragile surrounding environment. If you must leave the trail try not to step on any living plants. There has been considerable damage done to flora on Warderick Wells due to people leaving the trails. When you are finished with the trail maps please return them for the next hikers to come along.

At the southern end of Rendezvous Beach you will find a trail that winds around to the Loyalist Ruins on the western shore of Warderick Wells. Here you will find the ruins of three buildings dating from 1780 consisting of rock and conch shell mortar walls. Please do not disturb any artifacts that you may see here. Legend has it that the Loyalists did not leave Warderick wells of their own accord. It seems that there was some bad blood between the Loyalists and some pirates who still hung around these waters long after the great pirate era of the early 1700's. Legend has it that the Loyalists were massacred by the pirates who shortly thereafter also disappeared from the scene.

Just south-southwest of the Park Headquarters and approximately 200 yards to the west of Warderick Wells lies Emerald Rock (Chart #'s EX-15 & 16). The water around Emerald Rock is relatively shallow, less than 10'. The edges of Emerald Rock have deep undercut cave-like areas which support colonies of coral. It is an excellent site to examine hard corals but please do not disturb anything. Emerald Rock is the site of an ongoing research project that has been monitoring the growth on and around Emerald Rock for over 5 years. There are a few large heads ringing the rock within 100 yards that can easily be seen from a dinghy. Some cruisers like to anchor in this area, and if the north anchorage is full it would be a good alternative. From the banks, pass north of the Malabar Cays and south of the Malabar Shoal. Work your way in towards Warderick Wells on a heading of 55°-60° until you can anchor in 6'-8' of water at low tide just south or southeast of Emerald Rock.

THE SOUTH ANCHORAGE

Although not as popular as the north anchorage, the south anchorage (Chart # EX-17) has very good protection with four moorings and anchoring allowed. The anchorage is in the slot between the southeast corner of Warderick Wells and Hog Cay (once known as South Warderick Cay). The easiest entrance is from the north, entering from Exuma Sound (Chart # EX-15). As you head southward along the shore of Warderick Wells, about a mile south of the northern tip of Warderick Wells and a little less that one mile north of the south anchorage, lies a large rock a little more than ¼ mile offshore. Keep this well to starboard as you head south. A GPS waypoint of 24° 22.97' N, 76° 36.73' W will put you about ½ mile northeast of this anchorage and well southeast of the offlying rock in 21' of water. The entrance to the south anchorage is not immediately seen, but if you steer for the small beach (barely visible from seaward) on a course of 215°, the entrance will soon become evident. As you get closer you will see a small cairn on the north end of Hog Cay. Keep this to port as the anchorage opens up in front of you. Head in and keep a lookout for the stray head on your starboard side. The anchorage has a sandbar in the center of it, keep between the sandbar and the eastern shore of Warderick Wells. Anchor or moor anywhere here but not on the stromatolites in the center of the anchorage, they look like large, flat, square-sided rocks. Please do not touch, stand, or walk upon these reefs as the living sections of them are very delicate and are easily destroyed.

You may choose to head south a bit to anchor in the lee of Hog Cay. Pass between the sandbank in the center of the anchorage and the eastern shore of Warderick Wells and round up to port just north of Pegleg Rock to anchor off Hog Cay. If you take a mooring in the south anchorage, please alert the Park Headquarters and tell them which one you have picked up. Look towards the north end of Hog Cay at low tide and you will see a tunnel that goes through

Hog Cay and comes out into Exuma Sound. You can snorkel through this tunnel when the seas are calm. If anchoring use two anchors as the tidal flow through the anchorage is very strong, usually 1-2½ knots.

To enter the south anchorage from the cut at the northern end of Hall's Pond Cay (Chart #'s EX-17 & 18), a GPS waypoint at 24° 22.70' N, 76° 35.25' W will put you ½ mile northeast of the cut. If you don't have a GPS, stay ½ mile offshore until you can enter the cut at Hall's Pond Cay steering southwest towards the eastern end of White Bay Cay. Keep a lookout for shallow water on your starboard side. Once inside the cut turn to starboard and parallel the lie of Bonney Rock, Read Rock, and Teach Rock, keeping them to starboard, and pass between Teach Rock and Dinner Cay.

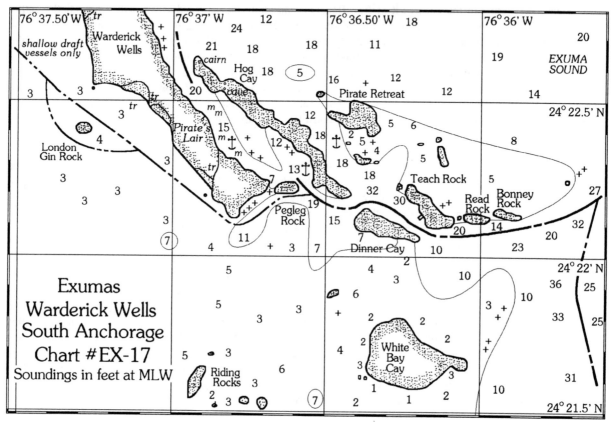

As you pass Dinner Cay, turn a little to port and keep the southeast end of Hog Cay to starboard. There is a small deep water channel to the south of Dinner Cay but it is not recommended due to the shoal building out from White Bay Cay. Keep an eye on tidal conditions in this area, especially between Dinner Cay and Pegleg Rock. Pass between Pegleg Rock and Hog Cay and you can turn to starboard to anchor or turn to port to enter the western side of the anchorage where the moorings are. Beware of the shoal area between Hog Cay and Warderick Wells, it is besprinkled with rocks, small heads, and many stromatolites.

You will notice that some of the smaller offlying cays between Warderick Wells and Hall's Pond Cay are named after pirates. Teach Rock was once the top prize in a Flying Treasure Hunt, the more popular second prize was a new car. The winner sold the cay to a German gentleman who built a dock to berth his sport fishing boat. When he found out the Park had a no-fishing regulation he abandoned the dock and has not returned. Teach Rock is named after the infamous Edward Teach, otherwise known as Blackbeard. Read Rock and Bonney Rock are named after female buccaneers Mary Read and Anne Bonney, the "Lady Pirates" of the early 1700's.

Ashore on Warderick Wells you can visit an area called the Pirates Lair, located towards the northern end of the anchorage. Just north of the casuarina and the mailbox, you will find a trail that is lined with conch shells leading inland to the Pirates Lair. A short walk through this narrow, palm frond lined path will take you to a small opening with a fresh water well. In this area grow tall cabbage palms (not indigenous to The Bahamas) and a certain type of grass usually found only in the Gulf Coast areas of Louisiana and nowhere else in the Exumas. It is believed to have gotten here aboard the pirate ships that used this anchorage. The Pirate's Lair itself was used as a meeting place for the pirates when ashore. They would bring their mats and loungings ashore (with the cabbage palm and grass seeds in them from when they were used on the Gulf Coast) and set them up in this area to sit, drink, talk, and do whatever it was that pirates did for recreation between boardings.

A pirate could take a draft of 12' into this anchorage day or night. The ridges on Warderick Wells at the mouth of the anchorage camouflaged his rigging while Hog Cay would conceal his hull from any ships sailing by offshore. In the early 1700's shipping traffic used The Wide Opening Channel to gain the banks, the channel being wide enough to sail through easily in almost any wind. Once on the banks, ships could make for the eastern entrance to Nassau or go around the western side of New Providence to enter Nassau from the west. Pirates lying at the south end of Warderick Wells could make easy prey of any vessel passing them headed for The Wide Opening Channel.

The last known inhabitant of the island was a man named "Davie" who lived at the southern end. In 1887, with his payments being in arrears, his land returned to the Crown. The ruins of his houses and a well can still be seen but must be searched for in the bush.

On the southwest side of Pirate Retreat is a pristine, though small beach; one of those types of beaches that you have come to The Bahamas to find.

THE PARK WARDENS

In 1981 Beryl Nelson became the first Warden of Exuma Park. Park super-volunteers, Anita Martinec and Bob Rader, cut trails so Beryl would have access to a high point to watch for poachers. Beryl lived on his houseboat on Beryl's Beach and was so allergic to poisonwood that he could not cut a trail himself. During Beryl's tenure as Warden, the laws pertaining to fishing in the Park were quite different. Then, local residents and visitors could catch for the family only. Generally this allowed up to a dozen each of fish, conch, and lobster. This was a very generous allotment but easily abused. With a greater influx of visitors every year, the marine life in the Park was seriously threatened. New fishing regulations were subsequently enacted through the efforts of Peggy Hall. Beryl Nelson resigned in 1983 and the search for a new Warden began. However, Beryl's surveys of the Park still stand today as invaluable references.

Photo courtesy of Kelly Becker

Ray Darville, Warden of the Exuma Cays Land and Sea Park.

Peggy Hall, then on the Board of the Trust, was responsible for finding a new Warden and began the search aided by Anita and Bob. After many unsuccessful attempts at finding a man with a boat who was willing to work for almost nothing, Anita and Bob suggested finding a woman for the job. Louise Fox of Long Island was suggested. Her husband had just died and she was extremely capable, however, she turned down the offer due to family reasons. Other candidates fizzled out for one reason or another and Peggy came to the conclusion that if a woman could do the job, then she could do it herself. She turned over her business to her manager and took on the responsibilities of the position of Park Warden in 1986. Peggy handled the job by herself until Anita and Bob became Deputy Wardens in 1988.

Peggy Hall came to the Bahamas from Ireland in the mid-1940's and established a plastics business in Nassau. She has owned a succession of sailboats by the names of *Arawak*, *Manatee*, and the current Lord Nelson Tug, *Moby*, which she lives on while in the Park. Peggy's contributions to the Park could comprise a book in themselves but her greatest role has been in making people aware of the Park and drawing them in to help. Peggy started the Support Fleet, a group of individuals, mostly cruisers, who have given of their time or money to the development of the Park. Membership includes use of a mooring and a regular newsletter that keeps members informed on what is happening in the Park. Anita specialized in the administrative aspects of the Park. She produced the newsletter and worked closely with visiting research groups. Anita gave regular lectures at the Headquarters for visiting cruisers to help acquaint them with the Park. Bob spent much time cutting trails all over the Park. Bob would crawl through the brush until he found a nice view, cave, or ruin, and then cut a trail to it. Bob has kept the trails narrow to avoid changing much of the environment. There are fantastic views from some of the high points of the cays that would be inaccessible if not for Bob's trails.

The team of Peggy, Anita, and Bob stayed together until the end of 1991 when Peggy retired and Anita and Bob returned to Florida. Peggy was replaced by Lester Albury and his wife Miranda. Lester and Miranda left in late 1992 and moved to Nassau.

In December of 1992, Gardner Young, Crystal Cheong, and several visiting yachtsmen took over as interim Wardens until a replacement could arrive at Warderick Wells. On February 1, 1993, Ray Darville began his current tenure as Warden.

Ray Darville probably has the best job in the world. He normally works 12 hours or more a day, seven days a week, and is on call 24 hours. His days are fraught with danger from the elements and from his fellow man. His salary is small and his expenses great. He has little in the way of recreation as you may be accustomed. No TV and very little radio. Those who benefit most from the job he does can in no way ever show him their gratitude. Considering everything, he would have it no other way.

Ray, a soft-spoken young Bahamian from Deadman's Cay, Long Island, is the Park Warden at The Exuma Cays Land And Sea Park. One would be inclined to believe he is American due to his accent, or lack of it. He was schooled in the United States and his accent reflects this, however, when he is around other Bahamians you may notice him slipping into his native Bahamian patois.

His entire life he has been a seaman just like his father was and his father before him. His background includes varied positions in the marine trades doing salvage work, ship refitting in the US. and Venezuela, and marine environmental work. He is descended from the pirates that roamed the islands and passages of The Bahamas centuries ago, but that is another story for another time. He looks like he would be at home with a cowboy hat and a badge as Marshall of some town in the Old West.

Ray grew up learning the ways of the sea and living off the bounty the ocean provides; conch, grouper, and lobster being the mainstays of one's diet, supplemented by the vegetables and fruits grown on the islands. While in many areas of The Bahamas the populations of these sea creatures are severely depleted, there is one area where they are still plentiful, thanks to Ray, and he intends to keep it that way. Ray has even named some of the more familiar denizens of the Park. There is Bubba the barracuda in the north anchorage, along with Boo Boo and his big brother, The Harbourmaster. Ray has even named some of the conch, there is Elvis, and Herman, and Chenille. His charges are very dear to him and he takes it personally when someone comes into the Park and molests them.

Ray was caretaking on Cistern Cay when he learned of the Park activities and soon volunteered as Deputy Warden to use his knowledge of these waters to help with the poaching problem. He assumed the position of Park Warden on Feb. 1, 1993 after Lester Albury resigned and moved to Nassau. Lester succeeded the popular Peggy Hall. Ray maintains the hard line approach that Peggy Hall brought to the position while continuing the outreach program to local schools.

His main problem as Park Warden lies with poachers; those that enter or pass through the park, fishing, conching, or lobstering, either for themselves or for profit. The largest majority of poachers are the visiting yachtsmen although they often take far less per instance than some of the locals (who can clean out a reef in a very short time and then sell their catches). On a daily basis, in season, there are more yachtsmen poaching than local Bahamians and Ray often gets caught in the middle. The yachtsmen claim that he is harsher on them, turning a blind eye to the locals, and the Bahamians complain that he lets the boaters, with their tourist dollars, go unscathed. Neither is the case. Ray is completely unbiased in his work. A poacher is a poacher, pure and simple. Many poachers either are unaware of, or simply do not consider, that the removal of even one breeder conch or lobster removes the possible hundreds of thousands of future conch and lobster from the Park. Those who are unaware, Ray educates. Those who refuse to consider will one day learn the lesson the hard way. There will be nothing to poach.

The visiting boaters' poaching leans toward trolling within the Park boundaries mostly, though some do anchor and dive on the reefs or coral heads in the area that are so rich with sealife. The locals however, know exactly where to go and have numerous "hot spots" which will yield exactly what they are looking for. Ray knows these "hot spots" well and daily risks his life in high speed chases with fast boats in shallow water. Poachers have even threatened his life but he is not to be deterred. After all, he's doing this for Bubba, and Elvis, and Herman, and Chenille.

Ray has received so many death threats from local poachers that The Defence Force has made Warderick Wells a permanent manned station. Currently one Defence Force seaman is rotated in and out of Warderick Wells every two weeks and rides with Ray on all patrols. This has resulted in more arrests for poaching and even a drug bust in 1996. Plans are under way for a new staff residence and permanent Defence Force quarters with housing for up to four Defence Force personnel and a dock for their boat.

In the summer of 1995, Ray Darville married Evelyn Hughes on Osprey Cay. The couple are currently living at the Park Headquarters along with their new son, Jonathon Robert Hughes-Darville, who was born in November of 1996. Congratulations Ray and Evelyn. A new Warden for the future perhaps.

THE PARK HEADQUARTERS

As you climb the steps of the Park Headquarters, one of the first things you will notice is the view. Don't forget your camera, this is the perfect time to capture your boat in a beautiful, peaceful anchorage. The point where the Headquarters stands is actually an island to itself, separated from Warderick Wells by a tidal creek. This creek, now shallow, was once deep water until the hurricanes of 1926 and 1929 filled it in. Warderick Wells was once known as "Warderick Wells and the island with the well." For some reason, many people thought the island with the well disappeared. It was not discovered until the 1960's that the island was still there and still separated from Warderick Wells by a shallow tidal stream that dried up at low water.

If you walk up from the beach side you will notice a bucket of water at the base of the steps to the Headquarters Building. It only takes a few visitors to deposit an incredible amount of sand on the floors of the Headquarters so please rinse off your feet here. If the bucket is empty, you don't have to be shy about filling it up at the beach. As you walk around the Headquarters feel free to enter the office area. There are many specimens of plant and animal life on display here including some minor oddities. Here also you will find the reference library with its many fine books on topics covering corals, sealife, animals, plants, birds and history. You can also pick up trail maps for the over 4 miles of trails on Warderick Wells. Just outside the door to the office is a small table with a hinged top. Inside there is usually a ziploc baggie with some sugar in it. You can put a little sugar in your hand and it won't be long before you have half a dozen Bananaquits eating right out of you hand. If you have any spare sugar, a donation to the Bananaquit fund would be appreciated.

The Headquarters now does double duty as a research center for visiting scientists and students. The office has t-shirts, postcards, mugs, and some excellent reference books, guides, and charts for sale. There is also an extensive book exchange where you can swap books 2 for 1. The Park asks that you refrain from entering the living quarters across the hall from the office, this is the Warden's home. Park Headquarters office hours are Monday through Saturday from 9:00 am until 12 noon, and then after a well deserved lunch break, from 1:00 pm until 5:00 pm. Sundays the Headquarters is open from 9:00 am until 1:00 pm. [When the closed sign is up (which is rare), please respect it and keep out of the Headquarters area. There are times when the Warden must work 24 hours a day due to emergencies or rescues, and he may be catching up on sleep. The Warden will soon open up the Headquarters again.] The Park currently hosts, during the season, Saturday afternoon happy hours on the deck at the Headquarters. For more information contact *Exuma Park* on VHF ch. 16.

You will probably notice the strong construction of the Headquarters. Led by Warden Peggy Hall and Deputy Warden's Anita Martinec and Bob Rader, volunteers from Operation Raleigh, with the assistance of some cruising boaters, built the Headquarters in 1989. On December 3, 1988 the first volunteers from Operation Raleigh arrived in Warderick Wells to cut trails and begin building the new Park Headquarters on Pepper Point in the north anchorage.

Operation Raleigh, organized under the patronage of Prince Charles in 1985, is made up of students from various countries who spend three months in another country. One month being spent in community service (repairs, building, cutting trails), one month was spent in research (surveys, reef projects), and one month for adventure (SCUBA diving in The Bahamas). They have a strenuous selection process and only one out of fifteen applicants is accepted and each person accepted must pay $5,000 for the privilege. Many hopefuls seek corporate support for their terms with Operation Raleigh, or Raleigh International as it is now known.

The first groups that came to Warderick Wells had to camp on the beach, carry water from the well, and eat dried rations. The initial group of 7 students and 2 staff put in the foundations and the floor. The second team had the roof on by the end of January and the final group finished the walls. Visiting cruisers assisted by hauling people and equipment in their boats, cutting trails, clearing the well, and building the dock as well as being involved in the actual construction of the building. Bob Rader and 6 students cut trails for three weeks as well as clearing the growth around the Loyalist ruins. Some of the trails, Julie, Ian, James, Ron, Theo, and Jenny are named after those volunteers. Before Christmas of 1988 there was a snag in material acquisition. At the last minute a gentleman by the name of Basil Kelly commandeered a Nassau freight boat, loaded it with building materials from his warehouses in Freeport, delivered it to Warderick Wells just a couple of days after Christmas, and then returned again with even more material. Donations from the Support Fleet more than paid for everything.

All in all, it took 140 volunteers the winter and spring of 1989 to finish the 30' x 60' building. The Park Headquarters and Visitor Information Center atop Pepper Hill opened on August 16, 1989, the day of a total lunar eclipse. Four days of festivities culminated in the raising of the Bahamian flag atop the Park Headquarters on August 19 by the Commissioner from George Town.

THE LORE OF WARDERICK WELLS

Warderick Wells is said to be haunted and it is reported that on moonlit nights the sound of a congregation singing hymns can be heard. When the singing ceases a number of voices can be heard calling to one another. There are three shipwrecks off the coast of Warderick Wells. The one in the vicinity of Boo Boo Hill reportedly was of a ship laden with missionaries. In 1989, then Assistant Warden Anita Martinec wrote to the Society for the Propagation of the Gospel, based in England, and they could not verify any missionaries sent to this area or any shipwreck. The term "Missionaries" at the time might have meant something other than religious missionaries, perhaps a government boat went down laden with bureaucrats bound for some "mission" on the outer islands. The boat may have been loaded with French Missionaries, some of which did land at Long Island. There is no verification of this and nothing in the Archives, but it makes for some very interesting nights at anchor.

The discovery of a human skeleton on the south end of the island and the circumstances that led to its final internment all add to the tale upon which ghost stories are built.

The 1978 BBYC Spring Cruise carried the participants through the Park on their way to Staniel Cay. The last night before arriving at Staniel the club anchored in the south anchorage at Warderick Wells. Most of the fleet took off the next morning except three boats who stayed behind for a couple of hours of exploring ashore. Coming up the west side of the cay they beached their dinghy and proceeded to walk inland. They had not gone very far when they discovered a human skeleton lying face down under a large bush. Closer inspection revealed it to be the bones of a male, about 6' tall with very good teeth. There were also remnants of a belt and some clothing around his midriff. He did not appear to have been there for very many years.

The cruiser's first reaction was to bury the poor fellow but with no means of digging soon gave up on this idea. One of the cruisers, an eye surgeon, was attracted to the skull because of some unusual bones at its base and insisted on taking the skull. After the rendezvous at Staniel Cay, two of the boats continued on to George Town where they decided to call on the Commissioner's Office and report the location of the skeleton. Feeling that a proper burial was more important than the possession of a medical specimen, they decided to turn over the skull. They began to wonder if they had done the right thing when the Commissioner asked them "Just exactly where is Warderick Wells?"

On the return up the Exuma chain, one of the boats stopped in at Warderick Wells, coincidentally on the same day that a burial party arrived from George Town. After introducing themselves and guiding the party to the remains, they learned that the skull had been left behind in George Town. The skeleton was buried, sans skull. So, if you happen to see a headless skeleton walking around one night, give him a bearing to George Town, he's probably just looking for his head.

The Rev. Kelly of Staniel Cay informed Peggy Hall of the following, possibly relative to this skeleton. In the 1950's two local fishermen marooned a third member of their party on Warderick Wells and went home. They were unable to return for him due to bad weather and it was only some time later that inquiries were instituted through the police. The police went to Warderick Wells to look for the missing man. After a careful search, they found some human bones in a hole and buried them, assuming them to have been what they came for. They found no signs of anyone else alive and no other recent remains.

One resident of the area who used to work the sailboat routes to Nassau and back a very long time ago related the following story. The workboats used the west side of Warderick Wells as an anchorage as it offered excellent protection from the prevailing winds. One time they pulled in to anchor and went ashore and discovered the beach and surrounding bush strewn with bones. There was also a set of footprints leading down to the water and back up into the bush. They remained there a couple of days and every day saw a new set of prints leading into and out of the water. They never found who made the prints. To this day, the narrator of this tale will not remain on Warderick Wells after sundown.

One longtime resident of Staniel Cay, a gentleman who has lived in this area for over fifty years, says that Warderick Wells is definitely not haunted. He tells how the charter boats from Nassau in the 1960's used Warderick Wells as a good all-weather anchorage and stopover. In order to keep it to themselves they apparently told ghost stories about the area to keep away those with faint hearts.

But on those special nights, when the moon is right, and you hear the sound of faint moans on the wind, and the very air seems to make the hairs stand up on the back of your neck, who's to say?

THE SOUTHERN PARK
Hall's Pond Cay to Conch Cut

HALL'S POND CAY

Hall's Pond Cay lies just southeast of Warderick Wells (Chart #EX-18). It is approximately 2 miles long and averages 700' wide. It has a total land area of about 200 acres. On the western shore are a series of high bluffs running lengthwise and projecting upward 30'-60'. Salt ponds take up about 15 acres of the interior of the cay. Along the northern shore are 4 caves with 4' headroom. One cave has 14 blow holes to the rock above. Three quarters of a mile from the southern end, on a high hill and flanking a deep bight, are the ruins of 4 houses. The last people to inhabit them, the Davis family, were driven away by the hurricane of 1926. Sisal, a major crop at that time, can still be found growing on the island. Northwest of the ruins about 300' is a cave hole with a fresh water well. Hall's Pond Cay is criss-crossed with various trails that cruisers can no longer traverse.

In 1996 Hall's Pond Cay was purchased by a wealthy Czech who has plans to build 28 buildings on the island. To say the island is now private would be an understatement. He has already installed several private moorings and the Park moorings have been removed. The owner has even purchased the *M/V Sampson* from Marcus Mitchell on Sampson Cay to use as his freight boat carrying supplies from Nassau to Hall's Pond Cay. The landmark Exuma Cays Club, sitting on a hill on the western shore, just south of the northern tip of the island, has been torn down. A new building will be going up on its base utilizing its cistern. It is the end of an era of Park history.

When entering from Exuma Sound, head for a GPS waypoint at 24° 22.70' N, 76° 35.25' W. This will put you ½ mile to the northeast of the cut in about 25' of water. Keep a sharp lookout for there are some shallow spots about ¼ mile offshore with less than 6' over them at low water. If you don't have a GPS, stay at least ½ mile offshore until you are northeast of the eastern end of White Bay Cay. Steer southwest on the eastern end of White Bay Cay and keep a lookout for the shallow water that lies to starboard just northeast of Bonney Rock. Once your clear the rock on your port side just inside the cut, turn to port to pass inside west of Hall's Pond Cay or to anchor off its western shore. The moorings you see along here are private so don't pick one up. Visits ashore are by invitation only. Do not plan to stay anchored here in the event of a frontal passage, instead move to the very calm and protected south anchorage at Warderick Wells. There is a small boat channel along the western shore that will take you to the Soldier Cay-Pasture Cay (Chart #EX-18) area. This is recommend only for vessels with drafts of 4' or less.

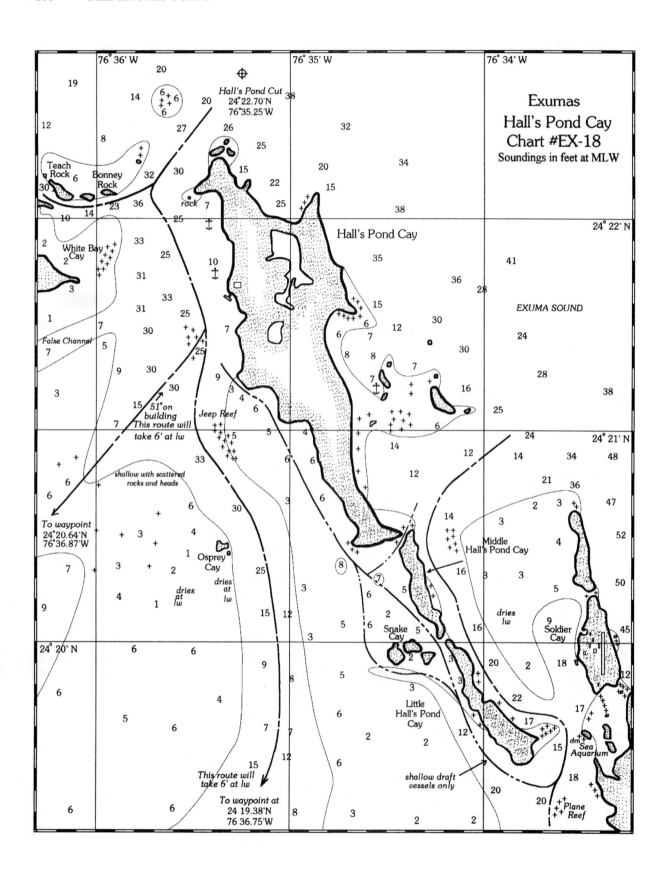

76° 36' W

76° 35' W

76° 34' W

19

20

14

6 + 6
+
6

20

Hall's Pond Cut
24°22.70'N
76°35.25'W

38

12

8

27

26

32

34

Teach
Rock   6

Bonney
Rock

32

30

26

25

15

Exumas
Hall's Pond Cay
Chart #EX-18
Soundings in feet at MLW

30

36

23

14

10

rock   7

25

15

22

25

38

24° 22' N

2

White Bay
Cay   2

33

25

3

31

10

25

Hall's Pond Cay

35

41

36

28

EXUMA SOUND

1

31

33

31

30

30

25

7

15

12

30

24

False Channel
7

5

9

30

25

7

6   8   8   30

28

3

9

25

15

51°on
building
This route will
take 6' at lw

7

9

3
4

Jeep Reef

5

6

9

16

25

38

7

6   7

6

24

24° 21' N

6

33

5   5

5
+   5

4

6

6

14

12

14

34   48

6

6

shallow with scattered
rocks and heads

30

3

6

12

21   36

2   3

47

To waypoint
24°20.64'N
76°36.87'W

3

4

6

14

3

52

7

3   2

1   Osprey
Cay

25

Middle
Hall's Pond Cay

16

3

4

5

50

9

4

1

dries
at
lw

dries
at
lw

3

6

5   5

2   16

dries
lw

9   Soldier
Cay

45

24° 20' N

6

6

9

5

9

Snake
Cay   5

20   2   18   12

6

8

5

2

3

22   17

17

5

4

6

7

Little
Hall's Pond
Cay

12

15

18

This route will
take 6' at lw

15

7

12

2

shallow draft
vessels only

20

dm Sea
Aquarium

To waypoint at
24 19.38'N
76 36.75'W

6

6

8

3

2

2

20   Plane
Reef

About 400 yards to the west of the central section of Hall's Pond Cay and along a line from the dock at the Exuma Cays Club to Osprey Cay, lies *Jeep Reef*. Out of sand and turtle grass beds small pieces of coral begin to appear, gradually developing into massive boulders standing up to 28' in height. The maximum consistent depth is around 35' and the whole reef takes on the appearance of large coral boulders separated by sand channels. There is a wreck of a jeep on the southwest side of this "J" shaped reef giving it its name. The main part of the reef lies within 200 yards of this jeep and continues to a greater extent to the northeast of the jeep. This is a very good spot for a tank dive but at slack water only due to the current. Begin your dive about ½ hour before slack tide and be careful. The fish on this reef are accustomed to humans and a few of the jacks can be petted. Just to the north of Jeep Reef is another smaller reef that is an excellent drift dive. It lies 500'-1000' north of Jeep Reef with the Exuma Cays Club bearing approximately ENE. Exercise caution with deep draft vessels along these reefs, some of the heads come to within 5' of the surface. If drift diving in the vicinity of Jeep Reef, lift your head out of the water every so often to make sure that you are still in a line with the Exuma Cays Club and Osprey Cay.

A deep water passage from the northern end of Hall's Pond Cay to the banks lies between Hall's Pond Cay and Osprey Cay (Chart # EX-18). From the northern end of Hall's Pond, head south in the deep water channel past Osprey keeping the dark patches that mark Jeep Reef well to port. Some of the heads that make up Jeep Reef only have 5' of water over them at low water. Keep the sandy shoal that stretches out south of Osprey Cay on your starboard and the sandy shoal to the west of Hall's Pond to your port. The further south of Osprey Cay that you go, the more you will turn to starboard, to the southwest and then west, until clear of the shoals. From the banks, head for the southern end of Osprey Shoal and, keeping it to port, head generally eastward, rounding up to north as you follow the lie of the shoal. A GPS position of 24° 19.38' N, 76° 36.75' W marks the southern end of Osprey Shoal. Caution should be exercised along this route as there are some shallow spots of 6' at low water.

Vessels drawing 5' or less may approach the northern end of Hall's Pond Cay directly from the Banks just southwest of Warderick Wells and White Bay Cay. From the Banks, steer towards the Exuma Cays Club on a heading of 51° magnetic. This is the old channel to the Exuma Cays Club and was once marked with red pennants, black flags, and a lighted range that stood just south of the Exuma Cay Club building just above the dock. This route will take you over a shallow sand bank with 5' at low water. For those with GPS, a waypoint at 24° 20.64' N, 76° 36.87' W will give you the position where this course crosses the shallow bank. Steering a reciprocal course of 231° with the Exuma Cays Club on your stern will bring you out onto the Banks.

Along the southeastern shore of Hall's Pond Cay is a beautiful long beach with some small offlying rocks. Access can be gained from Exuma Sound (Chart # EX-18). Although you can anchor a vessel here with up to 6' of draft, it is not recommended. This area is open to the prevailing winds and should only be used in settled weather, definitely not for overnight. If you decide to work your way into this area keep a sharp lookout, it is strewn with scattered heads and rocks. A visit to the long beach on this side is a must when exploring by dinghy.

Around the south tip of Little Hall's Pond lies a rocky bar that juts out eastward toward Soldier Cay and O'Brien's Cay. There are many stromatolites on this bar.

A unique tank dive in 80' of water lies off the northeastern end of Hall's Pond Cay along what is called *The Edge*. To find the reef, line up the northernmost rock at the north tip of Hall's Pond and the northernmost tip of White Bay Cay. Follow this line out to 80' of water and you will be on The Edge. The best part of the dive is an area in 80'-120' called the *Walled City* which consists of great spirals of coral reaching up from the depths resembling the skyscrapers of a large city. Divers should be extremely wary of the odd currents in this area.

South of Hall's Pond Cay lie Middle Hall's Pond Cay and Little Hall's Pond Cay. Little Hall's Pond Cay and its beautiful beach is off limits to cruising yachtsmen. The island is private and the owners request that visits ashore are by invitation only. It seems that some previous visitors were so callous as to leave their bags of garbage on the cay. This is not only improper (You wouldn't leave it on your neighbor's yard back home would you?), it is in violation of Park Regulations. Unfortunately there are many cruisers who seem to think they are above rules and regulations.

WHITE BAY CAY

White Bay Cay, originally called Hog Cay, lies just southwest of the cut north of Hall's Pond Cay (Chart #'s EX-17 & 18). White Bay Cay, a private island, has a few small beaches along its shore. The southern shore is very shallow and you will notice four pairs of small buoys stretching out towards the west in this area. Please do not disturb them as they are collectors in an ongoing research project. White Bay Cay is best explored by dinghy while you are moored or anchored at Hall's Pond or in the south anchorage at Warderick Wells

OSPREY CAY

Osprey Cay (Chart # EX-18), also known as Sandy Cay locally and on some charts shown as Little White Bay Cay, lies just to the west-southwest of Hall's Pond Cay. It is 400' across and has a land area of 2 acres and only rises to a height of 15'. There is a small cave just under the top of the hill. Osprey Cay is bordered by sandbanks on the east, west, and south sides. At low tide the sand banks lie 600' east to west and are 1000' long, while a narrow sand ridge extends southwest for ½ mile. On a full moon night and a low tide, walking the half mile to the end of the sand spit will be an experience you won't soon forget.

A very open island with no anchorages, Osprey Cay is best explored by dinghy. Under the casuarinas on the southern side you will find a pleasant place for a picnic with driftwood tables and seats. This is a very popular spot though you must watch out for scorpions on this cay. The northernmost rock just southeast of Osprey Cay is called Hawksnest Rock. The once prominent fishhawk's nest was often plundered by passing fishermen.

Osprey Cay and White Bay Cay are nesting sites for terns and other birds. If visiting these cays for a picnic or a swim, the Park asks you to shorten your stay if these birds are nesting as you will likely scare these birds away from their nests. Being driven from their nests for a period of as little as twenty minutes may cause them to abandon their eggs to rot and their hatchlings to perish. A little knowledge of the consequences of your actions can go a long way towards protecting the Park's wildlife.

This island is privately owned and no camping or fires are allowed without permission of the Park Warden. Call Exuma Park on VHF ch.16 to reach the Warden.

A hunt in the bush may reveal some human remains. Local legend has it that when you are sitting around a campfire on Osprey Cay you may feel what seems to be small raindrops. When you look up, you will not see a cloud in the sky.

SOLDIER CAY

Soldier Cay (Chart # EX-18), the only developed island in the southern half of Exuma Park, is a private island and visits ashore must be by invitation only. Soldier Cay is available for rent and is all inclusive. The entire cay is rented, including the use of Soldier Cay's boats. For information call 1-242-359-0285.

While the charts show that you can enter this area with a large vessel, it is not recommended due to the abundance of heads and rocks in the area. Do not attempt the cut between Hall's Pond Cay and Soldier Cay (Chart # EX-18) in strong onshore conditions. However, if you insist on entering the cut, stay about ½ mile offshore and line up with the northern end of the unnamed cay just to the south of Hall's Pond Cay. This will be very hard to pick out but it will be just to the south of the long beach and very low. When aligned with that point, head toward it on a course of 235° magnetic and watch out for stray heads and rocks. Keep clear of the large, shallow area to your port side. It fills up most of the cut and with good visibility you can't miss it. As you approach the point, round to port and stay close to the shore on your starboard side where you will have deeper water. Stay parallel to this shore until you can swing to port and clear the rocky bar that juts eastward from the south end of Little Hall's Pond. All in all, the cut at the north end of Hall's Pond Cay and the cut between O'Brien's Cay, and Little Bell Island are much safer and easier.

Anchoring between Soldier Cay, Pasture Cay, and Little Hall's Pond Cay is not recommended due to the fierce tidal flow. It is best to anchor at Hall's Pond, Little Bell or Bell and explore this area by dinghy.

PASTURE CAY

Pasture Cay (Chart # EX-19), once called Little Bell Island, lies between Little Hall's Pond Cay, O'Brien's Cay, and Bell Island. It was used as a cattle pasture until about 60 years ago. It is less than 1000' long, roughly 500' wide, and rises to a height of only about 10'.

Northeast of Pasture Cay lies Plane Reef, a triangle shaped reef of about 300 yards set in approximately 25' of water. To find it, line up the northwestern point of Pasture Cay and the end of the airstrip on Soldier Cay. Plane Reef consists of large boulders set amongst sandy gullies. The reef is in a very fast tidal channel between cays so slack tide would be the opportune time to view the reef. At one time the Park had set floating signs to mark this reef but the tide would turn them over and carry them away. On the southern edge you will see a wrecked light plane that allegedly ran drugs and crashed. The plane is held down by the weight of the engine in its nose and it is not unusual to find it turned in a different direction after a particularly strong tide or storm. These turbid water conditions have caused siltation damage to the reef, reducing the feeding ability of the coral polyps. Anchoring in the Pasture Cay-Soldier Cay area is not recommended due to this strong tidal action.

Pasture Cay is bounded on the south by the deep channel off the northern edge of Bell Island. When approaching from this channel heading west, be sure to clear the shoal area to your starboard side that works out from the southwest side of Pasture before making your turn to the northeast towards Soldier Cay. To the east, between Pasture Cay and O'Brien's Cay, lies shallow water with scattered heads and rocks.

O'BRIEN'S CAY

O'Brien's Cay (Chart # EX-19), named for Titus O'Brien who once worked on it, is rugged and rarely visited. There is a beach in a shallow bight on the north side. On its east side are bluffs up to 20' in height. and one can look inland and see a hill rising to 35'. The entire north side is very shallow and suitable for dinghy exploration only. Inside the northern end is an opening to a large salina that dries at low water. On the southwest side is an opening into another beautiful salina at Pam's Point that is also dry at low water. The western side of O'Brien's is shallow with scattered rocks and heads. Off the northwest side of O'Brien's is an offlying rock approximately 150' long that is the site of the Sea Aquarium. The Sea Aquarium, marked by a sign, is a beautiful miniature wall dive that is not to be missed. There are some very tame fish here.

Do not use the cut that lies between Soldier Cay and O'Brien's Cay as it is strewn with rocks, heads, and a rocky bar that works out from Soldier and stretches across the cut to O'Brien's. There is an 8' lemon shark that likes to patrol this cut. Although he has not been known to hurt anybody, please use caution if diving in this area.

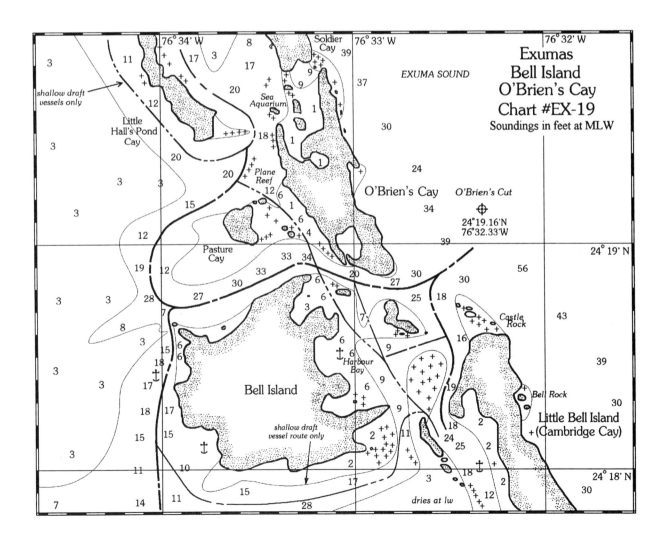

BELL ISLAND

Bell Island is quite private these days. Gone is the caretaker Clee. Gone is his clapboard house. Gone is the quiet ambiance this island exuded. In return we now have a wealthy owner who is overdeveloping the island with unsightly structures and a small private marina. His intention at this time is for the island to remain private for his own use and his staff but the future is uncertain and rumors abound. Sadly Bell Island as you may have known it is all but gone. Soon the anchorages around the cay will be unusable, they almost are now for all the construction traffic. If you get a chance to see it before too much future development consider yourself lucky. In another year or two we probably won't recognize the place.

If approaching from Conch Cut (Chart # EX-20), steer 360° from Conch Cut to Bell Island's westernmost point. Still heading north, just off the westernmost point of Bell Island, you will have a narrow gap to shoot through with 7' at low water. On your starboard side there will be a rock with a small submerged bar just behind it while to port you will see a sandy shoal with about 1' over it at low water. The gap between the two, approximately 50' wide, though narrow, should not offer any difficulty to the seasoned skipper. Once around this you may follow the channel to the north side of Bell Island in much deeper water or you may pass to the west of Pasture avoiding the shoal that lies to its southwest. If you proceed eastward along the north shore of Bell, just to your starboard is a nice beach and anchorage. The eastern side of Bell is usually not used for an anchorage as the western side of Little Bell is much more accommodating.

Along the eastern side of Bell are some very inviting beaches. In the southwest corner of the northernmost beach is a small mangrove swamp that is perfect for exploring. The middle beach, by far the prettiest of Bell's beaches, Harbour Bay, has a few casuarinas for shade. There is a prominent stand of casuarinas just to the south of Harbour Bay and inland. Here you will find a trail that crosses Bell Island to Clee's house. If walking this trail please do not pick any of Clee's produce.

If you wish to anchor off Harbour Bay or pass to the northern side of Bell and are approaching from Exuma Sound, enter the cut between Little Bell Island and O'Brien's Cay avoiding the shoals south of O'Brien's Cay and the rocks north of Little Bell Island. A GPS waypoint at 24° 19.16' N,76° 32.33' W will place you ½ nm northeast of O'Brien's Cut. If you wish to head to the north side of Bell, parallel the southern shore of O'Brien's Cay staying in the deeper, darker water where you will have 20'-33' at times. If you wish to anchor at Harbour Bay, once past the rocks north of Little Bell, steer towards Little Bell paralleling the lie of the rocks. When you are in line between the closest rock to Little Bell (Castle Rock) and the rocky outcropping at the south end of Harbour Bay, head directly for Harbour Bay. Keep the small cay in the center of the cut to your starboard and be sure to avoid the rocks and heads that lie just to the south of it. Eyeball navigation is essential in this area so be sure you have good light.

On the southern side of Bell Island is a deep channel that is not recommend due to scattered rocks and heads at the southeastern end of Bell Island and some shallow areas at the southwestern end.

Two nieces of Titus O'Brien, of O'Brien's Cay, took up their abode on Bell Island around 1862. Though diminutive in stature they were highly independent, relying only upon a dog and a gun for protection. They made their living by farming and diving for turtles. They allowed only a favored few to land upon Bell Island and assailed any trespassers who dared come ashore without permission. These eccentric ladies claimed ownership of the surrounding seas and everything that was in it as far as they could see. They would demand and attempt to exact a toll of fish or conch from any boat that stopped to fish nearby. On account of their age and stature they were usually humored although it is said a sailor threw one of them overboard when she attempted to collect her tax. Their house was destroyed in the hurricane of 1926 and they immediately set out building an improvised shack. They refused any and all offers of assistance in building another house. Eventually, the sister with the gun left to move back to Nassau. When the government found out that the other sister was on Bell living by herself (it was illegal for a woman to live alone on an island at that time), the government sent a boat to return the octogenarian to Nassau. She did not want to return to Nassau and the Government agent had to resort to trickery to get his unwilling passenger aboard.

LITTLE BELL ISLAND AND CONCH CUT

Little Bell Island was originally named Cambridge Cay after Alexander Cambridge who was granted the island in 1858. Little Bell is still shown as Cambridge Cay on some charts and many people still call it that. Little Bell is nearly a mile long and contains over 60 acres. About 1000' south of the extreme north end are several steep hills from 60'-75' high. About 1500' south of the northern side and about 120' out to sea stands Bell Rock. Fifty feet high, this sheer sided rock was once bell-shaped giving this cay and Bell Island their names many years ago. There is a much used trail leading to Bell Rock from the second beach south on the inside of Little Bell. Hardy climbers gaining the top of Bell Rock are rewarded with an excellent view. The cove on the southeast end of Little Bell has a nice beach called Honeymoon Beach that should be visited in settled weather.

To gain the anchorage at Little Bell from the north, good light and visibility are essential. Enter the cut between Little Bell and O'Brien's (Chart # EX-19) and once inside, head towards the shore of Little Bell paralleling the lie of the rocks off the northern end of Little Bell.

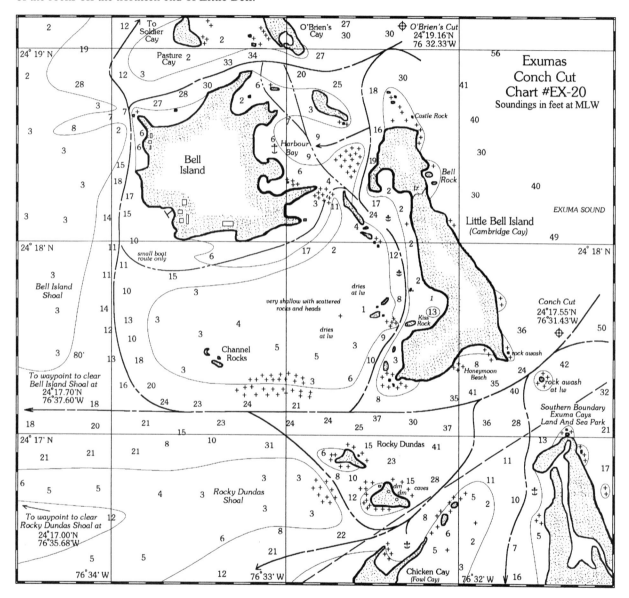

Somebody has set up a range for this made up of driftwood and floats hung from a casuarina. Coming in on this range is not recommended as it is not maintained and may not be there when you are. As you approach the shore of Little Bell Island, turn and steer parallel to the shore staying about 50-75 yards off. As you get closer to the turning point into the anchorage definitely favor Little Bell Island. You may need to get as close as 40-50 yards or less from shore. You will see some dark patches that you will be reluctant to pass over but rest assured, they are deep and an 8' draft will clear them. The danger lies on your starboard side where there lies a shallow bank with numerous rocks and heads that are easily seen with good light. As you approach the turn, swing a little towards the cay straight across from Little Bell to avoid the shoal to port at the turn, then swing back to port into deeper water and drop the hook wherever you wish; this is a wide, deep, anchorage.

To enter the anchorage from Conch Cut, either head east from the banks for Conch Cut (Chart # EX-20) or enter Conch Cut from Exuma Sound.

When approaching from the Banks, first clear Bell Island Shoal (Chart #EX-20). A GPS waypoint at 24° 17.70' N, 76° 37.60' W clears its western tip. Pass to the south of it and to the north of the sandy bar that reaches out to the west from the Rocky Dundas. A GPS waypoint at 24° 17.00' N, 76° 35.68' W marks the western end of this bar. Once between these bars you are in Conch Cut Channel. Head due east favoring the southern edge of the channel. When in the area of Channel Rocks, beware of the large reef system, partially awash, on the north side of the channel. Favor the Rocky Dundas side of the channel if in doubt or bad light. When you pass this reef system take up a course of 30° on Bell Rock. Please note, this is not the recommended route, the northern route is by far easier and safer. Good visibility and a sharp lookout is essential through here. Once abeam of the unnamed rock at the southwest tip of Little Bell, steer a little more northeast towards the offlying rock on the western side of Little Bell (called Kiss Rock because you have to come so close to it that you practically have to kiss it). There is a small rock cairn on its western end, steer for this. Pass this rock to starboard about 50'-75' off to avoid the mid channel reef to port. Take up a course to the next offlying rock on the western side of Little Bell. Take it to starboard between the submerged rocks that lie just off its western side and the submerged rocks to your port in mid channel. You are now in deeper water in the Little Bell anchorage.

If approaching from Exuma Sound, head for a GPS waypoint at 24° 17.55' N, 76° 31.43' W, placing you ½ mile northeast of Conch Cut. Enter the cut as shown on Chart # EX-20 between Little Bell and the rock that is awash at high tide. Stay on the north side of this rock as the south side has some large rocks with only 8'-9' over them at low water. Once in Conch Cut Channel, head for the southwest tip of Little Bell Island staying well to its south. After you pass the rock on the southwest shore of Little Bell, take up your course of 30° on Bell Rock and enter the anchorage as described above.

Little Bell is private but visitors are currently welcome ashore. Plans are in the works to develop the cay over the next few years so construction is imminent.

There is a huge elkhorn coral reef just inside the south point of Little Bell Island as you enter from Exuma Sound that is only surpassed by the magnificent stand of pillar coral near the brown bar on the northern edge of Conch Cut Channel, due west of Little Bell Island and north of the westernmost of the Rocky Dundas. This stand of pillar coral is over 4' high and extends over an area of 25' x 35'. It is one of the largest remaining stands of pillar coral in The Bahamas or Caribbean. Due to strong tidal action in this area, you may wish to wait until slack tide or just drift dive.

THE ROCKY DUNDAS

The Rocky Dundas, once known as Rockyadonda, are two rather high and forbidding islands on the southern side of Conch Cut (Chart # EX-20). On their windward side they are bluff sided and sheer, 30'-45' high. The southeastern cay has two mooring buoys just off its northeast side. Tie up your dinghy here in settled weather and visit one of the most attractive points in the Park. The cave here rivals, and may even best, Thunderball Cave at Staniel Cay. Besides the fish and coral formations, the Rocky Dundas boasts stalactite and stalagmite formations seen nowhere else in this area. If you are wondering how stalagmites can be formed underwater, remember that this area was once above water. The last major low sea level stand occurred about 15,000 years ago when the water level was approximately 300' or more lower than it is today. The Great Bahama Bank was one huge island then and a channel of only a few miles separated the "island" from Cuba. This is the period when the stalagmites would have formed. In comparison, if the water level today rose by as little as 10', 50% of the present Bahamian land area would be inundated.

You can anchor your boat off the Rocky Dundas making sure to avoid dropping your anchor on any coral. Most visitors anchor at Little Bell or out of the Park at Compass Cay or Chicken Cay (Fowl Cay) and dinghy over in calm weather. Anchoring at the Rocky Dundas is not recommended as it is notoriously poor holding and rife with currents. On an incoming tide there is a considerable northbound set to the current at the Rocky Dundas. It is advisable, when the current is strong, to tie your dinghy up to the northernmost mooring, visiting the northern cave first. Then swim down to the southern cave and when finished, ride the current back to your dinghy. Weak swimmers use caution. During a strong swell, when the waves are breaking along the eastern side of the Rocky Dundas, you can hear the sea thunder as it crashes against the bluffs and in the caves.

The area between and west of the two cays is shallow and foul with rocks and heads. On the leeward side of the Rocky Dundas you will see huge mounds of conch shells. Researchers dug down into these piles and dated the older conch shells near the center and the bottom. Tests indicated that those conch shells were placed there in the 1500's.

Legend has it that the Rocky Dundas were a holy place for the Lucayan Indians. There is an anchorage just off of the western shore of Compass Cay and one just north of Fowl Cay, known locally as Chicken Cay. At low tide, vessels with a 6' draft can pass between the southernmost of the Rocky Dundas and Chicken Cay and navigate between the two visible sandbars to join up with the Banks route.

THE
CENTRAL
EXUMAS

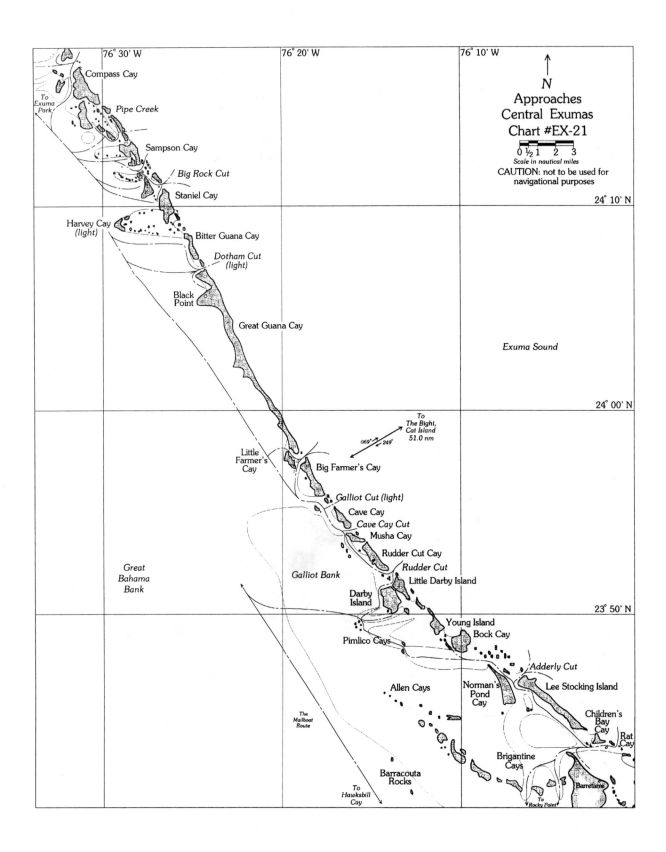

N

Approaches
Central Exumas
Chart #EX-21

0 ½ 1   2   3
Scale in nautical miles
CAUTION: not to be used for
navigational purposes

THE CENTRAL EXUMAS
Conch Cut to Rat Cay

APPROACHES TO THE CENTRAL EXUMAS

Vessels heading south on the Banks route, once clear of the sandbanks to the west of Bell Island and The Rocky Dundas, may cruise closer to the western shore of the cays, within a mile or less of the cays. From the Rocky Dundas to Little Farmer's Cay there are no large offlying sandbanks so characteristic of the more northern Exumas.

Once south of Conch Cut you may continue on your heading of 137° to bring you to Twin Cays, Sandy Cay, and Harvey Cay. Once past Harvey Cay you can take up a heading of 150° for Little Farmer's Cay. At Farmer's Cay Cut many vessels choose to enter Exuma Sound although a few head for Galliot Cut and then out into the Sound. Vessels with drafts of 5' can continue farther south past Rudder Cut Cay all the way to Barretarre and Soldier Cay on the inside. Vessels with a 6' draft can take the same route by playing the tides but should go outside at Rat Cay Cut. Proceeding southward on the Banks route, you will find that the deeper water tends to lie mostly to the west of your course line in the vicinity of Great Guana Cay and Little Farmer's Cay.

Vessels in Exuma Sound should stay at least ½ mile offshore to avoid any shallow areas such as the rocky bar with 7' over it that lies 250 yards east of Little Major's Spot. The route along the Exuma Cays in Exuma Sound is basically southeast paralleling the lie of the cays. There is excellent fishing in the deeper waters of Exuma Sound. The best cuts in bad weather would be Dotham Cut, Farmer's Cay Cut, Cave Cay Cut, and to a lesser extent, Rudder Cay Cut. Try to avoid Galliot Cut in bad weather or strong onshore conditions and an outgoing tide. Vessels approaching from Cat Island can take a heading of 249° from The Bight for 51.0 nm to arrive at Farmer's Cay Cut.

CHICKEN CAY (FOWL CAY)

Just south of the Rocky Dundas, and just outside the boundaries of The Exuma Cays Land And Sea Park, lies Chicken Cay (Chart # EX-22), often shown on charts as Fowl Cay. If you ask any resident of the area where Fowl Cay is they will direct you to the Fowl Cay that lies between Sampson Cay and Staniel Cay, about 3-4 miles further south. Chicken Cay is the name used to identify the cay just south of the Rocky Dundas and it will be known by that name in this guide.

Bounded on three sides by shallow sand banks, this u-shaped cay offers a small but secure anchorage off its north side with good protection except during a frontal passage (this anchorage is to be avoided in strong winds from west through north to east). The banks just to the east and southeast of Chicken Cay are excellent for conch (there is a reason that the cut just to the northeast of Chicken Cay is called Conch Cut). The anchorage may get a little rolly with a strong east or southeast wind.

To enter the anchorage from the eastern end of Conch Cut, Exuma Sound, or the Little Bell Island anchorage, pass just to the southeast of the Rocky Dundas and north of Chicken Cay. If approaching on the banks from the north (you will see the prominent white house of the caretaker, Clifford), head east down Conch Cut Channel towards Conch Cut and pass either just south of the Rocky Dundas, taking care to avoid the 6' shallows, or pass to the north of The Rocky Dundas in deep water with no obstructions. If approaching on the banks from the south, and you can pick out the darker water that will carry 6' at low tide, you may cut across the sandbank that lies just to the northwest of Chicken Cay about ¼ mile to the west of the cay. It is possible to pass between the sandbank that lies to the west of The Rocky Dundas and the Chicken Cay sandbank, but, once again, you will need good visibility to pick out the channel. If you cannot find this channel, proceed northwards until you can head east in Conch Cut Channel.

You can anchor in 8'-12' of water in the bight on the north side of Chicken Cay. Keep an eye out for the occasional stray coral head behind the Rocky Dundas as well as in the Chicken Cay anchorage itself. This anchorage is a good spot to begin your exploration of the Rocky Dundas and the large reef system just across Conch Cut Channel to the north of the Rocky Dundas. It is possible to work your way around the western side of Chicken Cay to anchor off the small bight on the southwestern shore, recommended only in settled weather or prevailing winds. As you work your way around, stay about 50 yards off following the channel between the shore and the obvious sandbank to the west of Chicken Cay. Vessels with less than 5' of draft may continue around the rock on the southeastern tip of Chicken Cay and round up to anchor off the eastern shore of Chicken Cay in 5' at low water. This is only recommended in settled weather or with winds from the west. Chicken Cay is private and visits ashore are by invitation only.

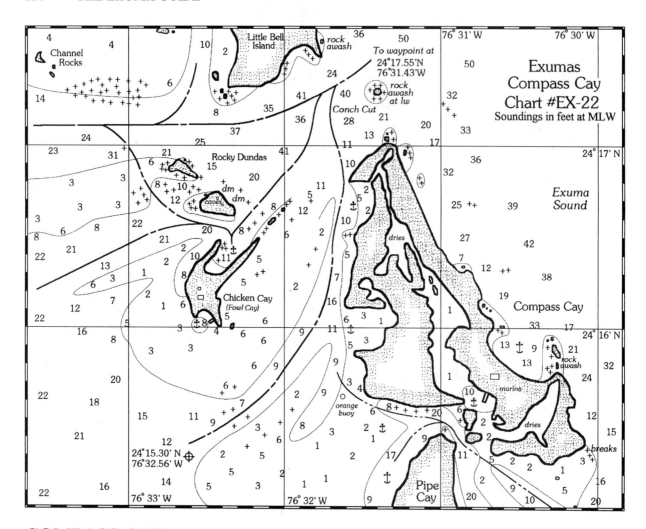

COMPASS CAY

Compass Cay's northern tip (Chart # EX-22) lies at the southern edge of Conch Cut and to the east of The Rocky Dundas and Chicken Cay. The cay is roughly a mile long with a very irregular shoreline and a 25 acre salina in its center. Earlier charts show the salina open to the Sound in two places but this has filled in over the years and the salina is now open only on the banks side at high water. Although parts of this salina dry at low water, there are navigable dinghy channels on a rising tide and there is said to be good bonefishing in the flats in this area. Compass Cay Marina is now open with space for 4 boats with 8' at low water (no fuel as of this printing). For info call *"Budget"* or *"Compass Cay Marina"* on VHF ch. 16.

Vessels entering Conch Cut may pass along the western shore of Compass Cay to anchor in winds out of the east and southeast or proceed out onto the banks for the trip south toward Sampson Cay. Boats with drafts of less than 6' may play the tides around the southwestern tip of Compass Cay (3' at MLW) and make for the entrance to Pipe Creek or to the anchorage that lies to the north and northwest of Pipe Cay. If it is not crowded you may enter the snug cove at the entrance to the salina in the center of Compass Cay.

If you are heading out onto the banks from Conch Cut along the Compass Cay shore, you must eyeball your way through two curving sandbanks. This route should not be taken if you have bad visibility as you must be able to see the sandbanks and the channel that leads you into the deeper water of the banks. When you enter from Conch Cut, follow close to the northwest tip of Compass Cay in 10' of water and head just west of south, paralleling the shore in 7'-10'. Take care to avoid the rocky bar that juts out westward from Compass Cay about ¼ mile south of the northwest tip. The bar is easily seen in good visibility. Roughly ¼ mile past the rocky bar the deep channel is split by a shallow sandbank. To gain the banks route you must follow the blue channel between the sandbank on your starboard and the sandbank that has just appeared in front of you, heading approximately southwest following the curvature of the sandbanks. Soon you will be heading west-southwest and you will come out in the deeper water of the banks after you clear a 7' (MLW) shallow spot. You must have good visibility to make this passage staying in between the two obvious sandbanks. If you wish to follow this route from the Banks to Conch Cut, a GPS waypoint at 24° 15.30' N, 76° 32.56' W will place you at the western starting point for this channel in 12' of water. Take up a course of approximately 70° on the hill that lies about ½ mile south of the northern tip of Compass Cay. Keeping between the very obvious sandbanks you will pass a curve in the banks and you will then take up a course of approximately 55° on the small hill that lies just south of the northern tip of Compass Cay. You will soon enter the deep channel that parallels the western shore of Compass Cay. These courses are approximate and are only suggested as references, the prudent mariner will use his eyes to follow the channel between the sandbanks.

If you wish to enter the Pipe Creek area from the western shore of Compass Cay, follow the channel southward along the Compass Cay shore until you come to the above mentioned split. At this point follow the channel that works along the Compass Cay shore keeping the orange buoy to starboard. This buoy was placed by Tucker Rolle of Compass Cay Marina to ease your entry to his facility. Vessels with drafts of 6' or less may play the tide and pass the 3' shallow area at the southwest tip of Compass Cay for the turn into the entrance to Pipe Creek (see next section: *Pipe Creek*). As you round the southwestern tip of Compass Cay, keep the easternmost of the Rocky Dundas on your stern as you cross the shallow area on a rising, almost high, tide. You may anchor just north of Pipe Cay in 20' or to the northwest in 9'-17'. This is a nice anchorage in winds from northeast through east to south but you must use two anchors in a Bahamian Moor for the anchorage is narrow and has a little current. The small, snug harbor inside of Compass Cay by the marina is good for all winds and has 10' at low water. If you do not head east around the southwest tip of Compass Cay you will see a deep blue channel leading off to the southwest that will lead you out onto the banks between two sandbanks, but only if you draw less than 5'. The Sound side of Compass Cay is very rocky with a beautiful, long, white, curving beach on its southeast side in the lee of some offlying rocks. You can anchor just off this beach in 13' of water in southwesterly or westerly weather but it is no place to be in any winds from northwest through east to south. There is a small underwater cave off the northeastern tip and about halfway down on the eastern side just before the small bight and rock. Just to the east-northeast of the large offlying rock, on its southeastern shore in 80' of water, is *The Crack*, an excellent tank dive.

PIPE CREEK: PIPE CAY TO OVERYONDER CAY

Pipe Creek is often referred to as the stretch of islands between Compass Cay in the north, and Staniel Cay in the south. Local residents of this area, when referring to Pipe Creek, mean the area between Compass Cay and Sampson Cay, comprised of the waters between Pipe Cay, Hattie's Cay, Little Pipe Cay (Kemp Cay), Wild Tamarind Cay, Joe Cay, Thomas Cay, and Overyonder Cay. This is the area that will be covered in this section.

Before you begin your exploration of Pipe Creek (Chart # EX-23), understand that this is one of those areas where careful attention to eyeball navigation is absolutely essential. Pipe Creek has some very shallow areas with numerous shifting sandbars and channels along with some large rocky bars to make things more interesting. If you choose to enter Pipe Creek, there will be spots where you must negotiate between rocky ledges and over areas that appear too shallow and mistakes can be costly if not deadly. The cuts in this area, although deep, have strong tidal currents which you must take into account as you maneuver through tight quarters between rocks and patch reefs. Please don't let these descriptions scare you away from enjoying the beauty that is Pipe Creek, instead, let these warnings cause you to keep an extra sharp eye out. Even novices on their first trip to these cays can enjoy Pipe Creek if they take the proper precautions and keep a sharp lookout.

Pipe Cay, although privately owned, has no restrictions about visits ashore. On the western side of Pipe Cay lies the remains of the old U.S. Navy Decca Station. You first inkling that this place is there are the four dolphins (pilings) that lead westward from the station. These are steel structures made of 5-6 steel I-beams approximately 16' above water. There are two at the entrance to the station and two more leading westward from it for about ½ mile. If you are on the banks and wish to enter the small cove at the station, keep these dolphins to your port and pass between the two inner dolphins and you will have no less than 8' all the way in at low tide. You will be heading in at approximately 95° but what is more important is to keep those dolphins to port. The dolphins also stretch across the banks to the Tongue of the Ocean and were used to lead U.S. Navy ships into the station. If you take up a course of 275° for approximately 36 nautical miles from the Decca Station you will reach the tongue of the Ocean with 12' of water almost all the way. If approaching from the south you may pass between the outlying unnamed cay just south of the westernmost dolphin and the small offlying rocks just west of Pipe Cay (Chart #EX-23), favoring the small offlying rocks and taking care to avoid the rocky bar that works eastward from the unnamed cay (do not attempt this route at night as you will not be able to see the rocky bar). If you are unsure about that route, it is best to pass to the west of the unnamed cay until you can line up the entrance channel and keep the two outer dolphins to port and split the two inner dolphins.

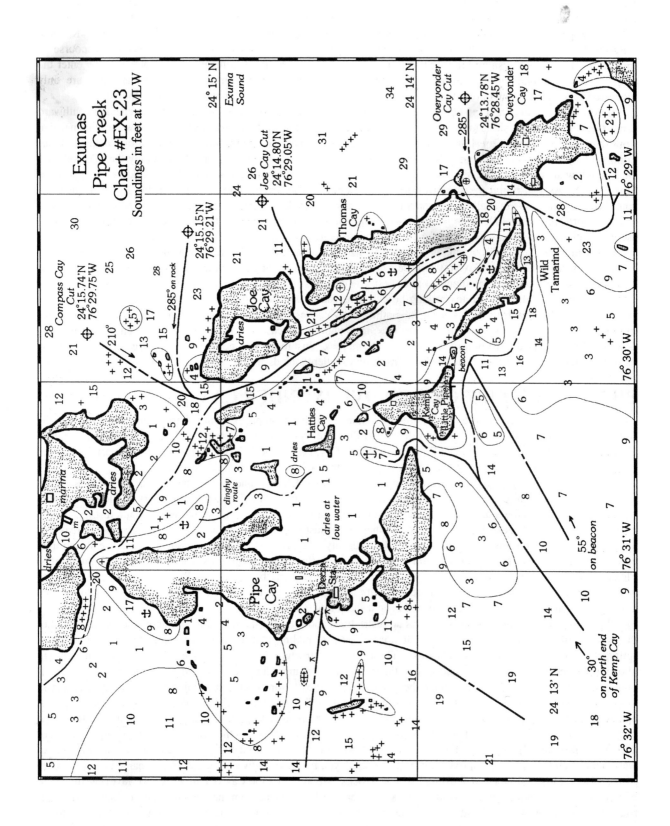

Exumas
Pipe Creek
Chart #EX-23
Soundings in feet at MLW

Once into the cove at the Decca Station there is room for two 40' boats to tie up to the concrete wall with 9' at low water. Anchoring is tricky here as there is little swinging room and the bottom is scoured so it might take a try or two to set your anchor. Ashore you can visit the remains of the station where there is little to see except an old, rundown building, however, just tying up to a wall overnight is a comfort to some. Be very careful when walking in this area as the building and grounds are covered with poisonwood. There are some nice beaches just behind the building to the south and others within dinghy range. A walk up the short hill to the east of the station will give you a nice view of the Pipe Creek area.

Skippers will find a small but calm anchorage just off the southeastern tip of Pipe Cay. To enter from the banks, steer an approximate 30° course on the western tip of Kemp Cay (Little Pipe Cay) until you can pick up the darker water that leads in between the two cays. Keep the shallow sandbar that lies just south of Pipe Cay well to port, the deeper water is to starboard so if you must stray, stray to starboard. As you enter the cut, keep the rocky bar that lies just to the northwest of Kemp Cay to starboard and you will have 9' of water. Once inside you must make a sharp turn to port between Pipe Cay and the small rock lying about 30-40 yards off. There is a small dark channel here that is easily seen and will take you into the narrow anchorage. It is best to do this on a rising tide as there is little margin for error. There is only room for about 4-6 boats in this anchorage and two anchors are necessary. Bonefish fanciers will love the shallow flats off the eastern shore of Pipe Cay.

Pipe Creek itself can be entered from the banks side or the Exuma Sound side from either the north or the south. If entering from the deep water channel that lies on the banks to the west of Compass Cay you must line up the easternmost of the Rocky Dundas on your stern and as you round the southwestern tip of Compass Cay. Vessels with a draft of 6' or less can enter here taking advantage of a rising, almost high, tide. Once over the shallow sandbank you will immediately pick up the deeper water. You can anchor to the north of Pipe Cay in 20' or to the northwest of Pipe Cay in 9-17'. This anchorage requires two anchors as it is narrow and has considerable current. To enter the Pipe Creek area avoid the rocky bar working out northward from Pipe Cay and pass through the cut between Pipe Cay and Compass Cay. At this point there will be a shallow sandbank directly ahead. If you take it to port you may anchor in 8'-17' in a small cul-de-sac. Keeping the sandbank to starboard you may proceed into Pipe Creek. There is a sandbank that lies off the southern shore of Compass Cay that must be kept to port. Steer towards the northern tip of Joe Cay and keep the rock in the center of Compass Cay Cut to port. Once past that rock you may proceed southeastward down the channel leading to Overyonder Cay and Wild Tamarind Cay. There is excellent snorkeling around the group of rocks that you will leave to starboard as you approach Joe Cay.

Skippers wishing to enter the north end of Pipe Creek from Exuma Sound may enter at Compass Cay Cut. There are two ways to enter this cut. First, a GPS waypoint at 24° 15.74' N, 76° 29.75' W will place you approximately ½ nm to the north/northeast of the cut. Take up a heading of 210° on the long beach that lies on the eastern side of Pipe Cay (easily seen from sea) and proceed into the cut keeping the small group of rocks that lie in the center of the cut and the shallow rocky shoal just north of them to port. You will pass over a dark brown bar but it will have 12'-15' of water over it at low water. Pass between the rock that lies well inside the center of the cut (keep it to starboard) and Joe Cay and then proceed down Pipe Creek.

A GPS waypoint at 24° 15.15' N, 76° 29.21' W will place you ½ nm east/southeast of the Compass Cay Cut. Take up a heading of 285° on the rock well inside the center of the cut and head in keeping the scattered heads and rocks off the north shore of Joe Cay to port and the group of rocks in the center of the cut to starboard.

Proceeding southeast along the channel you will pass Joe Cay to port. Joe Cay is almost ½ mile long and has a large salina in its interior that dries at low water. There is good diving along its north shore. The entire eastern and northern shore is rocky and barren with some large white bluffs along its southern shore.

Vessels can enter from Exuma Sound at Joe Cay Cut between Joe Cay and Thomas Cay. A GPS waypoint of 24° 14.80' N, 76° 29.05' W will place you ½ nm to the east/northeast of the cut. Take up a heading of 255° on the very conspicuous house that sits on Hattie's Cay and appears in the center of the cut. The cut is wide and deep with no obstructions. As you pass the northwestern tip of Thomas Cay you must round Thomas Cay to port. Do not attempt to keep heading towards the Pipe Creek channel as there is a large reef system with only 3' over it at low water. You may round Thomas Cay and anchor in its lee in 7'-12' of water. Keep a sharp lookout for the some shallow bars along its western shore with only 3' over them. From here you may pass southward into the Pipe Creek channel but keep an eye out to avoid any bars or rocks and work your way between them. Thomas Cay is approximately ¾ mile long and has a 60' hill.

As you pass southward along Pipe Creek channel, keeping between the Joe Cay, Thomas Cay, and the offlying cays to their west, you will need to close the southern tip of Thomas Cay very closely. There are some rocky ledges that lie southeastward across your route (easily seen with good light) and you must pass between them and Thomas Cay.

The cut between Thomas Cay and Overyonder Cay, although narrow, is straightforward and deep. On the western side of the small cay that lies between Overyonder Cay and Thomas Cay is a large rock that is awash at low tide. This rock is the only obstruction in this cut. A GPS position of 24° 13.78' N, 76° 28.45' W places you approximately ¼ nm to the east/southeast of the cut. Steer toward the center of the cut on a heading of 285° and watch out for strong currents. Once inside the cut you may head northward up Pipe Creek channel, enter the anchorage at Ray Cay, or pass to the south of Wild Tamarind Cay to head out onto the banks.

Overyonder Cay, with its 40' high hill and conspicuous blue house, is private and visits ashore are by invitation only. Besides the deep water cut to its north, vessels drawing 6' or less can pass between Overyonder Cay and Sampson Cay, and enter Exuma Sound in settled conditions. Do not try this cut in moderate to strong onshore conditions. Be wary of the strong current that flows through here at times. From the banks, enter the cut between Overyonder Cay and Sampson Cay favoring the Sampson Cay shore to avoid the rocky bar that is awash off the southwestern shore of Overyonder Cay. Pass the large red mooring buoy (a private mooring, please do not use it) and rock, keeping them to starboard, and enter Exuma Sound with 8' under your keel between Overyonder Cay and the small unnamed cay, actually little more than a large rock, in the center of the cut. This cut is definitely not a recommended passage but it is shown just for your information as quite a few local mariners make use of it. Snorkelers will enjoy the staghorn coral reef that lies to the south and west of the mooring and rock, and the heads off the southeastern shore of Overyonder Cay. Once again, watch out for the strong currents in this area. There is a very pretty beach on the north shore of Sampson Cay just inside the cut.

Wild Tamarind Cay is private and available for rental. See Enid or Pat Farquharson, the caretakers, or call *Little Mouse* on VHF ch. 16 for more information. If you would like an excellent guide to this area of the Exumas, contact Pat, he can assist you with diving and fishing sites. There is a very nice anchorage with 14' in places lying just off the dock on the northeastern side of Wild Tamarind Cay between Wild Tamarind Cay and the four offlying rocks. If you enter the cut between Overyonder and Thomas Cay, steer for the Wild Tamarind Cay shore and hug it as you enter avoiding the 4' bar lying southeast of the offlying rocks. You can also reach this anchorage from the banks. Vessels in the Pipe Cay anchorage may follow the shore of Kemp Cay and Wild Tamarind Cay, giving the southwestern tip of Kemp Cay a wide berth and the southeastern tip of Wild Tamarind Cay the same consideration. If approaching from the banks, take up a heading of 55° on the stone beacon (privately maintained, FL W ev 10 sec.) that lies just south of the large conspicuous house with the white roof on Kemp Cay. The beacon sits on a small rock in the cut between Wild Tamarind Cay and Kemp Cay. You will cross a small 5' deep spot on this route but once in the deeper water (15') you may follow the Wild Tamarind Cay shore around its southeastern tip. The Wild Tamarind Cay anchorage has a rather unusual tidal flow. When your stern is pointing towards the cut between Overyonder Cay and Thomas Cay you naturally think the tide is going out, but the tide is actually coming in. The west side of the Pipe Creek area is affected this way. Kemp Cay, locally called Little Pipe Cay, was named after Moses and Drucilla Kemp who worked nearby Overyonder Cay until 1929. Kemp Cay is private and visits ashore should be by invitation only.

SAMPSON CAY

Although there is no settlement on Sampson Cay (Chart # EX-24), it is one of the most visited cays in the entire Exuma chain, owing this distinction to the Sampson Cay Club and Marina. Once called Little Birnea, the cay was named after Israel Sampson who was granted the cay in 1810. The cay is a series of 50' high hills and small valleys.

The approach to Sampson Cay is very straightforward. As you head southeastward on the banks route, a GPS waypoint at 24° 12.30' N, 76° 30.84' W, places you approximately ¼ nautical mile west of Twin Cays. Once you round the Twin Cays, head eastward paralleling the lie of the rocks on your port side staying at least 150 yards off. There are some small patch reefs just south of the rocks with 7' over them at low water. If you avoid these reefs you will have 9' all the way into the anchorage just off the marina where you will find a minimum depth of 6' at low water. Just south of the entrance to the marina, between Sampson Cay and Dennis Cay, you can anchor off a small cove in 9' of water. Neither of these two anchorages are recommended in the strong westerly prelude to a frontal passage. If approaching from the south on the banks route, a GPS waypoint at 24° 11.05' N, 76° 30.15' W, places you ¼ nm west of Sandy Cay. Once you round Sandy Cay, head northeastward keeping the shallow sandbank that lies to the northeast of Sandy Cay to starboard. Vessels anchored to the west of Big Major's Spot may pass to the west of Fowl Cay, in the channel between the small cays that lie to the west of Fowl Cay and the shallow sandbank that lies further west. This route will accommodate a 6' draft vessel just after low water. Watch out for the stray heads at the entrance to the channel from the anchorage at Big Major's Spot.

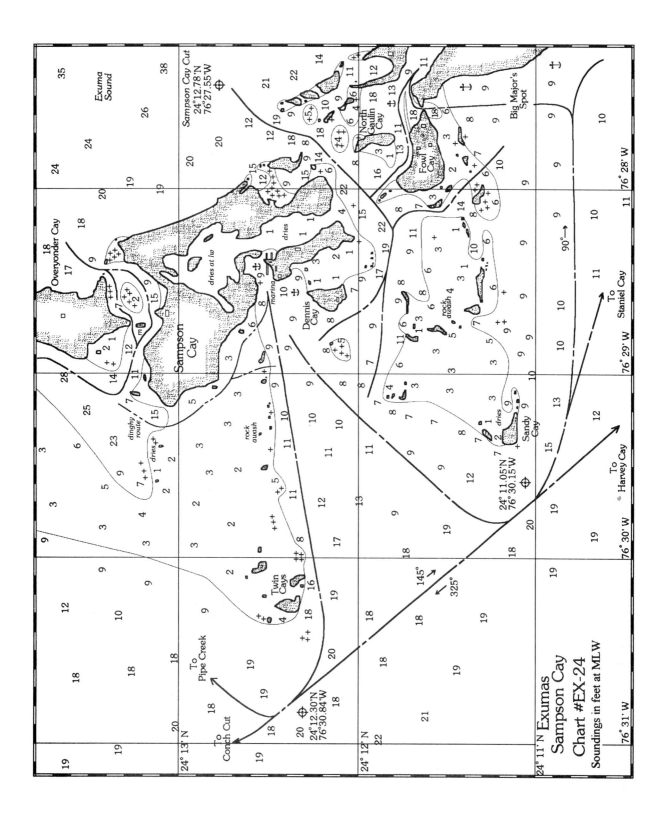

Exuma Sound

Sampson Cay Cut
24°12.78'N
76°27.55'W

Big Major's Spot

North Gaulin Cay

Fowl Cay

Overyonder Cay

dries at lw

marina

Sampson Cay

Dennis Cay

rock awash

90°→

To Staniel Cay

24°11.05'N
76°30.15'W

rock awash

Sandy Cay

dries

To Harvey Cay

dinghy route

rock awash

145°

325°

Twin Cays

To Pipe Creek

Conch Cut

24°12.30'N
76°30.84'W

24° 13' N

24° 12' N

24° 11' N Exumas
Sampson Cay
Chart #EX-24
Soundings in feet at MLW

76° 31' W

76° 30' W

76° 29' W

76° 28' W

Sampson Cay from the ESE.

Entering Sampson Cay Cut from Exuma Sound, a GPS waypoint at 24° 12.78' N, 76° 27.55' W, will place you approximately ¼ nm to the northeast of the cut in 29' of water. Head generally southwest into the cut and follow the darker water rounding the southern tip of Sampson Cay as indicated on Chart # EX-24. From Exuma Sound, you will notice the conspicuous casuarinas above the white beach on the southeastern tip of Sampson Cay.

The interior tidal flats at Sampson Cay dry at low water but are nice for dinghy exploration when the tide is rising. On the southwestern side of the flats is a long beach with a house on its northern end. Please respect the privacy of the owners of the house. In a small inlet just off the southeastern tip of Sampson Cay are some small isolated patch reefs in 9'-12' of water.

Sampson Cay Marina, open Monday through Saturday from 8-12 and 1-5, has slips for vessels with drafts up to 7', either on the outside or at the docks on the back side just up the small creek. This is a very safe place to leave your boat in the Exumas for any length of time. Do not enter the inner harbor in your vessel without first contacting the dockmaster Paul. The marina sells gas, diesel, water, and offers SCUBA tank refills, 110 and 220 volt electricity, and will dispose of garbage from guests at the marina. The small but well stocked store sells ice, spirits, cigarettes, canned goods, soft drinks, frozen meats and vegetables, and when available, fresh vegetables and bread. You can rent small outboards and snorkeling gear at the marina; see the dockmaster Paul. Ashore is the Sampson Cay Club, a nautical restaurant and bar serving breakfast, lunch, and dinner (reservations required) seven days a week. The stone walls and heavy nautical themes on the interior create a special ambiance. The cay even has air-conditioned cottages for rent and will provide transportation to and from the airport on Staniel Cay for guests.

For marine towing, salvage, or general repairs, contact Marcus Mitchell at *Sampson Cay* on or the *M/V Victoria*. Many previous visitors to the area will remember fondly the *M/V Sampson* as Marcus' primary vessel. Well Marcus sold the vessel in late 1996 and now uses the Victoria for salvage operations. Marcus, and his wife Rosie, managers of the marina, can fly guests in and out in Rosie's seaplane as well as offer aerial sightseeing tours of the Exumas. In case of emergency the Mitchells can be relied upon to offer fast, efficient, professional service, and can make arrangements to fly injured individuals to proper medical attention in Nassau. There are plans afoot for some moorings to be installed in the near future, sometime in 1997-1998, so keep your eyes peeled when anchoring off the marina. For information ask Paul at Sampson Cay.

DENNIS CAY

Dennis Cay (Chart # EX-24), approximately 1500' long, lies just to the southwest of Sampson Cay and is private, visits ashore should be by invitation only. The lone house is for rent and you may inquire about it at Sampson Cay Marina. The small group of five rocks that lie just southeast of Dennis Cay and southwest of Sampson Cay are good for snorkeling. Vessels entering or attempting to leave via the cut just south of Sampson Cay can pass to the west of Dennis Cay on either side of the small rock (stay at least 50 yards off the rock) and then pick up the deep water channel that leads to the cut.

FOWL CAY

Fowl Cay (Chart #'s EX-24 & 25) is private and has three residences and a small, private airstrip. Visits ashore should be by invitation only. The southern shore of Fowl Cay is very shallow with some small scattered rocks. The northern and northeastern shores are much deeper.

If entering from Exuma Sound through Samson Cay Cut and heading to the anchorage area between the Majors, pass between North Gaulin Cay and Fowl Cay, favoring the Fowl Cay shore to avoid the huge, shallow sand bar lying west of North Gaulin Cay. Keep away from the shallow sandbar that arcs out between Fowl Cay and Big Major's Spot. You will have no less than 9' of water through this route (see more on this anchorage in the section: *Little Major's Spot and Big Rock Cut*). There is excellent snorkeling around the heads that lie off the two small, unnamed cays that lie just to the northeast of North Gaulin Cay. North Gaulin Cay was once called Golden Cay and on it are the remains of an old sisal field.

BIG MAJOR'S SPOT

Big Major's Spot (Chart #'s EX-24 & 25) is a very popular anchorage in prevailing winds however it can be very uncomfortable and is not recommended in the westerly prelude to a frontal passage. Big Major's Spot is approximately one mile long and has a huge salt pond in its interior that was once worked by the people of Staniel Cay. The whole island is a series of steep hills and valleys. The western shore is primarily beaches while the eastern shore is mostly rocky and undercut from tidal action. On the long beach on the western shore you will see a sign concerning the "wild pigs" on the island. The pigs were placed there by a couple of Staniel Cay residents and were never really wild. It is fine to leave some food on the beach for them, some bread or lettuce, but no meat. Take care if approaching them. The pigs have been known to swim out a short distance to greet incoming dinghies.

Vessels wishing to enter the anchorage on the west side of Big Major's Spot may do so from five different directions. From the south, as you round Harvey Cay (24° 09.15' N, 76 °29.44' W) make a beeline for the west side of Big Major's Spot with good water all the way. If you are approaching from Staniel Cay, keep clear of the sandbar that lies south of Big Major's Spot until you can round its southwestern tip within 150 yards. If approaching from the north on the banks route, once you clear Sandy Cay (24° 11.05' N, 76° 30.15' W) turn to the east and head straight for the long beach keeping at least 200 yards off the rocks lying to your port side. Vessels entering from the cut south of Sampson Cay or from Sampson Cay itself have two different routes to take. The easiest is to pass to the west of Fowl Cay, between Fowl Cay and the sandbank to its west. Then, keeping the sandbank to starboard, pass the small unnamed cay to the west of Fowl Cay to port. As you round southern edge you will need to keep the small cay to its south with its small patch reef on your starboard side.

The trickiest entry is through the narrow cut between Fowl Cay and Big Major's Spot. This is a handy route for vessels riding out a front between the Major's who then want to return to the west side of Big Major's Spot after the winds have turned more into the north or northeast. It eliminates the need to go south past Big Rock Cut and its breakers to enter the Staniel Cay area and then work your way around the south end of Big Major's Spot. There is a very strong current in this cut and it should only be attempted with good visibility and at slack tide. From Little Major's Spot or Sampson Cay Cut approach the cut between Big Major's and Fowl Cay keeping an eye out for the sandbar that arcs out from Fowl Cay. At the eastern end of this sandbar there is a deep but narrow gap between the sandbar and Big Major's Spot. Enter the gap and you will be between the arcing sandbar to starboard and a sandbar that lies just off the north side of Big Major's Spot on your port side. You will be in 12'-18' of water between two sandbars at this point. Follow the curve of the deep water around until you can line up and pass through the cut. Wide multihulls should check the width of this cut first by dinghy before attempting to run it. Once inside, head to any spot you choose to drop your hook.

LITTLE MAJOR'S SPOT AND BIG ROCK CUT

Little Major's Spot (Chart # EX-25), approximately ½ mile long and ¼ mile wide, lies just to the east of Big Major's Spot on the edge of Exuma Sound. On its northern and southern end are high cliffs that rise to about 30'. There are a few small beaches on its western shore and one small beach on its eastern side. To the north of Little Major's Spot and just south of Sampson Cay you will see some large white rocks. This surreal, almost lunar, landscape was bleached white by the elements and is a must for exploring by dinghy in settled weather. Vessels paralleling the eastern shore of Little Major's Spot in Exuma Sound must keep a sharp lookout for the rocky bar with 7' over it that lies 250 yard to the east of Little Major's Spot.

Big Rock Cut is deep and has a tremendous current flowing through it. A surveyor in the 1920's said that the current ". . . pours through like a mill race and the average seaman cannot scull his boat against it." A GPS waypoint at 24° 11.66' N, 76° 26.38' W places you approximately ½ nm to the northeast of the cut in 50' of water. To enter the cut, head southwest and favor the northern half of the cut. There are some rocks in the center of the cut with only 8' over them at low water. Once through the cut you may head north to enter the anchorage between the Major's. Head in and keep the large rocky bar that is awash and breaking (very conspicuous) lying off the southwestern tip of Little Major's Spot well to starboard. Once past it turn to the north-northwest and parallel the Big Major's Spot shore and pick out a place to anchor. Do not anchor at the north end between the Major's. There is a white coral reef (5' over it) that is very difficult to make out and many people have hit it not knowing it was there. There is a private mooring here but please do not pick it up. A nice spot to anchor is in the bight at the southeastern tip of Big Major's Spot off the beach in 13' of water. Just follow the eastern shore of Big Major's Spot south until you find the place you wish to drop your hook. You can also enter this anchorage if heading north from Staniel Cay. Once you pass the southeastern tip of Big Major's Spot to port, pass between it and Crown of Thorns Rock and you will have 7' at low tide over a rocky bottom. The Crown of Thorns rock is the small but very dangerous rock in the middle of the channel between Big Major's Spot and Staniel Cay. It is best to try this route at slack tide because if you are not careful the current can push you onto the shallow area of the rocky bar with only 5' over it.

Vessels wishing to head south from Big Rock Cut to Staniel Cay will have deep water all the way with only one 8' spot over a rocky bar just before the Crown of Thorns Rock which must be kept to starboard. Watch out for the current here. Just past the rock, the current will let up slightly and you will enter the anchorage behind Thunderball Cave. If you proceed further south you will come to the Staniel Cay Yacht Club and the anchorage off Staniel Cay.

STANIEL CAY

Staniel Cay (Chart # EX-25), once known as Stanyard or Staniard Cay and corrupted to Staniel Cay, is one of the most visited cays in the Exumas. With two marinas (the Staniel Cay Yacht Club and Happy People Marina), three stores (the Pink Store, the Blue Store, and Isles General Store), two restaurants (SCYC and the Royal Entertainer), and three bars.(Thunderball's, SCYC, and the Royal Entertainer), some folks love this area so much that they make the Staniel Cay area their base for the season. Staniel Cay is actually two cays separated by a mangrove creek that is up to 100' wide in places. The cay is approximately 1½ miles long and about ½ mile wide. There is a 15 acre salt pond at the north end of the cay.

Vessels entering from Exuma Sound should follow the directions in the *section Little Major's Spot And Big Rock Cut* for entering the Staniel Cay area. As you enter the anchorage just below *Club Thunderball* you will notice five moorings between Thunderball Cave and the southern shore of Big Major's Spot. These moorings are for rent for $10 per night. The mooring in the center of the anchorage is for vessels to 200' and rates are available upon request, call Club Thunderball on VHF ch. 16. These moorings are installed by *STM (Sleep Tight Moorings)* and use the same mooring systems as are in place at the northern anchorage at Warderick Wells in Exuma Park. For more information call *Club Thunderball* on VHF ch. 16. If a mooring is vacant go ahead and pick it up and visit *Club Thunderball* after you have settled in to pay your bill. More moorings are slated for installation to the east of Thunderball Cave just below Club Thunderball.

Once past the anchorage to the east of Thunderball Cave, head southward paralleling the shore and you will approach the Staniel Cay Yacht Club on your port side. There is a good anchorage just south of the SCYC for 4-5 boats in a bight just south of SCYC. Pass between the SCYC and the shallow rocky bar that lies to its west and anchor in 5'-8'. Head west of the SCYC in the darker water and you will find plenty of room to anchor just west of the SCYC in 5'-20' over a sandy (lighter water) or grassy (darker water) bottom. Vessels wishing to tie up at the SCYC must approach it from the north to avoid the long rocky bar that lies to its west. Be advised that there is quite a lot of current in this area, it can push the inattentive skipper onto the bar if you try to pass it abeam too closely.

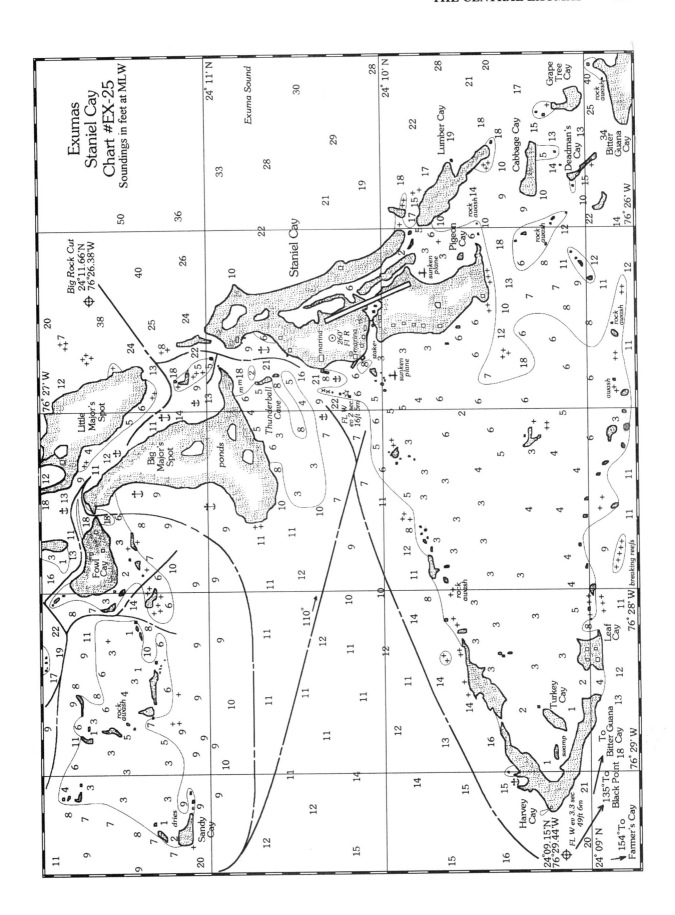

Exumas
Staniel Cay
Chart #EX-25
Soundings in feet at MLW

Photo courtesy of Nicolas Popov/Island Expeditions

Staniel Cay Yacht Club.

Vessels traveling south on the banks route may turn towards Staniel Cay as soon as they pass Sandy Cay. A GPS waypoint at 24° 11.05' N, 76° 30.15' W will place you ¼ nm to the west of Sandy Cay. Once you have rounded Sandy Cay, take up a course of 110° on the northern end of the very conspicuous 50' hill on Lumber Cay that appears just south of the Batelco Tower on Staniel Cay. On this course you will clear the large sandbank that lies just south of Big Major's Spot. As you head in, you will soon pick up the small rock that lies just west of Happy People Marina. On this rock sits a light (FL W ev 2 sec 16 ft 5 m) and a pole with a large "X" that looks like a railroad crossing sign. The proper course is to line up with the cross on a 109° heading, but from Sandy Cay it is hard to distinguish the cross from the background, even with binoculars. Taking up the 110° course on the hill will bring you safely in until you can pick up the "X" by eye and pilot your way in. The light on this rock may or may not be working when you pass through Staniel Cay.

Vessels heading north on the banks from Farmer's Cay or the Mailboat Route should round Harvey Cay and approach Staniel Cay on a 85° heading on the Batelco Tower. On this course you will have a minimum of 7' at mean low water. A GPS waypoint at 24° 09.15' N, 76° 29.44' W will place you ¼ nm west of Harvey Cay. The Staniel Cay Yacht Club and Marina has slips with 110v and 220v, a 7.5' depth, gas, diesel, and is the home of the Staniel Cay Yacht Club, a nautically flavored bar and restaurant with pool tables and satellite TV. The SCYC has long been the meeting place for cruisers with breakfast, lunch, and dinner with reservations. Happy People Marina has slips with electricity but no fuel. Happy People boasts The Royal Entertainer Lounge where owner Kenneth Rolle's wife, Theazil, is famous for her *Theazil Burgers*. Theazil offers breakfast, lunch, and dinner with advance notice. Hugh Smith's Pink Store and Burke Smith's Blue Store are just up the road from Happy People Marina. Just below the Batelco Tower is St. Luke's Clinic (which operates solely on your donations), a school, and a post office. St. Luke's Clinic is run by an American RN, Mary Lou Fadden. Mary Lou desperately needs any type of medical supplies you can donate, especially bandages and hydrogen peroxide. Club Thunderball, the large pink building on the hill overlooking Thunderball Cave, has two dinghy docks, one with moorings to tie your stern to, bar (serving delicious burgers and other delights), pool tables, and plenty of room for dancers.

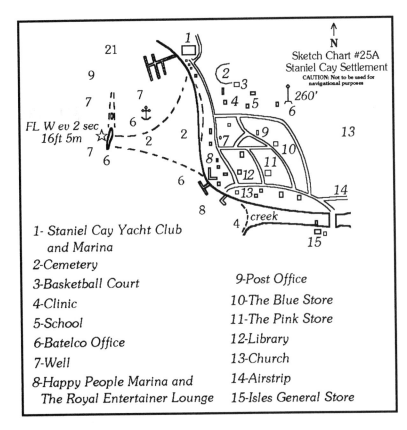

Sketch Chart #25A
Staniel Cay Settlement
CAUTION: Not to be used for navigational purposes

FL W ev 2 sec
16ft 5m

1- Staniel Cay Yacht Club
   and Marina
2-Cemetery
3-Basketball Court
4-Clinic
5-School
6-Batelco Office
7-Well
8-Happy People Marina and
   The Royal Entertainer Lounge

9-Post Office
10-The Blue Store
11-The Pink Store
12-Library
13-Church
14-Airstrip
15-Isles General Store

Photo courtesy of Nicolas Popov/Island Expeditions

Aerial view of Happy People Marina and the entrance to Staniel Cay Creek from the south.

Just past Happy People Marina and the Town Dock is the entrance to Staniel Cay Creek. Although the Staniel Cay area is known for its bonefish and its annual summer bonefishing tournament, this creek is a bonefish nursery and no fishing is allowed. About 100 yards up the creek you will see a concrete jetty on the south side. Tie up here and visit Vivian Rolle at her Isles General Store for groceries, gifts, marine supplies, propane, fresh baked bread to order, and ice cream. The gazebo on the waterfront is an excellent place to sit and enjoy a pint of Vivian's ice cream. Just past Isles General Store is the 3000' long airstrip where you can pick up guests arriving on Island Express Airlines. Charter flights can be arranged through the SCYC or Isles General Store.

As you dinghy along the very shallow creek, just past Happy People Marina on the north side of the creek you will see some sheds with a few Bahamian sloops of various sizes. If you are lucky you will see the *Lady Muriel*, the Staniel Cay entry and winner of the 1993 and 1994 Family Islands Regatta. You may also spy some other sloops such as the famous *Tida Wave* or *Sea Hound*, both former champions. Captain Rollie Gray, owner and skipper of the *Tida Wave*, once hosted H.R.H. Prince Philip aboard his vessel for a sail, the tiller of that sloop now presides at the bar in The Royal Entertainer Lounge. Staniel Cay itself hosts a very popular New Years Day Regatta where everyone wins a prize. The people of Staniel Cay are some of the best sailors in The Bahamas and have the trophies to prove it.

The highlight of the area for snorkelers is the famous *Thunderball Cave*, site of movies such as *Thunderball* and *Splash*. The cave is at the northern end of the longest of three cays that stretch from the southern shore of Big Major's Spot to just above the SCYC. There are two dinghy moorings off the western entrance to which you can tie to begin your exploration. The best time to dive the cave is at slack tide as there is a strong current through here. Carry a small bag of bread crumbs to feed the schools of small fish that will curiously accost you. The interior of the cave is like a small grotto with a large opening at the top where the sun shines through creating a dazzling effect in the water.

Photo courtesy of Nicolas Popov/Island Expeditions

Rebuilding the Lady Muriel.

For a good and reliable guide to the area, try Capt. Wade Nixon or Kenneth Rolle at the Happy People Marina, Burke Smith at the Blue Store, or Hugh Smith at the Pink Store.

Directly across from Happy People Marina sits a small scrub covered rock. Southwest of this rock about 100 yards is a sunken airplane with no tail section. It is almost awash at low water. There is another sunken plane just off the end of the runway south of Staniel Cay.

Lumber Cay, just southeast of Staniel Cay is ½ mile long and about 600' across with a very conspicuous 50' high ridge running along most of its length. Sisal was once farmed on Lumber Cay and nearby Cabbage Cay. Grape Tree Cay, just southeast of Lumber Cay is a rookery so please do not disturb any birds you may see nesting there.

HARVEY CAY

Harvey Cay (Chart # EX-25) is the site of Harvey Cay Light (FL W ev 2½ sec 49 ft 6 m). Once called Harbour or Harvest cay, its name has changed over the years to Harvey Cay. The automated light was once kept in operation by two light keepers. The area to the east of Harvey Cay stretching towards Staniel Cay is very shallow and the flats just to the east of Harvey cay make for excellent bonefishing. A small cay known as Turkey Cay, shown as a separate cay on all charts, is actually connected to Harvey Cay by a thick mangrove swamp that is rapidly silting in. Turkey Cay, once a sisal farm, will probably become part of Harvey Cay in the near future. There is a small anchorage in a bight on the northern side of Harvey Cay that is good in prevailing winds although surge does work its way around the tip of Harvey Cay and makes it uncomfortable in anything above light winds. A GPS waypoint at 24° 09.15' N, 76° 29.44' W will place you ¼ nm west of Harvey Cay.

BITTER GUANA CAY

Bitter Guana Cay (Chart # EX-26), is 1½ miles long and was named after the iguana population that once inhabited the cay. It was once three cays but the cuts have filled in forming one cay. At the southwest end, and to a lesser extent along the northern shore, are some blow holes which are the mouths of small submarine caverns. As the waves roll in the water is forced through the holes and sprays all over the nearby vicinity. It has two very conspicuous white cliffs at each end. Vessels may round Harvey Cay and proceed eastward and parallel the shore of the cays stretching towards Bitter Guana Cay in 8'-12' of water. There is a channel of deep water from the cut to the north of Bitter Guana Cay leading south-southwest. On the eastern side of this channel is a brown bar with 4'-5' over it at low water. Pass around the northern tip of this bar in 12' between the bar and the northern tip of Bitter Guana Cay. Anchor in 6'-9' off the long white beach in calm to light E-SE winds. There may be a little surge when the tide changes. The bodies of many Haitians are buried in a mass grave on Bitter Guana Cay. They died in a shipwreck just off the cay and were buried there by the people of Black Point.

GAULIN CAY

Gaulin Cay (Chart # EX-26), sometimes called Golden Cay, is named after the yellow crested night herons known as "gaul" and which some scientists write as "golden." The eastern shore is a series of cliffs 20'-50' high while the western shore has all the beaches. There are some caves along the northwestern shore. There can be a strong tidal flow between Gaulin Cay and Great Guana Cay of over 3 knots at times. It is thought there is a colony of iguanas on the cay but few people have claimed to see them. It is possible to anchor off the long white beach on the western shore but the anchorage is shallow and subject to tidal current and surge.

GREAT GUANA CAY AND DOTHAM CUT

Great Guana Cay (Chart #'s EX-26 and 27), almost 12 miles long, is the longest cay, with the exception of Great Exuma, in the Exuma chain. The only settlement is picturesque Black Point with its coconut palms and casaurinas, the largest and most traditional settlement in the northern and central Exumas. The residents rely on farming, fishing, and plaiting for their living. The men of Black Point are known for their fishing prowess. At the north end of Great Guana Cay is Dotham Cut, a major thoroughfare from the banks to Exuma Sound.

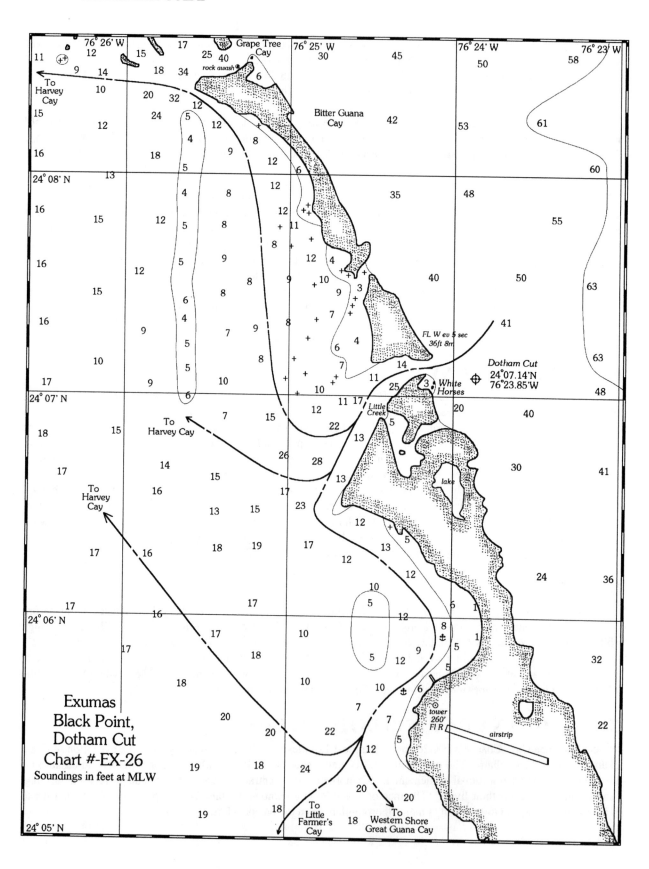

Exumas
Black Point,
Dotham Cut
Chart #-EX-26
Soundings in feet at MLW

Southbound vessels on the banks wishing to enter Exuma Sound at Dotham Cut may round Harvey Cay and head for Dotham Point. Avoid the shallow bar that lies to the west of Bitter Guana Cay until it is possible to round up into the deeper water of the cut. Vessels heading north on the banks may follow the shore past Black Point to enter the cut.

For those boaters on Exuma Sound wishing to visit Black Point or gain access to the banks, a GPS waypoint at 24° 07.14' N, 76° 23.85' W will put you in approximately 50' of water ¼ nm east of the cut which is very straightforward and deep. Dotham Cut Light (FL W ev 5 sec, 36 ft, 8 m) lies on the southeastern tip of Gaulin Cay. If you wish to head northward and cruise the shore of Bitter Guana Cay, follow the deeper water eastward inside Dotham Cut and, once clear of the shallow bar that works southwestward of Gaulin Cay, turn towards the shoreline of Gaulin and Bitter Guana. Vessels entering the cut and bound for Black Point should follow the northern shoreline of Great Guana Cay past Dotham Point to enter the anchorage off Black Point. Just south of Dotham Cut at the north end of Great Guana Cay lies the entrance to a shallow tidal creek whose interior is now a large mangrove swash. Dr. Evans Cottman, in his book *Out Island Doctor*, tells how he rode out a gale in this creek. One or two small vessels could anchor in the mouth of this creek in 5'-12' at low water. The creek is open to the west and northwest and two anchors are necessary due to the strength of the current. Vessels may anchor anywhere off the town dock at Black Point or the in the small cove to its east in 6'-12' of water.

The town of Black Point, the largest in the northern and central Exumas, has a 100' Batelco tower with a phone office by its base. There is a clinic with a nurse just across from the school which sits just southwest of the town dock. Lorene's Cafe is the spot for Bahamian fare and fresh baked bread. The Scorpio Inn is "THE" meeting spot in Black Point with its bar, Bahamian cuisine, and pool table. Adderly's Store, where the sign proclaims "Welcome to Adderly's Store-A Smile Awaits You," is run by the local constable. For guides to the area ask for Willie Rolle or Walter Robinson.

Off the eastern shore of Great Guana Cay, some 600' south of Black Point, are some white cliffs, 50' high and 600' long. Just south of Dotham Cut are some small rocks called the White Horses. Dr. Evans Cottman described them as appearing like three white horses rising up out of the crashing waves.

The western shore of Great Guana has some beautiful beaches and the rocky shore is pockmarked with caves awaiting your exploration. You can anchor almost anywhere off the western shore in northeast to southeast winds however a little surge works its way around the points in all but the lightest winds. Just south of Black Point, past Little Bay, are two pretty white beaches. There are some ruins of an old limestone house at the north end of the second beach. If walking ashore lookout for machineel which grows in abundance on Great Guana Cay. There are some nice heads for diving in the Little Bay area.

South of the two beaches along the rocky shore at Thatch Hill, the shoreline will reveal two conspicuous caves, one 6' above high water, and another whose mouth is at water level and is 12' wide and 6' high. The area around Thatch Hill is honeycombed with cave holes. The rocky shoreline does not seem as sharp and jagged as those further north, the rocks seem more rounded with small vertical grooves worn in them. There are plenty of heads in the waters awaiting your snorkeling expeditions.

In prevailing winds you can anchor off the long white beach just north of White Point but take care in setting your anchor as the bottom is rocky. There is good shelling on the beach and in the waters just off it. There is another long, curving beach just south of White Point where you may anchor in north-northeast winds. There are more caves just south of White Point at Hetty's Land and at the Crossing. Just south of White Point and west of Hetty's Land are some scattered patch reefs and heads approximately 200 yards offshore with 3' over them at low water. Do not try to cruise close along the western shore of Great Guana Cay from here southward in the early morning light as the sun will be right in your eyes. Without good light you will be unable to discern the black patches until you keel has picked them out for you.

The Crossing is a delightful little cove with some old caves in the vicinity and Exuma Sound just a short walk over the hills to the east. If you proceed south to enter the Little Farmer's Cay area from Oven Rock, beware of the shallow rocky bar that works out from the shore just below Kemp's Bay Bluff. There is a shallow bar with 5' over it at low water just to the west of Kemp's Bay. Oven Rock, the large conical rock that resembles a Bahamian stone oven lying off the southeastern shore of Great Guana Cay, bears 118° from this rocky bar. If you climb the hill that lies behind Oven Rock and walk down the back side, you will come to the opening of a large cave. This tremendous cavern descends some 90' and has two large freshwater pools at the bottom that make for a good tank dive. The pools go down about 70' and one branches out over 700'. Martin Rolle on Little Farmer's Cay is the best guide for this cave. He lives in the green house just past the town dock on Little Farmer's Cay.

Snorkelers will find some nice rocks and heads to dive on off the southeastern tip of Great Guana Cay around the large conical rock just offshore.

22   10   7   6
         ‡
              5   Black Point   30   48   63   **Exumas
12   Guana Cay
19   Chart #EX-27**
      23   45   Soundings in feet at MLW
                  Little   24° 05' N
        21   Bay   + +   +   22   10 fathoms
              20   12   ‡ 6   60
18   +   14   18   45
              18   12   +   24° 04' N
        19   12   +   caves   28
    To   Thatch   o oo   15   48
    Harvey Cay   Hill   10   +++   6   12   24   24° 04' N
                      13   + 6   6   Great Guana Cay
         18   12   Jack's   36
    18   Bay   6
                  Cove   10   6
                               10   24
         18   18   11 Jack's 10   24° 03' N
    13   Bay   12
                      11   10
                          11   ⊕   44
18   18   18   12   ‡ 5   18   37
              White Point ⊕ +
                      18   8
    13   18   + + Hetty's 13   33
18   18   Land
                          +   6+ 12   40
         13   18   ⊕   ‡ 11
                      15   ⊕ 8   18
                                   +   +   The   18   22
                          + 12   11   +   Crossing   24° 01' N
18   18   13   10   10   36
                          8   12
    18   18   13   Isaac Bay ‡ 12
                  13   10   13   23   33
                                        12   Bluff 14   24° 00' N
                  13   + + 4   Field
                      + 8 +   + 4   Bluff   15
              10   10   10   10   4
                               9   Bay   12
                                   Rush 4
                                   Bay   14
23° 59' N
                      10   10   8   ‡
9   9   9   9   10   8 Oven
                                        Rock
                               9   8 5
                          9   To   6   7
                               Little Farmer's   5
23° 58' N   9   Cay   6 7   5 5
76° 25' W   76° 24' W   76° 23' W   76° 22' W   76° 21' W 76° 20' W

LITTLE FARMER'S CAY AND FARMER'S CAY CUT

Little Farmer's Cay (Chart # EX-28), is one of those priceless little communities that one hopes to find in The Bahamas. It is said that there are 365 cays in the Exumas and the residents of Little Farmer's Cay say of those 365, pick one. It would be difficult not to choose this small but beautiful cay. The population of 55 are typical Exumians, very warm, open, and friendly. Little Farmer's Cay is approximately ¾ mile long and has a 2000' foot airstrip, marina, stores, restaurants, and a mangrove creek behind the marina at Big Harbour. The cay was first settled during the Loyalist period by two brothers, John and Anthony Smith who married two young ladies from Musha Cay, Christiana and Merciana Smith. John Smith discovered the Farmer's Cay area one day while exploring by boat from his home on Musha Cay. Liking the area, he and his brother moved their families here and the rest is history. At the turn of the 20th century some fruit was grown on the cay but the hurricane of 1926 destroyed all the trees although a few coconut palms still stand. There is a 260' tall Batelco tower on Little Farmer's Cay with a flashing red light at the top and a fixed red light at its mid-point.

Photo courtesy of Terry Bain

The Ocean Cabin Club on Little Farmer's Cay; a "must see" if you're in the area.

For vessels wishing to enter the Little Farmer's Cay area from Exuma Sound, a GPS waypoint at 23°57.95' N, 76° 18.32' W, places you ¼ nm east of Farmer's Cay Cut. Enter the cut between the northern tip of Big Farmer's Cay and the large rock in the center of the cut between Big Farmer's Cay and Great Guana Cay, watch out for the currents in this area. There is a deep hole to 70' just at the entrance to the cut and it probably adds to the seas that build in this cut. Do not pass between Great Guana Cay and the small cay in the center of the cut as there is a rocky bar with 6' over it in places. Once inside the cut you must watch out for the very visible shallow sandbank that lies slightly to port. You may pass this on your starboard side to enter a nice anchorage off the beach on the northern shore of Big Farmer's Cay while taking the sandbank to port will bring you into the Little Farmer's Cay area. Spelunkers will want to check out the caves on the northwestern tip of Big Farmer's Cay.

Vessels entering from the banks route have five choices and all require a sharp lookout and a little proficiency in the art of eyeball navigation. If you are approaching from the shore of Great Guana Cay, pass Oven Rock, the conical shaped rock that resembles a Bahamian stone oven, about 100-150 yards to its west and take up a course for the airstrip on Little Farmer's Cay. Steering approximately just west of south, keep between the shallow bar on the western shore of Great Guana Cay and the shallow bar to the west of Oven Rock. This route is good for 5' at low water.

Approaching from Harvey Cay, take up a course of 150° to a point approximately ½ nm west of Little Farmer's Cay. When just northwest of Little Farmer's Cay you may take up a course of 75° on the valley between the two small hills on Great Guana Cay that appear just north of Little Farmer's Cay. Follow this route around the northern tip of the cay keeping between the shallow sandbank to the west of Oven Rock and the shallows just off the beach on the northwestern shore of Little Farmer's Cay. This is a viable shortcut to the anchorages in the Farmer's Cay area for vessels with 5' draft at low water. The course of 75° is not as important here as is watching the water and staying in the channel.

A GPS waypoint 23° 57.40' N, 76° 20.90' W places your vessel about ½ nm to the west of the cay. From this point you may take up a course of 90° on the white house (Terry Bain's house) on Dabba Hill near the south end of the cay, you cannot mistake this house. Follow the route in and as you close the shore keep off approximately 30 yards in 7'-9' of water. Pass between Little Farmer's Cay and the large shallow bank that lies just to the southwest of the cay. As you round the southern tip of Little Farmer's Cay, steer wide of the rocky bar at the southeastern tip and bear approximately northward toward the anchorages off the harbors or proceed eastward between Big Farmer's Cay and the sandbank off its north shore to anchor in the small cove described earlier. This route is good for 5' at low water.

Vessels with deeper draft may proceed southward on the banks route a little more passing a 6' spot at low water. When you can line up the white roof of the small house on Big Farmer's Cay on a 74° course, head in on that bearing until you can round up in to the Little Farmer' Cay area. This route is direct and deep with at least 6' at low water all the way in. This route is the easiest in terms of pilotage as well as being deep.

Further south is a route that some recommend as the best. On the banks route, pass Little Farmer's Cay until you can line up the southeastern tip of Little Farmer's Cay on a 22° heading and follow that in with 6'-7' all the way. This route entails a little extra mileage (not much) but there are no shallows between this route and the route which calls for a 74° heading on the house.

Whichever route you choose you may anchor in the deep water just off Big Harbour (the large cove on the northeastern shore of Little Farmer's Cay) in 10'-20', or off the southeastern cove on Little Farmer's Cay. If you approach Big Harbour from the south, pass between the rocky bar off the eastern shore of Little Farmer's Cay and the rocky bar on the southwestern tip of Great Guana Cay. A very popular anchorage lies off the southwestern shore of Great Guana Cay. The narrow entrance is between the rocky bar off the southwestern tip of Great Guana Cay and the shallow sandbank between Great Guana Cay and Little Farmer's Cay. Pass between the bar and bank in 7' at low water and take care that the current does not push you either onto the bank or the bar. Once inside you will find a narrow anchorage which thins at its northern end. Once again, two anchors is a must here due to the tidal flow.

If you are having trouble negotiating the entrances, call Terry Bain at *Ocean Cabin* or Roosevelt Nixon at *Farmer's Cay Yacht Club* for information on VHF ch.16, they will be happy to assist you.

Little Farmer's Cay has the last fuel before Barretarre for boats heading south. At the northern tip of Big Harbour be sure to stop in at the Farmer's Cay Yacht Club and Marina where manager Roosevelt Christopher Nixon will ably assist you. He is open seven days a week and offers diesel, gas, oil, water, ice, laundry service, showers, 110v and 220v electricity, garbage disposal, and can accommodate 4-6 boats with 8' at low water. He also has four moorings in the harbor for $10.00 per night. Inside the marina building you will find a delightful restaurant and bar with satellite TV serving Bahamian cuisine for breakfast, lunch, and dinner, reservations requested. Roosevelt also has double occupancy rooms available and takes credit cards. Roosevelt is planning to open a laundromat and small grocery store on the premises by 1995. At this time the only marine supplies he carries are a few fuel filters and belts. There is a Batelco phone booth on site.

Farther south is another smaller cove called Little Harbour where you may tie up to the town dock. If you put your dinghy on the beach allow for the tidal fall. Just past the town dock you will find a small green and white house where Hallan Rolle lives. Hallan and his two sons, Martin and Stanley, can be called on as excellent guides to this area. Spelunkers will want Martin to take them to Great Guana Cay and the cave previously mentioned that descends to 90'. Hallan and Stanley are regarded as excellent guides for diving and fishing. Hallan can also supply you with propane, call *Little Jeff* on VHF ch. 16, Hallan's wife, Mavis, also runs a small grocery store. Mavis' father, J.L. Maycock, built the famous Bahamian sloop *Brothers* on Little Farmer's Cay.

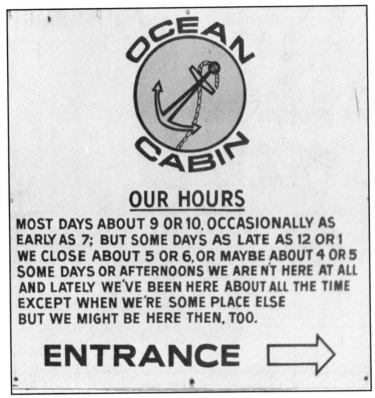

OUR HOURS

MOST DAYS ABOUT 9 OR 10, OCCASIONALLY AS
EARLY AS 7; BUT SOME DAYS AS LATE AS 12 OR 1
WE CLOSE ABOUT 5 OR 6, OR MAYBE ABOUT 4 OR 5
SOME DAYS OR AFTERNOONS WE ARE N'T HERE AT ALL
AND LATELY WE'VE BEEN HERE ABOUT ALL THE TIME
EXCEPT WHEN WE'RE SOME PLACE ELSE
BUT WE MIGHT BE HERE THEN, TOO.

ENTRANCE

Photo courtesy of Terry Bain

Sign showing the hours of the Ocean Cabin on Little Farmer's Cay.

Just up from the town dock you will find Duke and Eugenia Percentie's Little Harbour Super Market. They have a good selection of canned goods, drinks, meat, cheese, eggs, and vegetables when available. Eugenia is known as quite a cook and also runs the small liquor store in back of the grocery store where she can serve you up a cold beer upon request. If you take a left up the path just before the grocery store, a short walk up the hill will bring you to a pink house with a huge wooden carving in front. Here you will find JR, the local woodcarver who has quite a talent and is willing to deal with you on prices.

As you proceed up the hill past the Little Harbour Super Market you will find Corene's Post Office and Grocery Store in the small green building on your left. If the store or Post Office is not open check across the path at the Ocean Cabin.

Ocean Cabin is run by Terry Bain and his wife Earnestine and was originally built in 1969 by Captain Henry Moxey, Terry's grandfather. Capt. Moxey was widely known throughout The Bahamas as an excellent pilot, sailing the world over on all manner of sailing ships. The restaurant and bar is a "do not miss" attraction in the Exumas. Terry and Earnestine serve cold drinks, American and Bahamian fare, ice cream, and they also have a library of paperback books for trade. Terry is quite the world traveler and philosopher and it is easy to spend hours engrossed in conversation with him. Ask him to show you his Mediterranean toilet.

Terry and Ocean Cabin put on the annual 5F (Farmer's Cay First Friday in February Festival) party. First begun in 1986, the festival has gained quite a reputation as the place to be in February when the harbors around Little Farmer's Cay are brimming over with boaters. The Festival features three legged races, sailboat races, raffles, food, drink, a chicken run (ask Terry), donkey dancing, men and women's best legs contest, and a wet T-shirt contest. Your cruise through the Exumas will be lacking if you miss this party.

Just over the hill from Ocean Cabin is the Batelco tower and phone office. To its left is the clinic run by Roosevelt Nixon's wife Boleyn.

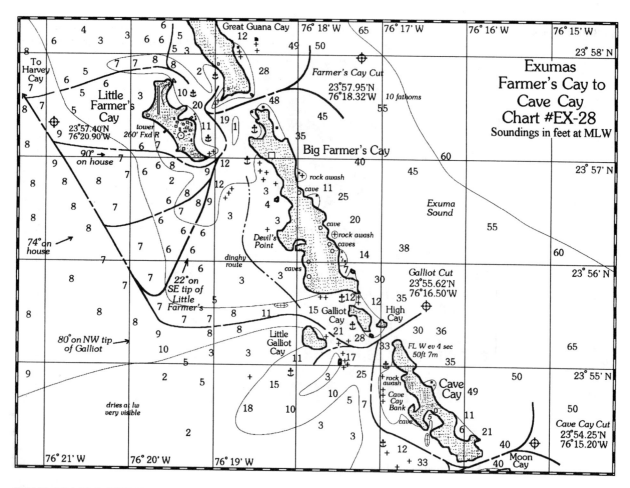

BIG FARMER'S CAY

Big Farmer's Cay (Chart # EX-28), once called Wilshire or Wilthshire's Cay and often called just Farmer's Cay, is approximately 2½ miles long. The island's only inhabitants are some goats that Terry Bain from Little Farmer's Cay placed on the island.

It's eastern shore is pockmarked with small caves and beaches and is very deep. Off the southeastern tip on the Sound side is a small cove with a curving beach. This is a nice day anchorage in calm or westerly weather. The curving beach is covered with all manner of flotsam and jetsam for your investigation. The cove will take 7' at low water but watch out for some rocky ledges as you enter.

The western shore is shallow and only shoal draft vessels (less than 4') and small outboards may run its shore at high water. About ¾ of a mile south of the northwestern tip lies a large rock about 12'-15' high just offshore with a small cave on its southern side. Close to the southern end, just south of Devil's Point, lies a small cove with a creek that leads to a large mangrove marsh.

Just off the southwestern tip of the cay, at the edge of bank alongside the deep water channel from the banks route to Galliot Cut, lies the wreck of the *Drake*, an old Bahamian mailboat. The Drake was making for George Town in Exuma Sound when she began taking on water. In order to save the passengers, the crew brought her in the cut and put her aground on the edge of the bank southwest of Big Farmer's Cay. The wreck is not hard to find, simply proceed along the edge of the bank in your dinghy and you will soon be able to make out its dark shape on the bottom in 6'-13' and it may or may not be marked by a small buoy. There is a good anchorage at the southern end of Big Farmer's Cay that will be covered in the next section *Galliot Cay and Galliot Cut*.

GALLIOT CAY AND GALLIOT CUT

Galliot Cay (Chart # EX-28) is a small cay, only about ½ mile, long lying just south of Big Farmer's Cay. Galliot Cay is a reserve for the protection of wild birds. There is a popular anchorage in the cut between Galliot Cut and Big Farmer's Cay where two anchors are called for due to the strong tidal current. Do not attempt to enter this anchorage from Exuma Sound through this cut. There is a rocky bar at its entrance with less than 2' over it at low water. Galliot Cay was once used by local farmers for growing sisal.

If southbound on the banks route, proceed past Little Farmer's Cay until you can turn and steer towards the western tip of Galliot Cay on an 80° heading. If you fail to make this turn and head towards the deeper water to the west of Galliot Bank, you will encounter difficulty trying to cross Galliot Bank until west of Darby Island. As you proceed past Little Farmer's Cay you will notice the very visible sandbanks that are awash at high water directly in front of you. Do not panic. You will make your turn well before you reach this curving sandbar which is quickly becoming an island. The sandbar is excellent for shelling, especially after a westerly blow. You will have a least depth of 7' along this route once you clear the 6' bars to the west of Little Farmer's Cay. These depths will slowly deepen until you are between Little Galliot, Galliot, and Big Farmer's in 15'-25'. From this point you may anchor north of Galliot Cay or south of Little Galliot Cay, venture out into Exuma Sound via Galliot Cut, or proceed south inside Cave Cay.

For vessels wishing to enter Galliot Cut from Exuma Sound, a GPS waypoint at 23° 55.62' N, 76° 16.50' W will put you approximately ¼ nm east of the cut. To enter Galliot Cut, pass between Cave Cay to the south and High Cay which lies directly to its north across the cut. High Cay can be identified by its 45' high, white, overhanging cliffs. On the north end of Cave Cay sits Galliot Light (FL W ev 4 sec, 50 ft. 7 m). Galliot Cut is wide and deep, and is a virtual river when the current flows through it. This cut has earned a nasty reputation over the years. In early years it was said that ". . . weak nerves do not suit this place."

Galliot Cut will often have what is called a "standing wave" across its entrance. This may appear to be a 4' wall of water that does not seem to move in either direction. It is similar to an overfalls. It is created by an outgoing tide and anything over moderate onshore winds may swamp a small boat or dinghy. Do not try this cut in strong onshore conditions, use Cave Cay Cut instead, it is safer though narrower.

A visit to Little Galliot Cay, which is actually much bigger than Galliot Cay, will reveal a natural stone bridge along its southern shore, a small cave along its eastern shore, and some lignum vitae trees and large buttonwoods. There is an excellent tank dive on some beautiful reefs in the deeper water between Galliot Cay and Little Galliot Cay and just off the eastern shore of the small cay that lies southeast of Little Galliot Cay.

CAVE CAY AND CAVE CAY CUT

Cave Cay (Chart # EX-28), is approximately 1½ miles long and rises to 35' at its south end. Cave Cay is actually two cays, a longer eastern cay and a smaller western cay, that are joined together by an isthmus. There is a small pond on its western shore that could be used as a hurricane hole or as a refuge in the event of a frontal passage if needed. There is 4' over the bar at the entrance at low water. To enter follow the channel around to port, the sides dry at low water, until the inner anchorage opens up where there is room for 2-3 boats in 5' at low water. There is a good anchorage over a sandy bottom lying just off the western shore of Cave Cay near the entrance to the cove. The area around this anchorage and to its west has many small coral heads scattered throughout. Just to the west of the mouth of the cove lies the remains of a sunken ferrocement sailboat. With no anchor light on, she was run over one dark and stormy night by a mailboat and sank. That incident alone should be sufficient reason to burn an anchor light in these waters and some of the local residents who remember the incident well may remind you to turn on your anchor light.

Cave Cay earned its name from the caves and cave holes that honeycomb this island. About 500' north of the southwestern tip is a large cave from which local farmers removed bat guano for fertilizer. Further south are two smaller caves. There are some very prominent ruins just north of the entrance to the cove on the western shore. From the anchorage you can see the ruins of some pasture walls running down to the edge of the rocks. On the hill above the walls lies a large walled in pen about 40' square.

Just off the northwestern tip of the cay lies a long, curving, sandy beach. Follow this beach until the end, or round the rocky point to its southwest, and you will come upon a beautiful hidden grotto. The roof of the grotto is 10'-12' high and the green water below it is 9'-10' deep. If proceeding southward on the inside, pass to the west of Cave Cay giving Cave Cay Bank a wide berth to port while keeping to starboard the section of Galliot Bank that reaches eastward toward Cave Cay. The usual route through here called for lining up the white cliffs on High Cay and the western edge of the beach on Lansing and proceeding on that route with 7' at low water. That passage has shoaled slightly over the years and the deeper water now lies more to its west. Now you should line up the white cliffs on High Cay with the two small offlying rocks (known locally as Shark Rocks because of the sand sharks that live in that area), that lie well to the west of Lansing until you clear the Cave Cay Bank. You will have 7' at low water on this route with up to 9' just to the west. Once through this area you may anchor off Cave Cay, proceed out into Exuma Sound through Cave Cay Cut, or stay on the inside past Musha Cay to Rudder Cut Cay. Once again I must remind you that vessels with a draft of 5' can pass on the inside relatively easy all the way to Barretarre and Soldier Cay. Watch out for the shallow spot at Jimmy's Cay (see *Rudder Cut Cay and Rudder Cut*). Vessels with a draft of 6' can also be taken through here but very close attention must be paid to the state of the tide and they should exit at Rat Cay Cut to Exuma Sound.

Cave Cay Cut is one of the best cuts in this stretch of the Exuma Cays. Wide and deep, it is not as dangerous as Galliot Cut. Entering Cave Cay Cut from Exuma Sound, a GPS waypoint at 23° 54.25' N, 76° 15.20' W places you ¼ nm east of the cut. Enter the cut between the south end of Cave Cay and Moon Cay that lies to the north of Musha Cay. Moon Cay is so named because its white cliffs give it a lunar landscape appearance. There is a cross atop the cliffs that is used as a navigational landmark but do not count on its being there when you enter. The cut is wide and deep and the strength of the current makes for rough conditions when it opposes a strong wind.

There are currently about a dozen goats on Cave Cay that are the property of the caretaker, Kirkie, and a gentleman on Little Lansing Cay. Kirkie is one of the last of what is best described as the "Old Man of the Sea" in The Exumas. Picture the Exumas forty years ago when Kirkie was much younger. Unlike today, there were very few modern yachts passing through and for the most part they stayed in Exuma Sound on their way to George Town. The only sailors to ply these waters were the local men who had to scull their boats when there was no wind or the current was fiercely against them. These sailors knew the waters well enough to traverse them at night and could forecast the weather by the look of the sky and the way the air felt. Kirkie is one of the last of this proud, dying breed. Unfortunately his future is in doubt. Cave Cay has two new owners who have big plans for the cay. Beginning in February, 1997, the inner harbor will be dredged to make way for a marina, fuel dock, restaurant, and hotel complex. The new development will aim at the Sportfishing enthusiast. The owners are planning to place FADs, fish attracting devices, offshore in hopes of making the surrounding waters even richer. Their plans are to host tournaments and even get on the Bahamas Billfish Circuit. Good news for sportfishing aficionados.

MUSHA CAY

Musha Cay (Chart #EX-28) was once known as Moosha Cay and Little Toucher's Hole. It was once two cays but over the years has filled in. The cay is private and visits ashore are by invitation only. Musha Cay has become one of the largest new job sites in The Bahamas. The hotel complex being constructed currently employs over 80 people and will offer employment to over 100 during 1997. The exclusive resort will be available for rent sometime in late 1997. You can anchor off the western shore in 10'-12' in a good holding sandy bottom and don't forget to use an anchor light here. There is a lot of traffic between Musha Cay and Little Lansing Cay. Although it may not appear to be, this is actually a good anchorage in all but the most severe frontal passages as the shallow sandbanks to the west and north break the seas. However you do get a little chop which works its way in and a strong south to southwest wind will also create a chop in this anchorage. To enter from the north, pass between the northwestern tip of Musha Cay and the tip of Galliot Bank that stretches towards it from the north side of Lansing Cay. Probably 10 boats a year go aground on this bar which partially dries at low water. Use caution in this area and favor the Musha Cay shore when entering the Musha Cay anchorage.

On the northeastern shore of Musha Cay is a large cove with some small offlying rocks. There are two beautiful elkhorn and staghorn coral reefs in this area whose tops are awash at low water. One reef lies just northwest of the pretty beach at the western end of the cove while the other reef lies at the extreme eastern end of the cove. At first glance, the easternmost reef appears as it might be a wreck with its ribs protruding above the water. In the waters surrounding the reefs are numerous soft corals and sea fans. Please do not anchor on the coral and keep an eye out for fire coral.

If proceeding southward towards Rudder Cut Cay on the banks, you will pass between the shallow bank that lies to the east of the Lansing Cays and the bank between Musha Cay and Rudder Cut Cay. Favor the eastern side of the channel (stay 20-30 yards west of the bank) and watch out for a 5' spot at low water just north of Jimmy's Cay (see *Rudder Cut Cay and Rudder Cut* for more on this route). The sandbank between Musha Cay and Rudder Cut Cay dries almost completely at low water and is excellent for finding sanddollars. Please do not take any live sanddollars. There are plenty of dead, bleached white ones to add to your shell collection. For an excellent guide to the area, or if you simply wish to purchase some grouper, conch, or lobster in season, call Richard Ellis, *Little Gwen* on VHF ch.16. Although almost every Exumian you meet is friendly, Richard may actually be the friendliest. Give him a call, he almost always has grouper available.

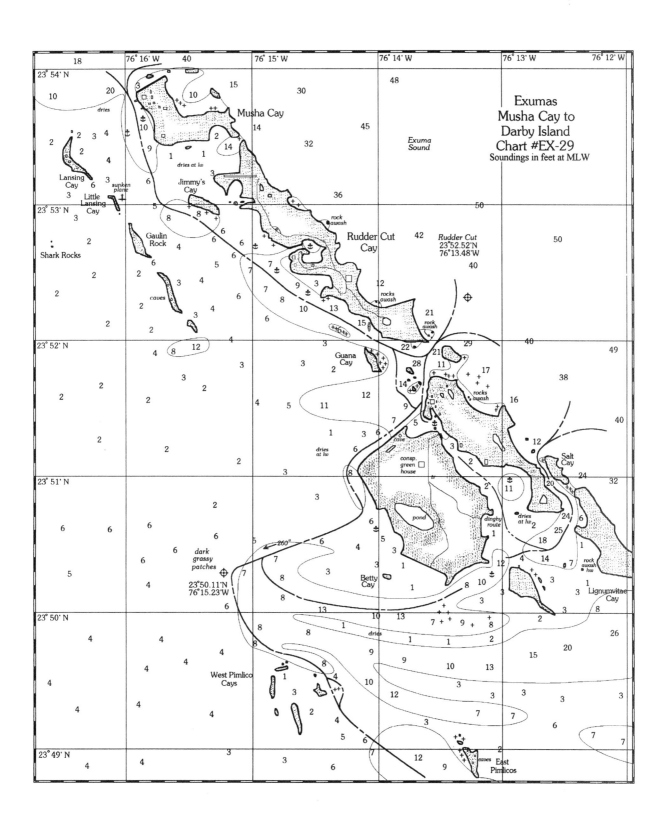

Exumas
Musha Cay to
Darby Island
Chart #EX-29
Soundings in feet at MLW

LANSING CAY

Lansing Cay (Chart # EX-28) was named after Col. Cleveland Lansing who purchased it in 1935. The cay, as well as Little Lansing Cay just to its southeast, is private and visits ashore are by invitation only. To the east of Little Lansing Cay lies the remains of an Aerostar airplane in 3'-4' of water. To find it, run just south of a line from the cut between Musha Cay and Rudder Cut Cay and the northernmost house (highly visible; it sits on stilts) on Little Lansing Cay. The plane rests on the bottom about 150 yards to the east of Little Lansing Cay. This is a good spot to take the kids snorkeling. Just south of Little Lansing lies Gaulin Rock where you will find sea grapes growing in abundance.

RUDDER CUT CAY AND RUDDER CUT

Rudder Cut Cay (Chart # EX-29), once called Big Toucher's Hole or Hog Cay, is 2½ miles long with a cove off its western shore that could be used as a hurricane hole or as a refuge from a frontal passage. The cay's most prominent feature, either from the banks or Sound side is the large domed house that sits on a 60' high hill about one mile north of the southern end of the island.

The north side of the cay is very shallow and sections of it dry at low water. Just north of the center of the cay along its western shore is a dredged channel leading to a small lake. The entrance has shallow bars both north and south of the entrance. The channel will accommodate a 6' draft vessel at low water however there is a 5' bar just at the entrance to the lake at low water. Once inside there is room for 8 boats in 6'-8' of water. The previous owner of the cay used to keep a chain across the channel to prevent boaters from entering. The owner was indicted in Florida when his Insurance Company went belly up and the State of Florida laid claim to Rudder Cut Cay. His once elegant former residence quickly became overgrown and was vandalized.

Rudder Cut Cay was purchased in January of 1997 for over $6 million dollars by the same people that own Musha Cay. The owners also purchased Little Lansing Cay in the process. Current plans call for the reconstruction of the airstrip and the building of private residences on the cay for the owners and their guests. Also in the works is a possible bridge linking Musha Cay and Rudder Cut Cay spanning the narrow cut between the two islands to permit easy access to the airstrip for guests and staff of the Musha Cay Resort.

Cruisers will be sad to learn that the pond, that secure anchorage that so many people call home for months at a time will be chained off in early 1997 so construction can begin on a private dock in the interior of the pond. Boaters cruising the Exumas during hurricane season should remember that it is a Bahamian law that all owners of private harbors must make them accessible to boaters seeking refuge from oncoming hurricanes. Along with the loss of the pond is the loss of a fantastic source of fresh water in the cisterns near the dock along the entrance to the pond. This island has been open to cruisers for the last few years and unfortunately some have done little to take care of it. Boat after boat after boat have come ashore and taken advantage of the water and left behind their garbage. This is to cease with the chaining of the harbor. Visits ashore will once again be by invitation only.

If approaching Rudder Cut Cay on the banks side from Musha Cay, pass between the very obvious sandbank between Musha and Rudder Cut Cay and the not so obvious sandbank to its west. Favor the Musha Cay side of this route staying about 20-30 yards west of the sandbank. This route will accommodate a 5' draft at low water except for a low spot of 4.8' just off Jimmy's Cay. Once past Jimmy's Cay steer towards a point between the domed house and the point of land to its west where you will see the opening of a large cavern that appears as a very dark area in the bluff. The water begins to deepen the further south you go. You can anchor in the pond or just off the western shore of the cay. If anchoring west of the entrance to the lake make doubly sure your anchor is properly set. The bottom has places which are packed quite hard due to the scouring action of the tide through here. The wreck of the *S/V Red Stripe* on the western shore of Rudder provides proof of the holding here.

Vessels in Exuma Sound may enter at Rudder Cut (Chart #'s EX-29 and 29A), so named because a ship once hit a large fish, local legend says a margate, and lost its rudder in the cut. Another tale is that the rocks just inside the cut resemble a ship's rudder from offshore. The cut can be absolutely deadly in strong onshore winds and an outgoing tide. Even in light onshore winds and swell coupled with an outgoing tide you will see small breakers forming over ½ mile offshore. The current flows like a river for quite a way into Exuma Sound. A GPS waypoint at 23° 52.52' N, 76° 13.48' W places you approximately ¼ nm mile to the north/northeast of the cut. From this point line up on the house on Little Darby on a heading of 185° and enter the cut passing between the southern tip of Rudder Cut Cay and the small unnamed cay to the north of Little Darby Island. An approach from this heading instead of coming in on a more easterly heading will help you avoid the main flow of the breakers until you are almost in the cut itself. Keep a sharp lookout for the rock that is awash at high tide about 50 yards off the southeastern tip of Rudder Cut Cay. Do not attempt to pass between the unnamed cay and Little Darby Island, this cut is foul with rocks and heads. Once inside Rudder Cut you may either turn to starboard towards the anchorages off Rudder Cut Cay or head to port to the Darby Island anchorage or the banks route through the Pimblico Cays. Landmarks in the area of Rudder Cut are the prominent stand of casuarinas and palm trees on the northern tip of Little Darby Island, the houses on Little Darby Island, and the conspicuous green house on Darby Island.

If heading for the anchorages off Rudder Cut Cay, follow the shore northward passing between Rudder Cut Cay and Guana Cay that lies off its southwest shore. Do not confuse this cay with the large rock that lies off Rudder Cut Cay's southern shore just inside Rudder Cut. This cay has a large rocky bar to its east with a large rock that is awash at high water. Keep an eye out for the large reef system that lies just to the west of the first beach you pass heading north along the shore of Rudder Cut Cay. You can pass this reef either to port or starboard. There is 12' over the majority of the heads but a few have only 4' over them at low water. Just inside Rudder Cut you will see a group of five large rocks. The northernmost rock, the largest, has a small tunnel on its southern end that you can swim through. The mushroom-shaped rock to its south has an osprey nest on it. Although these rocks have deep water running through them, they also have a tremendous current which can set the unwary skipper upon them. Follow the prescribed routes with the big boat and explore these rocks by dinghy.

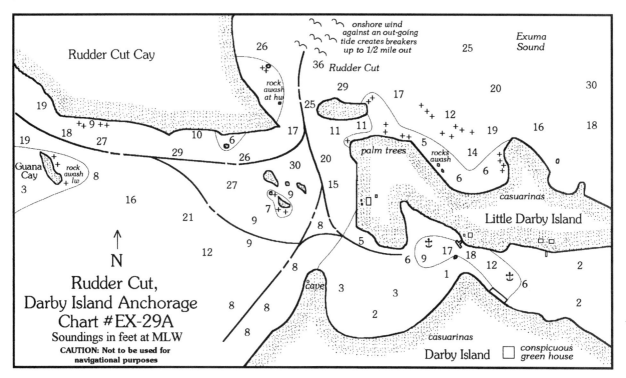

THE DARBYS

Little Darby Island (Chart # EX-29), is 2½ miles long with a prominent stand of palm trees and casuarinas on its northern tip. There is an 80' high hill on the northern end with a very conspicuous house on it. There are several buttonwood ponds in the interior of the cay. One pond extends across almost the whole island. Throughout the center of the southernmost pond run two stone causeways. There is no record of this pond ever being worked for salt although the owner who built the causeways in the early 1900's was a salt pond enthusiast.

Just to the west of Little Darby Island lies the much larger Darby Island. The most prominent feature on Darby Island (Chart # EX-29) is the large green house on the hill known as *The Castle*. The house was built by the owner in 1939, a man who was a bit of an eccentric. He had a first rate radio room and machine shop where he built some beautiful wicker furniture that still remains in the house to this day. He hired local workers for the labor force, which certainly helped out the economy, but he was very stingy and did not pay them much at all. The island was so buggy that the workers would sleep at night on the beach on the last rock south of Lansing Cay. He planted over 20,000 coconut palms and imported herds of cattle, sheep, and goats with the intention of operating a full-time coconut plantation. He was a known German sympathizer who was not very popular after the outbreak of World War II.

Dredging the channel between the Darbys, he built a concrete dock to allow U-boats to enter and tie up. It is doubtful that any U-boats ever entered the harbor as the entrance channel, which he did not dredge, was still too shallow. It is rumored that he would ferry supplies out to U-boats in Exuma Sound and even gave sanctuary to a few survivors of a U-boat sunk by the Allies in the vicinity. He was eventually asked to leave the islands. The islands are now private and visits ashore must be by invitation only.

There is a good anchorage between the Darbys (Chart # EX-29A) in this former U-Boat harbor. Once inside Rudder Cut, follow the shore of Little Darby Island keeping the small group of rocks to starboard. Round into the anchorage about 50'-75' off the tip of Little Darby Island and watch out for the 5' bar at low water. Once inside you may anchor in 6'-15'. Further in past the dock is a very protected anchorage, a great spot to ride out a frontal passage with depths from 6'-12'. Pass between the dock on Little Darby Island and the rock off Darby that is almost awash at high water. You must use two anchors here due to the current and the size of the anchorage (4 boats maximum although we have seen more in there). Further south between the Darbys lies a deep hole that is 11' deep at its center at low water. A vessel with a 3½' draft can pass over the bar from the inner anchorage between the Darbys and anchor here and be very protected. To enter the anchorage between the Darbys from the banks side of Rudder Cut Cay pass between Guana Cay (watch out for the rocky bar off its eastern shore), which lies to the southwest of Rudder Cut Cay, and the offlying rocks between Rudder Cut Cay and Little Darby Island. There is a least depth of 9' on this route. There is a very nice anchorage on the western side of Darby Island just about 150 yards off the beach in 5'-7' at low water. This anchorage is very good in northeast to southeast winds but if the winds are from any other direction, go between the Darbys. This is a good spot to begin a southbound cruise through the Pimblicos. To reach this anchorage, pass along the northern shore of Darby in 6'-7' of water past the entrance to the anchorage between the Darbys until you can round the western tip of Darby Island. Watch out for the shallow water just off this tip and the very visible 3' spot (you will notice it by the turbulent water flowing over and around it) just to the northwest of this route. Round the tip and head in as close to the beach as your draft will allow. Five feet of draft will have no problem finding a place to anchor further in towards the long beach in a sandy bottom. One anchor is fine here in the prevailing winds but if any windshift is expected use two anchors to keep from being blown into the shallows off the beach. Betty Cay, Goat Cay, and Salt Cay, all of which lie just off the Darbys, are designated bird sanctuaries. They are breeding grounds for white crowned pigeons and Bahamian ducks. If you see any nesting birds on these cays please do not disturb them.

There is a little known and seldom used anchorage off the southern shore of Darby Island that is good when the wind picks up from the north and the anchorages at Rudder Cut Cay and between the Darbys are full. To enter the anchorage pass to the west of Darby Island and when you can place the point of land south of the first beach on your stern, then turn and steer approximately 260°. You will pass over a shallow 3'-4' (at low water) area with many soft sandy humps that lies between two shallow sandbanks, one that works out from the southern end of Darby past Betty Cay, and the other which is actually a part of the Galliot Bank. This is also the beginning of the route through the Pimblico Cays (see next section *The Pimblico Cays*) and should only be attempted in good light on a rising tide. On this heading you will come to a dark patch of grass which is the turning point for both the Pimblico route and the entrance to the anchorage at the south end of Darby. A GPS waypoint at 23° 50.11' N, 76° 15.23' W places you almost on top of the grass in 7'-8' of water. At this point, turn to port and take up a course for a position just to the south of Betty Cay. You will be between two sandbanks once again.

To port will be the sandbank that works out from the south end of Darby Island and to starboard is one of three sandbanks that lie to the east of the West Pimblicos. The deeper, dark water between the two will be very obvious in good light. Morning is not the time to try this route as the sun will be right in your eyes, wait until at least 1100 before attempting this passage. The water will deepen to 13' in places as you pass Betty Cay abeam. As you approach the south end of Darby another sandbank will appear to the south of Darby Island working out from Goat Cay. You must pass between that sandbank and Darby Island in 8' at low water. Anchor anywhere you prefer between Darby Island and Goat Cay. Once past Goat Cay the water thins quickly. This anchorage is good in any northerly winds although a strong northeast or east wind may build up a little chop over the exposed shallow water between you and Little Darby Island. It is possible to pass over the shallow bar north of the dock on Goat Cay and enter the deeper water for an exit into Exuma Sound between Salt Cay and Little Darby Island. This is not a recommended pass into Exuma Sound but local mariners use it and the cautious skipper would be able to take advantage of it. Watch out for the current in this passage and the rocky bar that works westward on the northwest tip of Salt Cay.

For a guide to this area call Clay Rolle, the caretaker on Little Darby Island, he is *Rocket* on VHF ch.16.

THE PIMBLICO CAYS

The Pimblico Cays, named after the native migratory bird known in The Bahamas as *pimlicos,* are divided into two separate groups, the East Pimblicos and the West Pimblicos. The Pimblicos are best explored by dinghy as there are no anchorages in their immediate area although in calm weather it is possible to anchor near them for an exploratory outing. There are numerous heads that are good for snorkeling in their immediate area. Check the banks around the cays for conch.

The West Pimblicos (Chart # EX-29), 9 in number, range from small rocks to small cays over ¼ mile long. The waters around and between them are shallow. There are some small caves in the bluffs above the high water mark on the larger cays.

The East Pimblicos (Chart # EX-30), 8 in number, are generally larger and higher than the West Pimblicos. The northernmost large cay has a very conspicuous large cave on its western shore, easily seen when proceeding south along the Pimblico route.

The Pimblico route is very narrow and shallow in two places, both when rounding the Pimblico Cays themselves. The controlling depth for the Pimblico route is 4' due to the shallows just west of Darby Island and along the route past the western Pimblicos.. A vessel with a 5' draft can take this route shortly after low tide while vessels with a 6' draft should plan to pass the shallow spots no sooner than mid-tide. Although it is an excellent passage for boats heading north or south when Exuma Sound kicks up, it should only be attempted on a rising tide with good visibility and not with the sun in your eyes. Follow the directions and the charts exactly or you may wind up between two sandbanks with no place to go except back. Do not let these warnings prevent you from attempting this route, it is a very good alternative to going out into Exuma Sound when the weather is bad. Your piloting skills will indeed be tested through here.

Heading south from Rudder Cut Cay or the Darbys, pass to the west of Darby Island as described in the previous section and line up the point of land south of the first beach on your stern. Then steer approximately 260° between the sandbank lying to the northeast of Darby Island and the sandbank that works westward from the south end of Darby Island. You will soon come upon some dark, grassy patches. A GPS waypoint at 23° 50.11' N, 76° 15.23' W will place you almost on top of the grass in 7'-8' of water (you can reach the mailboat route from the grassy patches by steering 270°-300° for 5 miles). From the grassy patches steer towards the eastern side of the West Pimblicos and the water will gradually deepen to 10' at low water just north of the cays. At this point you will begin to steer more to port and you will pass between a sandbank and the West Pimblico Cays. The sandbanks along this route are all very visible in good light. As you round the eastern side of the cays you must pass very close to the two easternmost rocks, between them and the point of the sandbank which curves westward just north of the West Pimblicos. The darker, deep water to the east of this sandbank will make it appear that you should pass this sandbank and the cays to starboard (heading south) but do not. Mistakenly following this dark water will take you into a long deep bight which leads to the cut between Young Island and Bock Cay (see Chart # EX-30). Passing correctly between the easternmost rocks and the sandbank (a narrow passage) you will see a brown bar which southbound vessels should pass on their starboard side. Be careful here, the water shallows to 4' at low water. This is one of the two truly shallow spots on this route. Once past this shallow area begin steering for the East Pimblicos following the curve of the sandbank to port. The water will gradually deepen from 5' to 9' just before the East Pimblicos. Vessels drawing less than 5' can play the tides and pass to the west of the West Pimblicos and steer around their southern tip, then head toward the East Pimblicos. There is only 3' or less at low water through here and you must dodge some coral heads just off the southern tip of the West Pimblicos.

Leaving the West Pimblicos, follow the curve of the sandbank to the East Pimblicos and pass between the two largest cays. The northernmost cay will have a large conspicuous cave about 20' above the water on its western shore. Once between the two cays it is once again time to pay close attention to where you are steering. The natural tendency is to stay in the dark water but it will only bring you into a bight that shallows just to the west of Melvin Cay with a passage into the deeper water between Young Island and Bock Cay (see Chart # EX-30) after you cross a 4' bar at low water. To stay on the Pimblico route you must turn sharply to starboard and pass along the eastern shore of the large cay. Keep at least 50 yards off the cay to avoid the shallows on its eastern shore. As you approach its southern tip you must "thread the needle" so to speak. Pass between the southern tip of the cay and the sandbank to port and do not let the strong current push you onto either one. Once again, there is a shallow spot of 4' through here at low water. Once past this spot the water will deepen again to 7'. Begin steering approximately 120° until you can pick up the dark, deeper water that will soon appear off your starboard bow. You are once again between two sandbanks but the water will only get deeper from here. Follow the darker water to starboard and head for the northern tip of Norman's Pond Cay and you will soon be in 10'-20' of water. Well now, that wasn't so bad was it? You have probably gained a little more confidence in your piloting abilities after this one.

YOUNG ISLAND

Young Island, (Chart # EX-30) was once called Prime Cay and Passy Cay. As Passy Cay it was named after Passy Lloyd, a squatter who died in the 1920's. The cay is 1½ miles long with a creek in the middle of the cay on its western side that runs for ¼ mile into the interior and is 3'-4' deep. It is said that the locals used to raise turtles in this creek. Between the creek and the southern end of the cay are some small buttonwood ponds in the interior. Young Island is private and visits ashore must be by invitation only as signs ashore will remind you.

There is a deep but narrow passage into Exuma Sound to the north of Young Island between Young and the first small cay to its north. Although there is 20' through here at low water, this route is not recommended as Rudder Cut and Adderly Cut are very close and much safer. Local mariners use this cut often and it is included for that reason.

Southwest of Young Island there is a good anchorage in the deep water along the shore with plenty of good diving on the soft coral reef in the channel and the heads around the three rocks which lie to the southwest of Young Island. This anchorage can be gained from the Pimblicos route or from the cut between Young Island and Bock Cay.

On the southeastern shore of Young Island is a small cove that would be a good day anchorage in settled weather only. There are some excellent reefs in this area and the long beach is excellent for beach combing.

BOCK CAY

Bock Cay (Chart # EX-30) was once called Peace and Plenty, The Low Cay, and Old Buck Cay. It is 1¼ miles long and has several separate hills climbing to 45' in height and, except for these hills, it is a very low cay. On its southwest side is a 2 acre buttonwood pond. Bock Cay and Melvin Cay are private and visits ashore must be by invitation only. There is a 100' tall Batelco tower on the southwestern tip of Bock cay with a fixed red light.

You can anchor between Bock Cay and Melvin Cay in two small, shallow bights. Each will hold 1-2 boats in 6' at low water. To enter the anchorage at the northern end of the passage between Melvin Cay and Bock Cay, either enter from the Pimblico route from the East Pimblicos, or from Bock Cay Cut between Young Island and Bock Cay. From the Pimblico route, pass to the north of Neighbor Cay (4' at low water) and turn to starboard between Neighbor Cay and Wooby Cay and proceed to the anchorage between Melvin Cay and Bock Cay. To enter from Bock Cay Cut, pass close to the northeastern tip of Bock Cay and favor its northern shore. There are some very shallow, dangerous rocks and reefs in this area so hug the northern shore of Bock Cay staying 50 yards off. Round the western tip of Bock Cay and you are in the anchorage.

To enter the south anchorage between Melvin Cay and Bock Cay, enter from the Pimblico Route avoiding the shallow sandbar which juts out from the southeast tip of Melvin Cay. Pass between the small cay and the sandbar and work in between the docks on Melvin and Bock and anchor in 6' at low water. Although small, this is a good anchorage in which to ride out a frontal passage. Use two anchors due to the tide.

LEAF CAY

Leaf Cay (Chart # EX-EX-31), lies just to the northeast of Norman's Pond Cay. It is approximately 3000' long and 600'-1000' wide. There are two ponds in the interior, one of 1½ acres off the southwest side and one of 4 acres in the center of the cay. There is a beautiful small beach in a small bight on the western shore. There is a good spot to anchor in northerly winds off the southern shore of Leaf Cay. Boats have been known to ride out frontal passages here although holding is fair at best. The best holding is in sand and grass just south of Leaf Cay. This is a good spot when winds are out of the east and southeast as the swell is broken at Adderly Cut before it has a chance to get to Leaf Cay.

To the west of Leaf Cay, between Leaf Cay and Norman's Pond Cay, are numerous heads lying in 15' of water that make for good snorkeling. The small cays and rocks to the north and east of Leaf Cay are strewn with heads and reefs and good diving abounds in this area.

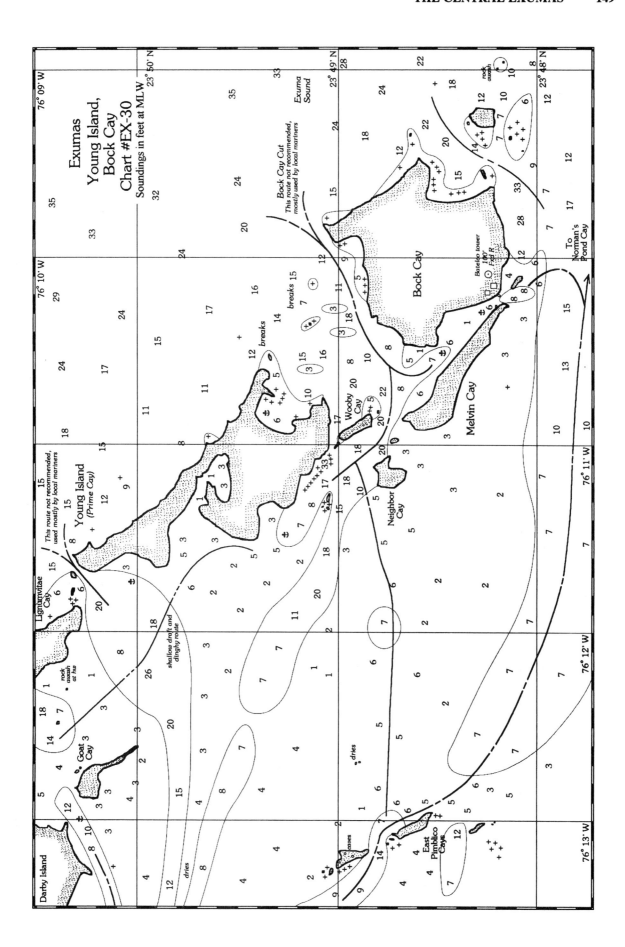

Exumas
Young Island,
Bock Cay
Chart #EX-30
Soundings in feet at MLW

Bock Cay Cut
This route not recommended,
mostly used by local mariners

Exuma
Sound

Bock Cay

Batelco tower
100'
Fxd R

To
Norman's
Pond Cay

Melvin Cay

Wooby
Cay

Neighbor
Cay

breaks

breaks 15

Young Island
(Prime Cay)

This route not recommended,
used mostly by local mariners

Lignumvitae
Cay

rock
awash
at hw

Goat
Cay

shallow draft and
dinghy route

dries

dries

caves

East
Pimblico
Cays

Darby Island

rock
awash

rock
awash

NORMAN'S POND CAY

Norman's Pond Cay (Chart # EX-31), is approximately 2¼ miles long and almost ¾ mile wide. On its southern end is a large 48 acre salt pond just south of a 50' high hill. A poorly constructed canal once connected this pond to the sea. A dinghy can enter the pond but only at or near high tide due to the canal wall that blocks the way at low water. There is said to be good bonefishing in this pond. Ashore you will find the ruins of buildings from the salt pond days including a 6' deep turtle kraal and some pasture walls. The rocky shoreline on the eastern side of Norman's Pond Cay is excellent for beach combing with all manner of flotsam and jetsam washing ashore through Adderly Cut. The western shore is almost all beach with some very rocky sections.

North of Norman's Pond Cay lies Guana Cay with a nice beach on its western side. There is a colony of rock iguanas on the cay so do not bring your dog ashore or feed the iguanas, they are protected by the Bahamian government. There are the remains of an old pasture wall on the cay. To the east of Guana Cay lies Dildo Cay, so named because of the abundance of dildo cactus which grows there. All around the rocks that lie to the east of Norman's Pond Cay, between Bock Cay to the north and Adderly Cay to the south, are scattered heads, rocks, and ledges making for excellent snorkeling.

If approaching from the Pimblicos, pass between the northern end of Norman's Pond Cay and Guana Cay. Watch out for the small reef that is almost awash at high water off the northeastern tip of Norman's Pond Cay. It is possible to anchor off the northwestern tip of Norman's Pond Cay in prevailing winds. There is a fantastic submarine cave just inside the entrance to this anchorage. Look for the opening in the rocks just below the hill with the large dildo cactus on it. The entrance will look like a small green pool just a few feet in from the rocky shoreline. This is a magnificent network of caves and a must for tank divers. The cave drops in three steps with large cathedral ceilings at a 45° angle down to about 120'. At that depth a diver can still see the light of the opening and the cave branches out into other caves while one opening drops straight down. One diver who was familiar with the cave said it went well over 250' down while locals say it is bottomless. At one time, a scientist from the Caribbean Marine Research Center on Lee Stocking Island used the cave to play a practical joke on some visiting researchers. He planted a plastic human skeleton deep in the cave and invited his victims to dive the cave with him. That was probably a very memorable dive. A colony of small green iguanas inhabit the island and are often seen around the mouth of this cave. If approaching from Adderly Cut, pass between Leaf Cay and Norman's Pond Cay, round the northern tip of Norman's, and enter the anchorage. A deep water channel (Chart #'s EX-34, 35, & 36) leads from this anchorage to Clove Cay Cut and the cut between Brigantine Cay and New Cay.

Some cruisers choose to anchor off the southern tip of Norman's Pond Cay. To enter this anchorage simply follow the eastern shore of the cay around until you find the spot where you want to drop your hook in 5'-7' at low water.

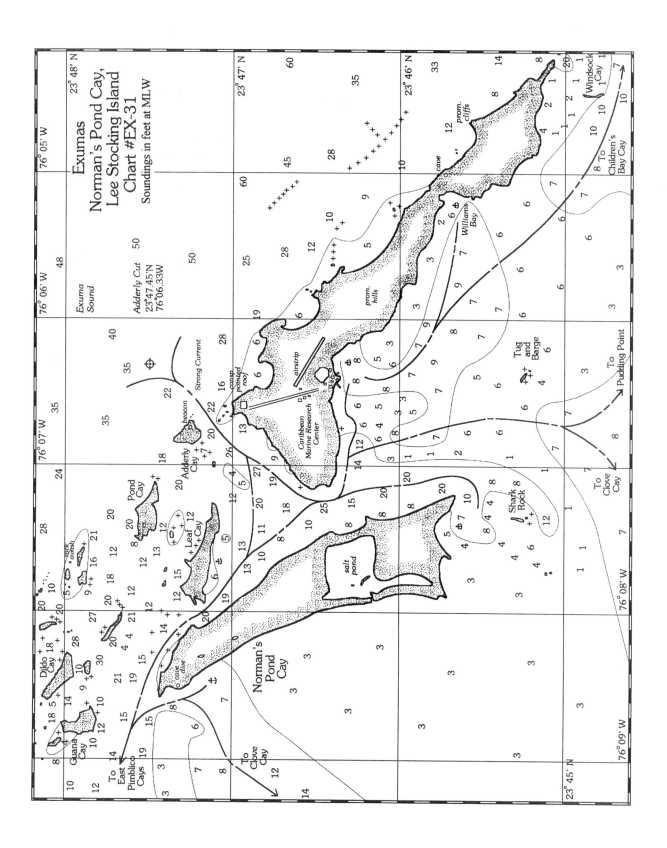

Exumas
Norman's Pond Cay,
Lee Stocking Island
Chart #EX-31
Soundings in feet at MLW

Exuma
Sound

Adderly Cut
23°47.45'N
76°06.33W

ADDERLY CAY AND ADDERLY CUT

Adderly Cay (Chart # EX-31), is approximately ¼ mile long and half as much wide. It is the site of Adderly Beacon, the navigational landmark for Adderly Cut. About 200' from its south end, Adderly Beacon sits 20' above high water. The beacon shaft sits on a base that is 5' square and 5' high. It is topped by a concrete cap 3" thick. The shaft of the beacon is circular and approximately 20' tall with a 5' diameter at its base. On the cay itself you will find some sea grape trees. There are some heads and rocks just off the southwestern tip of Adderly Cay that are worth investigating by dinghy.

A GPS waypoint at 23° 47.45' N, 76° 06.33' W, will place you ¼ nm northeast of the cut. The entrance to the cut is wide, deep, and very straightforward. As you enter the cut you may see some small buoys placed here and there in the waters between Lee Stocking Island, Adderly Cay, Leaf Cay, and Norman's Pond Cay. These are not to be confused with navigational aids. They are markers for some of the ongoing research being conducted at the Caribbean Marine Research Center on Lee Stocking Island.

Photo courtesy of Nicolas Popov/Island Expeditions

A traditional Bahamian racing sloop.

LEE STOCKING ISLAND

Lee Stocking Island (Chart # EX-31) is approximately 4 miles long and the southern section, sometimes called Williams Cay, was once a separate cay but the cut between the two has filled in over the years. There is a well protected anchorage that makes a good stop on the way to George Town or just to ride out a front. Enter from Adderly Cut and swing close around the western tip of Lee Stocking Island. Heading in towards the anchorage area you may or may not see a large white buoy that says "No Wake" on it. If it is there, pass it to port as there are some shallow rocks between the buoy and shore, then angle in towards the dock slightly until you enter the deeper water of the anchorage. This anchorage is a good refuge in the event of a frontal passage but it is wide open to strong winds from south-southeast through south to southwest.

If you pass through the anchorage and head south along the western shore of Lee Stocking Island, avoiding the shallow sandbank that lies on its western shore, you will soon come to Williams Bay, another good anchorage in 6' at low water but also open to south and southwest winds. Just north of Williams Bay is a small curving beach. With its palm tree lined shore and backdrop of a steep rocky hill covered with dense jungle-like vegetation it may remind you of a South Pacific island. If you proceed further south along the shore of Lee Stocking Island you can pass south of Windsock Cay and head towards Children's Bay Cay and Rat Cay. To the south of Lee Stocking Island you will see two rocks called Tug and Barge because they resemble a small tug pulling a barge.

Lee Stocking Island is the home of the Caribbean Marine Research Center. The CRMC is a one of the National Oceanic and Atmospheric Administration's (NOAA) National Undersea Research Centers (NURC). The center is affiliated with Florida State University, the University of South Carolina, Oregon State University, the Virginia Institute of Marine Sciences, and the United States Geological Survey. The CRMC offers scientists a complete marine field laboratory with easy access to pristine marine environments including coral reefs, shoals, mangrove swamps, sea grass beds, deep hardgrounds, and carbonate mud beds.

The principal projects being conducted at the CRMC are the study of the habitat, lifestyles, feeding patterns, and growth cycles of the Queen Conch, Nassau Grouper, the Red Tilapia, and the Spiny Lobster. Saltwater aquaculture studies being done at the Center are designed to enhance stocks of these important food sources. Because so much research on this work is being done in the waters surrounding the Lee Stocking Island area, the researchers at Lee Stocking Island respectfully request visitors not to spearfish, line fish, or take any conch, corals, or shells anywhere in the vicinity of Lee Stocking Island from Bock Cay south to Rat Cay. This is little to ask in view of the good it will bring in the long term. The average cruiser may think that taking one grouper for dinner won't matter but they are quite wrong. One grouper can have a dramatic effect on the studies in the area. If you insist on taking fish in the area, wait; take a tour of the Center first. If you witness the marvelous work that they are doing you may think twice about fishing in the area and disturbing their ongoing research projects. Anyone wishing to tour the facilities can call the Center, "*Bahama Hunter*," on VHF ch.16 and ask about a tour. The Center requests that groups of boats join together for tours for obvious reasons and please not go ashore without permission. The staff will be more than happy to show you the facilities if you ask. A popular attraction with the kids is the 2 man submarine, the *Gamma Neckton*. Able to cruise for seven hours at depths up to 1000' on one charge of its 24 volt system, this tiny submersible is in almost daily use charting the waters and giving scientists a first hand look at the local marine life. Sorry, the CMRC cannot take the kids for a ride.

A very interesting feature at the CMRC is the tidal gauge. This is simply a shaft leading down to water level which is fed inland a short distance by an underwater tunnel. By means of a gauge and chart recorder, the scientists at the CMRC are able to accurately measure true Atlantic Ocean tides and contribute important data to the Permanent Service on Mean Sea Level. Underwater caves surveyed by the scientists in the area provide more than 125,000 years of geological history showing natural changes in sea level during prehistoric times. One interesting discovery that they have made is that extreme tides, though not all extreme tides, may forewarn of impending natural disasters. Four hours before the devastating 1989 earthquake in San Francisco, the chart recorder measured an all time record high tide of 8" above the highest spring high tide ever recorded in this area. Scientists are hoping that one day they will be able to identify and predict certain disasters and possibly avert bigger catastrophes by using this tidal information.

The CRMC also monitors seawater temperature which can confirm a global warming trend. The Center also measures harmful UV-B radiation and its effects on DNA, the basic genetic material found in cells. The DNA is placed in quartz tubes and deployed in the ocean where the device absorbs UV-B radiation from all angles in the same way as marine organisms. Experiments conducted near this lab have discovered that the amount of UV-B radiation striking organisms at the ocean surface is up to twice as high as predicted under conventional theories.

The center is also actively involved in taking core samples for recording geological records and ancient climatic cycles. In 1987, corals throughout the Caribbean lost their bright colors and turned bone white, signaling severe stress on the fragile coral reefs. The CRMC was part of a National Science Foundation rapid response team mobilized at that time to study the coral bleaching throughout the Caribbean.

CHILDREN'S BAY CAY AND CHILDREN'S BAY CUT

Children's Bay Cay (Chart # EX-32), approximately 1¼ miles long, was once known as the "Showcase of the Exumas." The Cay's previous owners, Hume Cronyn and the late Jessica Tandy, reportedly sold it in the mid-1960's for one million dollars to Pickle King H.J. Heinz II and his socialite wife Drue. It seems that Drue had difficulty adjusting to island life. Wanting to go to a market she had heard about in George Town she had a worker take her there. When he set her off in front of a small, dilapidated building she asked her guide where the market was. He told her, "This is it." She was shocked and told her guide to take her to George Town. It took a while for him to convince her that this also was "it." Long before Children's Bay Cay became such a beautiful development it was worked for its sisal. The cay is private and visits ashore must be by invitation only.

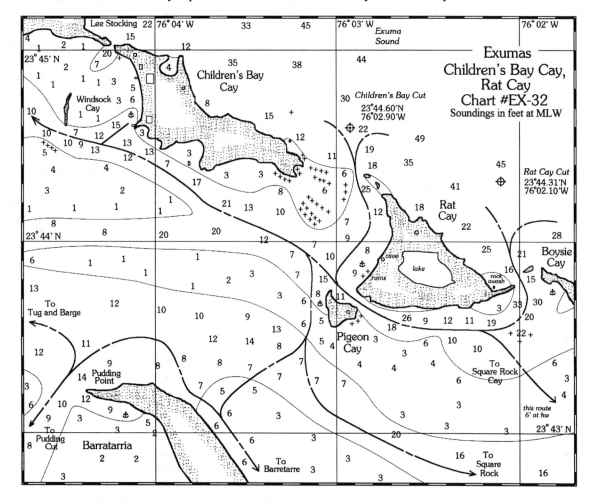

If approaching from Lee Stocking Island, round the southern tip of the island and pass to the south of Windsock Cay. Pass close to Windsock Cay to avoid the soft coral reef with 5' over it just to the south. The best anchorage at Children's Bay Cay is just off the long curving beach on its northwestern shore. Pass between the dock and the sandbank that lies to the east of Windsock Cay and anchor in 6' over a sand and grass bottom. The anchorage is open to the south-southwest through west. Another anchorage you may consider is further south about ¼ mile just off the curving beach. You will not be able to work in very close because the water shallows quickly but this spot offers protection in winds from north through northeast to east.

Children's Bay Cut is very dangerous and should not be attempted as Rat Cay Cut is just another mile or so south and much safer. For those who wish to enter Children's Bay Cut, a GPS waypoint at 23° 44.60' N, 76° 02.90' W will place you approximately ¼ nm mile north of the cut. To enter the cut you must pass between Children's Bay Cay and the second small cay that lies to the north of Rat Cay. Pass within 50 yards of this small unnamed cay and favor the Rat Cay shoreline. Any attempt to head more towards the Children's Bay Cay side of the cut will only put you upon some treacherous reefs. If in doubt, stay out! Use Rat Cay Cut instead, it is much safer and easier on the blood pressure.

RAT CAY AND RAT CAY CUT

Rat Cay (Chart # EX-32), is approximately ½ mile long and has a large 10 acre pond in its interior. The cay has a nice beach along its northwestern shore facing Children's Bay Cay. There is a cave and the ruins of a pasture wall just south of this beach. There are some heads and rocks in the deep water just off the southeastern tip of Rat Cay. There is a herd of goats living on the cay that were placed there by residents of Barretarre, please do not bring your dog ashore here.

Approaching on the banks from Children's Bay Cay head straight for the gap between Rat Cay and Pigeon Cay in the deep water channel between Children's Bay Cay and the shallow sandbanks that lie to the southwest of the cay. You can anchor off the beach along the northwestern shore of Rat Cay (rolly) or behind Pigeon Cay in 6' at low water. If anchoring at Pigeon Cay, head as far as possible to the westernmost tip before dropping your hook in sand. The bottom along the deep channel is rocky and difficult to set a hook in. Pigeon Cay is a designated bird sanctuary so please do not disturb any birds you notice nesting upon the cay.

If entering Rat Cay Cut from Exuma Sound, a GPS waypoint at 23° 44.31' N, 76° 02.10' W will place you approximately ¼ nm north of the cut. Enter the cut between Rat Cay and the small rock to the northwest of Boysie Cay in 16'-20' of water. Follow the shoreline of Rat Cay favoring the Rat Cay shore as you approach Pigeon Cay. Watch out for the shallow sandbank off the southeastern tip of Rat Cay.

Just to the east of Rat Cay lies Boysie Cay with a very pretty small beach on its southern shore. Boysie Cay is also a location of several blowholes. Vessels heading south with a 5½' draft or more are advised to head outside at Rat Cay Cut. Vessels with 5½' draft or less can play the tides and venture further south on the inside (See *The Southern Exumas; Square Rock Cay and Square Rock Cut*).

ALLEN CAYS

The Allen Cays (Chart #'s EX-33 & 34), lie to the northwest of Gold Ring Cay, the westernmost of the Brigantines and stretch to the northwest to Kelly Rock. These cays are little more than rocks and their only redeeming features are the few coral heads that make for good diving in the area. The largest cay in the group is Bo Cat Cay (Chart # EX-34), just northwest of Gold Ring Cay. Bo Cat Cay has a small beach on its western shore and a tidal creek into its interior. Well to the south and west of Bo Cat Cay lie West and East Barracouta Rocks which mark the eastern edge of the mailboat route.

THE BRIGANTINE CAYS

The Brigantine Cays (Chart #''s 34, 35, & 36) are 40 in number, 8 larger and 32 smaller cays. They have a different quality about them as they are uninhabited (with the exception of the one house on Clove Cay) and seldom visited by yachts. The waters surrounding the cays are shallow but there are deep water passes between almost all the cays. The diving in the area is superb and the cays are laced with mangrove swamps. There are two routes through the Brigantines which will take you onto the rarely cruised shallow waters off the western shore of Great Exuma Island and eventually out to the mailboat route. The runs from Norman's Pond Cay, Lee Stocking Island, and Pudding Point must all be done on a rising tide with good light. The ability to read water is essential when cruising the Brigantines because you often must dodge shallow bars.

From the east, the first deep cut is called Pudding Cut and lies between False Cay and Jimmy Cay. From Lee Stocking Island head south between the bar that lies to the east of Norman's Pond Cay and Tug and Barge. Once past this steer towards Pudding Point staying between the sandbank just south of Tug and Barge (Chart #'s EX-31 & 36) and the sandbank that works northward from Clove Cay and Jimmy Cay. Once in the vicinity of Pudding Point, follow the curve of the sandbank to the southwest of Pudding Point staying between it and the Clove Cay-Jimmy Cay sandbank. Just before you enter Pudding Cut you must make a dogleg to port to avoid the point of the sandbank that juts out into the channel. Exercise caution here, this is a shallow bar with only 1'-2' over it at low water. Once through the cut take up a course of 190° to a point just west of Rocky Point if you wish to cruise the western shore of Great Exuma.

Clove Cay Cut, also a route to Rocky Point, can be reached from two directions. If approaching from Norman's Pond Cay, enter the anchorage off the northwestern tip of Norman's Pond Cay (Chart # EX-31) and proceed along the darker, deep water towards Clove Cay (often called Cluff's Cay) Cut. From Tug and Barge, round the sandbank just south of Norman's Pond Cay and head for the cut. The cut can be recognized by the prominent stand of casuarinas and the house that lie just to the east of the cut. Steer to the west of the casuarinas. As you get closer you must make a dogleg around a shallow bar to enter the deeper water of the cut. From the cut to Rocky Point you must steer around some dark grassy patches and soft sand ledges on the southern side of the cut until you can enter the area of water that is generally 5'-6' deep at low water. From there take up a heading of 160° to Rocky Point.

It is possible to anchor in the deep water between the cays and explore them by dinghy. The absolute best diving is in the cut between Brigantine Cay and Lily Cay (Chart # EX-35). This area has many ledges and walls that drop vertically from 5' to 22'. The best way to explore this cut is by dinghy from Lee Stocking Island or Norman's Pond Cay, or, if you prefer, you can anchor your boat in the cut between Brigantine Cay and New Cay. To approach this cut from Norman's Pond Cay, enter the anchorage on the northwestern tip of Norman's Pond Cay and follow the deeper water towards the cut between Brigantine Cay and New Cay and anchor in this cut. Brigantine Cay is also the home of tropic birds in season and is good for beach combing along its rocky shore. In the cut between Brigantine Cay and New Cay is another area of good diving on numerous ledges. In the center of Brigantine Cay are two hills behind which lie two ponds. In one of these ponds are the remains of a Long Island sailing vessel driven there by the hurricane of 1926.

New Cay (Chart # EX-34), has a curbed well that you can reach by a path which lies approximately 600' north of the southern tip of the cay. There is a beautiful long white beach backed by sandy dunes on the northern shore of New Cay. The beach and dunes resemble white cliffs from Norman's Pond Cay.

On Long Cay (Chart # EX-35), approximately 700' northwest of the southeastern tip is a point of land almost 15' high. There is a small pile of rocks here built to mark the resting spot of a vessel after the 1926 hurricane. Jimmy Cay was once called Well Cay for its well which lies east of the high hill on the cay.

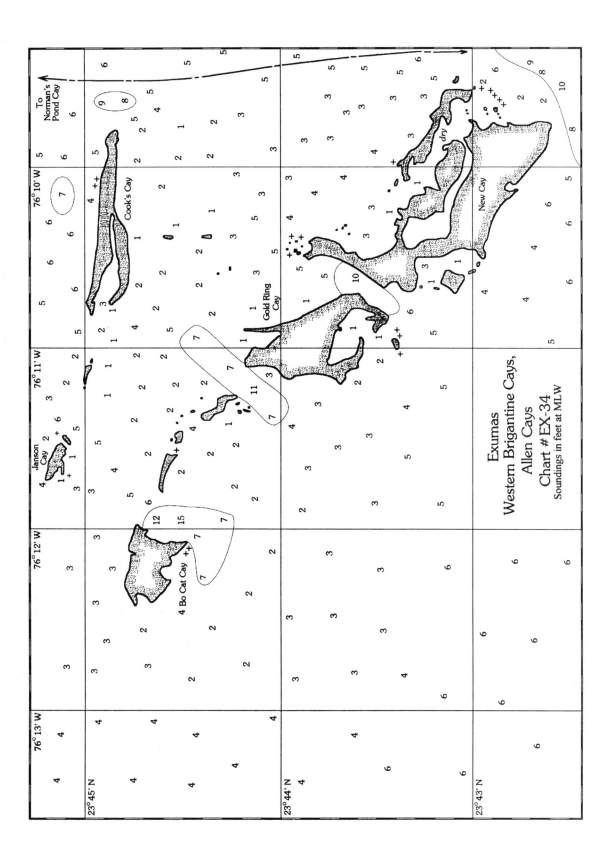

Exumas
Western Brigantine Cays,
Allen Cays
Chart # EX-34
Soundings in feet at MLW

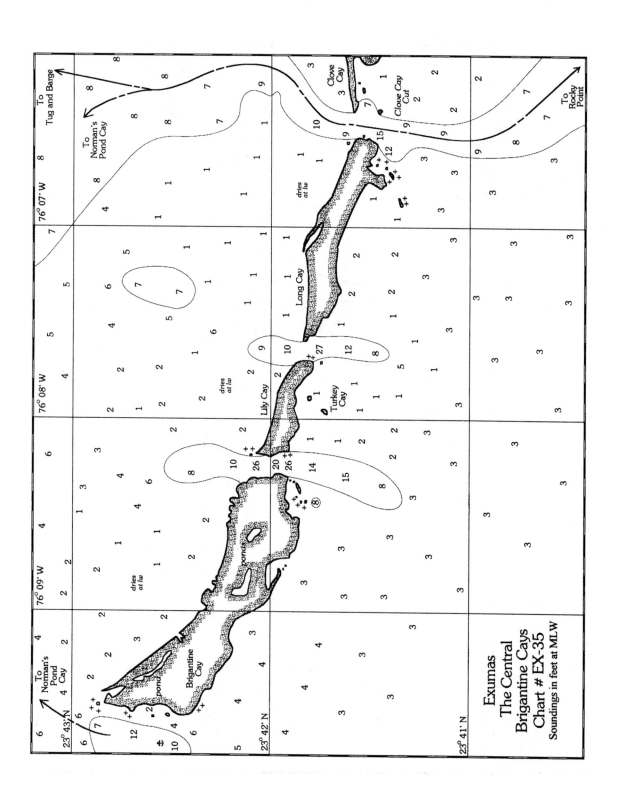

Exumas
The Central
Brigantine Cays
Chart # EX-35
Soundings in feet at MLW

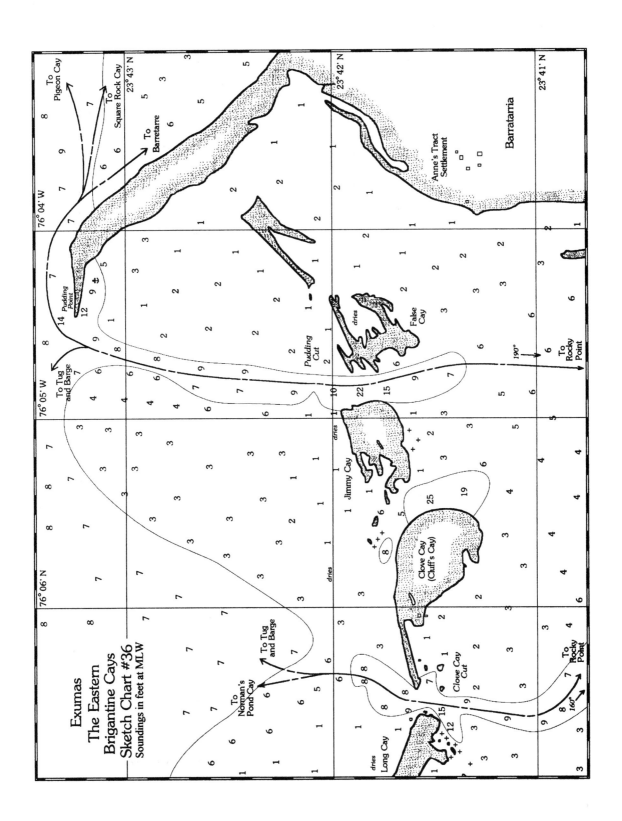

Exumas
The Eastern
Brigantine Cays
Sketch Chart #36
Soundings in feet at MLW

THE
SOUTHERN
EXUMAS

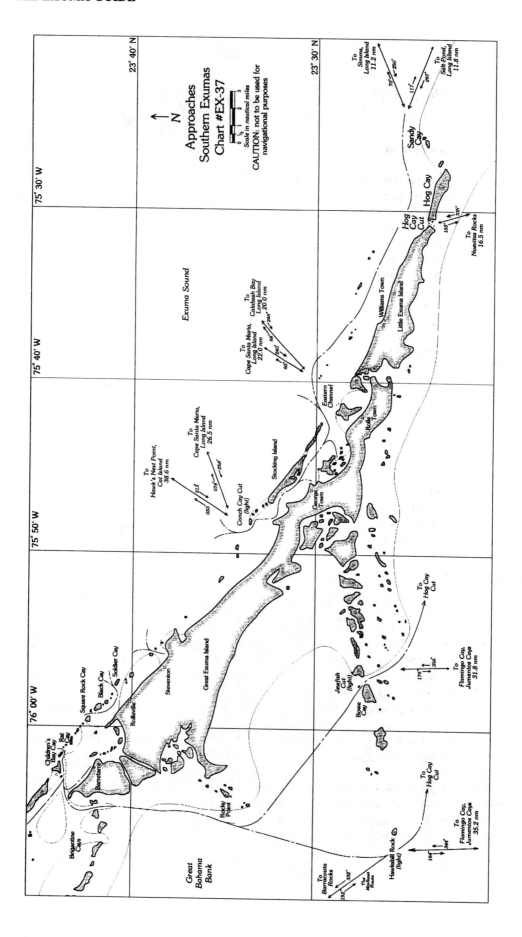

N

Approaches
Southern Exumas
Chart #EX-37

0 ½ 1   2   3
Scale in nautical miles
CAUTION: not to be used for
navigational purposes

THE SOUTHERN EXUMAS
Barretarre to Hog Cay

APPROACHES TO THE SOUTHERN EXUMAS

Vessels approaching the southern Exumas from the north can proceed outside in Exuma Sound, staying at least ¼ nm offshore, or inside on the banks depending on their draft. Vessels with drafts of 5' or less can stay inside all the way to Soldier Cay before having to exit into Exuma Sound while vessels with a draft of 6' should exit at Rat Cay Cut.

From Hawk's Nest Point at the SW tip of Cat Island (Chart # EX-37), laying a course of 213° for 38.6 nm will bring you to the western entrance of Elizabeth Harbour at Conch Cay Cut. The ODAS Buoy at 23° 50.40' N, 75° 43.20' W is the only hazard to navigation on this route. When the U.S. Navy is performing underwater tests in this area you will have to avoid the buoy by 5 miles as is done at the ODAS Buoy in north Exuma Sound.

From the Caribbean most vessels will round the northern tip of Long Island at Cape Santa Maria. Vessels heading for the southern Exumas from Long Island have a few routes to take depending on their location. Vessels rounding Cape Santa Maria should steer 240° for 22.0 nm to reach the Eastern Channel entrance to Elizabeth Harbour. A course of 258° from Cape Santa Maria for 26.5 nm will place you at the western entrance to Elizabeth Harbor at Conch Cay Cut. If you are at Salt Pond, Long Island, a course of 297° for 11.8 nm will bring you to a position just north of the northeastern tip of the sandbank that lies to the NE of Sandy Cay. From here you can follow the shore to the Eastern Channel or pass through Hog Cay Cut. Vessels leaving Simms, Long Island, can take up a course of 250° for 11.2 nm to reach the same location.

From Flamingo Cay in the Jumentos, a course of 344° for 35.2 nm will bring you to a position just to the west of Hawksbill Cay on the old mailboat route, well to the west of Great Exuma. If you take up a course of 356° for 31.8 nm you will arrive at Jewfish Cut. Vessels wishing to depart from Flamingo Cay to Hog Cay Cut must detour around a large area of coral heads and a very shallow sandbank. For this reason no courseline is given for this route. You must pilot by eye for the first third of the journey at least. Vessels departing Nuevitas Rocks at the north end of the Jumentos can take up a course of 335° for the 16.5 nm run to Hog Cay Cut.

Vessels leaving Nassau wishing to follow the old mailboat route along the backside of Great Exuma may set a course of 152° from Porgee Rocks for 96.5 miles to arrive at West Barracouta Rock. At this point you should alter course to 141° for 4.0 miles to a point west of East Barracouta Rock. From this position you can take up a course of 137° for 18.9 miles to Jewfish Cut. A course of 163° for 16.2 miles from East Barracouta Rock will bring you to a point just west of Hawksbill Rock where you can set your course for the Jumentos or Hog Cay Cut. For more information on the old mailboat route, see the section *The Mailboat Route*.

BARRETARRE

Barretarre (Chart # EX-38 & 39) is a small island, about 1¾ miles long, lying just off the northwestern tip of Great Exuma and connected by two bridges (built in the 1980's) to the mainland. The shore of the island is essentially rocky with its western and southern shores bounded by mangroves.

When anyone mentions Barretarre they usually are referring to the settlement of Barretarre which lies about midway along the eastern shore of Barretarre. No one seems really certain as to the origin of the name of this cay although the popular telling is that the spongers used this cay as a "bar" to "tarry" on before going to the mainland. Others say that it comes from the French term *bar terre* which means *land obstruction*. Still others say it originated when pirates roamed these waters and named the land after Barataria, a small coastal area in Louisiana on the United States Gulf Coast. In fact, on Nassau Land and Survey Department charts the area is called *Barratarria*. There is only one church in the community, the Ebenezer Baptist Church, which was first opened around 1840 and was blown down by gales in 1926 and 1930. Barretarre is your typical Bahamian community with vividly painted houses in various pastel colors.

Just up from the government dock you will find Circle T's, one of the two local bars, and just across the street, RayAnn's Variety Store where you can purchase fresh fruit, vegetables, and sundry items. If you tie your dinghy up at the Fisherman's Inn dock, the large concrete structure just north of the town dock, you can walk straight up the hill and visit Norman Lloyd at his Fisherman's Inn.

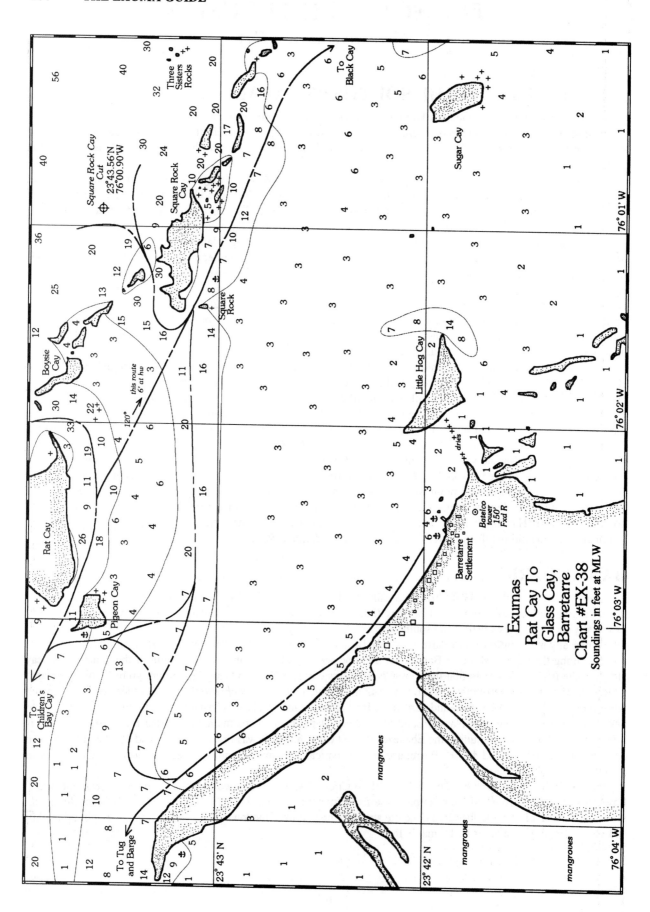

Three Sisters Rocks

Square Rock Cay Cut
⊕ 23°43.56'N
76°00.90'W

Square Rock Cay

Square Rock

Boysie Cay

Rat Cay

Pigeon Cay

To Children's Bay Cay

To Tug and Barge

120°

this route 6' at hw

dries

Little Hog Cay

Sugar Cay

To Black Cay

Barretarre Settlement

Batelco tower 150' FxdR

mangroves

mangroves

mangroves

**Exumas
Rat Cay To
Glass Cay,
Barretarre
Chart #EX-38**
Soundings in feet at MLW

23° 43' N

23° 42' N

76° 04' W   76° 03' W   76° 02' W   76° 01' W

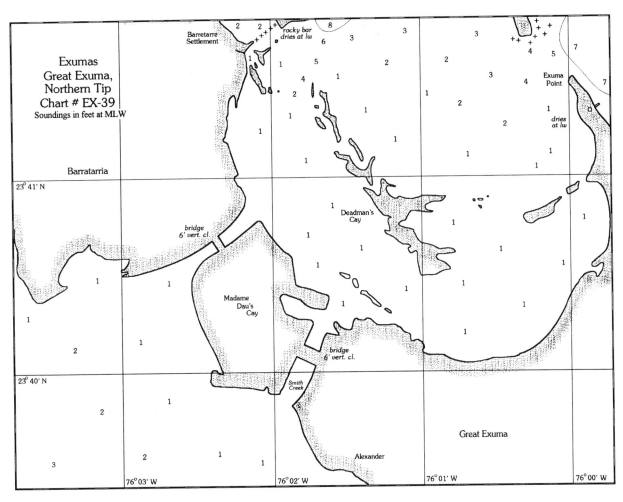

Exumas
Great Exuma,
Northern Tip
Chart # EX-39
Soundings in feet at MLW

Watch out for the pieces of steel re-bar that rise out of the water awaiting passing inflatables on the eastern side of this dock. Fisherman's Inn is a must see in this area and has a beautiful view of the waters which stretch eastward into Exuma Sound. Fisherman's Inn is open at 8 a.m. serving breakfast, lunch, and dinner with reservations. As the name implies they serve native seafood and the sign above the bar states that "Seafood eaters make better lovers." Norman and his wife are excellent cooks and can serve up some of the best cracked conch you will ever have along with grouper, turtle steaks, and ice-cold drinks. Norman also runs a taxi service for trips to George Town and the airport. This is extremely helpful if you have guests arriving or leaving and you can't or don't want to go all the way to George Town. Fisherman's Inn also has ice, a pool table, DJ's on Thursday through Sunday nights, and occasionally, live music.

Across the road to the north of Fisherman's Inn you will find McKenzie's Food and Liquor Stores. Here you will meet Wilhemenia McKenzie who operates the establishment selling food staples, spirits, and quality Bahamian crafts, shells, and T-shirts. McKenzie's monitors VHF ch.17 and Wilhemenia also offers deep sea and bonefishing charters. The flats to the south and west of Barretarre are excellent for bonefishing. For guides to this area call Cely Smith at 242-358-0027 or Tony Smith at 242-345-2305. For fuel see Rev. McKenzie who has the small dock north of Fisherman's Inn and you will notice it by the Shell flag flying there.

There is a 4' controlling depth on the channel into Barretarre at low water. The channel parallels the shore southward from Pudding Point. You can anchor in front of the Government Dock or The Fisherman's Inn concrete dock in two holes which have 6' at low water. These anchorages can accommodate 2-3 well anchored boats but this is no place to be in strong winds from northwest through north to east. Pudding Point can be gained from Lee Stocking Island, Rat Cay, and Square Cay. To approach Pudding Point from Lee Stocking Island, head south between the bar that lies to the east of Norman's Pond Cay and Tug and Barge. Once past this area, steer towards Pudding Point staying between the sandbank just south of Tug and Barge (Chart #'s EX-31 & 36) and the sandbank that works northward from Clove Cay and Jimmy Cay. At Pudding Point follow the eastern shoreline southward staying between the shoreline and the shallow bar that lies to the east of it. As you pass the first houses on the northern outskirts of the settlement the water shallows quickly to 4' at low water and the best water, in the mailboat channel, lies closer to the shore. Residents of Barretarre say that the mailboat follows the shore so closely that the crew can reach over the side and touch the land. The water deepens to 6' at low water just off the Fisherman's Inn dock and then shallows again to 4' at low water until you are off the town dock, once again in 6' at low water.

If approaching from Rat Cay or Square Rock, there is a deep water channel leading to Pudding Point (Chart # EX-38). From Rat Cay, pass to the north of Pigeon Cay staying about 50 yards off as there is a shallow sandbar to its north. You will find 5' through here at low water. When in the deeper water steer towards Pudding Point. From Square Rock Cay simply steer straight for Pudding Point staying in the deep water between the two obvious sandbanks. From Pudding Point follow the shoreline as described in the last paragraph.

There is an anchorage good for prevailing winds in the area to the west of Pudding Point although it can be quite buggy on still nights due to the mangrove swamps in the area.

SQUARE ROCK CAY AND SQUARE ROCK CAY CUT

Square Rock Cay (Chart # EX-38), is often called simply Square Cay and is approximately 2000' long. Once called Square Island, Square Rock Cay is a white-crowned pigeon rookery so please do not disturb any birds that you might see on your visits ashore. There is a well about 50' inland in the middle of the cay on the south side that is of little use nowadays. Square Rock lies 200' south of Square Rock Cay and is very conspicuous as its name implies and has some cave holes along its south shore. The rock is also the site of an osprey nest.

There is a good anchorage in the lee of Square Rock Cay between the cay and Square Rock in 8'-12' at low water and is open to the east through southeast to southwest. The approach from Rat Cay (Chart # EX-38) can be tricky but there are two routes to take. From the southern shore of Rat Cay steer approximately 120° for the gap between Square Rock and Square Rock Cay. This route has 6' at high water but you must dodge sand ridges with only 4'-5' over them. The better route is to pass on the northern side of Pigeon Cay staying about 50 yards off in 5' at low water and avoiding the shallow bar to the north. Once past Pigeon Cay you will be in deeper water that will lead directly to Square Rock and Square Rock Cay. Watch out for the two obvious shallow sandbanks on both sides of the channel. This anchorage has some ravenous mosquitoes wandering about when there is no wind.

For vessels wishing to enter Square Rock Cay Cut from Exuma Sound, a GPS waypoint at 23° 43.56' N, 76° 00.90' W will place you approximately ¼ nm east-northeast of the cut. Enter between Square Rock Cay and the small unnamed island to its north. You will find 9' in the cut once you clear the 6' shallow bar at low water that lies just outside the cut. Once inside the cut round the tip of Square Rock Cay to port and take Square Rock to starboard to enter the anchorage area.

Vessels heading south from Square Rock Cay and drawing over 5' should consider going outside at Square Rock Cay Cut. You can exit into Exuma Sound at Square Rock Cay and enter again at Glass Cay Cut if you wish to visit Rolleville. Vessels drawing 5' or less must play the tide to pass around Glass Cay and beyond as their is a 3' sandbar at low water lying to the northwest of Peggy Wild Cay that you must cross. High tide will give you just over 6' on this bar so it is best to attempt it at mid-tide or better. Pass along the western shore of the small cays between Square Rock Cay and Glass Cay in 6'-10' of water at low tide. There are heads scattered throughout these cays and snorkelers will wish to visit them all.

East-southeast of Square Rock Cay and just off Levi Cay lie the Three Sisters Rocks named after three sisters who drowned just off these rocks. Deep water surrounds them and it is possible to pass between the Three Sisters and Levi Cay. Do not confuse these rocks with the set of rocks named the Three Sisters that lie close offshore at Mount Thompson further south on Great Exuma. Do not attempt to run between the GPS waypoints for Square Rock Cay Cut and Glass Cay Cut as your course may take you directly into the Three Sisters Rocks. Once again, a gook lookout is imperative. Once you clear the Three Sisters Rocks you should be able to make out the large wedge shaped mass of Stocking Island that marks the George Town area on the southern horizon.

GLASS CAY, BLACK CAY

Vessels traveling south inside Glass Cay (Chart # EX-40) must cross a shallow bank, 3' at low water, that lies to the northwest of Peggy Wild Cay (often called Levi Cay). Do this on a rising tide at mid-tide or better with good light and 5' will pass through here with no problem. Vessels with a draft of 5'-6' will have to steer around the occasional sand ridge. Once clear of the bar, swing towards the deeper water that lies to the east of Sugar Cay. At this point you can proceed into the anchorage behind Black Cay or head southward in the deep water towards Soldier

Cay. Sugar Cay lies northwest of Rolleville just off Exuma Point and is approximately 1300' long. There is a cave with an entrance on the western shore about 400' south of the northern tip.

Black Cay (Chart # EX-40) is almost ½ mile long and lies almost due north of Rolleville. There is a very good anchorage off the western shore in prevailing winds. To enter the anchorage at Black Cay from Exuma Sound, a GPS waypoint at 23° 42.50' N, 75° 59.20' W places you approximately ¼ nm north of Glass Cay Cut. The best route passes between Glass Cay and the small cay between Glass Cay and Black Cay. Watch out for the rocky bar working south from Glass Cay and the smaller rocky bar working north from the unnamed cay. One can also pass between Black Cay and the unnamed cay but this pass is narrower and slightly shallower with some scattered heads with 9' over them at low water. Once inside the cut, round the end of Black Cay and drop your hook before the second beach where the water thins quickly. Two beaches to your south from this anchorage is the home to the Black Cay Yacht and Tennis Club opened in 1993 by the sailing vessels *Wanderer* (not the *Wanderer* of Eric Hiscock fame) and *Reality*. This a very pretty beach with clear deep water and palm trees with some driftwood furniture that is perfect for lounging about. Divers and snorkelers will love exploring the beautiful reefs surrounding the small cays between Black Cay and Soldier Cay.

ROLLEVILLE

Rolleville (Chart # EX-40) is the northernmost settlement on the eastern shore of Great Exuma Island. It is a fairly large settlement, some say the largest, and very traditional. Many of the residents still cook in outdoor ovens and some even have thatched roofs. Rolleville has a 260' tall Batelco tower with a red flashing light at its top and a red fixed intermediate light. The first regatta held in Exuma was held at Rolleville.

Although it is possible to anchor off town itself about ¼-½ mile out, the best way to see Rolleville is to visit it by dinghy while anchoring in the lee of Black Cay. You will have to anchor or pull your dinghy up on the beach by what used to be the town dock and now is little more than a boardwalk to the beach. At the head of the walkway is the Rolleville Post Office and just to the right in the green building is the Police Station. A short walk up the hill past the school is Kermit Rolle's Hilltop Restaurant and Tavern. Kermit, or his brother Clayton, will gladly assist you with cold drinks while you sample the magnificent view of the surrounding waters. Hilltop serves breakfast, lunch, and dinner and requests you call them on VHF ch.16 in advance (call *Hilltop*) so your food will be prepared upon your arrival. Kermit has a huge open air dance floor with live music on weekends. Check with Kermit for the availability of water and ice. There is a small cannon guarding the front of the restaurant which was once one of a pair of cannons that were mounted on the highest hill in Rolleville, overlooking the waters between Rolleville and the outlying cays. You may think that it seems foolish to place cannons atop the hill when a deep draft vessel cannot get within ½ mile of the town, but up until about 30 years ago, there was as much as 7' of water right up to the town dock. It has since filled in over the last 20 years or so.

There are two small stores in town, one to the north of Hilltop and one to the south, where you can purchase some staples as well as fresh fruits and vegetables in season. Just below Kermit's Hilltop is the smaller Club Little Savoy. There is no fuel and no means of garbage disposal in Rolleville.

Stuart Manor and Curtis are two small settlements a good distance inland from the main road and shore to the northeast of Rolleville. The residents are primarily engaged in farming, fishing, and plaiting.

SOLDIER CAY AND SOLDIER CAY CUT

Soldier Cay (Chart # EX-40) is the exit point to Exuma Sound for all but the shallowest draft vessels. The cay itself is ½ mile long and its prominent 55' hill is easily seen. Soldier Cay as well as Bob's Cay just a little further south is a bird preserve, so again, please don't disturb any birds you may see nesting there. Bob's Cay, lying ½ mile southeast of Soldier Cay was once owned by Denys Rolle and commuted by Lord John Rolle. There is not a suitable anchorage for anything other than in flat calm weather in the Soldier Cay area.

The approach to Soldier Cay on the inside from Black Cay follows the darker water between Rolleville and the outlying cays. From the anchorage at Black Cay, head towards Rolleville until you can clear the shallows lying to the southwest of the Black Cay anchorage. At this point you may steer more southeastward paralleling the lie of the outlying cays. A shallow bank works out from White Bay Cay and you must angle over towards Rolleville somewhat to pick up the channel of darker, deeper water. Follow this as it curves around towards Soldier Cay and proceed out either one of the two cuts.

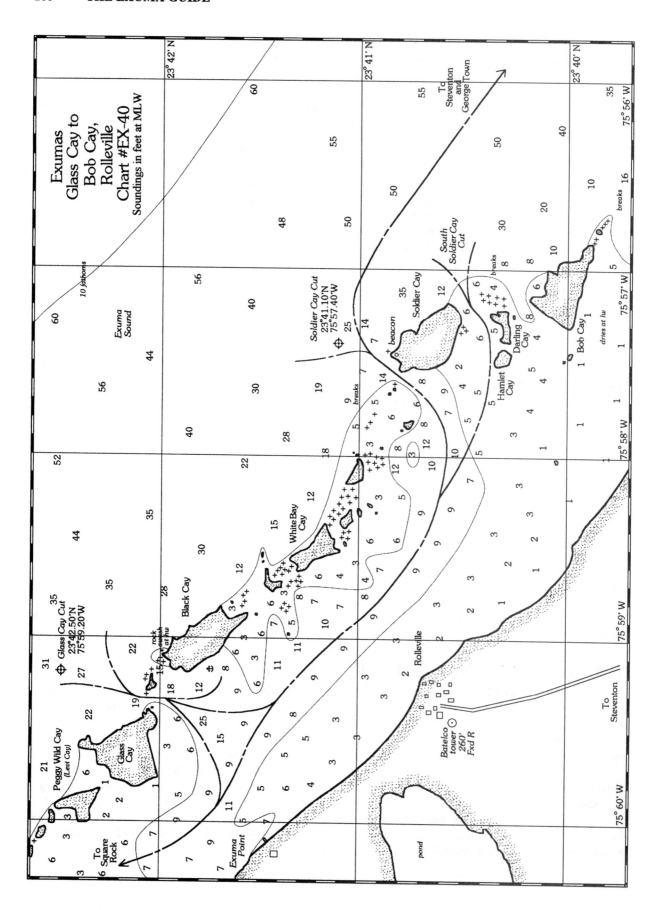

Exumas
Glass Cay to
Bob Cay,
Rolleville
Chart #EX-40
Soundings in feet at MLW

Soldier Cay has two entrances into Exuma Sound along its shores. The northern route, called Soldier Cay Cut and marked by a 25' tall, pointed, stone beacon, is the better of the two. A GPS waypoint at 23° 41.10' N, 75° 57.40' W places you approximately ¼ nm northeast of the cut. From the inside, pass just south of the small cays to the northwest of Soldier Cay and hug the Soldier Cay shore on the way out the cut. Be very careful of the rocky bar that works southward from the small unnamed cay that lies to the northwest of Soldier Cay. Pass between the rocky bar and the Soldier Cay shore. Keep and eye out for the rocks awash at low water just at the tip of Soldier Cay. This channel, although narrow, is much preferred over South Soldier Cay Cut.

South Soldier Cay Cut is not recommended unless you have excellent visibility and reasonably calm weather. Soldier Cay Cut, the preferred route, is much easier. For this reason there is not a GPS waypoint given for South Soldier Cay Cut. From the inside, proceed as above but when you are in the vicinity of Soldier Cay steer south of the cay towards Hamlet Cay and Darling Cay and pass along their northern shore. Hug Darling Cay on your way out to avoid the shallows and the reef off the southern shore of Soldier Cay. Once past this visible, breaking reef, you must dogleg slightly toward Soldier Cay and out the cut to avoid the reef that lies just off the north side of Darling Cay. This "S" route through these reefs combined with the 6' depths at low water over some rocky bars is what makes this route so difficult. Locals use this cut often but then again, they have lived here all their lives and know these waters like you know the streets in your hometown.

From this point southward, with the exception of the cut into Steventon, you will be in Exuma Sound where you should stay a minimum of ¼ nm offshore (and preferably further offshore) to avoid any reefs in the Steventon area. The waters from Steventon to Conch Cay Cut run very deep close to the offlying cays but are shallow yet navigable between the cays and Great Exuma.

STEVENTON

Although Steventon (Chart # EX-41), situated on the shore of Great Exuma just south of Bob's Cay, has little in the way of shoreside facilities, it more than makes up for that with its superb diving. The residents of Steventon make their living from farming and fishing the reefs off their shore. The long white beach, conspicuous tall palm trees, and gaily painted houses mark the community from well out in Exuma Sound. The Steventon Clinic, built in 1958, is in the pink building on the northern end of the long beach in Flamingo Bay. There is a good anchorage in the lee of the settlement of Roker's Point in 7' at low water which is protected from winds from southeast through south to northwest. Do not attempt to ride out a frontal passage here as strong northeast to east winds make this anchorage untenable.

The entrance to Steventon is between two small unnamed cays (little more than two large rocks) that lie just to the northwest of Guana Cay. A GPS waypoint at 23° 39.68' N, 75° 55.70' W will put you approximately ¼ nm northeast of the pass between the rocks. Line up the large rock that lies just off the beach at Steventon between the two small cays and head straight in for that rock. There is a conspicuous white house and the remains of an old rusting bulldozer lying just to the south of the rock on the beach. On the southernmost of the two small outlying cays that you are steering between lies a boulder about 6' in diameter which may help you locate this small cay. Once inside the cut steer toward the rock off the beach and then turn more southeast to anchor in the lee of Roker's Point. You can anchor within 150 yards of the shore in 7' at low water. The route through Flamingo Bay is strewn with coral heads and small reefs over a sandy bottom. Steer around any large dark spots you see, some of the heads leading to the anchorage have less than 6' over them at low water. Some large reef systems lie well in towards the Steventon shoreline and have less than 3' over them at low water.

The waters around the Steventon area abound in reefs and reef structures. In particular, the area off Roker's Point is strewn with massive reefs of elkhorn and fire coral. There are numerous fringing reefs from Guana Cay southeastward past Roker's Point. Most of these reefs are fished out by the residents of Steventon but they are still beautiful to see. If you do see some food fish around these reefs please spare them, save them for the people of Steventon.

North of Steventon, just past the very conspicuous white house with the red roof, lies the entrance to Ann's Creek. This creek, with its many branches, is similar to the creeks of Shroud Cay in The Exuma Cays Land And Sea Park. It is a mangrove lined creek which leads to a large mangrove swamp. Here you are apt to see all kinds of fish from sharks to rays to snappers.

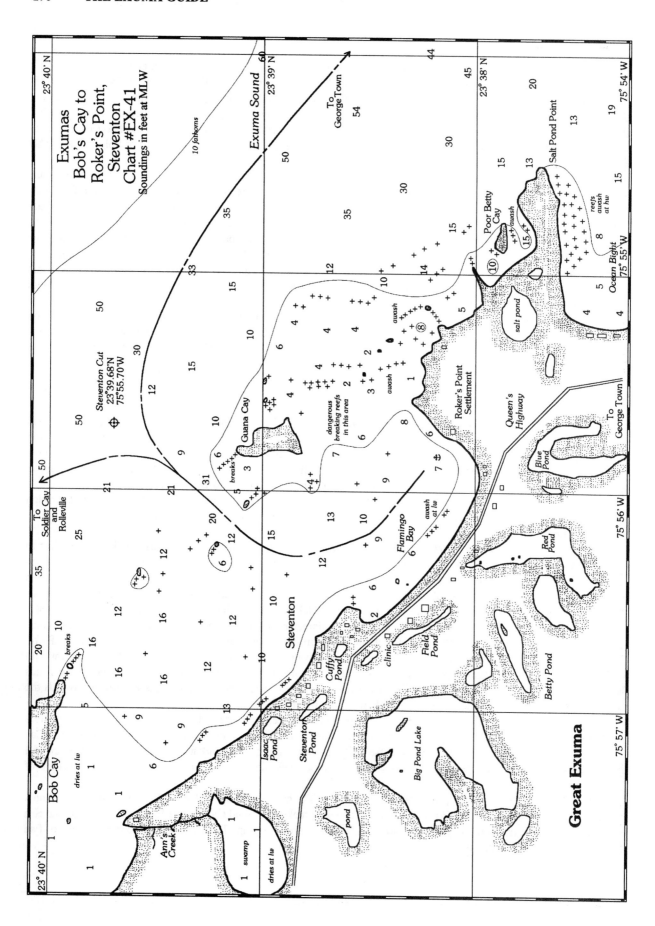

Exumas
Bob's Cay to
Roker's Point,
Steventon
Chart #EX-41
Soundings in feet at MLW

Exuma Sound

To
George Town

10 fathoms

Steventon Cut
23°39.68'N
75°55.70'W

Guana Cay

dangerous
breaking reefs
in this area

awash

awash

Poor Betty
Cay

Salt Pond Point

reefs
awash
at hw

Ocean Bight

salt pond

Roker's Point
Settlement

Queen's
Highway

Blue
Pond

To
George Town

Red
Pond

Flamingo
Bay

awash
at lw

To
Soldier Cay
and
Rolleville

Steventon

clinic

Field
Pond

Betty Pond

Cuffy
Pond

Steventon
Pond

Isaac
Pond

Bob Cay

dries at lw

Ann's
Creek

swamp

dries at lw

pond

Big Pond Lake

Great Exuma

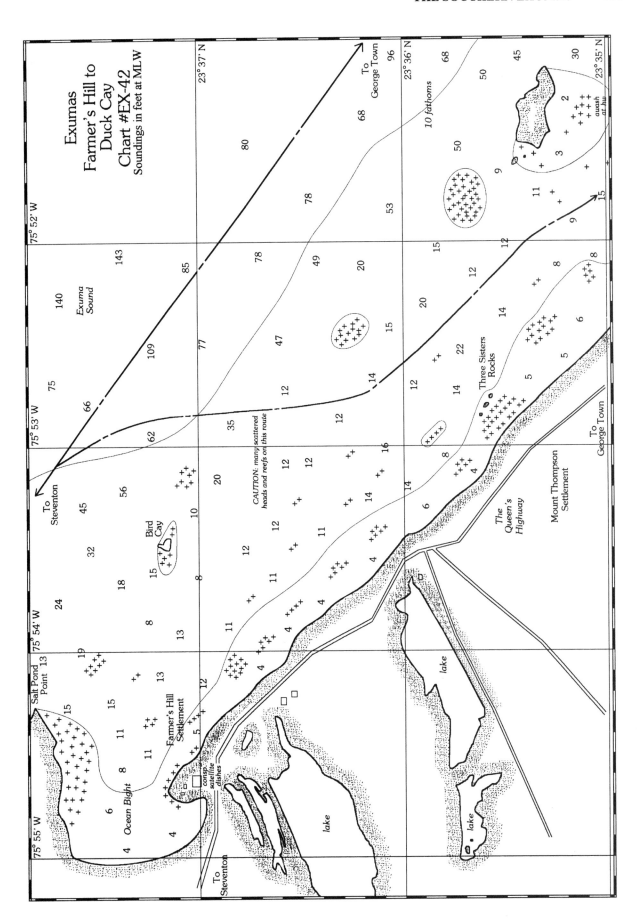

Exumas
Farmer's Hill to
Duck Cay
Chart #EX-42
Soundings in feet at MLW

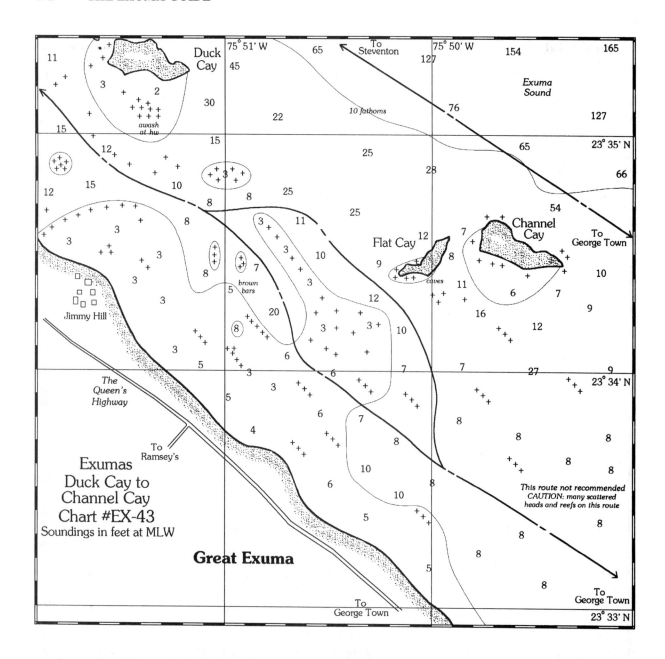

Exumas
Duck Cay to
Channel Cay
Chart #EX-43
Soundings in feet at MLW

Great Exuma

Just south of Roker's Point, inside Salt Pond Point is a massive shallow water reef system that is awash at high water. On the hill at the southern end of Ocean Bight there is a conspicuous Batelco station with two large satellite dishes (Chart # EX-42). Just below the Batelco station is the settlement of Farmer's Hill. On older charts you will notice that at one time there was a deep water creek from the lakes in the interior to Ocean Bight that has filled in over the years. Bird Cay, just south of Salt Pond Point is a white-crowned pigeon rookery so please do not disturb any birds you may see nesting there.

South of Farmer's Hill, just off the eastern shore of Great Exuma Island and north of Conch Cay Cut, are some small offlying cays named Duck Cay, Flat Cay, and Channel Cay. Although Duck Cay has a small pond in its interior, Flat Cay (Chart # EX-43) has the most interesting features. Flat Cay is approximately 1600' long and on its northwest shore is a cave with a blue hole 30'-40' deep. Off its southwest point is a tunnel leading in from the sea. Along the south shore are two smaller caves, one shallow cave leads 75' inland.

The waters between Salt Pond Point and Conch Cay Cut (Chart #'s EX-42, 43, & 44) are deep enough for navigation however anyone passing through this area will have to dodge numerous sandbars, rocky bars, and coral reefs. Keep an extra sharp eye out for the two shallow breaking reefs that lie in 15' of water on a line between Bird Cay and the northwest tip of Duck Cay. For these reasons we recommend that cruisers take the traditional entrance to Elizabeth Harbour and George Town at Conch Cay Cut. This is not to say that the experienced skipper who has the ability to read the water, good visibility, calm weather, and an adventurous spirit, cannot safely traverse this area.

CONCH CAY CUT: THE ENTRANCE TO GEORGE TOWN

You are now approaching the one cut that so many cruisers dread the most. Ironically, or maybe fittingly, it is the entrance to George Town, the destination of most of the cruisers that visit the Exumas. There certainly are narrower cuts, cuts with more current, and much shallower cuts, however Conch Cay Cut has one of the worst reputations. It is indeed a dangerous cut in bad conditions or with poor visibility but then again, most cuts in the Exumas can also be described that way.

What is so dangerous about this cut is the reef that lies to the west and north of Conch Cay Light. This is compounded by a reef on the inside that one must turn to port to avoid. With a little swell running the outer reef breaks and can be seen easily while calm seas will hide it from view until you are almost upon it. In heavy weather the cut is impassable as it will break for most of the distance from Conch Cay to Channel Cay. The inner reef is much harder to see in poor conditions. There have been a number of vessels lost on the outer reef in recent years and better navigational aids are called for here. Some local Exumians have suggested that the Bahamian Government place a light on Simon's Point but don't bet on it happening anytime soon. Although in good conditions you can easily pilot by eye through here passing around the inner reef, for safety's sake we recommend that cruisers stick to the traditional routes that mariners have been using for many years to enter Elizabeth Harbour.

A GPS waypoint at 23° 34.30' N, 75° 48.50' W, will place you approximately ½ nm north-northwest of Conch Cay Cut. Prior to Hurricane Lili you could take up a heading of 165° on the large privately maintained daymark above Simon's Point. It was a large square board with a vertical white stripe between two black stripes and it had a radar reflector mounted on its top. The daymark sat atop the hill on Simon's Point just west of the very conspicuous palm trees. The daymark is gone now but may be replaced by the time you arrive in George Town. If the daymark has not been replaced don't panic, the palm trees are very easy to pick out silhouetted against the sky and you can take up a heading of 165° on them. Just to the east of the palm trees (the trees will appear to your left if you are offshore looking at them) are two pink (at this writing) houses (the houses will appear to your right if you are offshore and looking at them). You may actually take up a heading of 165° on the either the daymark, the palm trees, or the pink houses. There is a very conspicuous two-story house with a gabled roof to the east (left) of the pink houses just past Simon's Point. Do not take up your course on this house as it may put you on the reef.

Once past the outer reef, and when Conch Cay Light bears 90°, change course and steer approximately 130° for the beacon on Stocking Island. At this point you will be between Conch Cay and the inner reef that lies approximately ¼ mile west-southwest of Conch Cay. The inner reef is easily seen in good conditions as a brown bar. Once clear of this inner reef their are two basic routes to take. The first route, the one most local mariners take, is to clear the inner reef and take up a heading of 154° on the Batelco Tower at George Town. This route will take you clear of the three shallow sand ridges lying south of Lily Cay. Once on a line between the pink houses on Simon's Point and the beacon on Stocking Island, turn towards the beacon and follow the shoreline of Stocking Island (Chart # EX-46) in the dark water to your desired anchorage. This route is much favored by local boat traffic.

Another traditional route to take once you have cleared the inner reef is to take up a heading of 173° on the daymark on Simon's Point. When you are approximately 200 yards off Simon's Point, take up a heading of 128° until you are on a line between the pink houses on Simon's Point and the beacon on Stocking Island. Turn and steer towards the beacon and pass along the Stocking Island shore in the dark water avoiding the shallow sandbank just to the west of Hamburger Beach. This route also clears the sand ridges south of Lily Cay.

In 1995, PVC bouys were placed in the cut by yachtsmen according to Nassau Port Authority waypoints. With the exception of a green striped buoy off Simon's Point these buoys are no longer there. When entering Conch Cay Cut do not attempt to follow waypoints. You must rely on your eyes to maneuver safely here. Unfortunately many people pass around waypoints as if they were answers to prayers. Any skipper (spelled **F-O-O-L!**) who attempts to enter Elizabeth Harbour through Conch Cay Cut using **anyone's** waypoints deserves whatever ill befalls him. Ed Haxby of Exuma Fantasea, informs me that four of the six yachts that went aground and were lost trying to enter Conch Cay Cut in 1995 were attempting to follow waypoints. The prudent mariner will use every method of navigation available to them, yet the prudent cruising guide writer will never attempt to give you waypoints through such an area. I suggest that you do not attempt to use *anyone's* waypoints through Conch Cay Cut. The risk is far too great and the level of accuracy in GPS in tight quarters is far too small. Trust your eyes.

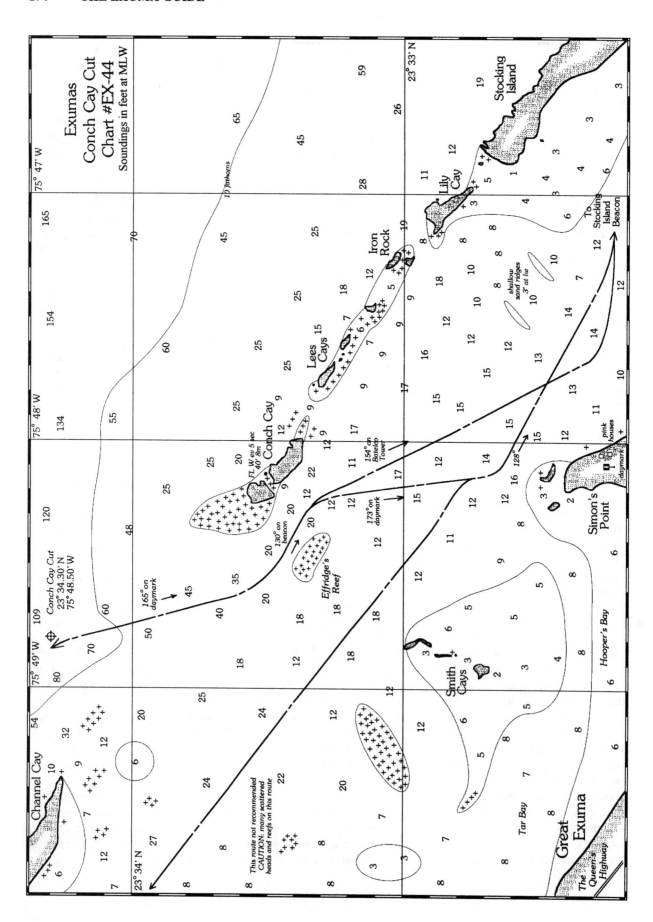

Exumas
Conch Cay Cut
Chart #EX-44
Soundings in feet at MLW

Channel Cay

Conch Cay Cut
23° 34.30' N
75° 48.50' W

165° on daymark

130° on beacon

Effridge's Reef

Conch Cay
FL W ev 5 sec
40' 8m

154° on Batelco Tower

173° on daymark

This route not recommended
CAUTION: many scattered
heads and reefs on this route

Smith Cays

Tar Bay

Great Exuma
The Queen's Highway

Hooper's Bay

Simon's Point
pink houses
daymark

128°

To Stocking Island Beacon

shallow sand ridges
3' at lw

Lees Cays

Iron Rock

Lily Cay

Stocking Island

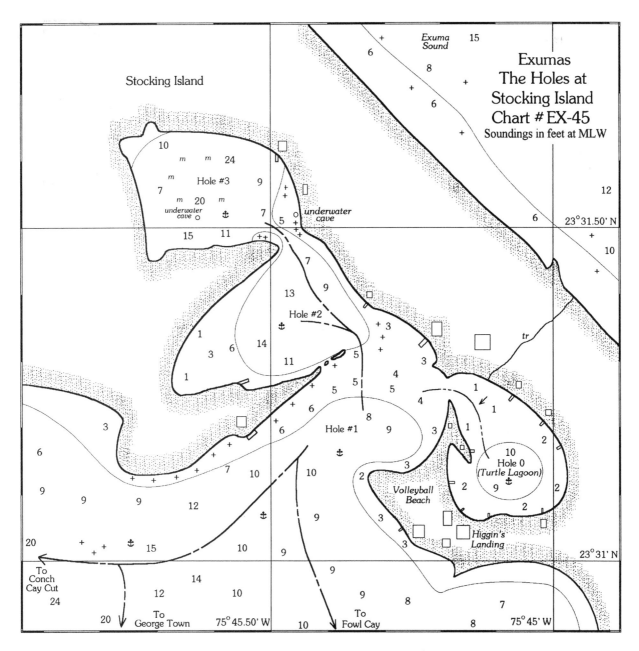

The Holes at Stocking Island — Chart # EX-45

If you would like a local guide (for a fee) to assist your entry you can call Wend MacGregor (*Little Toot*), Brian Collins *(Native Son)* or Wendall Cooper *(Interlude)* on VHF ch.16. If none of these guides is available try Ed Haxby (*Exuma Fantasea*), also on VHF ch.16.

The reef to the north of Conch Cay Light is a good dive in calm weather. Depths range from 3'-20' with many shallow walls and wide ledges.

STOCKING ISLAND

Stocking Island (Chart #'s EX-44, 45, 46, & 47), is the focus for beach/water fun and games in the Elizabeth Harbour area. Good diving can be found all around Stocking Island. Adjacent to Lily Cay, just north of Stocking Island, lies Coral Reef and Sting Ray Reef. Depths here range from 20'-40'. Coral Reef is home to an array of trumpet fish, barracuda, turtles, and large schools of grunts and yellowtail snappers. Sting Ray Reef, lying just to the east, has few corals but many rays. Long Reef, just off the southern tip of Stocking Island is a maze of staghorn and elkhorn coral where you may find turtles, grunts, and hogfish in depths from 25'-60'.

Stocking Island's high shape is easily recognized from over 10 miles away. It is capped by a 25' high stone beacon atop a 100' hill. During the winter cruising season all along the shore of Stocking Island you will see numerous boats lying at anchor. As you enter from Conch Cay Cut, all you can see is a forest of masts starting at Hamburger Beach and proceeding past Volleyball Beach and the entrance to the holes all the way to Sanddollar Beach.

Hamburger Beach, just below the beacon, is a popular spot for boaters to congregate for swimming and eating. The Peace and Plenty Hotel runs a small concession here with food and drinks and an occasional barbecue. Boats anchored off the beach here should remember to use an anchor light at night and to allow boat traffic use of the deep channel to the west of Stocking Island. The mailboat or occasional freighter comes through here at night and they have been known to run aground to avoid carelessly anchored boats in the area.

Boats may anchor along the Stocking Island shoreline from here southeastward but most prefer to anchor just off the holes. The holes at Stocking Island (Chart #EX-45) are packed in the winter when boaters often cram themselves in, lying to two or more anchors to avoid swinging into their nearby neighbors. The entrance is called Hole #1 and is open to the west and southwest. It lies just off Volleyball Beach (The Weather Rock Yacht Club), a very popular gathering spot with almost daily volleyball games organized by the cruisers.

A draft of 6' can be taken from Hole #1 into Hole #2 just past low tide. As you enter the cut between the two holes watch out for the curving reef to starboard, keeping more to the port side of the channel and keeping an eye out for the occasional rock to port. Once in Hole #2 you may anchor in a secure little cove protected from all directions. Proceed into Hole #3 in the same manner, keeping to the port side in the channel to avoid a reef to starboard. The third hole is deeper and has two underwater caves to interest snorkelers. One cave is said to come out on the ocean side. There are some moorings in this hole that are frequently used by people who keep their boats here on a long term basis. If you need to store you boat here indefinitely call Wendall MacGregor, *Little Toot* on VHF ch.16. He will help you arrange for a mooring. The entrance from Hole #1 into Hole 0 is for shallow draft vessels only. The narrow, twisting, shallow channel (marked by stakes) can only be maneuvered at high tide by the shallowest of drafts. For this reason Hole 0 is often referred to as Multihull Hole. There is deep water, 6'-10' at low tide, if you can make it inside. Just inside the entrance to Hole 0 is a trail leading to the ocean side of Stocking Island. The eastern shore of Stocking Island has many offshore reefs and a beautiful long white beach with good shelling. The many offshore reefs are quite popular for spearfishing.

Inside Hole #0 is a small dock leading to Higgin's Landing, a very eco-conscious resort. The facility offers true gourmet dining at 7pm (with reservations by noon), cottage rentals, and transportation to and from George Town. The resort runs entirely on 12 volt and relies on solar panels for power. The toilets are self-composting types which create a very fertile growth medium. This allows the owners to raise a very nice vegetable garden that is nearly impossible to achieve on the rocky cay were it not for the compost.

Proceeding southeastward along the Stocking Island shore there is plenty of room to anchor and the water deepens to 20' and more just a short way off the beaches. The long curving beach before the end of Stocking Island is called Sanddollar Beach and is another popular spot for the cruiser.

If you are heading southeasterly from Stocking Island, bound for Red Shanks or perhaps Fowl Cay for a jump off to Long Island, you will find that good light is essential. These waters are strewn with small, shallow, dangerous patch reefs that are easily seen and avoided. They appear as dark black or brown areas, often surrounded by a ring of brighter green water which is the sand bottom showing through. I cannot overemphasize the importance of paying attention to what you are doing and keeping a sharp lookout at all times. If you turn your head away for a few minutes to talk to someone you may run right up on a head so be careful.

The first obstruction you will come to is a large patch reef lying just south of the southern tip of Stocking Island (Chart # EX-46) off Sanddollar Beach. At the time of this writing the southern tip of the reef was marked by a large black barrel, which may or may not be there when you pass through so keep a good lookout; it is easily seen. The local residents usually keep some kind of marker on this reef. You may pass either north or south of the reef as you head southeastward. There are two reefs you must pass between or go around lying just south of Elizabeth Island. We will discuss these in the section *Elizabeth Island to Fowl Cay*.

Photo courtesy of Nicolas Popov/Island Expeditions

Elizabeth Harbor and George Town - Aerial view showing George Town from the southeast with Rolle Cay and Crab Cay in the Foreground.

GEORGE TOWN AND ELIZABETH HARBOUR

Well, this is it. The turn-around point for most, a stopover for some, the winter refuge for others, but whatever it means to you personally, George Town is the cruising Mecca for east coast sailors. George Town is over 200 years old, initially established in August of 1792. During the season George Town often hosts 300 plus boats with the high to date slightly over 400 during the Cruising Regatta in March of 1994. It seems likely that George Town will soon be able to boast 500 boats in its waters. Part of George Town's popularity is its huge harbour (Chart # EX-46) with many places for the voyager to anchor, either close to town among other like-minded boaters or away from everything with few if any other boats around.

George Town itself has many facilities to equip the boater in need as well as to satisfy the greatest thirst or hunger. There is a dentist's office, a clinic with a nurse and doctor on duty, and a nearby airport with easy connections to Nassau and the United States. If you have some time to spend while at the airport visit Kermit Rolle's Airport Restaurant and Bar, open from 7:30 a.m.-8:00 p.m.. UPS even has an office in George Town that will facilitate your receiving that much needed part.

When approaching George Town from Stocking Island, steer slightly southwest from Hole #1 towards Regatta Point and the anchorages off George Town proper. You can anchor off the Peace and Plenty Hotel in 6'-8' or in Kidd Cove off Regatta Point and Exuma Docking Services in 5'-8'. Elizabeth Harbour was dredged in 1942 when the United States opened a U.S. Navy Seaplane base in George Town but the harbour has been filling in slightly over the years and you will find some spots that have only 3'-4' over them at low water (see Chart # EX-46).

A large cruising community such as is George Town every winter can be quite a problem for boaters and local residents alike. Complaints are often heard concerning the absence of anchor lights and boats blocking the channel to the town dock and Exuma Docking Services. Anchor lights are imperative in a harbour this crowded; not only to protect people in small boats and dinghies, but to protect you as well, especially when the mailboat comes through at night. Everyone knows where the channel is so please do not block it; there is plenty of room to anchor outside the channel. Kidd Cove often develops a sanitation problem with so many boats in the cove and no real flushing action by the tide. Some local residents are studying the problem and welcome any ideas that cruisers may have regarding how to address this problem.

The cruising community usually has a very organized VHF net every morning with weather, announcements, and sometimes news. At 0810 on VHF ch.16 you will be asked to switch to ch.68. If the news is given you will first hear a brief newscast followed by weather and different announcements from local businesses or cruisers seeking mechanical help, a hard to find part, someone to share a taxi to the airport, or a missing dinghy oar (very common). Taxis in George Town monitor VHF ch.16 which makes it very easy to arrange a trip to the airport. Sandy Minns at Exuma Markets will receive faxes and phone messages for you and announces every morning on the net who has faxes or messages waiting at the market. Sandy plans to be able to send faxes for boaters by 1995.

Every March George Town is the scene of a cruiser's party called The Cruising Regatta. Festivities include races, games, sand sculptures, dances, peas and rice eating contests, kid's contests, and a talent show. The Regatta is organized by the local cruising community with the help of some local residents and the proceeds go to help George Town put on the Family Islands Regatta.

After the Cruising Regatta is over, George Town hosts the Family Islands Regatta, the "World Series" of Bahamian sailing. The Regatta, usually held in late April, draws hundred of visitors, Bahamian and foreign alike, who crowd the small settlement and pack the hotels, bet heavily, drive fast boats around the anchorages (once again, don't forget your anchor light), and eat heartily at any of the many eateries quickly set up along the government dock. The festivities are highlighted by the appearance of The Royal Bahamian Police Force Band in their very formal uniforms wrapped in the traditional leopard skins.

Photo courtesy of Nicholas Popov/Island Expeditions

Lady Muriel sails in the Family Islands Regatta.

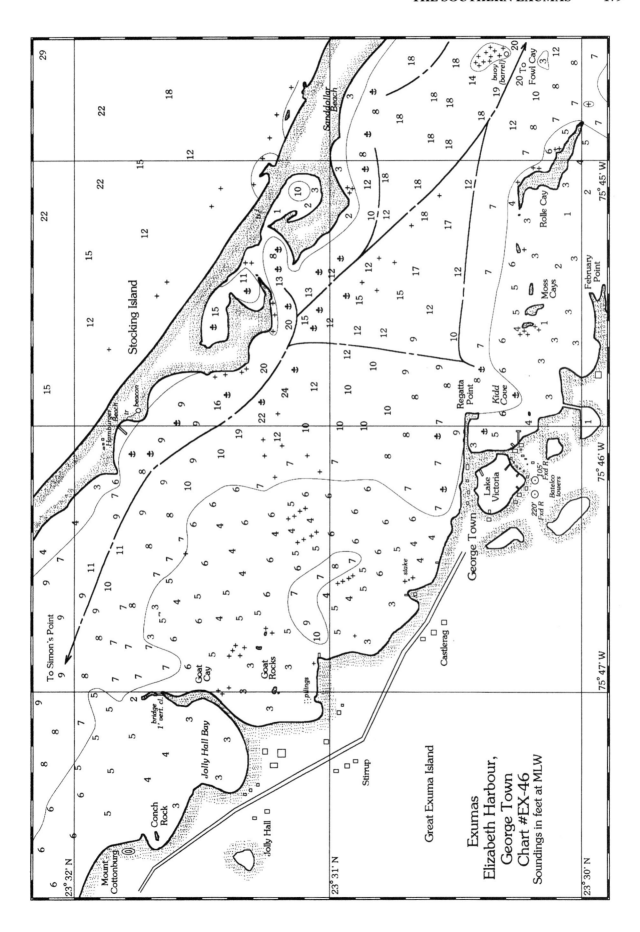

Exumas
Elizabeth Harbour,
George Town
Chart #EX-46
Soundings in feet at MLW

Photo courtesy of Nicolas Popov/Island Expeditions

Royal Bahamas Police Force Band playing at the Family Islands Regatta.

The idea of holding a regatta for Bahamian working sailing craft was conceived by a group of Bahamian and American yachtsmen in the early 1950's. As the age of working sail was drawing to a close and the general condition of the Bahamian fleet was deteriorating, it was felt that the condition of the vessels would be improved by the preparations necessary to ready the vessels for competition. Besides being a fine showcase for Bahamian sailors and boat builders, it would give all a chance to share in the glory as well as introducing visiting yachtsmen to the magnificent cruising grounds that are the Exumas.

It was in late April, 1954, when nearly 70 Bahamian sloops, schooners, and dinghies gathered in Elizabeth Harbour for three days of racing and related activities. The success of this first Regatta prompted the organizers to establish the Out Island Squadron which was to organize and secure funding for more Regattas. Made up of dedicated Bahamian and American yachtsmen, the Out Island Squadron directed the Regatta from its birth in 1954 to its place as one of the outstanding annual Bahamian events. His Royal Highness, Prince Philip visited the Family Islands Regatta in 1959 and his picture from that visit hangs in the Peace and Plenty. In 1973, as part of The Bahamas Independence Celebrations, the annual Regatta was held in Nassau. To organize the race a National Regatta Committee was formed. Since that time, the committee has staffed the Regatta every year in George Town. Today, the people of Exuma raise the better part of the funds and supply the manpower needed for the running of the Regatta.

Initially, the contestants in the early Regattas were working vessels. When they were not racing they were fishing, hauling goods, or in general, earning a living for their owners and crews. It was not long before the seeds of rivalry were sown and the builders were building new boats and the sailors striving for that extra fraction of a knot of speed. The prize money was such that it was not a bad investment to build a boat whose sole purpose was to win the Regatta. The race committee was soon faced with the problem of keeping the competition fair and carrying out the principles on which the Regatta was founded. Over the years the committee successfully managed the transition from working sailboats to racing thoroughbreds and today the Regatta draws entries from all over The Bahamas. The racing rules state that a vessel must be Bahamian designed, built, owned, and sailed. Also, wherever possible, restrictions on materials used or allowed have been introduced to keep these boats as closely related to their working forebears as possible (for instance-no winches). Spectators are allowed to follow the sloops around the race course in their dinghies to watch the often intense competition up close which is also a fantastic opportunity for photographers wanting action shots.

George Town has a number of businesses around the shore of Lake Victoria, usually called "the pond." Let us take a tour of the businesses (Chart # EX-46A) from the Exuma Markets dock where the majority of dinghies tie up, and proceed southward around the pond to Harbour View Laundry. From there we will back up and begin again at Exuma Markets, proceeding northward.

As you enter the pond from Kidd Cove you will pass under an arched bridge. The vertical clearance is 8' and the horizontal clearance is little more than that. There are signs above the arch stating a 3 mph speed limit through the bridge. Dinghies on the inside wishing to go out into Kidd Cove have a sign above the arch specifying for them to yield to incoming traffic. Often during the Family Islands Regatta you will see some visiting Bahamians in high powered small boats such as Boston Whalers playing chicken with the bridge. They will gun their boats, bringing the bow almost vertical heading straight for the bridge at high speed. The first one to drop their bow loses. It is quite interesting to watch no matter how reckless you perceive it. Since most dinghies coming through the bridge are not attempting to play chicken with it, it is advisable to slow down as you come through and not leave a wake for the people tying up at the Exuma Markets dock just to your left upon entering the pond.

Exuma Markets Ltd., the pink building at the head of the dock, is owned by Sandy and Michael Minns. They are most congenial and very helpful to the boating community. As mentioned earlier, Sandy will receive faxes and phone messages for the boaters. The store itself is a fully stocked grocery store where you will find almost anything you need including fresh meat, frozen foods, milk, soft drinks, canned goods, batteries, film, and reading material. There is free well water at the dock, it may taste a little brackish to some folks but it is very good for washing dishes

Photo courtesy of Nicolas Popov/Island Expeditions

The Family Islands Regatta.

and showering. Exuma Markets is open Monday through Friday from 8-6, Saturday from 8-7, and on Sunday from 8-10 a.m.. Exuma Markets will receive mail for you and place it alphabetically in boxes just to the left inside the front door. Have your mail addressed to you, aboard your vessel, care of Exuma Markets, P.O. Box EX29031, George Town, Exuma, Bahamas. Their phone number is 242-336-2033 and their fax number is 242-336-2645.

Exuma Markets allows boaters to deposit their garbage for free in the bins at the northern end of the store by the bridge.

Walking up from the dock at Exuma Markets look to your right where you will see Denzella's N & D Produce. Here you can choose from a large selection of fruits and vegetables along with cold drinks and ice cream. N & D also rents bicycles. Next to N & D is Freda's. Here Freda Rolle serves lunch and baked goods every day except Sunday. Across the street from Exuma Markets is The Scotia Bank building with travel services and real estate businesses on the upper floors along with Brianne's Nail Salon. In the same building is Thompson's Rentals where you can rent a bicycle, scooter, or a car. Just south of the bank is Shaquille's All In One Store with groceries and sundries on the upper floor and Exuma Master Tailors on the ground floor. Next door is Sam Gray's Enterprises and Liquor Store with car rentals. Behind the liquor store is the entrance to Exuma Docking Services which also has laundry facilities. The marina answers to *Sugar One* and has slips with 110v and 220 v with a depth of 5'-8' at low water while the channel approaching the dock has 6' at low water. The marina answers to *Sugar One* and has slips with 110v and 220v electricity with a depth of 5'-8' at low water, the channel approaching the dock has 6' at low water. The marina sells diesel, gas, oil and they take Visa. Take care to secure your boat during heavy east winds as the docks are exposed in that direction. In the same small complex you will find a pay phone, laundromat, Scentious Perfumes, Gray's Electronics, and Sam's Place, a very nice restaurant and bar upstairs overlooking the marina. Between the school and the bank you will see the Mom's Bakery van, Monday through Saturday during the season. Mom has a small bakery in Williams Town and comes to George Town every day with a truckload of goodies. Every purchase gets a hug and a "Praise the Lord" from Mom. Mom is one of the sweetest people you could want to meet and is a heck of a baker.

Walking south along the road you will come to the new Exuma Dive Center. Managers Johnny and Connie Dey offer SCUBA lessons, snorkeling and dive trips, dive equipment rentals, scooter rentals, and boat rentals. Just across the street and further south you will come to the Minister of Finance office where business licenses can be purchased. Across the street is Seaside Realty and Seaside Tours where you can make arrangements to tour the island's historic sites or anyplace else that interests you. Next door is Antiola Gelin's Dress Shop. If you cross the street again you will find Olga's Variety Store where you can purchase foodstuffs and canned goods. South of Olga's is the building that once was M & L Quality Meats. Although M & L's is out of business here, the dock is still standing and as of this writing there is still water to the dock. If you cross the street again you will come to Clarke Hardware which carries a few marine supplies. Just past Clarke's and on the other side of the street is Tino's Restaurant and Bar overlooking Lake Victoria. At the fork in the road you will find the monument to the first squatters who settled this area. Heading north around the pond the first place you will come to is the Batelco office where you can make phone calls during business hours. There are also pay phones at Exuma Docking Services, the Two Turtles Inn, and the Peace and Plenty Hotel. Just around the corner to the left of the Batelco building is Corene Rolle's red cottage where she will do your laundry and upholstery covers for you. North of Batelco is Exuma Auto Parts, The Hillside Bar, and Eddie's Edgewater Club. Eddie's serves fine Bahamian cuisine and is usually crowded during the season so you may want to make a reservation on VHF ch. 16. Eddie's Rake And Scrape nights never fail to draw a big crowd.

Further north on Lake Victoria is a small dock. This was the dinghy dock for Harbour View Laundry, the large pink multi-storied building on the hill overlooking Lake Victoria. The laundry has just re-opened to a great welcome by the cruising community who missed doing laundry while watching the traffic pass below in Lake Victoria or in Elizabeth Harbour.

O.K., back to Exuma Markets and from there northward along the road. The road itself is one-way with traffic heading south. Just across the bridge on the right you will find Muck a Mucks, a very nice ladieswear shop. Next to Muck a Mucks is Exuma Cleaners, where you can have your laundry done for you, and Tranee's Beauty Salon where you can have your hair styled. On the floor above Exuma Cleaners is Munning's Sportswear. On the left as you cross the bridge you will come to Marshall's Liquors and Marshall's Supplies and Gas Station. Drop off your propane tank here for a refill. Behind Marshall's is the Town and Country Cafe open for breakfast, lunch, and dinner by request. They also sell fresh baked bread and some wonderful baked goods that are in high demand. Just past Marshall's is the UPS office which also houses Express Courier and Wally's Photography Studio. To your right you will see Regatta Park, host of the talent show and many other activities during the George Town Cruising Regatta as well as the Family Islands Regatta. Across the street and next door to UPS is the new Top II Bottom. Top II Bottom has a great selection of marine supplies and hardware including hard to find stainless steel nuts and bolts, hydraulic fittings, paints, general hardware, and various sundry goods. Across the street and just past the park is Exuma Supplies and Hardware which also has apartments for rent. Further northeast is the government dock and in the yellow building, the Produce Exchange, where fresh produce is on sale every Wednesday and Thursday.

To your left and across from the park is the Two Turtles Inn. The Inn is one of the most popular gathering spots for the cruising community. It is a welcome shady spot during the day where you can have lunch or a cold drink and a crowded nightspot on Tuesdays and Fridays when they host the Two Turtles Barbecue. The 2-T's has air-conditioned rooms for rent as well as bike and scooter rentals. Next door is the Public Library and school. The Library has a book swap for members of the Library Association which only costs $2 to join. Across the street under the huge shady tree is the straw market where local women sell their handmade plaited goods along with T-shirts, hats, and jewelry. Unfortunately the tree was severely damaged during Hurricane Lili and many of the large limbs that spanned the street had to be removed. A sad sight to veteran George Town cruisers.

Looking northward towards Elizabeth Harbour you will see the large pink Government Building. The building, modeled after the Government House in Nassau, houses the Police Department, Commissioners Office, Post office, and other government offices including Customs and Immigration. Vessels clearing in are required to tie up at the government dock just south of the building. North of the Government building is the large, pink, Peace and Plenty Hotel which boasts 35 air-conditioned rooms and a very nice restaurant and lounge. Their once large dinghy dock was destroyed by Hurricane Lili and will be rebuilt. On some nights there is live music on the outside terrace overlooking Elizabeth Harbour. The Peace and Plenty was named after the ship that transferred Lord John Rolle's many slaves to the Exumas and slaves were once bought and sold on the site where the hotel now sits. In the early 1900's the building was the sight of a sponge warehouse and auction. The fireplace is the oldest part of the building.

Directly across the street from the Peace and Plenty you will find the building that once was Minn's Water Sports. The building is now a government office and its future is uncertain. Next door is the Sandpiper owned by Diane Minns. Diane sells clothes, ceramics, postcards, T-shirts, jewelry, and a good selection of paperback books. Diane is quite the artist and you can purchase prints of her many Bahamian scenes. Down the hill, on the edge of the pond sits Exuma Fantasea. Owner Ed Haxby is a dealer for Johnson Outboards, Boston Whaler, and Carib Inflatables. His crew repairs outboards and inflatables as well as running a first class dive operation. Ed sells and rents scuba equipment, offers PADI instruction, refills scuba tanks, and takes visitors on diving tours of the many reefs and caves in the area. Ed is a marine biologist and an expert on coral reef ecology. Divers attempting to try any of the caves in the area should try going out with Ed before diving on the caves by themselves. Cave dives are especially tricky and one should learn from the expert in this area about what safety precautions to take.

Proceeding northward on the road is the Peace and Plenty boutique with a good fashion selection. Next to the boutique, high on the hill overlooking the town, is the St. Andrew Anglican Church which first opened its doors in 1802. Just past the church, on the same side of the street, is the dentist's office and clinic. The clinic, which is staffed by a doctor and a nurse, opens at 9:00 am and it is advisable to get there early. Fees are very reasonable and the care is excellent. Anything that they cannot treat in George Town will be referred to Nassau. Three miles west of George Town is Darville Lumber for all your construction needs. If you need an electrician or refrigeration mechanic call *Turtle Maintenance* on VHF ch. 16.

Now that you are familiar with George Town, settle in and enjoy it; stay a few days or the whole season. If you head south to the Caribbean or north back to the States, chances are you will see George Town again. You may leave George Town but George Town rarely leaves you.

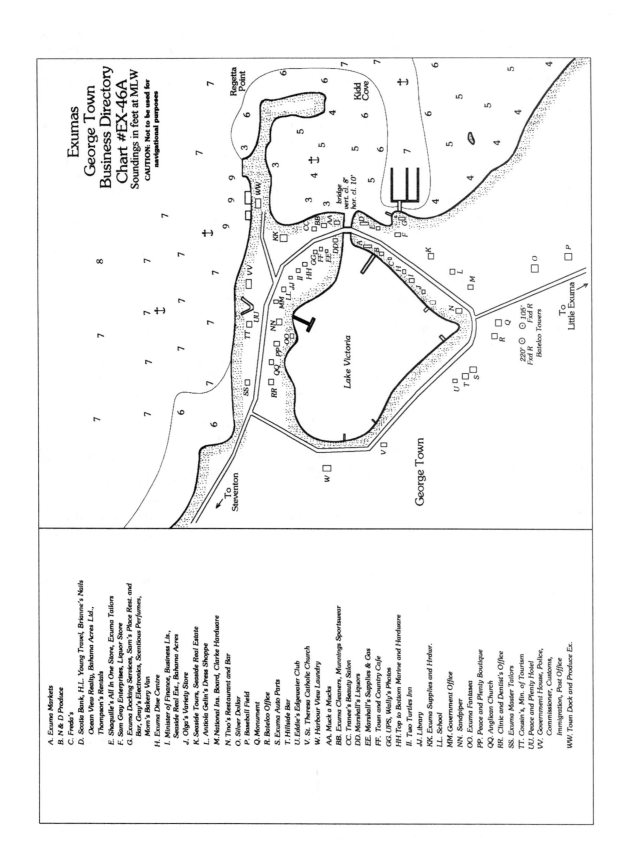

Exumas
George Town
Business Directory
Chart #EX-46A
Soundings in feet at MLW
CAUTION: Not to be used for
navigational purposes

Regetta Point

Kidd Cove

bridge
vert. cl. 8'
hor. cl. 10'

Lake Victoria

George Town

To Steventon

To Little Exuma

Batelco Towers
220' ⊙ 105'
Fxd R ⊙ Fxd R

A. Exuma Markets
B. N & D Produce
C. Freda's
D. Scotia Bank, H.L. Young Travel, Brianne's Nails
    Ocean View Realty, Bahama Acres Ltd.,
    Thompson's Rentals
E. Shaquille's All In One Store, Exuma Tailors
F. Sam Gray Enterprises, Liquor Store
G. Exuma Docking Services, Sam's Place Rest. and
    Bar, Gray's Electronics, Scentious Perfumes,
    Mom's Bakery Van
H. Exuma Dive Centre
I. Minister of Finance, Business Lis.,
    Seaside Real Est., Bahama Acres
J. Olga's Variety Store
K. Seaside Tours, Seaside Real Estate
L. Antola Gelin's Dress Shoppe
M. National Ins. Board, Clarke Hardware
N. Tino's Restaurant and Bar
O. Silver Dollar
P. Baseball Field
Q. Monument
R. Batelco Office
S. Exuma Auto Parts
T. Hillside Bar
U. Eddie's Edgewater Club
V. St. Theresa Catholic Church
W. Harbour View Laundry
AA. Muck a Mucks
BB. Exuma Cleaners, Munnings Sportswear
CC. Tranee's Beauty Salon
DD. Marshall's Liquors
EE. Marshall's Supplies & Gas
FF. Town and Country Cafe
GG. UPS, Wally's Photos
HH. Top to Bottom Marine and Hardware
II. Two Turtles Inn
JJ. Library
KK. Exuma Supplies and Hrdwr.
LL. School
MM. Government Office
NN. Sandpiper
OO. Exuma Fantasea
PP. Peace and Plenty Boutique
QQ. Anglican Church
RR. Clinic and Dentist's Office
SS. Exuma Master Tailors
TT. Cousin's, Min. of Tourism
UU. Peace and Plenty Hotel
VV. Government House, Police,
    Commissioner, Customs,
    Immigration, Post Office
WW. Town Dock and Produce Ex.

THE ISLAND OF GREAT EXUMA

The island of Great Exuma is best explored either by rental car or on one of the local sightseeing tours. I have found Christine Rolle's *Taxi 25* to be the most unique and informative, if not the most entertaining, of the tours. Christine, the unofficial "Official Ambassador of Great Exuma," will pick you up at 10:00 am in front of the Peace and Plenty for a four hour tour of the island of Great Exuma. Along the way she will tell you of the history of the island and introduce you to bush medicine. Christine is the author of a book on the subject and she will often stop along the way to pull some leaves and demonstrate what they are and what they can do for you. After a stop for lunch you will arrive back in George Town all the wiser for your experience. Words cannot do this tour justice, you must spend a day with Christine, call *Taxi 25* on VHF ch.16.

Heading north from George Town, the first settlement you will come upon is The Hermitage. The Fergusons, Loyalists from the Carolinas, settled here after the American War of Independence. There are several tombs dating back to the 1700's in the area. Just inland from the western shore of Great Exuma is Moss Town, a small farming settlement. Further north you will come to Ramsey, named after the family who settled there in the 1850's. There is a gas station, restaurant and bar, and the Central Highway Inn in Ramsey.

Mount Thompson was named after the first settlers and the fact that the area appears mountainous. Mount Thompson is the farming center of Exuma with the only Agriculture Farm Packing House on the island. Fresh produce is brought in daily and onions, which are so plentiful that they are on the Exuma Coat of Arms, are exported in great quantities. The settlement lies just above the Three Sister's Rocks (Chart # EX-42) which are not to be confused with the Three Sister's Rocks between Square Rock Cay and Glass Cay. The Forest is the next small community you will come to on your northbound journey. It is a small community which practiced tenant farming until the last 20 years after much confusion between the owners and the tenants in the 1960's.

Farmer's Hill has the highest point on Great Exuma, Gun Hill, with a beautiful view overlooking almost the entire island. The Batelco station with its large satellite dishes mark this community from well offshore. Steventon, Roker's Point, and Rolleville are all covered in previous sections.

Stuart Manor and Curtis are two small settlements a good distance inland on the northwestern tip of Great Exuma. The few residents are mainly involved with farming for a living. There is a bakery in Stuart Manor. Richmond Hill, once a flourishing community, is now all but extinct. Southbound on the Queen's Highway are some residential developments and little else until you reach The Ferry.

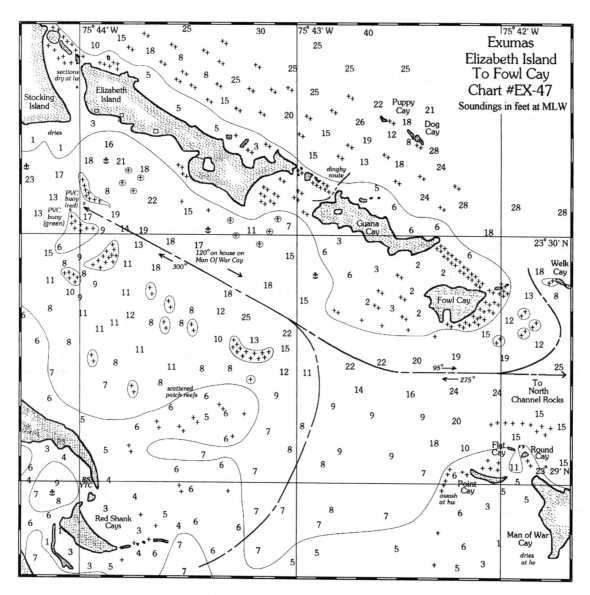

ELIZABETH ISLAND TO FOWL CAY

Elizabeth Island (Chart # EX-47) lies just southeast of Stocking Island and is approximately 1 mile long. Its main attraction, besides its good lee anchorages, is the multitude of reefs lying just off its eastern shore. If coasting down its eastern shore you will want to give this cay a wide berth, some of the reefs have only 4'-6' of water over them. In a small bight on the southern shore of Elizabeth Island is a shallow, narrow mangrove creek which leads inland to a small lake on whose shore sits the not too old remains of a house with a concrete dock and cistern.

The cuts between Stocking Island, Elizabeth Island, Guana Cay, and Fowl Cay are all almost entirely blocked by reef structure, some of which dries at low water. Guana Cay is approximately ½ mile long and was once worked for Sisal. Guana Cay is now private and visits ashore should be by invitation only. Fowl Cay, as befits its name, is the home of white-crowned pigeons, doves, and Bahamian Ducks. Please do not disturb any of these creatures as they nest. There is a little cave on the southern shore of Fowl Cay that may be entered by a small diver in calm weather.

All the cays from Stocking Island southeast to Fowl Cay offer good lee anchorages although they are no place to be caught in the prelude to a frontal passage. From Stocking Island follow the lay of the islands southeast avoiding the numerous shallow patch reefs that are scattered throughout these waters.

Heading southeast from Stocking Island you will come across two large patch reefs that lie virtually across the center of Elizabeth Harbour (Chart # EX-47). You may pass these either to the north, along the shore of Elizabeth Cay (watch out for stray heads), or to the south, along the shore of Crab Cay. Most people choose to pass between the two. The passage between the reefs is well marked as of this writing. The southern tip of the northern reef is marked with a 10" PVC buoy with red stripes while the northern tip of the southern reef is marked by a PVC buoy with green stripes. Remember, red-right-returning, proceeding southeast you are leaving the harbour and heading out to sea. Once you clear the reef marked by the barrel off Stocking Island, line up the conspicuous house that sits atop the hill on Man Of War Cay between the two buoys and steer for this on an approximate heading of 120°. You will pass between the buoys in 19' of water at low tide. From this point you may steer toward Fowl Cay to anchor or head to the entrance to Red Shanks. If you are bound for Long Island it is best to anchor in the vicinity of Fowl Cay at the eastern entrance to Elizabeth Harbour the night before your planned departure. This will give you a better angle on the wind and make the journey a few miles shorter than leaving from the western entrance at Conch Cay Cut.

If you are leaving Elizabeth Harbour by the Eastern Channel, the best route is to stay in the deep water between Fowl Cay (watch out for the patch reefs to the south of Fowl Cay) and Man Of War Cay and take up a heading of 95° on the largest of the North Channel Rocks. There is a passage out between Fowl Cay and Welk Cay but it involves steering between some patch reefs and can often be a very violent cut (as can the entire eastern entrance). The Eastern Channel heading towards North Channel Rocks is much wider, deeper, and safer. Unless you are heading north into Exuma Sound the pass between Welk Cay and Fowl Cay will gain you nothing.

CRAB CAY AND RED SHANKS

Crab Cay (Chart # EX-48), lying just southeast of George Town and south of Stocking Island, is approximately 1½ miles long. It has many interesting ruins or buildings, gates, and fences ashore and boasts a couple of underwater caves.

In 1782, a British naval officer, in a report to the Duke of Richmond, stated that "Crab Cay, in the harbour of Exuma, is well suited for a town." In 1784, William Walker, a Loyalist from west Florida, sought refuge in The Bahamas, eventually settling in the Exumas and receiving title for Crab Cay. Walker had access to considerable funds and built a plantation as nice as any in The Bahamas. The arched windows in the buildings and the carved stonework of the gates testify to the quality of the stoneworkers and the construction. All that remains of the manor house is the foundation but the flying buttresses will give you an idea as to the size of the original structure. The house was originally built of brick and stood two stories tall with an impressive view of Elizabeth Harbour and Great Exuma. All the bricks in the construction have long since been taken and some locals say one shipload of them lies at the bottom of Elizabeth Harbour just off Fowl Cay. There are two large columns and steps to the northeast of the manor house which were part of an extensively terraced area in the front of the house. The cook house lies at the southwest corner of the manor house and is still essentially intact but as time passes is rapidly being vandalized as are all the ruins. There was a gun placement on the cay to protect the inhabitants from pirates who still plagued the area. To the west of the cookhouse are the remains of a walled garden with beautiful, round carved stone pillars for gates on the east and west sides. Crab Cay was abandoned around 1830 and was returned to the Crown sometime prior to 1843.

The ruins are easily seen from the southern shore of Crab Cay and a well marked trail leads to it from the small beach. If you plan to visit the ruins bring some bug spray. There are trails leading up from Ruins Bay where you can anchor in 6'-7' at low water. From Kidd Cove pass around Rolle Cay and follow the shore until you can make the turn into Ruins Bay. Watch our for the reef in the center of the entrance and steer to one side or the other to avoid it. A shallow mangrove creek separates Crab Cay and Little Crab Cay and you can dinghy through it at high tide. There are two caves on the eastern shore of Crab Cay.

On the northeastern shore of Crab Cay, just south of Little Crab Cay lie the remains of the *Exuma Pride*. Before the *Grandmaster* became the official George Town mailboat, the community went through a period of no regular mailboat service. Several local businessmen got together and bought the *Exuma Pride* and put her into service. For reasons that are unclear, she became embroiled in a series of legal squabbles and one night she broke from her mooring and wound up where she now lies. All that is left now is her rusting hull, anything of any value long since removed. There is an underwater cave around the corner in the next bight just south of the freighter.

The area between Crab Cay and the mainland of Great Exuma is very shallow and sections of it dry at low water. The people of George Town are trying to establish this as a marine park to protect the fish in the area. At one time there were schools of small tarpon in these waters and the local residents want to bring them back. There is a blue hole in 8' of water at low tide between Kelsall Cay and Crab Cay. The blue hole, home to a large nurse shark, is more of a crevasse than a hole, stretching downwards some 90'. Kelsall Cay, once called Burrows Cay, has the ruins of an old wall cutting across the island. John Devine Cay, once called Sylvanus Cay after a former squatter, was also once called Mowbray's Cay after a John Mowbray.

Below the southeastern tip of Crab Cay is the entrance to the Red Shanks anchorage. This is a very popular spot during the season for those who wish to anchor away from the hustle and bustle of George Town. The anchorages in the Red Shanks area are very well protected in all directions and you will be quite safe and snug there. The Red Shanks anchorage is home to the Red Shanks Yacht and Tennis Club. The facilities are right on the beach at the southeastern tip of Crab Cay. During the season there is usually some sort of get-together every night at the RSYTC. If you wish to join, look up the Commodore when you arrive. Unfortunately, the RSYTC does not have beach barbecues during high tides.

To enter Red Shanks from George Town you have two routes from which to choose. If you round Rolle Cay (Chart # EX-48) and follow the eastern shore of Crab Cay you will have to weave your way through some small but shallow patch reefs near the southeastern end of Crab Cay. The water will shallow to 5'-6' at low tide but with good light you can easily pilot your way through. The best route is to pass through the reefs that are marked by PVC buoys just south of Elizabeth Island (see previous section *Elizabeth Island to Fowl Cay*) and take up a course of 120° on the conspicuous house on Man of War Cay. When the southeastern tip of Crab Cay begins to come abeam, look for the large patch reef that lies well before the shallows west of Man of War Cay. Pass either side of the reef although the better water is to the east of it. Steer approximately southwest until you can round up into the Red Shanks anchorage passing John Devine Cay to port. There are actually three areas to anchor here. The first one lies in the deep water just south of Crab Cay and west of Red Shanks Cay. The other two anchorages lie more to the west along the Crab Cay shore. The entrances to both should only be attempted at high tide and with good visibility. To enter the first inner hole, head toward the southern shore of Crab Cay to clear the shallows that work northward from John Devine Cay and parallel the shore into the hole. You can take 6' through here at high tide. The entrance to the second hole is slightly more difficult as you must pass between two sandbars in a channel that will take 6' at high water. The deeper water lies slightly closer to the Crab Cay shore and you must steer around the point to avoid a shallow bar. The bottom here is generally sand and if you take it slow and easy you should not run into trouble. It is a short 5-10 minute dinghy ride to George Town from Red Shanks depending on the size of your outboard motor. Rowing will take you quite a bit longer.

A very nice anchorage lies to the west of Red Shanks, inside the western arm of Crab Cay. This anchorage is good for vessels with drafts slightly exceeding 6'. There is 7'-9' at low water in places here and the holding is good. This anchorage is usually occupied by shoal draft multihulls due to the shallows in the approach channel from Red Shanks. Some multihulls gain access to the anchorage by using the traditional dinghy route from George Town to Red Shanks leaving Flamingo Bay to starboard and passing through Cottage Cut. For deeper draft vessels the entrance lies between the first two anchorage basins in Red Shanks, just southwest of the Red Shanks Yacht And Tennis Club. The entrance is over the shallow sandbank between the two holes and should only be attempted at high tide or just before high tide. Steer between John Devine Cay and the small rock that lies to its northwest, favor the small rock but not too closely. Round the narrow unnamed cay to starboard in 4'-6' at low water and pass into the deeper depths (7'-9') that lie to its west. Watch out for the rocky bar that runs eastward from the small cay that lies to the south of the anchorage area as shown on Chart EX-48.

If Red Shanks is too crowded you can anchor behind Isaac Cay in Master Harbour. Approach the harbour as you would to enter Red Shanks and steer around the tip of Isaac Cay. This route has a few 4' spots at low water but it deepens the further inside you get. Do not block this channel as there is a little commercial traffic to the dock on the shore of Great Exuma. This anchorage is shallow so check the depths before you decide to anchor and the tide goes out on you leaving you aground and embarrassed. Ashore by the wreck of the tug sits the new George Town Marina And Repair. This new boat yard has been in construction since 1996 and the first phase is scheduled for opening sometime in mid to late 1997. A travel lift will allow cruisers to haul their boats and do their own work if they wish, or if they prefer, the yard will handle it. A marine store, docks, slips, and fuel sales will all follow in due time. There is a small mooring between the marina area and Isaac Cay that is private.

Isaac Cay has a hill on its southwest side that rises to 45'. On the southeast side of this hill in the cliffs is a bat cave with several rooms and an entrance about 20' above the high water mark. This cave is not easy to find so bring a machete and bug spray if you intend to search for it. Isaac Cay is separated from the mainland by a small tidal creek that dries at low water. Along the shoreline of Great Exuma, just southeast of Isaac Cay are several very conspicuous caves and one especially large structure that appears to be more of a natural bridge than a cave.

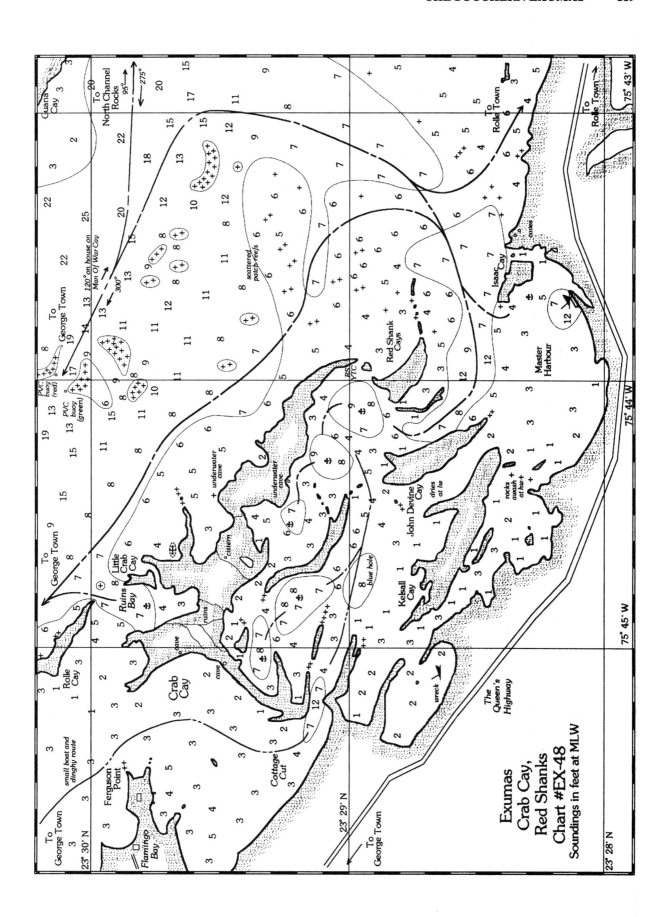

Exumas
Crab Cay,
Red Shanks
Chart #EX-48
Soundings in feet at MLW

Photo courtesy of Nicolas Popov/Island Expeditions

Two-hundred year old tombs in Rolle Town.

MAN OF WAR CAY, ROLLE TOWN

Man of War Cay (Chart # EX-49), lying just offshore and east of Rolle Town, is home to the remains of an ancient battery built of rubble masonry, which once guarded the entrance to George Town harbour. Actually, any vessel entering from Little Exuma was protected by the hills lying southeast of the battery which were higher than the battery at that time. The battery was very small with room for only one gun. This cannon, which has been recovered, was 5' 9" long with a bore of 4¾" and its shot weighed 14 pounds. Lobster Reef lies in the Eastern Channel just north of Man of War Cay. Here you will find huge coral formations teeming with fish life (if they haven't all been fished out by the time you get there).

There is a small anchorage that would be good in west or northwest winds just south of the eastern point of the cay. To enter the anchorage pass between the large reefs lying just off Man of War Cay and the north shore of the cay. You will be in 10'-15' of water through here but should give the eastern point of the cay a wide berth. The anchorage is not recommended in winds from any easterly direction. Good visibility and weather is a must to pilot through the reefs in the area.

Moriah Harbour Cay is approximately 1 mile long and lies just to the southeast of Man of War Cay. It has a good lee anchorage in settled weather but a little swell does works its way in around the point. Enter the anchorage from the north passing between South Channel Rocks and Middle Channel Rocks, or by heading across from the east point of Man of War Cay. Watch out for small patch reefs and steer around them. The entire western shore of Moriah Harbour Cay is shallow and most of it is beach. The southern shore has a small channel that allows dinghies and small boats to reach The Ferry. The area between Moriah Harbour Cay and Little Exuma is very shallow and most of it dries at low water.

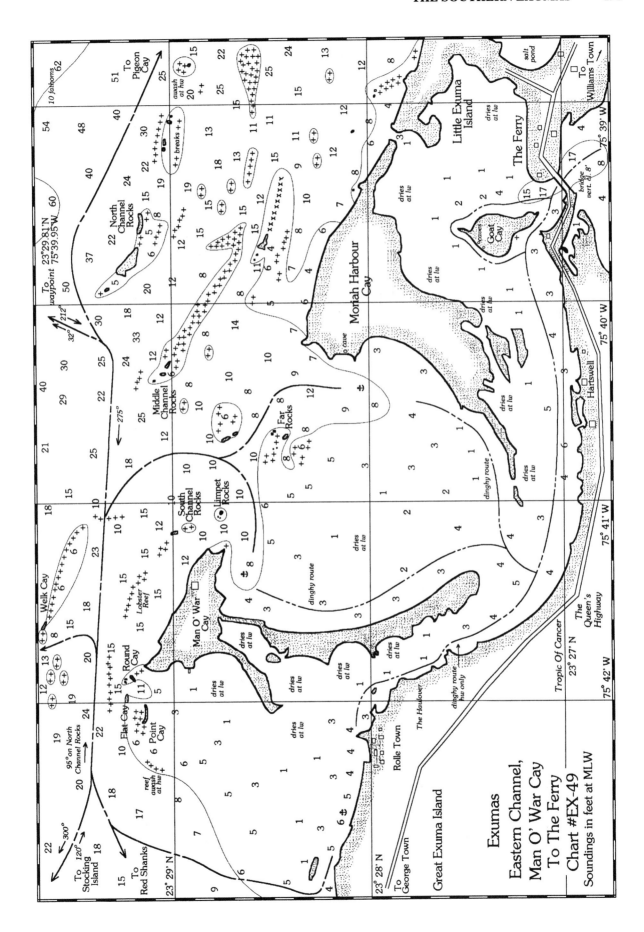

Exumas
Eastern Channel,
Man O' War Cay
To The Ferry
Chart #EX-49
Soundings in feet at MLW

Rolle Town lies atop a hill on Great Exuma overlooking Man of War Cay. Vessels drawing up to 6' can enter the channel along the shore of Great Exuma east of Isaac Cay at high tide and anchor in pockets of deep water 5'-6' deep at low tide in places. Rolle Town is generation land, deeded to Rolles in perpetuity, and there are tombs in Rolle Town that date back 200 years. The area where Rolle Town sits has a large fresh water well which dates back to slave days when it was used by the plantation. Television star Esther Rolle was born in Rolle Town.

From Rolle Town to The Ferry there is a high tide only dinghy route with a very interesting feature. Just south of Rolle Town is The Haulover, a series of rock walls that you must take your dinghy through. These walls were built very long ago, no one can really say when, by the people of Rolle Town. They were constructed in the water to provide a passage through this extremely shallow area. You may have to tilt your dinghy engine up slightly to get through in spots over a sandy bottom.

Hartswell is a small community between Rolle Town and The Ferry along the small boat route to the Ferry. There are a few families living here who rely on farming and fishing for their living.

THE EASTERN CHANNEL

The Eastern Channel (Chart # EX-49) is a deep draft entry to Elizabeth Harbour. It is the likely entrance to Elizabeth Harbour if you are coming from Simms or Salt Pond, Long Island, or if you have rounded the tip of Cape Santa Maria on your way north from the Bahamian Out Islands or the Caribbean.

If approaching from Long Island, a GPS waypoint at 23° 29.81' N, 75° 39.95' W places you approximately ¼ nm northeast of the eastern entrance to Elizabeth Harbour in about 75' of water. From this point line up Middle Channel Rocks and Far Rocks on a heading of 212° and steer that course until you can make a turn to starboard and steer 275° with the largest of the North Channel Rocks on your stern. Do not confuse Far Rocks with the small unnamed rocks that lie more to their northwest. Watch out for the reef that works its way southeastward from Welk Cay into the channel. Where the southeastern tip of this reef approaches the channel you will cross a shallow area with 10' over coral. Make sure that the current does not push you onto the Welk Cay reef. To approach the Stocking Island area, turn to starboard slightly to a heading of 300° when you can place the conspicuous house on Man of War Cay on your stern.

If you are departing Stocking Island or Elizabeth Island by way of the Eastern Channel, take up a course of 120° on the house on Man of War Cay. When the largest of the North Channel Rocks bears 95°, change course and take up that heading. Once again, watch out for the large reef system that works southeastward from Welk Cay and the 10' shallow spot over coral at low water. As you get closer to the North Channel Rocks and fall in line with Middle Channel Rocks and Far Rocks, place them on your stern and steer 32°. This will take you out into deeper water where you may take up a heading for Cape Santa Maria or Salt Pond, Long Island by way of the sandbank north of Sandy Cay. A course of 113° for 17.5 miles from the entrance to Eastern Channel will bring you to the GPS waypoint at 23° 24.93' N, 75° 21.62' W which lies ½ nm north of the sandbank. From this point you can take up a course for Simms or Salt Pond, Long Island. Remember, if you run from the GPS waypoint at Eastern Channel to the waypoint north of Sandy Cay be sure to keep an eye out for the Black Rocks lying well offshore of Little Exuma. Vessels proceeding southeastward to Pigeon Cay or Hog Cay Cut should follow the lie of the small rocks just southeast of North Channel Rocks. Stay about ¼ nm off the rocks and you will be in 30'-50' of water. You can pass inside these rocks along the shore of Little Exuma but there are many scattered reefs that you must avoid, some with only 3' over them. If you choose this route good light and weather is essential, do not attempt this route on a cloudy day or with the sun in your eyes. This is not an area you wish to be in with a heavy ground swell running.

THE ISLAND OF LITTLE EXUMA

Just south of Great Exuma lies the island of Little Exuma. The closest anchorage, and the last good lee before Hog Cay Cut, is at Pigeon Cay (Chart # EX-50). The beach on the western shore is good for shelling as are the eastern beaches after strong onshore winds. To enter the anchorage, proceed out the Eastern Channel and parallel the lie of the rocks to the southeast of North Channel Rocks staying about ¼ nm mile off. When you pass the last small rock steer towards Pigeon Cay and enter from the north side. You can anchor just off the beach in 10'-12' over a sandy bottom. The beach is steep-to and is a good place to careen your boat for a bottom job in calm weather. As mentioned earlier, it is possible to pass between the outlying rocks and the shore of Little Exuma. The route is tricky at best with numerous reefs to be avoided and it is much easier and safer to go outside. Boats anchored at Moriah Harbour Cay may attempt this inshore route but only because it would be much shorter.

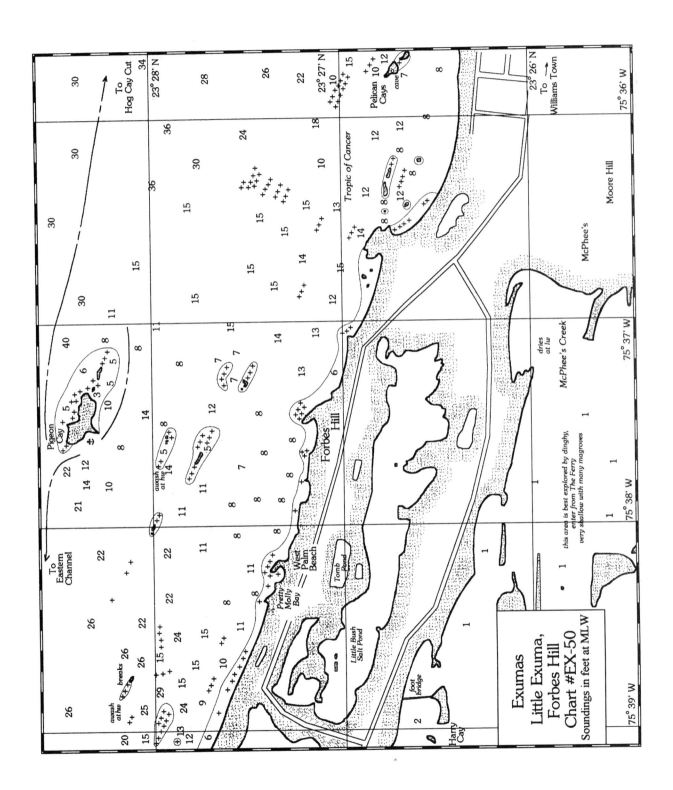

Exumas
Little Exuma,
Forbes Hill
Chart #EX-50
Soundings in feet at MLW

The first settlement on the northwestern tip of the Little Exuma is The Ferry. The two islands, now connected by a bridge, were once separate and the only means of crossing was by a ferry whose remains may still be seen on the south end of Great Exuma. The small cay between Great Exuma and Little Exuma is called Goat Cay and was home to the local ferryman. The office of ferryman entailed operating the ferry between Great Exuma and Little Exuma and was an important position even though it did not pay well. Goat Cay was given to the ferryman by the local Board of Works of Exuma so that he could better support his family by the sweat of his brow. The Board had no real authority to do this and several times the Crown said that its ownership of the cay should be respected and that the local officials, who quite often ignored this request, had no right to give it away. There are the ruins of some pasture walls on Goat Cay and two small, but interesting caves along its western shore just above the waterline.

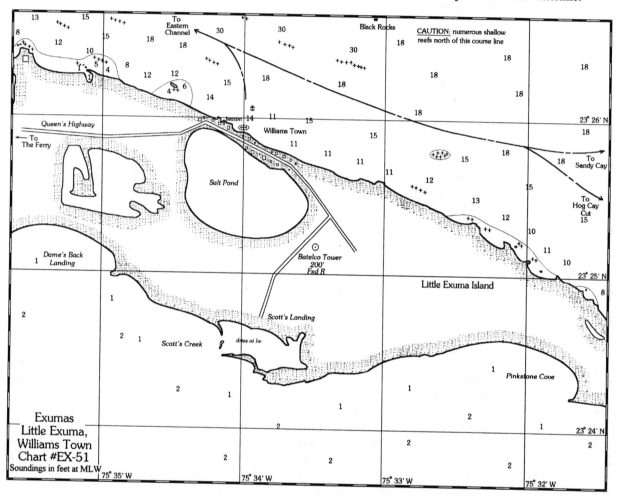

Exumas
Little Exuma,
Williams Town
Chart #EX-51
Soundings in feet at MLW

The oldest building in The Ferry is the Cotton House, home of George and Gloria Patience which was once a post office. Gloria is locally known as *The Shark Lady* as the sign in her front yard proudly proclaims to the numerous tourists who find their way here daily. In the almost 20 years since she and her husband retired here, she has landed over 1000 sharks in her 13' Boston Whaler including an 18' tiger shark with a partially digested 7' lemon shark in its stomach. She sells the teeth and is an archeologist, artist, and sailor, being the only women to skipper a boat in the Family Islands Regatta. Ask her about her all girl topless crew.

There is a small boat dinghy route to the Ferry that leads in from Man of War Cay and the western shore of Moriah Harbour Cay (Chart # EX-49). Just to the west of Goat Cay are some concrete pilings in about 3' of water with 4" x 4" wooden beams rising out of the water at odd angles so be careful. Just across from Goat Cay on the southern tip of Great Exuma is the new Peace and Plenty Bonefishing Lodge which runs bonefishing expeditions in the nearby shallow waters. The owners are building an 8 room lodge adjacent to the main building which should be open in 1995. For information contact the Peace and Plenty Hotel in George Town or call 242-345-5555. The small cays on the south side of The Ferry are only accessible by dinghy or small boat as they are very shallow with many mangroves and good bonefishing on the flats on both sides of the bridge. The bridge at The Ferry has an 8' vertical clearance and is almost as wide between the support pilings.

Further south, just before you get to Forbes Hill, named after early settlers, are the remains of a once exclusive resort called the Sand Dollar Beach Club which actually sits on Pretty Molly Bay and was once called the Pretty Molly Bay Club. Pretty Molly was a slave girl who is believed to have grown so despondent about her status that she walked into the bay one night and never came out. She did not disappear completely as generations of local residents have claimed to see her on the beach on moonlit nights.

Just south of Pretty Molly Bay is La Shante, a restaurant and bar with cottages to rent on a beautiful crescent beach. For lunch or dinner reservations call BM, the manager, on VHF ch.16, he answers to *La Shante*. Just off the point to the northwest of La Shante is the site of a wreck of an old rum runner. Old bottles are often found on the rocks to the northwest of the restaurant and around the corner by the next beach is a large anchor and some chain in about 5'-10' of water, probably from the same wreck.

In 1892, the British built a fort at Forbes Hill on a nearby hill just north of the settlement. The Fort was surrounded by a wall 4' high. It consisted of two main buildings with four cannons placed along its perimeter. The Fort sits above Fort Bay, the sight of a beautiful beach and home of a legendary mermaid who sits on the shore on moonlit nights combing her long hair. There is a tree in Forbes Hill which gives off a substance the color of blood every Good Friday.

South of Forbes Hill are some small cays called the Pelican Cays. The largest and most northern is Pelican Cay which has a cave with an arched mouth 12' wide running inland about 75'. It is 30' wide inside with a shaft rising up. South of Forbes Hill the small, shallow patch reefs that you have been avoiding become fewer, deeper, and less of a hazard to navigation. After Williams Town they disappear completely, the only reefs you will find in that area will be along the shore and a huge area of reefs about two miles offshore that parallel the islands of Little Exuma and Hog Cay for a couple of miles, favor the shoreline in these areas. These reefs are extremely shallow and there are only a few breaks through them. If paralleling the shore of Little Exuma southeastward you must also keep an eye out for the very conspicuous Black Rocks. There are two groups of 4 rocks, each lying east-southeast of Forbes Hill and two smaller rocks lying off Williams Town. If you plan to steer a course from Eastern Channel to the GPS waypoint off the sandbank north of Sandy Cay you must keep an eye out to avoid these rocks which lie well offshore.

Williams Town (Chart #EX-51), a settlement of about 200 people with many old buildings, lies midway along the eastern shore of Little Exuma. It is most notable for its abandoned salt pond which for years made Williams Town the center of a huge salt industry employing over 800 people. Today, fishing, farming, and plaiting makes up the mainstay of existence for the residents. The stone beacon, reminiscent of a Greek column and built over 200 years ago, once guided ships which picked up salt for export to Nova Scotia and North America. There is a marker on the beach at Williams Town showing where the Tropic Of Cancer crosses the island. Although many places up and down through this area claim that the Tropic of Cancer passes through them, the Tropic of Cancer actually passes through The Ferry and Forbes Hill at 23° 27' N (Please note that the Tropic of Cancer is actually a moving position and can change slightly from year to year, I am using 23° 27' N as referenced in *The American Practical Navigator-Bowditch*, if you have any complaints write to Nathaniel Bowditch).

There are many ruins in the area and the most interesting are the ruins of the Hermitage Estate adjacent to the salt pond. It originally processed cotton for the Kelsall family, Loyalists who moved here in 1790 in the schooner *Eliza*. You will also find the ruins of the Gin House, the oldest building, the Guava Factory, a gin mill, Nigger House where slaves were kept, and tombs of what is believed to be the Kelsall's children.

Mom's Bakery (remember Mom and her van from George Town?) does good business in Williams Town. There are two stores in Williams Town. The Coin Shop sells groceries, meat, and fresh fish. Bullard's sells groceries and wholesale liquors. There is a 200' Batelco Tower in Williams Town with a fixed red light at its top.

HOG CAY AND HOG CAY CUT

Hog Cay (Chart # EX-52), is 3¼ miles long and lies just south of Little Exuma. Hog Cay is private and visits ashore should be by invitation only. Hog Cay once had the rather unique name of "Captain Mingo Rolle-God Rest The Dead Cay."

Vessels heading for Simms or Salt Pond, Long Island can head south from Williams Town and parallel the shore of Hog Cay, staying at least ½ nm off to avoid the shallows. A GPS waypoint at 23° 24.93' N, 75° 21.62' W will place you approximately ½ nm mile north of the northeastern tip of the shallow sandbank that lies to the northeast of Sandy Cay (Chart # EX-53). Remember, if you run from the GPS waypoint at Eastern Channel to this waypoint to be sure and keep and eye out for the Black Rocks lying well off Little Exuma.

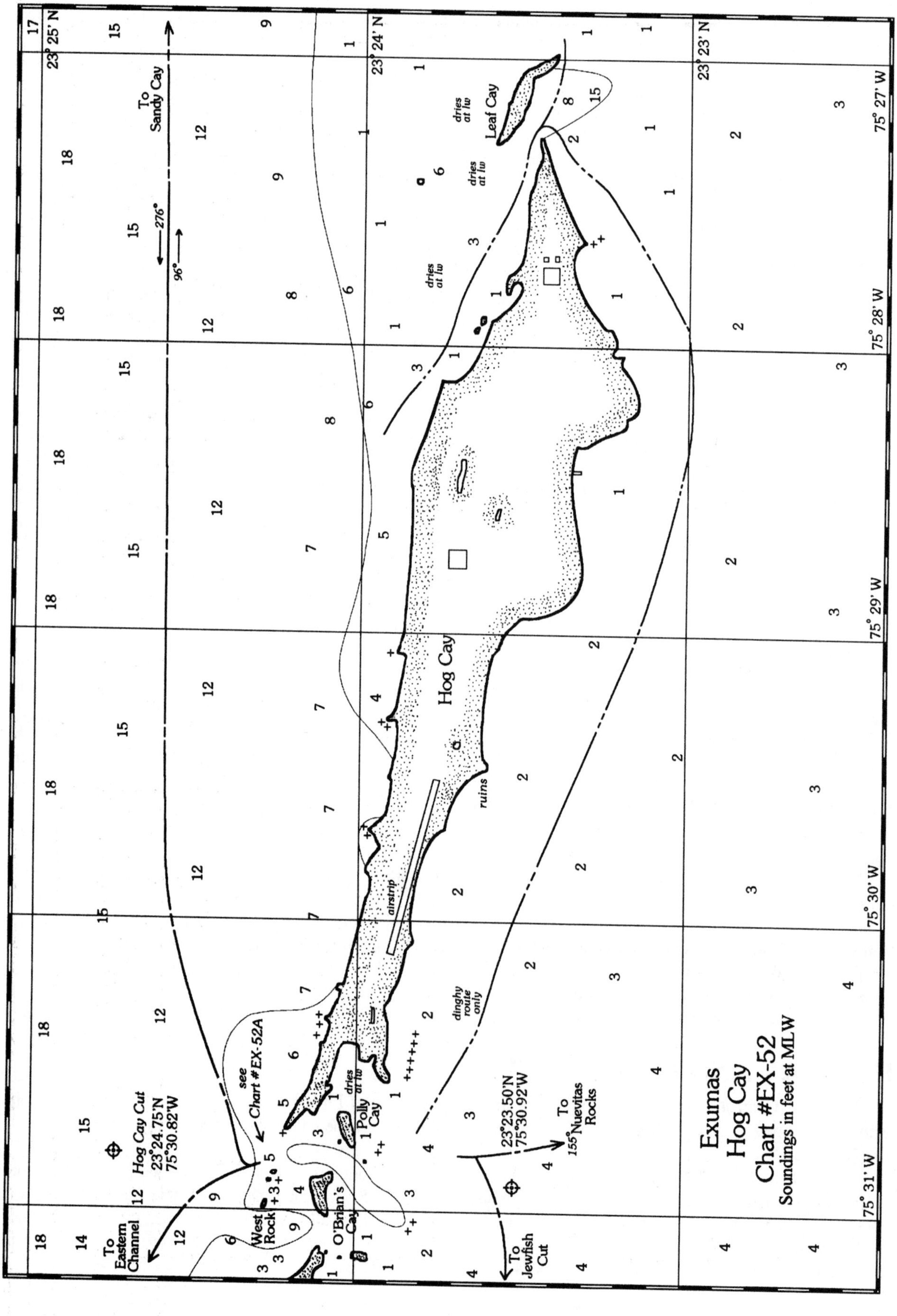

Exumas
Hog Cay
Chart #EX-52
Soundings in feet at MLW

To Sandy Cay

Leaf Cay

dries at lw
dries at lw
dries at lw

Hog Cay

ruins

airstrip

dinghy route only

dries at lw

see Chart #EX-52A

Hog Cay Cut
23°24.75'N
75°30.82'W

West Rock
O'Brian's Cay

Polly Cay

To Eastern Channel

To Jewfish Cut

23°23.50'N
75°30.92'W
155° To Nuevitas Rocks

276°
96°

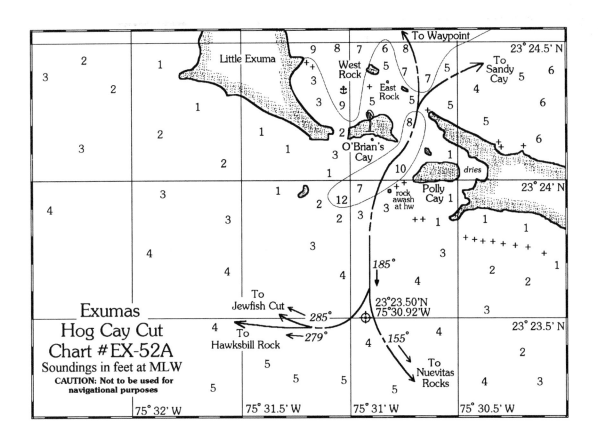

Exumas
Hog Cay Cut
Chart #EX-52A
Soundings in feet at MLW
CAUTION: Not to be used for
navigational purposes

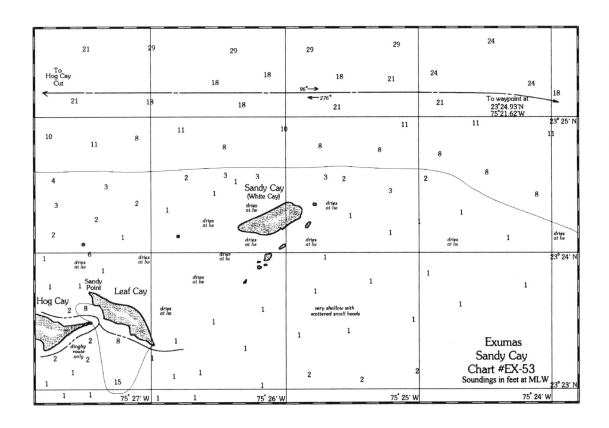

Exumas
Sandy Cay
Chart #EX-53
Soundings in feet at MLW

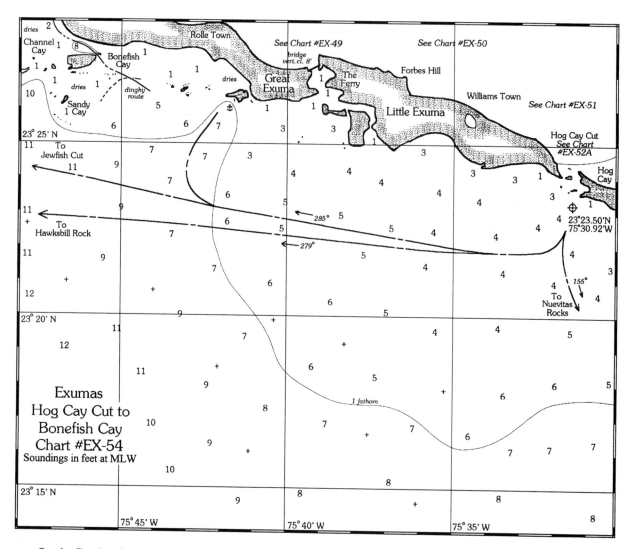

Exumas
Hog Cay Cut to
Bonefish Cay
Chart #EX-54
Soundings in feet at MLW

Sandy Cay is often shown on charts as White Cay but is called Sandy Cay locally and shown as such on Land and Survey Department Maps. After you clear the sandbanks that lie to the north and east of Sandy Cay you can take up a course of 70° to Simms and 117° to Salt Pond. There is a very visible arm of the same sandbank that reaches to the east a little further south of the GPS waypoint that you will cross on your route to Salt Pond. The shallowest spot in this area is 6' at low water. Skippers wishing to arrive at the Eastern Channel from the Sandy Cay sandbank must steer 293° for 17.5 miles making sure to avoid the Black Rocks off Williams Town. From the north side of Hog Cay Cut it is 8.46 miles on a course of 96° to the GPS waypoint off Sandy Cay.

Sandy Cay is home to a group of friendly iguanas. They are not quite the same species as the rock iguanas at Allan's Cay in the northern Exumas, the ones on Sandy Cay tend to be more orange in color. Please do not take your dog shore on Sandy Cay to avoid confrontations with the iguanas. The waters around Sandy Cay are very shallow and many sections dry at low water so it is best to approach the cay by dinghy on a rising tide just before high and leave shortly after high.

Hog Cay Cut (Chart # EX-52A), although being of the trickiest cuts to maneuver through safely, will reward you with the opportunity to cruise the western side of Great Exuma. Once through the cut you can pass through the cays lying to the west of Great Exuma at Jewfish Cut, continue out to the mailboat route and bypass the shallower waters by rounding Hawksnest Rock, or head south for the Jumentos Cays. Your piloting skills, which you have probably honed to a fine edge by the time you have gotten this far, will certainly be tested in Hog Cay Cut as you must pass over a 3' (at low water) hard bar on the southern side of the cut. It should go without saying that good visibility and fair weather are very important to making an uneventful passage through here. You can easily take a draft of 5½' through here at high water and 6' depending on the tide and your skills at eyeball navigation. There is a strong tidal current through the cut which is most apparent on the southern side at the shallow 3' bar. It is best to run the cut at high slack but bear in mind that if you run aground at slack tide the water has nowhere to go but out leaving you high and dry for about 11 hours. If you need to anchor for a while to await the tide you can drop the hook between West Rock and Little Exuma in 6'-9' at low water. Use two anchors and allow for a strong current.

A GPS waypoint at 23° 24.75' N, 75° 30.82' W will place you approximately ¼ nm mile to the north of Hog Cay Cut. Enter the cut (Chart # EX-52A) on a southerly heading by passing between East Rock and the northern tip of Hog Cay slightly favoring the East Rock side. There is 5' at low water through this entrance. Once past East Rock the water will deepen to 10' between Polly Cay and O'Brian's Cay. Watch out for the rocky bar and rock that is awash lying to the southwest of Polly Cay. The conspicuous lone palm tree on O'Brian's Cay is your turning mark. There is a 3' (at low water) hard bar that runs across the cut just southwest of Polly Cay extending all the way across in a westerly direction. You must cross this bar to get to the deeper water on the other side. To the west of Polly Cay there is an obvious area of bright green water with a depth in one spot of 12'. The naturally tendency for many mariners is to head for that green spot. Do not do this! The waters south and west of the spot are 1' shallower than the hard bar. As you pass between Polly Cay and O'Brian's Cay, place the lone palm on your stern and steer 185° and you will cross the bar with 5½'-6½' at high water depending on that particular high tide. The shallow part of the bar is not very wide, perhaps a boat length or two, and then you will be back in water that is 4'-5' at low water. If for some reason the lone palm tree is not there, there is a small rock lying just off the western shore of O'Brian's Cay below where the palm tree stands. Line this up on your stern and steer 195° to clear the bar. Both the palm tree and the rock lie approximately in the middle of O'Brian's Cay.

If approaching Hog Cay Cut from the Jumentos or somewhere along the mailboat route, a GPS waypoint at 23° 23.50' N, 75° 30.92' W will put you ¼ nm south of the rocky bar. Take up a heading of 005° on the lone palm on O'Brian's Cay and once you are over the bar steer between O'Brian's Cay and Polly Cay and through the cut to the north side.

THE WESTERN SHORE OF GREAT EXUMA

Once through Hog Cay Cut you can cruise the seldom visited western shore of Great and Little Exuma Islands (Chart #'s EX-54 & 55) or proceed south to the Jumentos Cays. If you are headed to the Jumentos, once through Hog Cay Cut take up a heading of 155° for 16.5 nautical miles and you will come to Nuevitas Rocks.

If you are headed north you have two routes to take. From the south side of Hog Cay Cut a course of 279° will bring you to a GPS waypoint at 23° 25.31' N, 76° 06.31' W, approximately 200 yards west of Hawksbill Rock Light (FL W ev 3.3 sec 40ft 6m, Chart # EX-55) where you will pick up the mailboat route. The waters from Hog Cay Cut to Hawksbill Rock get progressively deeper the further west you travel from Great Exuma or Little Exuma with scattered coral heads. Watch out for the rocky brown bar that extends northward from Hawksbill Rock. From this position you can take up a course of 020° to Rocky Point and then on to the Brigantines or you may proceed along the mailboat route (see the next section: *The Mailboat Route*).

The second northbound route follows the shoreline of Little Exuma and Great Exuma and passes through Jewfish Cut where you pick up the Long Island Mailboat Route. The anchorages through here are basically lee side anchorages. There is good protection from the east and west in the cut between Jewfish Cay and Bowe Cay but you will be open to the north and south. Once clear of Hog Cay Cut, take up an approximate heading of 285° and parallel the shore staying about one mile off. Bear in mind that the deeper water will lie to the westward of your position on this route. The waters close inshore are very shallow and should only be explored by dinghy. In the vicinity of The Ferry (Chart # EX-54) the water will begin to shallow outward from the Great Exuma shore until you clear the area of Sandy Cay and Bonefish Cay. There is a good lee side anchorage on the western shore of the small unnamed cay about 1½ miles northwest of The Ferry. The waters to the west of Great Exuma are strewn with many small rocks and heads that are definitely worth investigating. These waters are rife with sponges and you may see a Long Island sponge boat working this area.

Follow the lay of the cays and rocks until you clear the last set of three small rocks and can take up a heading of 350° for Jewfish Cut. A GPS waypoint at 23° 25.37' N, 75° 56.25' W will place you approximately 1 mile south of Jewfish Cut with the cut bearing 350°. It is possible to anchor in Jewfish Cut just off the Jewfish Cay shore with good protection from the west and east. It is absolutely imperative to burn an anchor light if you intend to anchor here and try not to anchor in the central traffic lane.

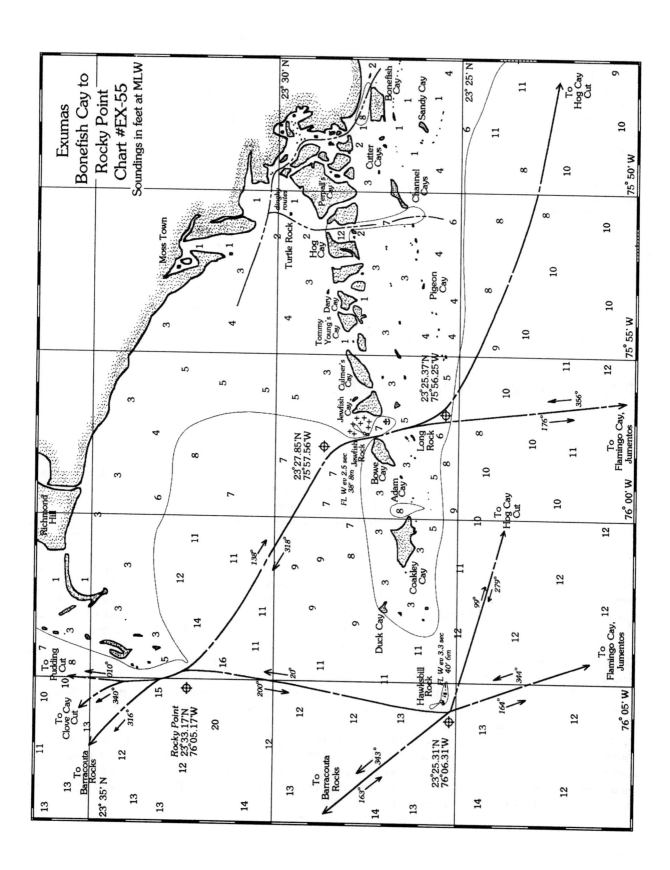

Passing through Jewfish Cut (Chart # EX-55), the deeper water and obstruction free channel lies between Bowe Cay and Jewfish Rock where Jewfish Cut Light (FL W ev 2½ sec 38ft 8m) is located. Both Jewfish Cut Light and Hawksbill Rock Light are extremely unreliable. Pass between Jewfish Rock and Bowe Cay and head approximately north, avoiding the shallow areas to port and the rocky bars to starboard. A GPS waypoint at 23° 27.85' N, 75° 57.56' W will place you 1 mile north of Jewfish Cut. From this point you may take up a course of 318° for Rocky Point and then the Brigantines.

As you approach Rocky Point watch out for the shallow sand bank that lies in an east-west direction just south of the cays off Rocky point. A GPS waypoint at 23° 33.17'N, 76° 05.17'W places you approximately 3/4 nm southwest of the small cays off Rocky Point. From this position you can take up a heading of 010° to Pudding Cut, 340° to Clove Cay Cut, or 316° to the Barracouta Rocks and the mailboat route.

All the small cays along this route are worth investigating by dinghy. The waters are extremely shallow with many mangrove creeks for exploration and excellent fishing grounds for those who wish to pursue the elusive bonefish. A reported navigable route passing between Bonefish Cay and Great Exuma Island has filled in to depths of 1'-2' at low water as have the waters between Bonefish Cay and Perpall's Cay. This route is only recommended for shallow draft vessels and dinghies. The route from the Channel Cays to Perpall's Cay is only navigable for part of that distance as it shallows to 2' at low water also. There are small boat and dinghy routes between most of the major cays lying from Great Exuma all the way out to Jewfish Cay. Jewfish Cay is private and visits ashore should be by invitation only.

Bowe Cay has a 35' hill lying ½ mile from its northern tip. Approximately 800' west of this hill are the ruins of pasture walls that run from the sea to a mangrove swash. About 600' east of the southwest point of Bowe Cay are two cave holes 60' apart, one is 20' across and the other is 7' wide. They are near shore and connected by a subterranean tunnel with 5' of water at high tide. Sixty feet southwest of these holes is a shaft 20' inland with a 4' diameter and 4' deep. At the bottom of this shaft is a tunnel that leads out to sea.

Perpall's Cay, once called Long Cay or Powell's Cay has the ruins of many small pasture walls and numerous cross walls. About a quarter of a mile east of the western end of the cay are the ruins of a small house. Most of the cays between Hawksbill Rock and Great Exuma are home to ruins of pasture walls and cave holes and are worth the time it takes to explore them. This is a rarely visited area and you will likely have the waters entirely to yourself.

THE MAILBOAT ROUTE

By utilizing the old mailboat route it is possible to cruise from Nassau to George Town (by way of Hog Cay Cut) and rarely get in water over 25' deep. Most cruisers who take advantage of the deep protected water on this route are heading northward along the western side of Great Exuma after passing through Hog Cay Cut or heading north from the Jumentos. This route has been used for years by Bahamian mailboats and Haitian vessels and it is not unusual to see an old working sailboat still plying the waters along this route. The northern section of this route, from Farmer's Cay to Nassau, has no obstructions to keep a vessel from turning eastward and enjoying the cays from Great Guana northward. Shallow sandbanks, primarily the Galliot Bank and the shallows in the area of the Pimblicos and Brigantines, offer only minor inconveniences to mariners wishing to pass into the more traveled waters that lie closer to Exuma Sound.

Heading northward from Hog Cay Cut your will first pick up the mailboat route at Hawksbill Rock (see previous section: *The Western Shore of Great Exuma*). From here you can steer 343° to pass west of East Barracouta Rock. A GPS waypoint at 23° 40.14' N, 76° 13.23' W will bring you to a position approximately ¾ mile to the west of East Barracouta Rock (Chart # EX-34). From here a course of 321° for 4.0 miles will bring you to a GPS waypoint at 23° 42.95' N, 76° 16.32' W which lies approximately ¾ mile west of West Barracouta Rock. Give the Barracouta Rocks a wide berth to avoid the rocky bars that run on a northwest/southeast line at each rock. Once clear of the Barracouta Rocks you may take up a heading for Harvey Cay or Little Farmer's Cay. If you wish to proceed to Darby Island and Rudder Cut you can continue on a 335° heading until you can steer towards the conspicuous green house on Darby Island on a heading of 100°-130° and work you way to the western shore of Darby Island by passing north of the Western Pimblicos (Chart # EX-29). From West Barracouta Rock a heading of 332° for 96.5 miles will bring you to Porgee Rocks.

Vessels leaving Nassau may set a course of 152° from Porgee Rocks for 96.5 miles to arrive at West Barracouta Rock. At this point alter course to 141° for 4.0 miles to a point west of East Barracouta Rock. At this point you can take up a course of 137° for 18.9 miles to Jewfish Cut. A course of 163° for 16.2 miles will bring you to a point just west of Hawksbill Rock where you can set your course for the Jumentos or Hog Cay Cut.

EXUMA RECIPES

Bahamian cuisine is quite unique in itself. Bahamian cooks tend to use a lot of hot sauce, peppers, basil, and thyme, so be prepared for some spicy dining. Peas and rice is a staple dish and almost always served with the entree in every Bahamian restaurant. Bell peppers, limes, sour orange, grits, sweet potatoes, tomatoes, onions, pumpkin squash, fish, conch, and lobster are all staples and usually a part of the daily menu. On many of the cays you will likely find some ladies that bake some excellent bread although the loaves do not keep well due to the lack of preservatives. On the other hand, the bread is so tasty that it won't last long anyway.

The following are traditional Bahamian recipes prepared in a traditional way.

Conch Salad

Conch salad can be found everywhere in the Exumas, from sidewalk vendors at the Family Islands Regatta to the best restaurants. The conch is added raw with the lime juice or sour orange marinade serving to "cook" it, similar to seviche.

Ingredients: 3 fresh raw conch, 6 tomatoes, 2 onions, 2 green peppers, cucumbers, juice of 6 key limes and 1 sour orange (can be bottled), bird peppers or goat peppers to taste.

Directions: Dice conch, tomatoes, onions and green peppers into ¼" size pieces. Skin cucumbers and dice. Add diced ingredients to a large bowl and pour in the juice of 6 key limes or one sour orange. Stir conch salad and let the juice saturate every piece. If you need more juice, add more, there should be about 1" of juice in the bottom of the bowl. Dice some hot bird or goat peppers and add to taste.

Gin and Coconut Water

In an area where one would think rum to be the traditional drink, Gin and Coconut Water is immensely popular. Numerous songs have been written about this concoction and its effects. If you indulge freely you must be very careful if you get up and walk out into the fresh air, for some reason this is the last thing many remember until the next morning. You will find that quite a few Bahamians have a Gin and Coconut Water story to tell.

Ingredients: 1 bottle of fine Gin; 1 can sweetened condensed milk; 6 jelly coconuts; large pieces of ice.

For those who are unsure what exactly a jelly coconut is, it is the young, newly formed and still green coconut. If you look up at a coconut tree you will see three types of coconuts. The smaller coconuts, whose tips are still unformed, are too young to be of any use yet. The jelly coconuts are larger and fully formed. They have a soft green color and are very young looking. Their fleshy insides, dry in an older coconut, are very soft and jelly-like. The older coconuts with the drier meat are the ones that are starting to tan and discolor. If you are able to find the yellow or gold coconuts, they are much sweeter and more desirable than the green coconuts.

Directions: Take the water of six jelly coconuts and place in a large container (a five gallon bucket is called a Bahamian cocktail shaker). Add gin to taste. Add one can of sweetened condensed milk until you get a sweet taste, usually about 1 can for ½ bottle of gin. Add a little more gin to taste. Carefully scrape out the coconut jelly from the shell making sure not to remove any of the brown skin that lies just under the shell. The brown skin can give the drink a sour taste. Shake contents and pour over large chunks of ice.

Peas and Rice

Peas and rice is *the* staple Bahamian dish. It is served with virtually every entree in every restaurant. You will rarely sit down to a Bahamian meal without peas and rice somewhere on the table. There are as many ways to cook peas and rice as there are cooks. After sorting through numerous recipes this one proved to be an almost foolproof method of creating a tasty peas and rice dish with little chance of error as long as directions are followed correctly.

Ingredients: 2 oz. salt pork, 2 tbs. olive oil, 3 cups white or brown rice, tea kettle of hot water, large Exuma onion, 16 oz. can of pigeon peas or 16 oz. hardened pigeon peas, 2 tbs. tomato paste, fresh thyme, salt, 2 tbs. *Kitchen Bouquet*.

Directions: Put on kettle of hot water and bring to boil. As you are boiling water, dice onion and cut up salt pork into ¼" cubes. In large frying pan, sauté onion and salt pork in olive oil until onion is fairly crisp. Add rice. Stir rice well until it becomes almost translucent (brown the rice). In a separate bowl mix tomato paste, thyme (heavily season to taste), and *Kitchen Bouquet*. Add ½ cup of hot water and stir. Turn heat up on rice to high and fry for an additional minute, then add tomato paste mixture and stir. Stir in a 16 oz. can of pigeon peas or 16 oz. of hardened pigeon peas that have been soaked overnight and are pre-cooked. Pour in boiling water from the kettle until rice is just covered, bring to a boil and stir, reduce heat, cover, and do not stir again. Check water in pan every few minutes. Take a tbs. of hot water and pour it on the rice, if it sizzles there is no water in pan and you must add just a little, no more than ¼ cup at a time. When rice is done to taste, uncover and simmer for five minutes. Fluff rice with a meat tine, never with a spoon. Eat heartily.

Scorched Conch

This is a good recipe to try when you are cleaning a large number of conch. As you are cleaning them, scorch a few and eat them as you finish your job. Be sure and have some milk or fresh water handy as scorched conch can be quite hot.

Ingredients: Small bottle of Bahamian Sour Orange or Key Lime juice; 1 Bahamian red pepper per conch; 1 conch per person depending on appetite; salt.

Directions: Take a freshly cleaned conch and score it diagonally ¾ of the way through the meat, first one direction and then the other, leaving a criss-cross pattern of ¼" squares. Take a Bahamian Red Pepper and cut the end off. Rub the pepper up and down each and every score. Sprinkle a little salt over the conch. Place conch in a container or plastic baggie. Squeeze the juice of a Sour Orange or Key Lime (depending on your taste) into the container and let soak for as little or as long as you like. Open mouth and take a bite of the conch. Have milk or water handy for relief.

REFERENCES

AND SUGGESTED READING

A Checklist of the Amphibians and Reptiles of the Exuma Archipelago; Richard Franz, Fla. Museum of Natural History, 1989

A Cruising Guide to the Caribbean and the Bahamas; Jerrems C. Hart and William T. Stone, Dodd, Mead and Company, New York, 1982

A Cruising Guide to the Exumas Cays Land And Sea Park; Stephen J. Pavlidis with Ray Darville, Night Flyer Enterprises, U.S.A. 1994

A Field Guide to the Sandy and Rocky Seashore; The Bahamas National Trust, 1979

A History of the Bahamas; Michael Craton, Collins Press, London, 1969

A History of the Bahamas; Michael Craton, San Salvador Press, Ontario, Canada, 1986

A Preliminary Report on the Early History of Crab Cay; Bob Rader and Anita Martinec, 1979

A Study of the Coral and Fish Species of the Exuma Cays Land and Sea Park; Alastair Bramwell 1989

American Practical Navigator; Nathaniel Bowditch, LL.D., DMA Hydrographic Center, 1977

An Introduction to Oceanography; Cuchlaine A. M. King, M.A., Ph.D., McGraw Hill, 1966

Bahamas Handbook and Businessmen's Manual; Etienne Dupuch, Jr., Etienne Dupuch Jr., Publications, Nassau, Bahamas, 1960

Bahamas Handbook and Businessmen's Manual; Sir Etienne Dupuch, Jr., Etienne Dupuch Jr., Publications Ltd., Nassau, Bahamas, 1991

Bahamian Bush Medicine; Christine Rolle, Farmer's Hill, Exuma, Bahamas, 1992

Birds of The Bahamas; Andrew Paterson, Durrell Publications Inc., 1972

De Orbe Novo; Peter Martyr (1511), translated by F.A. McNutt, New York, 1912

Dictionary of Bahamian English; John A. Holm, Lexik House Pub., Cold Springs, N.Y., 1982

Exuma Historical/Pictorial Guide; Exuma Historical Publications, Nassau, 1988

Exuma: The Loyalist Years 1783-1834; W. H. James, W. H. James, Mamaroneck, New York, 1988

Guide to the Shallow Water Marine Habitats and Benthic Invertebrates of The Exuma Cays Land and Sea Park; Kathleen M. Sullivan, Ph.D., Sea and Sky Foundation, 1991

Journal of the Bahamian Historical Society; Vol. 5, #1, May 1983

Legislation Affecting Wildlife and National Parks in The Bahamas; The Bahamas National Trust, 1992

Out Island Doctor; Dr. Evans W. Cottman, Hodder and Stoughton, London, 1963

Postage Stamps And Postal History Of The Bahamas; Harold G. D. Gisburn, Stanley Gibbons, Ltd., London 1950

Rediscovering the Park; Beryl Nelson, Warden of the Exuma Cays Land and Sea Park, 1985

Report of the Exuma Cays Park Project; Carleton Ray, New York Zoological Society

Reptiles and Amphibians of The Bahamas; Bahamas National Trust, 1993

Sailing Directions For The Caribbean Sea; Pub. #147, Defense Mapping Agency, #SDPUB147

The Aranha Report on the Exuma Cays; Land and Surveys Dept., Nassau, New Providence, Bahamas 1928

The Bahamas Rediscovered; Nicolas and Dragon Popov/Island Expedition, MacMillan Press, Ltd. London 1992

The Ephemeral Islands, A Natural History of the Bahamas; David G. Campbell, MacMillan Education, 1990

The Life Story of the Queen Conch; Katherine S. Orr, World Wildlife Fund, 1985

The Life Story of the Spiny Lobster; Katherine S. Orr, World Wildlife Fund, 1988

The Ocean Almanac; Robert Hendrickson, Doubleday, New York, 1984

The Pirates Own Book; published by A. & C. B. Edwards, New York, and Thomas, Cowperthwait, & Co., Philadelphia, 1842

The Statute Law of The Bahamas; Revised Edition 1987, Chapter 355

The Yachtsman's Guide to the Bahamas; Meredith Fields, Tropic Isle Pub., 1994

Wind From The Carolinas; R. Wilder, Norman S. Berg, 1983

APPENDICES

APPENDIX A: Navigational Aids in the Exumas

All navigational aids are listed in order from north to south.

Lights

Navigational lights in The Bahamas should be considered unreliable at best and their characteristics may change without notice. It is not unusual for a light to be out of commission for long periods of time.

LIGHT	CHARACTERISTICS	COLOR	HT.	RNG.
Beacon Cay	FL ev. 3 secs.	W & R*	58'	8m
Elbow Cay	FL ev. 6 secs.	W	46'	11m
Staniel Rock	FL ev. 2 secs.	W	16'	5m
Harvey Cay	FL ev. 2½ secs.	W	49'	6m
Dotham Cut	FL ev. 5 secs.	W	36'	8m
Galliot Cut	FL ev. 4 secs.	W	50'	7m
Conch Cay	FL ev. 5 secs.	W	40'	8m
Jewfish Cut	FL ev. 2½ secs.	W	38'	8m
Hawksbill Rock	FL ev. 3.3 secs.	W	40'	6m

*Shows red when your bearing to light is 292° to 303°.

BATELCO Towers

Towers over 50' should have red lights at their tops, either fixed or flashing (Fxd or Fl). Taller towers may have fixed red lights at intermediate levels. Positions are approximate.

LOCATION	LIGHT	HT.
Highborne Cay	R-Fl	260'
Staniel Cay	R-Fl	260'
Black Point	R-Fxd	100'
Little Farmer's Cay	R-Fxd	260'
Bock Cay	R-Fxd	100'
Lee Stocking Island	R-Fxd	100'
Children's Bay Cay	unlit	30'
Clove Cay	unlit	50'
Barretarre	R-Fxd	150'
Rolleville	R-Fxd	260'
Farmer's Hill	unlit	40'
George Town	R-Fxd	220'
George Town	R-Fxd	105'
Williams Town	R-Fxd	200'

There is an unused radio tower on Norman's Cay that should not be confused with a Batelco Tower. The towers at Children's Bay Cay, which looks like a private VHF tower, and Clove Cay, which has a wind-generator at its top, resemble private towers as opposed to the huge red and white Batelco towers that one normally sees.

Beacons

Beacons are simply large rock or brick cairns that are used as navigational aids. With the exception of the beacon on Little Pipe Cay (Fl W ev 10 sec.) which is privately maintained, the beacons are unlit so do not expect to use them at night.

Little Pipe (Kemp) Cay
Adderly Cay
Soldier Cay (Southern Exumas)
Stocking Island
Williams Town

APPENDIX B: Marine Facilities in the Exumas

Some of the marinas listed below may be untenable in certain winds and dockside depths listed may not reflect entrance channel depths at low water. Check with the dock master prior to arrival. All the marinas can handle your garbage disposal problems however some may levy a charge per bag for those who are not guests at their docks.

MARINA	FUEL	SLIPS	DEPTH	PROPANE	GROC.	SPIRITS	DINING
Highborne Cay	D & G	17	8'	Y	Y	Y	Cater
Sampson Cay Marina	D & G	25	7'	N	Y	Y	Y
Happy People	NONE	6	6'	N	N	Y	Y
Staniel Cay Yacht Club	D & G	12	7½'	Y	N	Y	Y
Farmer's Cay Yacht Club	D & G	6	7½'	Y	Y	Y	Y
Exuma Docking Services	D & G	52	7'	Y	Y	Y	Y

APPENDIX C: GPS Waypoints in the Exumas

Waypoints are listed from north to south. Latitude is "North" and longitude is "West." *Caution*: GPS Waypoints are not to be used for navigational purposes. GPS waypoints are intended to place you in the general area of the described position. All routes, cuts, and anchorages must be negotiated by eyeball navigation. The author and publisher take no responsibility for the misuse of the following GPS waypoints.

#	DESCRIPTION	Latitude	Longitude
1.	Nassau Harbor-W entrance, R "2"	25° 05.33'	77° 21.35'
2.	Porgee Rocks-500 yards S	25° 03.50'	77° 14.55'
3.	Beacon Cay-500 yards NW	24° 53.18'	76° 49.50'
4.	Beacon Cay/Ship Channel-2 nm SE of Beacon Cay	24° 51.73'	76° 47.81'
5.	Ship Channel Cay Anchorage-¼ nm W	24° 47.63'	76° 50.40'
6.	Long Rock Cut-¼ nm NW	24° 46.78'	76° 50.30'
7.	Long Rock Cut-¼ nm SE	24° 46.38'	76° 49.39'
8.	Allan's Cay-¼ nm W of entrance to anchorage	24° 44.74'	76° 50.91'
9.	Turning point to Highbourne Cay from Nassau-1 nm W of Cay	24° 42.40'	76° 51.40'
10.	Highborne Cay Cut-¼ nm ESE	24° 42.20'	76° 48.60'
11.	Long Cay Cut-¼ nm E	24° 39.30'	76° 48.25'
12.	ODAS Buoy in North Exuma Sound	24° 38.20'	76° 31.30'
13.	Norman's Cay Cut-¼ nm E	24° 35.76'	76° 47.48'
14.	Norman's Spit-¼ nm W	24° 35.64'	76° 51.96'
15.	Wax Cay Cut-½ nm NE	24° 34.76'	76° 47.01'
16.	Elbow Cay -¼ nm W	24° 30.90'	76° 49.25'
17.	Cistern Cay Cut-½ nm NE	24° 27.31'	76° 44.10'
18.	Coral Cut-½ nm NE	24° 25.98'	76° 42.23'
19.	The Wide Opening Channel-½ nm NE	24° 25.51'	76° 40.00'
20.	Warderick Wells Cut-½ nm N	24° 24.86'	76° 38.24'
21.	Warderick Wells South Anchorage-½ nm NE of entrance	24° 22.97'	76° 36.73'
22.	SW edge of sandbank N of Wide Opening Channel	24° 22.81'	76° 44.14'
23.	Hall's Pond Cut-½ nm NE	24° 22.70'	76° 35.25'
24.	S tip of Malabar shoal-turn to Warderick Wells from banks	24° 21.79'	76° 39.81'
25.	SW edge of sandbank for turn into Warderick Wells from banks	24° 21.60'	76° 42.40'
26.	Shallowest point on 51° course to Exuma Cays Club from banks	24° 20.64'	76° 36.87'
27.	SW end of deep water channel between Osprey and Hall's Pond	24° 19.38'	76° 36.75'
28.	O'Brien's Cut-½ nm NE	24° 19.16'	76° 32.33'
29.	Conch Cut-½ nm NE	24° 17.55'	76° 31.43'
30.	W tip of Bell Island sandbank	24° 17.70'	76° 37.60'
31.	W tip of Rocky Dundas sandbank	24° 17.00'	76° 35.68'
32.	Compass Cay Cut-½ nm N	24° 15.74'	76° 29.75'
33.	Compass Cay Channel-W point of deep water channel	24° 15.30'	76° 32.56'

34.	Compass Cay Cut-½ nm ESE	24° 15.15'	76° 29.21'
35.	Joe Cay Cut-½ nm E	24° 14.80'	76° 29.05'
36.	Overyonder Cay Cut-¼ nm E	24° 13.78'	76° 28.45'
37.	Sampson Cay Cut-¼ nm NE	24° 12.78'	76° 27.55'
38.	Twin Cays-¼ nm W	24° 12.30'	76° 30.84'
39.	Big Rock Cut-½ nm NE	24° 11.66'	76° 26.38'
40.	Sandy Cay-¼ nm W	24° 11.05'	76° 30.15'
41.	Harvey Cay-¼ nm W	24° 09.15'	76° 29.44'
42.	Dotham Cut-¼ nm E	24° 07.14'	76° 23.85'
43.	Farmer's Cay Cut-½ nm E	23° 57.95'	76° 18.32'
44.	Little Farmer's Cay-½ nm W	23° 57.40'	76° 20.90'
45.	Galliot Cut-¼ nm E	23° 55.62'	76° 16.50'
46.	Cave Cay Cut-¼ nm E	23° 54.25'	76° 15.20'
47.	Rudder Cut-¼ nm NNE	23° 52.52'	76° 13.48'
48.	ODAS Buoy in South Exuma Sound	23° 50.40'	75° 43.20'
49.	Grassy patches-turning point for Pimblico route	23° 50.11'	76° 15.23'
50.	Adderly Cut-¼ nm ENE	23° 47.45'	76° 06.33'
51.	Children's Bay Cut	23° 44.60'	76° 02.90'
52.	Rat Cay Cut-¼ nm N	23° 44.31'	76° 02.10'
53.	Square Rock Cay Cut-¼ nm ENE	23° 43.56'	76° 00.90'
54.	West Barracouta Rock-¾ nm W	23° 42.95'	76° 16.32'
55.	Glass Cay Cut-¼ nm N	23° 42.50'	75° 59.20'
56.	Soldier Cay Cut-¼ nm NE	23° 41.10'	75° 57.40'
57.	East Barracouta Rock-¾ nm W	23° 40.14'	76° 13.23'
58.	Steventon Cut-¼ nm NE	23° 39.68'	75° 55.70'
59.	Conch Cay Cut-½ nm NNW	23° 34.30'	75° 48.50'
60.	Rocky Point-½ nm SW	23° 33.17'	76° 05.17'
61.	Eastern Channel, Elizabeth Harbour-¼ nm NE	23° 29.81'	75° 39.95'
62.	Jewfish Cut-1 nm N	23° 27.85'	75° 57.56'
63.	Jewfish Cut-1 nm S	23° 25.37'	75° 56.25'
64.	Hawksbill Rock-200 yards W	23° 25.31'	76° 06.31'
65.	Hog Cay Cut-¼ nm N	23° 24.75'	75° 30.82'
66.	Sandy Cay- ½ nm N of NE tip of sandbank	23° 24.93'	75° 21.62'
67.	Hog Cay Cut-¼ nm S	23° 23.50'	75° 30.92'
68.	Salt Pond, Long Island-¼ nm SW of Indian Hole Point	23° 20.87'	75° 09.55'

APPENDIX D: Distance Table

LOCATION	Nass	Allan	WW	Stan	Farm	GT	SPLI
Nassau, N.P.		33	59	75	90	127	165
Allan's Cay	33		26	42	57	94	132
Warderick Wells	59	26		16	31	68	106
Staniel Cay	75	42	16		15	52	90
Farmer's Cay	90	57	31	15		37	75
George Town	127	94	68	52	37		38
Salt Pond, L.I.	165	132	106	90	75	38	

These distances are in nautical miles and should be considered approximate.

APPENDIX E: Metric Conversion Table

Visitors to the Exumas will find the metric system in use and many grocery items and fuel measured in liters and kilograms. As a rule of thumb, a meter is just a little longer than a yard and a liter is very close to a quart. If in doubt use the following table.

1 centimeter (cm) = 0.4 inch	1 inch = 2.54 cm
1 meter (m) = 3.28 feet	1 foot = 0.31 cm
1 m=0.55 fathoms	1 fathom=1.83 m
1 kilometer (km) = 0.62 miles	1 yard = 0.93 m
1 km=0.54 nautical miles	1 nautical mile=1.852 km
1 liter (l) = 0.26 gallons	1 gallon = 3.75 l
1 gram (g) = 0.035 ounce	1 ounce = 28.4 g
1 metric ton (t) = 1.1 tons U.S.	1 pound = 454 g

APPENDIX F: Weather Broadcast Frequencies

All frequencies are upper sideband

Voice Broadcasts

NMN-Coast Guard Portsmouth, Virginia

AREA	TIME UTC	FREQ. KHz
Offshore Forecast- W Central and SW No. Atlantic west of 65° W, Gulf of Mexico and Caribbean Sea	0400	4426, 6501, 8764
Offshore Forecast-same as above plus the offshore waters east of New England	1000	4426, 6501, 8764
	1600, 2200	6501, 8764, 13089
High Seas Forecast-North Atlantic west of 35° west, Gulf of Mexico and Caribbean Sea	0530	4426, 6501, 8764
	1130, 2330	6501, 8764, 13089
	1730	8764, 13089, 17314
Gulf Stream Location	1600, 2200	6501, 8764, 13089

WLO-Mobile, Alabama

AREA	TIME EST	FREQUENCY KHz
Gulf of Mexico	0100, 0700, 1300, 1900	4396, 8806, 13152, 17362, 22804
Caribbean	0100, 0700, 1300, 1900	4396, 8806, 13152, 17362, 22804
SW North Atlantic	0100, 0700, 1300, 1900	4396, 8806, 13152, 17362, 22804

WOM-Miami, Florida

AREA	TIME UTC	FREQUENCY KHz
Gulf of Mexico	1300, 2300	4363, 8722, 13092, 17242, 22738
Caribbean	1300, 2300	4363, 8722, 13092, 17242, 22738
SW North Atlantic	1300, 2300	4363, 8722, 13092, 17242, 22738

CW Broadcasts

WLO-Mobile, Alabama

AREA	TIME UTC	FREQUENCY, KHz
Gulf of Mexico	0400, 1000, 1600, 2200	4343, 6416, 8514, 12886.5, 17022.5, 22487, 26135
Caribbean and SW No. Atlantic	0500, 1100, 1700, 2300	4343, 6416, 8514, 12886.5, 17022.5, 22487, 26135

AMTOR/SITOR

WLO-Mobile, Alabama

AREA	TIME UTC	FREQUENCY KHz DEC. 1- MAY 31	FREQUENCY KHz JUNE 1-NOV. 30
Gulf of Mexico	0435, 1035, 1635, 2235	4343, 6416, 8514, 12886.5, 17022.5, 22487, 26135	4462.5, 6344, 8534, 12992, 16997.6, 22688, 26144
Caribbean and SW No. Atlantic	0535, 1135, 1735, 2335	4343, 6416, 8514, 12886.5, 17022.5, 22487, 26135	4462.5, 6344, 8534, 12992, 16997.6, 22688, 26144

NAVTEX

STATION	TIME UTC	FREQUENCY
NMA-Miami, Fla.	0000, 0400, 0800, 1200, 1600, 2000	518 KHz

TIME

STATION	FREQUENCY
WWV-Ft. Collins, Colorado	2.5, 5, 10, 15, 20, 25 MHz
WWVH-Kekaha-Kawai, Hawaii	2.5, 5, 10, 15, 20 MHz.

The National Bureau of Standards broadcasts time signals continuously 24 hours a day and storm alerts at 8-10 minutes after the hour.

APPENDIX G: Logarithmic Speed Scale

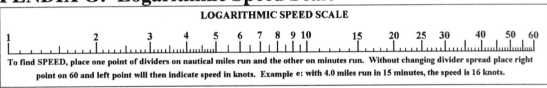

APPENDIX H: Depth Conversion Scale

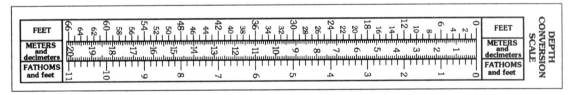

INDEX

D

E

Y

Z

About The Author
Stephen J. Pavlidis

Stephen J. Pavlidis has been cruising and living in the Bahamas aboard his 40' sloop *IV Play* since the winter of 1990. In February of 1993, he met Ray Darville, the new Warden of the Exuma Cays Land And Sea Park. Ray soon drew him into a working relationship with the Park as a volunteer Deputy Warden. In this role he quickly gained an intimate knowledge of the waters of the Exumas. Realizing that The Exuma Cays Land and Sea Park deserved a bit more recognition than is given in even the best guides to the area, he and Ray produced *A Cruising Guide to the Exuma Cays Land And Sea Park*. The favorable response to that publication in turn led to the publication of *The Exuma Guide* which covers the entire Exumian island chain in addition to The Park. *The Exuma Guide* was originally published in 1995. For this second edition, Steve completely resurveyed the entire region, produced all new, improved charts in lieu of the original sketch charts, and updated all information contained in the guide. Steve, N4UJP, is a member of the Waterway Radio and Cruising Club.

Courtesy of Jack Blackman

About the Cover Artist
Jack Blackman

Jack Blackman, the artist of *Tida Wave at Rest* on the front cover, has had a varied and successful career as an artist and designer. His fine art studies were obtained from The School of Fine Arts at Columbia University and The Art Students League in New York City. Jack's talents have involved many disciplines, such as designing sets for The Broadway Stage, network television, and Art Direction for major motion pictures. A small sampling of his design credits include: *One Life To Live*, *As The World Turns*, *House Sitter*, *What About Bob*, and *Fatal Attraction*. Several years ago, Jack sailed his cutter *Sea Rogue* to the Bahamas, where he fell in love with the brilliant colors of the islands and their waters. Since then, his watercolors have been inspired by the graceful lines of racing sloops, time worn facades of Out Island buildings, and the warm, honest Bahamian people at work and play. Having had a number of shows, many of Jack's paintings reside in private collections internationally, as well as The Bahamas. His original works and reproductions are well represented in local galleries. Jack has a studio in the Berry Islands where he paints daily, completing commissions and new works for his next show.

Photo courtesy of Lady E

Author aboard the Carolina Skiff that was supplied as a courtesy of the manufacturer.

Publishers Note

Seaworthy Publications supports the Exuma Cays Land and Sea Park and is a

Member of the Bahamas National Trust.

We strongly encourage those with an interest in this region to join the Support Fleet.

These islands and their surrounding waters are among the most beautiful cruising regions to be found anywhere. Become a member of the Support Fleet using the form on the following page. As a Support Fleet Member, you will be helping to keep The Exuma Cays Land and Sea Park a pristine ecological wellspring that will pay dividends for generations to come.

EXUMA CAYS LAND AND SEA PARK

Date______________
Cash______________
Check_____________
Decal_____________
*****
EP Class__________
BNT______________
Ed/Sec____________
For Office Use

SUPPORT FLEET

MEMBERSHIP APPLICATION

(Block Capitals Please)

NAME (s)____

ADDRESS____

CITY__________________ STATE_______________ ZIP________

BOAT NAME____

SUBSCRIPTION: $30 ( ) $50 ( ) $100 ( ) MORE ($)

WORK ( ) RESEARCH ( ) MATERIALS ( )

DETAILS____

Please make checks payable to:
"EXUMA CAYS LAND AND SEA PARK"

For U.S. tax-deductible contributions of $50 or more, please make checks payable to:
"ENVIRONMENTAL SYSTEMS PROTECTION FUND"

A contribution of $25 or more automatically constitutes an annual membership to
THE BAHAMAS NATIONAL TRUST.

Name of all current Support Fleet members will be posted in the Park Headquarters.

Members contributing $1,000 or more will be listed on a plaque at the Park Headquarters.

BAHAMAS NATIONAL TRUST
EXUMA CAYS LAND AND SEA PARK
P.O. BOX N3189
NASSAU, BAHAMAS

NOTES